Elements of Jaina Geography

Elements of Jaina Geography

The Jambūdvīpasaṃgrahaṇī
of Haribhadra Sūri

critically edited and translated
with the commentary of Prabhānanda Sūri

FRANK VAN DEN BOSSCHE

MOTILAL BANARSIDASS PUBLISHERS
PRIVATE LIMITED • DELHI

First Edition: Delhi, 2007

ISBN: 81-208-2934-4

MOTILAL BANARSIDASS
41 U.A. Bungalow Road, Jawahar Nagar, Delhi 110 007
8 Mahalaxmi Chamber, 22 Bhulabhai Desai Road, Mumbai 400 026
236, 9th Main III Block, Jayanagar, Bangalore 560 011
203 Royapettah High Road, Mylapore, Chennai 600 004
Sanas Plaza, 1302 Baji Rao Road, Pune 411 002
8 Camac Street, Kolkata 700 017
Ashok Rajpath, Patna 800 004
Chowk, Varanasi 221 001

Printed in India
BY JAINENDRA PRAKASH JAIN AT SHRI JAINENDRA PRESS,
A-45 NARAINA, PHASE-I, NEW DELHI 110 028
AND PUBLISHED BY NARENDRA PRAKASH JAIN FOR
MOTILAL BANARSIDASS PUBLISHERS PRIVATE LIMITED,
BUNGALOW ROAD, DELHI 110 007

for Gisela

Contents

Preface

Willibald Kirfel's basic work on ancient Indian cosmography and geography '*Die Kosmographie der Inder; nach den Quellen dargestellt*' first appeared in 1920. It treated the Brahmanic, Buddhist and Jaina views on the construction of the universe and of our 'middle' world and, it was entirely based on primary sources. However, since then relatively little work has been carried out in the field of Indian cosmology and geography. In particular editions and translations of basic post-canonical texts, whether extensive (*Bṛhad*) or concise (*Laghu* or *Saṃgrahaṇī*), are lacking.

The primary literature on the building of the cosmos that originated in India is extensive. Especially the Jaina tradition is rich in cosmological and geographical texts. The Jaina Āgama or Siddhānta already contains numerous cosmological and geographical data. The *Jīvājīvābhigama*, *Prajñāpanā* (Pkt. ***Paṇṇavaṇā***), *Sūryaprajñapti* (Pkt. ***Sūriẏapaṇṇatti***), *Jambūdvīpaprajñapti* (Pkt. ***Jambuddīvapaṇṇatti***), *Candraprajñapti* (Pkt. ***Caṃdapaṇṇatti***) and *Nirayāvalī* contain materials that are essential for the study of Jaina cosmography. But it was primarily in the post-canonical tradition that cosmographical and geographical treatises abound. In the first part of the 'Bibliography' included in this work a tentative list of Jaina treatises on the matter, Śvetāmbara and Digambara, is given.

I fully realise that, in the first place, a thorough analysis of the canonical cosmographical and geographical data is needed. However, the Jaina Āgamas still require extensive and profound critical editions. But I also think that, meanwhile, editions of the minor and major post-canonical texts can already be undertaken in order to pave the way for a profound analysis of the canonical data. I have opted for a critical edition and annotated translation of the *Jambūdvīpa-saṃgrahaṇī* for two reasons. First, Kirfel included this text and its commentary in the primary sources for his analysis of Jaina cosmography. The second reason was less deliberate. For, initially, I thought that the composer, Haribhadra Sūri, was the same as the famous author of a number of important post-canonical texts such as the *Anekāntajayapatākā*, *Ṣaḍdarśana-samuccaya*, *Yogabindu*, etc. I was wrong here, but the *Jambū-dvīpasaṃgrahaṇī* and its commentary by Prabhānanda Sūri proved important and informative enough for the study of Jaina geography in general to start an analysis of the basic Prākrit text together with its Sanskrit commentary.

I wish to thank the following persons for their valuable support and advice: Prof. Dr. R.I. Nanavati of the Oriental Institute, Vadodara; the Profs. Dr. S.D. Laddu and A.M. Ghatage of the Bhandarkar Oriental Research Institute, Pune; Prof. Jitendra B. Shah and Dr. Lalit Kumar of the L.D. Institute of Indology, Ahmedabad; Prof. V.P. Jain and Mrs. Dr. Aruna Anand of the Bhogilal Leherchand Institute of Indology, Delhi; Dr. K.C. Sogani of the Apabhrams Sahitya Akadami, Jaipur; Dr. Eva De Clercq and Mrs. Hilde De Keukelaere of Ghent University. Especially I want to express my gratitude to Pt. Amrit Patel for his assistance in tracing the Āgamic origins of a number of quotations, Dr. Jean-Michel

Delire of the University of Brussels for his persistent help in unravelling the mysteries of Jaina mathematics.

Frank Van Den Bossche
Ghent University

Abbreviations

BKSJ	the *Bṛhatkṣetrasamāsa* of Jinabhadragaṇi (ed. Bhadraṃkara Prakāśana, 1978-79)
JDP	the *Jambūdvīpaprajñaptisūtram* (ed. Shāha Naginbhai Ghelābhāi Javeri, 1920)
JDSH	the *Jambūdvīpasaṃgrahaṇī* of Haribhadra Sūri
JDSU	the *Jambūdvīpasamāsa* of Umāsvāti (ed. Satyavijaya Granthamālā, 1922)
JRK	the *Jinaratnakośa* of H.D. Velanker (Poona: Bhandarkar Oriental Research Institute, 1944)
Kirfel	*Die Kosmographie der Inder* of W. Kirfel (1920)
Pkt.	Prakrit
sū.	*sūtra*
Skt.	Sanskrit

Except for the quotations, Sanskrit words and passages in the transliterated texts are invariably put in *italics* while Prākrit words and passages are put in the ***bold-italics*** letter type.

1 Introduction

1.1 Jaina cosmography and geography

Jaina cosmography and geography excel, even more than their Brahmanic and Buddhist counterparts, in their systematic and mathematical approach. The Jaina vision of the universe and the world is complicated, inventive, and above all, extremely idealized. No doubt, a number of the Jaina views on the universe and its parts, however small, is based on facts. For instance, the descriptions of the celestial bodies and of Bharata as the Indian subcontinent are partly based on empirical observations. However, even the shapes, dimensions and eventually the movements of these factual entities are moulded into a quasi-perfect image that satisfies the almost aesthetic demand for symmetry and relative proportion. In Jaina cosmography and geography, the endeavour of the human mind to grasp his universe and his world in idealised patterns is illustrated at its best.

Jaina cosmography and geography forms an essential part of Jainism as a religion. Jainism is very holistic. It organises all elements of the human and the non-human world into an integrated whole of which cosmography and geography are fundamental parts. Jainism presents a worldview that leaves very little to imagination though its contents may look largely imaginary indeed.

Since the *Jambūdvīpasaṃgrahaṇī* of Haribhadra Sūri deals with Jaina geography only, I will not go into detail here regarding the views on the construction of the universe itself.[1] More or less elaborate and illustrated descriptions of its constituents and its form and shape can be found in several works on the Jaina doctrines as e.g. in Caillat, C. & Kumar, R. (1981), Guérinot, A. (1926), pp. 174-79, Padmanabh, S. Jaini (1979), pp. 127-131, Schubring, W. (1962), pp. 204-246 and von Glasenapp, H. (1964), pp. 214-243. The most comprehensive and detailed exposition, however, will be found in Kirfel, W. (1920): *Die Kosmographie der Inder; nach den Quellen dargestellt*, pp. 208-339.

In the centre of the middle part (Madhyaloka[2]) of the Jaina universe, between the upper world consisting of seven heavenly regions and the lower world consisting of seven hellish abodes, Jambūdvīpa, the island of the Rose Apple tree (Jambū), lies.[3] This Madhyaloka is a vast flat disc made up of

---

[1] Fig. 1, p. 266 gives a general idea of the layout of the Jaina universe.

[2] Also Tiryagloka, the world of creatures moving horizontally, viz. animals, birds, men, etc.

[3] For a general view, see Figs. 2*ff*, pp. 267*ff*. Near the centre of Jambūdvīpa, in Uttarakuru (See Fig. 10, p. 275 and the description in *sū.* 11 & 12, pp. 151*ff*), a unique specimen of the Jambū tree grows that gives this land part of its name. There has been some discussion about the identification of this 'canonical' Jambū tree with a living species. D. Wujastyk in his 'Jambūdvīpa: Apples or Plums', in: *Studies in the History of the Exact Sciences in Honour of David Pingree*, edited by Charles Burnett, Jan P. Hogendijk, Kim Plofker and Michio Yano, Leiden: Brill, 2004, identifies it with the *Eugenia jambolana*, the Jambul or Black Plum, not with the Rose Apple as it is done erroneously in the dictionaries. Only for tradition's sake I have kept the name 'Rose Apple tree'.

an innumerable amount of oceans and lands concentrically surrounding the core, being Jambūdvīpa itself. Jambūdvīpa is a vast stretch of land also in the form of a disc with a diameter 100,000 *yojanas*[1]. It is completely encircled by the Lavaṇa Samudra or the Salt Ocean. That is the reason why it is called an 'island'. It is rimmed by a wall and is divided into seven continents by six huge 'continent-supporting' (Varṣadhara-parvata) mountain ranges that extend from east to west, from one side of the Lavaṇa Ocean to the other.[2] Each continent is again subdivided by fourteen great rivers (Mahānadī)[3] each with many tributaries, smaller mountain ranges (Vaitāḍhya), single mountain peaks (Kūṭa), and is characterized by forests (Vana), lakes (Hrada), lotus ponds, etc.

Haribhadra Sūri treats all topics mentioned above very succinctly in his *Jaṃbūdvīpasaṃgrahaṇī* (*JDSH*). This concise presentation of the subject matter is carried out in the typical aphoristic *sūtra* style, originally intended to be memorized. However, this very sketchy geographical information is fortunately rather elaborately commented upon by Prabhānanda Sūri. In fact, without Prabhānanda's commentary, the basic text of the *JDSH* would be quite unintelligible for a reader not already familiar with Jaina geography.

---

[1] One Yojana is the distance traversed 'in harnessing or without unyoking', sometimes regarded as equal to four or five English miles, but more correctly four Krośas or about nine miles. According to other calculations, it is two and a half English miles.

[2] See Fig. 3, p. 268.

[3] See Fig. 4, p. 269.

1.2 The *Jambūdvīpasaṃgrahaṇī* and its *Vṛtti*

1.2.1 Haribhadra Sūri and Prabhānanda Sūri

The name Haribhadra Sūri, or simply Haribhadra, is well known in the Jaina tradition. Many works in different fields of the Jaina lore, written in Sanskrit as well as Prākrit, are attributed to him. However, there is more than one Jaina author bearing the name of Haribhadra (Sūri).[1]

Haribhadra Sūri 1 or Haribhadra 'Virahāṅka' flourished around 529 A.D.[2] He is the author of the *Pañcāśakas* written in Prākrit[3]. The concluding verses of each of its 19 parts contain the word '*viraha*' or '*bhavaviraha*'. Therefore, the author is named 'Haribhadra (Bhava-)Virahāṅka'[4].

Haribhadra Sūri 2 or Haribhadra 'Mahattarā-Yākinī-putra'[5] lived around 750 A.D.[6] This is the most famous Haribhadra,

---

[1] Klatt in his *Specimen of a Jaina Onomasticon* (Leipzig, 1892, p. 7; ref. found in Williams, R., 1959, p. 12) lists eight Haribhadra Sūris! For an overview of all Haribhadras and their works as listed in the *Jinaratnakośa* (*JRK*), see 'Appendix 2', p. 1252.

[2] Williams, R. (1963), pp. 4*ff*.

[3] Also called *Pañcāśakasūtra* or *Pañcāśakaprakaraṇa*, *Pañcāśakāni*, *Pañcāsaya*, *Pañcāsaga*, *Pañcāsagapagaraṇa*, etc., Tripāṭhī (1975), p. 203. See also the same, Mss. entries 144H and 145H, pp. 202-205. In its colophon MS 144H, p. 203 mentions Haribhadra as the author: ...-*śrī-haribhadra-sūri-viracita-paṃcāśakâkhya-ṭīkêti*.

[4] As it is explicitly mentioned in the commentary of Abhayadeva on the Pañcāśaka: *iha ca viraha-śabdena (śr)ī-haribhadrācārya-kṛtatā prakaraṇasya sūcitā, virahâṅkatvāt tasyêti* ..., ibid.

[5] Lit. '[spiritual] son of the most respectable [nun] Yākinī'.

[6] Williams, R. (1963), pp. 7-8, who follows Muni Jinavijaya.

author of the *Anekāntajayapatākā* (Victory Banner of Relativism) with an auto-commentary (*Ṭīkā Svopajña*) and a *Vivaraṇa* by Municandra Sūri, and of numerous other works on Jaina Āgama, philosophy and yoga.[1]

Haribhadra Sūri 3 is the author of the *Nemināthacarit(r)a* (*Nemināhacariya*) which narrates the life story of Neminātha, the 23th Tīrthaṃkara.[2] The *Nemināthacarita* was written, in

[1] The other works of this Haribhadra Sūri 2 are: the *Anekāntapraghaṭṭa*, *Anekāntavādapraveśa* and *Anekāntasiddhi*, a *Laghuvṛtti* on an *Anuyogadvārasūtra*, a (*Bṛhad*)*Vṛtti* or *Siṣyahitā* on Bhadrabāhu's *Āvaśyakasūtraniryukti*, a *Ṭīkā* on the *Daśavaikālikasūtranirukti* of Bhadrabāhu, the *Dharmabindu* and *Dharmasaṃgrahaṇī*, a *Laghuvṛtti* on the *Jīvājīvābhigamasūtra*, the *Lokatattvanirṇaya* and *Lokavinīśika*, a *Vivaraṇa* on the *Nandīsūtra*, a commentary on Śaṃkarasvāmin's *Nyāyapraveśa*, the *Pañcāśakasūtra*, a *Ṭīkā* on Cirantanācārya's *Pañcasūtra*, a commentary on Umāsvāti's *Praśamaratiprakarana*, the *Ṣaḍdarśanasamuccaya*, *Śāstravārttāsamuccaya*, *Ṣoḍaśakaprakaraṇa* and *Tattvaprakāśa*, a *Laghuvṛtti* on Umāsvāti's *Tattvārthasūtra*, the *Upadeśapada*, *Yogabindu*, *Yogadṛṣṭisamuccaya*, *Yogaviṃśika*, *Yogaśataka* and *Viṃśatīviṃśikā*. See Potter, K.H. (1983): *Bibliography of Indian Philosophies*', pp. 183*ff* or consult Potter, K. (2004), the same but updated on-line version of *The Encyclopedia of Indian Philosophies*, developed and maintained by Christine Keyt: http://faculty.washington.edu/kpotter/ (consulted on 02.06.04). See also H. Jacobi: 'Haribhadra's Age, Life and Works', in: Jina Vijaya Muni: *Dhūrtākhyāna of Haribhadra Sūri*, 1944, and Banerjee, N.R.: 'An Introduction to the life and Works of Haribhadra Suri, A Jaina Scholar-Saint of the 8th century', in: S.D. Trivedi (ed., 1989): *Essays on Indology, Polity and Administration, In honour of Padmabhushan Sh. R. K. Trivedi* (Vol. I). Delhi: Agam Kala Prakashan, pp. 257-267.

[2] The Apabhraṃśa portion, the *Sanatkumāracarita* was edited separately by H. Jacobi, Munchen, 1921. It was fully edited by Bhayani, H.C. & Modi, M.C. (1970 & 1971) as: *Haribhadra's Nemināhacariya*.

Apabhraṃśa, in Saṃ. 1216 at Ahnilwad during the reign of King Kumārapāla of Gujarat. The author was member of the Vaṭa Gaccha and his teacher was Candra Sūri.[1]

Haribhadra Sūri 4 is the author of one of the 18 versions of the *Maṇipaticarit(r)a* or *Munipaticarit(r)a* (MPCH) dated Saṃ. 1172.[2] According to Desai, Haribhadra Sūri, the author of the *Maṇipaticarita*, was a pupil of Jinadeva Upādhyāya of the Bṛhad Gaccha. He composed a commentary on the *Karmagrantha* (Saṃ. 1172), on the *Praśamarati* (Saṃ. 1185) and also composed a certain '*Kṣetrasamāsa*'.[3]

I order to investigate the matter more closely, let us first have a look at the information relevant to the figure of Haribhadra Sūri as found in the *JRK* starting from Desai's statement that the Haribhadra Sūri of the *Maṇipaticaritra* was

---

Lalbhai Dalpatbhai Series 23 & 25, Ahmedabad: Lalbhai Dalpatbhai Bharatiya Samskriti Vidyamandir.

[1] *JRK*, p. 217.

[2] See Williams, R. (1959): *Two Prakrit Versions of the Maṇipati-carita*, p. 12. Verse 645 reads: *nayaṇa-muṇi-rudde saṃkhe Vikkama-saṃvaccharaṃmi*. The same is noted by Schubring in the Berlin Ms. of the *Maṇipaticarita*: *Vikramāditya thī saṃvatsara saṃsyā etale saṃ. 1172 raci che*. See also the *JRK*, p. 311.

[3] M.D. Desai in: Fattehcand Belānī: *Jaina grantha aur granthakār*. Benares, 1946 (ref. found in Williams, R., 1959, p. 12). Regarding this identification Williams, R. (ibid.) says: "... but his identification with the author of the *MPCH*, however probable, seems to rest only on the coincidence of date". For the *MPCH*, see Tripāṭhī (1975) Mss. nos. 209H, 210H, 211H and 212.

a pupil of Jinadeva of the Bṛhad Gaccha. The *JRK* links Haribhadra and Jinadeva in the following manner[1]:

JRK	**author**	**relationship(s) & work(s)**	**dates & places**
21	Haribhadra	- pupil of Jinadeva of the Bṛhad Gaccha; - author of *Vṛtti* on the *Āgamanikavastu-vicārasāraprakaraṇa* (= *Ṣaḍaśīti*) of Jinavallabhagaṇi of the Kharatara Gaccha.	Comp. Saṃ. 1172 at Ahnilvad.
72-73	Haribhadra	- pupil of Jinadeva; - author of a *Ṭīkā* on the (*Bṛhat* or *Prācīna-*) *Karma-vipāka* of Gargarṣi; - author of a *Ṭīkā* on the (*Bṛhat* or *Prācīna-*) *Karmastava* of Jinavallabha.	No date.
281	Haribhadra	- pupil of Jinadeva Upādhyāya of the Bṛhad Gaccha; - author of a *Ṭīkā* on the *Bandhasvāmitva*.	Id.
300, 311	Haribhadra (Sūri)	- pupil of Jinadeva, pupil of Mānadeva of the Bṛhad Gaccha; - author of *Maṇipaticaritra* (Pkt., = *Munipati-caritra*).	Comp. Saṃ. 1172.
399	Haribhadra	- pupil of Jinadeva of the Bṛhad Gaccha;	

[1] The data given here are drawn from my list of references to the Haribhadras mentioned in the *JRK* and presented in the 'Appendix 2', p. 252. The numbers in the first columns refer to the pages in the *JRK*.

		- author of the *Śreyāṃsacarita.*	Comp. Saṃ. 1172.

Next there is the statement that the Haribhadra Sūri of the *Maṇipaticaritra* also wrote a commentary on the *Karmagrantha* composed in Saṃ. 1172. This must be the same as the *Ṭīkā* on the (*Bṛhat* or *Prācīna-*)*Karmavipāka* of Gargarṣi or the *Ṭīkā* on the (*Bṛhat* or *Prācīna-*)*Karmastava* of Jinavallabha.[1] Concerning the assertion that the same Haribhadra Sūri also wrote a commentary on the *Praśamarati* in Saṃ. 1185, we indeed find in the *JRK*:

273	Haribhadra	- pupil of Mānadeva of the Bṛhad Gaccha; - author of a *Ṭīkā* on the *Praśamarati.*	Comp. Saṃ. 1185.

The information obtained so far does not contain any anomaly. Now we have to consider Desai's assertion that the same Haribhadra Sūri also wrote a certain '*Kṣetrasamāsa*'. The *JRK* lists twelve *Kṣetrasamāsas* authored by Umāsvāti[2] (Skt.), Jinabhadragaṇi[3] (Pkt.), Somatilaka Sūri (Pkt.), Ratnaśekhara Sūri, Devānanda, Candraprabha, Padmadeva Sūri, Śrī Candra Sūri, Hemācārya (?), Jayaśekhara and two anonymous ones. Therefore, Haribhadra Sūri cannot be linked directly, viz. as author, to a work named '*Kṣetrasamāsa*'. However, we indeed find a Haribhadra, author of a *Vṛtti* on the

---

[1] See *JRK*, p. 69.

[2] Also named *Jambūdvīpasamāsa.*

[3] Also named *Bṛhatkṣetrasamāsa* (*BKSJ*).

(Bṛhat-)Kṣetrasamāsa of Jinabhadragaṇi.[1] Maybe Desai reference is only to this commentary on the *BKSJ* and not to the basic text of Jinabhadragaṇi. However, there is another possibility. The words '*kṣetra*' and '*jambūdvīpa*', and '*samāsa*' and '*saṃgrahaṇī*' are readily interchanged in several works on Jaina geography, and the title '*Kṣetrasamāsa*' applies entirely or partly to works of different authors.[2] In the introductory stanza of Prabhānanda's commentary on the *JDSH* the alternative title '*Kṣetrasaṃgrahaṇī*' is explicitly used for the *Jambūdvīpasamāsa*.

Next, let us have a look at all the Haribhadras mentioned in the *JRK* who wrote a basic work or a commentary on Jaina cosmography and geography in general.

98	Haribhadra	- author of a *Vṛtti* on the *BKSJ*.	Comp. Saṃ. 1185.
130	Haribhadra	- author of *Ṭīkā* (Pkt.) on the *Jambū-dvīpaprajñapti*.	No date.
131, 336	Haribhadra Sūri	- author of the *Jambūdvīpasaṃgrahaṇī* (Pkt., 30 gāthās, = *Laghusaṃgrahaṇī*) with *Vṛtti* of Prabhānanda Sūri.	Comp. Saṃ. 1390.
286	Haribhadra	- author of the *Munipaticaritra* and of - a *Vṛtti* on the *Bṛhatsaṃgrahaṇī* of Jina-bhadragaṇi.	No dates.

[1] *JRK*, p. 98.

[2] See 'Bibliography, Primary sources', pp. 278*ff.*

Here we find Haribhadra Sūri as the author of the *Jambūdvīpasaṃgrahaṇī* (≐ *Laghusaṃgrahaṇī*) with a *Vṛtti* of Prabhānanda Sūri dated Saṃ. 1390. Now, firstly, the *Vṛttis* mentioned on pp. 98 and 286 of the *JRK* must be the same since the *Bṛhatkṣetrasamāsa* and the *Bṛhatsaṃgrahaṇī*, both of Jinabhadragaṇi, are definitely identical.[1] Secondly, the author of the *Maṇipaticaritra* (or *Munipaticaritra*) is indeed the same as the author of the *Vṛtti* on the *BKSJ*. Thirdly, we have to record the facts that the Haribhadra of the *Munipaticaritra* wrote a commentary on the *BKSJ*, and that there is also a Haribhadra who wrote a commentary on the *JDP*, which both are quoted in the commentary of Prabhānanda Sūri on the *JDSH*. So, we may conclude for the moment that Haribhadra Sūri, author of the *JDSH* (also named *Kṣetrasamāsa* ?), was a pupil of Jinadeva and, directly or indirectly, of Mānadeva, both of the Bṛhad Gaccha, and that he is likely to be also the author of:

1. a *Vṛtti* on the *Āgamanikavastuvicārasāraprakaraṇa* (= *Ṣaḍaśīti*) of Jinavallabhagaṇi of the Kharatara Gaccha composed in Saṃ. 1172 at Ahnilvad,
2. a commentary on the *Karmagrantha* composed in Saṃ. 1172, being the *Ṭīkā* on the *(Bṛhat or Prācīna-) Karmavipāka* of Gargarṣi or the *Ṭīkā* on the *(Bṛhat or Prācīna-)Karmastava* of Jinavallabha,

[1] K. Potter also mentions a Haribhadra Sūri being the author of a *Vṛtti* on Jinabhadra's *Kṣetrasamāsa*. See Potter, K. on-line (2004), entry 646 (consulted on 2.06.04). The date given for Haribhadra here is 1129 A.D. or Saṃ. 1186, which does agree with the dates for Haribhadra Sūri given above. According to the same source this Haribhadra Sūri was also the author of the *Darśanasaptatiprakaraṇa* and the *Jñānādityaprakaraṇa*.

3. a *Ṭīkā* on the *Bandhasvāmitva*,
4. the *Maṇipaticaritra* (Pkt. = *Munipaticaritra*) composed in Saṃ. 1172,
5. the *Śreyāṃsacarita* composed in Sàṃ. 1172,
6. a *Ṭīkā* on the *Praśamarati* composed in Saṃ. 1185,
7. a *Vṛtti* on the *BKSJ* or *Bṛhatkṣetrasaṃgrahaṇī* of Jinabhadragaṇi composed in Saṃ. 1185,
8. a *Ṭīkā* (Pkt.) on the *Jambūdvīpaprajñapti* and, finally,
9. the *Jambūdvīpasaṃgrahaṇī* (Pkt., 30 *gāthās*, = *Laghu-saṃgrahaṇī*) with a*Vṛtti* of Prabhānanda Sūri which was allegedly composed in Saṃ. 1390.

The information on Jinadeva and Mānadeva in the *JRK* is, however, scanty:

72	Jinadeva	- teacher of Haribhadra Sūri.	No date.
294	Id.	- teacher of Malliṣeṇa.	Id.
311	Id.	- teacher of Haribhadra Sūri, author of the *Munipaticaritra*.	Comp. Saṃ. 1172.
317	Jinadeva Sūri	- author of the *Yatipratiṣṭhāsthāpana-sthala*.	Comp. Saṃ. 1185.
305	Mānadeva Sūri	- teacher of Śīlācārya, author of the *Mahāpuruṣacarita* (Pkt.).	Comp. Saṃ. 925.
306	Id.	- teacher of Deva Sūri, author of the *Mahāvīracarita* (Pkt.).	No date.
311	Mānadeva	- of the Bṛhad Gaccha, teacher of Jinadeva.	Id.

From this we may conclude that Jinadeva (and maybe also Mānadeva) of the Bṛhad Gaccha was teacher of Haribhadra

Sūri. Jinadeva can be dated ca. Saṃ. 1185. Now we can have a closer look at Prabhānanda, commentator of the *JDSH*:

44	Prabhānanda	- pupil of Devabhadra who was pupil of Abhayadeva.	No date.
58	Id.	- pupil of Devabhadra; - author of a *Ṭīkā* on the *Ṛṣabha-pañcāśikā* (= *Dhanapālapañcāśikā*) of Dhanapāla Kavi.	Id.
131	Id.	- of the Śrīkṛṣṇa Gaccha; - pupil of Haribhadra Sūri; - author of a *Vṛtti* on the *Jambūdvīpa-saṃgrahaṇī* of Haribhadra Sūri.	Comp. Saṃ. 1390.
362	Id.	- successor of Devabhadra of the Kharatara Gaccha; - author of a *Ṭīkā* (= *Durgapada-prakāśa*) on the *ītarāgastotra* (= *Viṃśatiprakāśa*) of Hemacandra[1].	No date.
461	Prabhānanda Sūri	- pupil of Devabhadra who was pupil of Abhayadeva Sūri; - spiritual brother of Paramānanda Sūri; - author of the *Hitopadeśāmṛta* with *Vṛtti* of Paramānandasūri.	Comp. Saṃ. 1304.

So, Prabhānanda was (1) a pupil of Devabhadra who himself was a pupil of Abhayadeva Sūri, and (2) he had a spiritual brother named Paramānanda. This means that both

[1] See M.B. Emeneau, 1935, entry no. 4198.

Prabhānanda and Paramānanda must have lived at about the same time. Paramānanda wrote a *Vṛtti* in Saṃ. 1304 on the *Hitopadeśāmṛta* of his spiritual brother Prabhānanda. This suggests that the date of Saṃ. 1390 associated with Prabhānanda's commentary on the *JDSH* is doubtful, if not altogether wrong.

The relevant data on Paramānanda found in the JRK are:

72	Paramānanda	- pupil of Abhayadeva; - author of a *Ṭīkā* on the *Karmavipāka* of Gagarṣi.	No date.
100	Paramānanda Sūri	- pupil of Bhadra Sūri.	Id.
272	Id.	- pupil of Abhayadeva Sūri, pupil of Bhadreśvara Sūri; - author of the *Pravrajyāvadhāna* (= *Pravrajyākulaka*).	Id.
280	Id.	- guru of Kṣamāratna.	Id.
432	Id.	- pupil of Abhayadeva Sūri; - author of the *Samācārī*.	Id.
461	Id.	- pupil of Devabhadra, pupil of Abhayadeva Sūri; - spiritual brother Prabhānanda; - author of a *Vṛtti* on the *Hitopadeśāmṛta* of Prabhānanda.	Comp. Saṃ. 1304.

Finally, let us have a look at the information contained in the *JRK* on Abhayadeva Sūri and Devabhadra[1] in relation to Haribhadra Sūri, Prabhānanda Sūri and Paramānda Sūri:

47	Haribhadra Sūri	- successor of Abhayadeva Sūri.	No date.
230 - 231	Haribhadra	- author of the *Pañcāśakasūtra* (19 Pañcāśakas) with *Vṛtti* of Abhayadeva Sūri and, with *Cūrṇi* (Pkt.) of Yaśodeva with own (?) *Ṭīkā*.	Comp. Saṃ. 1124, comp. Saṃ. 1172.
44	Devabhadra	- pupil of Abhayadeva.	
44, 58, 131, 362, 461	Prabhānanda Sūri	- pupil and successor of Devabhadra, pupil of Haribhadra Sūri; - spiritual brother of Paramānanda Sūri; - author of a *Vṛtti* on the *Hitopadeśāmṛta* of Paramānanda Sūri.	Comp. Saṃ. 1304.

[1] Potter (on-line edition, 2004, entries 593, 647, 727, 741 & 1461, consulted on 2.06.04) lists five Devabhadras: a Devabhadra 1 dated 1027 A.D. (= Saṃ. 1084), author of a *Vivaraṇa* on the *Darśanaśuddhiprakaraṇa* (with the help of Śāntibhadra Sūri) and of a *ṬṬippaṇa* on Siddhasena Divākara's *Nyāyāvatāra*, a Devabhadra 2 dated 1130 A.D. (= Saṃ. 1187), author of a *Vṛtti* on Jinavallabha's *Dvādaśakulaka* and a *Vṛtti* on Padmajineśvara's *Upadeśaratnamālā*, a Devabhadra 3 dated 1240 A.D. (= Saṃ. 1297), author of a commentary on Candra Sūri's *Kṣetrasamāsa*, a *Ṭippaṇa* on Siddharṣi Gaṇi's *Nyāyāvatāravivṛti* and a *Vṛtti* on Candra Sūri's *Laghusaṃgrahaṇī*, and a Devabhadra 4 dated 1251 A.D. (= Saṃ. 1308), author of the *Pramāṇaprakāśa* and a *Vṛtti* on Jinavallabha Sūri's *Dvādaśakulaka* (This last must be wrong since it is listed twice).

This means further that (1) Haribhadra Sūri 4 was successor of Abhayadeva (which not necessarily means that he was his pupil) who flourished arround Saṃ. 1124[1], (2) that Devabhadra was a pupil of Abhayadeva and (3) that Prabhānanda Sūri was a pupil and successor of Devabhadra and (4) that Prabhānanda Sūri had a spiritual brother, Paramānanda Sūri, who wrote a commentary on one of his works in Saṃ. 1304.

Conclusions: (1) The author of the *JDSH* (also called *Kṣetrasamāsa* ?) is Haribhadra Sūri 4 (See above, ca. Saṃ. 1180 or 1123 A.D.), pupil of (→) Jinadeva and successor of (→|) Abhayadeva Sūri (ca. Saṃ. 1124 or 1067 A.D.). (2) Prabhānanda Sūri was the spiritual brother of (⇆|) Paramānanda Sūri and pupil of Devabhadra 2 (ca. Saṃ. 1184 or 1241 A.D.). Prabhānanda Sūri cannot have composed his *Vṛtti* on the *JDSH* in Saṃ. 1390. (3) The date of Paramānanda, Saṃ. 1304 is also improbable. The final conclusions, put into a scheme, are as follows:

---

[1] The dating of the different Abhayadevas (AD) is no easy task since there are at least three of them: AD 1, ca. Saṃ. 1120 (*JRK*, pp. 55, 64, 147, 224, 231, 290 & 407); AD 3, ca. 1160 (*JRK*, pp. 28, 57, 143 & 431); AD 3 ca Saṃ. 1242 (*JRK*, p. 133) and AD 4 ca. Saṃ. 1451 (*JRK*, pp. 181, 292, 364). Probably this Abhayadeva can be identified with the Abhayadeva Sūri (1060 A.D. = Saṃ. 1117) of the *Bhāṣya* on Jinacandra's *Navatattvaprakaraṇa*. See Potter, K. on-line (2004) entry 610. K. H. Kamdar in his E-article 'The Anuttara Upapatika Sutra', *http://www.ibiblio.org/jainism/database/ ARTICLE/anuttar.doc* (consulted on 08.06.04), is very precise concerning the date of Abhayadeva Sūri: "Abhayadeva Suri of the Chandra Gachcha and the disciple of Jineshwar Suri (...) was ordained a monk in Vikrama Samvat 1088 at the age of ten years and he died in Vikram Samvat, 1135, at Kapadavanj, Khaira district, Gujarat".

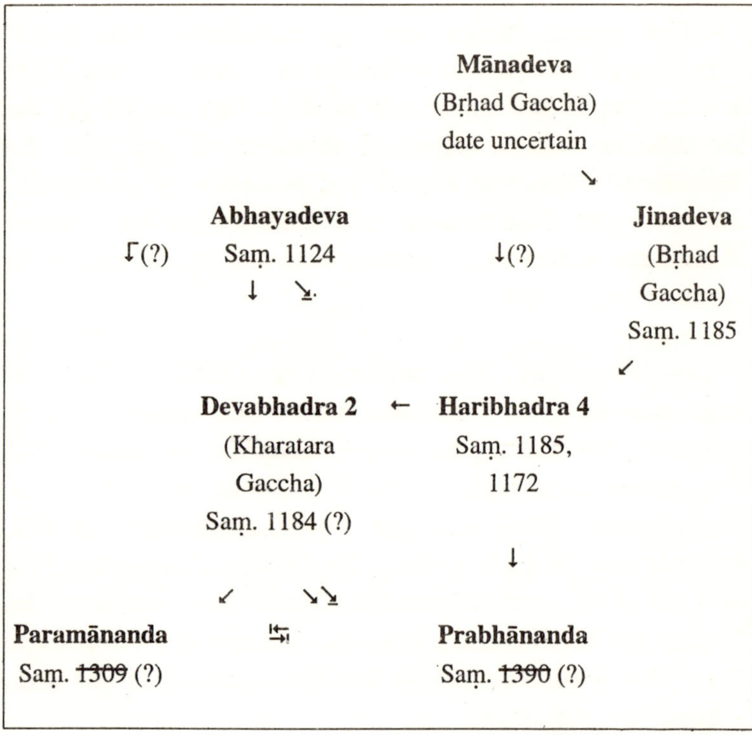

1.2.2 The text

The *JDSH* is one of the minor (*Laghu*) texts on Jaina geography written in standard Māhārāṣṭrī. It is also named *Kṣetrasaṃgrahaṇī*, *Laghusaṃgrahaṇī* or *Laghusaṃghayaṇī*, *Jambūdvīpasaṃghayaṇī* or *Jaṃbūdīvasaṃghayaṇī*, or simply *Saṃgrahaṇī* or *Saṃghayaṇī*. It consists of thirty *gāthās* or *āryās* and describes the structure of Jambūdvīpa in a very concise manner. It relies on canonical sources such as the *Jambūdvīpaprajñapti* and *Jīvājīvābhigamasūtra*, and on post-canonical works such as the *Bṛhatkṣetrasamāsa* of

Jinabhadragaṇi and the *Jambūdvīpasamāsa* of Umāsvāti Vācaka.

1.2.3 The subject matter: the ten topics

After the Maṅgalācaraṇa or salutatory formula in *sūtra* 1, Haribhadra Sūri introduces the subject matter of the *JDSH* in *sūtra* 2 in the form of ten topics[1]: 1. the Sectors (*khaṇḍa*, Pkt. ***khaṃḍa***), 2. the Yojanas (Pkt. ***joẏaṇa***), 3. the Continents (*varṣa*, Pkt. ***vāsa***), 4. the Mountains (*parvata*, Pkt. ***pavvaẏa***), 5. the Peaks (*kūṭa*, Pkt. ***kūḍa***), 6. the Fortresses (*tīrtha*, Pkt. ***tittha***), 7. the Rows (of abodes of the gods: *śreṇi*, Pkt. ***seḍhi***), 8. the Provinces (*vijaya*, Pkt. ***vijaẏa***), 9. the Lakes (*hrada*, Pkt. ***daha***) and 10. the Rivers (*salilā*, Pkt. ***salilā***).[2]

Topic 1 - the Sectors - *sūtras 3-5*. With Bharata as standard measure Jambūdvīpa counts 190 sectors or, more precise, sector-widths. A sector or *khaṇḍa* is defined as the width of Bharata being $^1/_{19}$ of the diameter of Jambūdvīpa which is 100,000 *yojanas*. Therefore, a sector measures 526 $^6/_{19}$ *yojanas*. These sector widths increase and decrease progressively from south to north in the proportions 1 - 2 - 4 - 8 - 16 - 32 - 64 - 32 - 16 - 8 - 4 - 2 - 1 for alternately continents and world mountain ranges, viz. Bharata, Himavat, Haimavata, Mahāhimavat, Hari, Niṣadha, Mahāvideha, Nīla, Ramyaka, Rukmin, Hairaṇyata, Śikharin and Airāvata.

---

[1] *dvāra*. (Pkt. ***dāra***).

[2] This is exactly the order of topics as given in the *JDP*, *sū.* 125 (ed. Javeri, 1920, p. 425).

Topic 2 - the Yojanas - *sūtras 6-10*. Distances and surface areas are measured in *yojanas* and square *yojanas* respectively. The circumference of Jambūdvīpa, being a perfect circle, is the square root of ten times the square of its diameter, which is 100,000 *yojanas*. The outcome is a bit more than 316,227 *yojanas*. Its surface area is the circumference multiplied with a quarter of the diameter. The result is 7,905,694,150 square *yojanas*. Prabhānanda Sūri's commentary calculates both in detail.[1]

Topic 3 - the Continents - *sūtra 11a*.[2] The continents are, from south to north, 1. Bharata(varṣa)[3], 2. Haimavata(v°)[4], 3. Hari(v°)[5], 4. Videha(v°)[6], 5. Ramyaka(v°)[7], 6. Hairaṇyata(v°)[8] and 7. Airāvata(v°)[9].

Topic 4 - the Mountains - *sūtras 11b-12*. There are four curved and thirty-four elongated Vaitāḍhya or Vijayārdha mountains and sixteen Vakṣaskāra mountains. There are also Citra and Vicitra, two Yamaka mountains, two hundred Kāñcana mountains and four Gajadanta mountains. There is also Meru or Mandara in the centre of Jambūdvīpa. Finally, there are six great world mountain ranges, viz. from south to

---

[1] See 'Appendix 1', p. 278, for additional information on the calculation.

[2] See Fig. 2, p. 267.

[3] Pkt. Bharaha.

[4] Pkt. Hemavaī.

[5] Pkt. Harivāsa.

[6] Or Mahāvideha, Pkt. id.

[7] Pkt. Ramma(ẏ)a.

[8] Pkt. Heraṇṇava(ẏ)a.

[9] Pkt. Erāva(ẏ)a.

north: 1. Himavat[1], 2. Mahāhimavat[2], 3. Niṣadha[3], 4. Nīla[4], 5. Rukmin[5] and 6. Śikharin[6].

Topic 5 - the Peaks - *sūtras 13-17.* The sixteen Vakṣāra mountains have four peaks each, Saumanasa and Gandhamādana seven, and Rukmi and Mahāhimavat eight. The thirty-four Vaitāḍhya mountain ranges and also Vidyutprabha, Niṣadha, Nīlavanta, Mālyavat and Suragiri possess nine peaks each. On Himavat and Śikharin there are eleven peaks. There are thirty-four Ṛṣabha peaks in the provinces and eight on Meru, on the Jambū tree, in Devakuru and on both the Harikūṭa and Haritsaha.

Topic 6 - the Fortresses - *sūtra 18.*[7] All provinces in Mahāvideha as well as Airāvata and Bharata have three fortresses: Māgadha, Varadāma, and Prabhāsa.

Topic 7 - the Rows - *sūtra 19.*[8] On the Vaitāḍhya mountain ranges there are two rows of palaces of the Vidyādhara and Ābhiyaugika gods.

Topic 8 - the Provinces - *sūtra 20a.*[1] There are thirty-four provinces: Bharata and Airāvata plus thirty-two smaller ones in Mahāvideha.

---

[1] Also Himavanta, Kṣullahimavat, Kṣudrahimavat, Pkt. Cullahimavanta.
[2] Pkt. Mahāhimavanta.
[3] Pkt. Nisaha.
[4] Also Nīlavat, Pkt. Nīlavanta.
[5] Pkt. Ruppi.
[6] Pkt. Sihari
[7] See Fig. 6, p. 271 and Fig. 11, p. 276.
[8] See Fig. 12, p. 277.

Topic 9 - the Lakes - *sūtra 20b.*[2] There are six great lakes on top of the world mountain ranges: Padma, Mahāpadma, Ti(ṅ)giccha, Keśarin, Mahāpuṇḍarīka and Puṇḍarīka. In de Kuru regions there are ten smaller lakes.

Topic 10 - the Rivers - *sūtra 21-26.*[3] The main rivers are: the Gaṅgā and the Sindhu, the Raktā and the Raktavatī, the Rohitāṃśā and the Rohitā[4], the Rūpyakūlā and the Suvarṇakūlā[5].

In the *sūtras* 27-28 the *JDSH* discusses what actually should have been included in topic 4. Both verses treat the height and colour of the world mountain ranges. In *sūtra* 29 the Niṣadha and Nīlavat mountains are dealt with. Finally, *sūtra* 30 represents the closing formula.

1.2.4 The critical edition

The present critical edition of the *JDSH* is based on three printed editions and twenty-three manuscripts. Below both types of sources are listed under their respective abbreviated titles of reference.

---

[1] See Fig. 7, p. 272.
[2] See Fig. 5, p. 270.
[3] See Fig. 4, p. 269.
[4] Also Rohit.
[5] Also Svarṇakūlā.

1.2.4.1 The printed editions

Ed1: *Śrī-Haribhadra-Sūri-viracitā Jambūdvīpa-saṃgrahaṇī, Śrī-Prabhānanda-Sūri-viracitayā Ṭīkayā Samalaṅkatā.* Nyāyāṃbhonidhi Śrīmad-Vijayānanda-sūrīśvara Pādacaraṇāṃbhojacaṃcarikeṇa. Bhāvapura Vāstavya Śā. Āṇaṃdajī Puruṣottamasya Dravya-sāhāyyena, Prakāśayitrī. Śrī-jaina-dharma Prasāraka Sabhā - Bhāvanagar. Saṃ. 1972 or 1915 CE.

Ed2: Shah, M.J.: *Śrī Gajasāra Muni Viracita Daṇḍaka Prakaraṇa tathā Pū. Ā. Śrī Haribhadra Sūri Viracita Jambūdvīpa Saṃgrahaṇī.* Mahesāṇā: Śrī Bābūlāl Jeśiṃgalāl Mehetā, Saṃ. 2054 or 1997 CE.

Ed3: *Sūri-purandara-Śrī-Haribhadra- Sūri-viracitā Jambūdvīpa(laghu)-saṅgrahaṇī Paramapūjya Ācārya-Śrī-Vijayodaya- Sūri-viracita-vṛtti-sahitā.* Paramapūjya Ācārya Śrī-Vijaya-sūryodaya- Sūri-śaṣyamuni Nandīghoṣa-vijayaḥ. Śrī Jaina-grantha-prakāśanasamitiḥ. Vi. Saṃ. 2045 or 1988 CE.

1.2.4.2. The manuscripts

The following Mss. of the *JDSH* are kept at the L.D. Institute of Indology, Ahmedabad:

	Catalogue No.	Title	folios
LD1	947	*Jaṃbūdvīpasaṃgrahaṇī + Stabaka*	8
LD2	3916	*Jaṃbūdvīpasaṃgrahaṇī + Ṭīkā* of Prabhānanda Sūri	15

The following Mss. of the *JDSH* are found at the Oriental Institute of Vadodara (Baroda):

	Catalogue No.	Title	folios
Brd1	1606/16233	*Jaṃbūdvīpasaṃgrahaṇī*	6
Brd2	1607/16239	*Jaṃbūdvīpasaṃgrahaṇī*	4
Brd3	1607/16292	*Jaṃbūdvīpasaṃgrahaṇī*	5

The following MS of the *JDSH* was obtained from the South Asia Collection of the Universitaetsbibliothek in Tuebingen, Germany[1]:

	Catalogue No.	Title	folios
Tueb	2287	*Jaṃbūdvīpasaṃgrahaṇī*	4

The following Mss. of the *JDSH* are preserved at the in the Bhogilal Leherchand Institute of Indology, Delhi:

	Catalogue No.	Title	folios
Bhog1	312	*Jaṃbūdvīpasaṃgrahaṇī*	2
Bhog2	4236	*Jaṃbūdvīpasaṃgrahaṇī*	8
Bhog3	4237	*Laghusaṃgrahaṇīprakaraṇa* + *Vṛtti*	14
Bhog4	4239	*Jaṃbūdvīpasaṃgrahaṇīprakaraṇa*	9
Bhog5	4240/4	*Saṃgrahaṇīprakaraṇa*	4
Bhog6	4212	*Kṣetrasaṃgrahaṇī*	3

1 I obtained a copy thanks to Dr. George Baumann of the Universitätsbibliothek. This Ms. of the *JDSH* cannot be the same that Kirfel used as one of his sources for his *Kosmographie* which was kept at the Königl. Bibliothek in Berlin since this Ms. also contained the commentary of Prabhānanda (See Kirfel, p. 208).

Bhog7	4217	*Laghusaṃgrahaṇī + Stabaka*	14
Bhog8	4228/1	*Jaṃbūdvīpasaṃgrahaṇī + Pudgalakulaka*	2
Bhog9	4251/1	*Jaṃbūdvīpasaṃgrahaṇī*	3
Bhog10	4276	*Laghusaṃgrahaṇī (Saṃghayaṇīsūtra) + Stabaka*	5
Bhog11	4281	*Jaṃbūdvīpasaṃgrahaṇī*	3
Bhog12	4283	*Jaṃbūdvīpasaṃgrahaṇīprakaraṇa*	6
Bhog13	4297	*Jaṃbūdvīpasaṃgrahaṇīprakaraṇa (Jaṃbūdīvasaṃghayaṇī)*	6
Bhog14	4317	*Jaṃbūdvīpasaṃgrahaṇī (Jaṃbūdīvasaṃghayaṇī)*	12
Bhog15	4271	*Laghusaṃgrahaṇī*	5
Bhog16	4298	*Jaṃbūdvīpasaṃgrahaṇīprakaraṇa*	23
Bhog17	4767	*Jaṃbūdvīpasaṃgrahaṇīprakaraṇa*	4

Common mistakes in the Mss. of the basic text of the *JDSH* are the following. The ***o***, ***u*** and ***uṃ*** are often interchanged. The semivowel &य&, which in Jaina Mss. is generally written before ***a*** and ***ā*** and not elsewhere, is often omitted. I have consequently written &य& and &या& where required. There is often interchange of इ and ई. The *anusvāra* is frequently dropped or added. The '`' of standard Nāgarī, as for instance in 'के', is often written in the Jaina manner as 'ाक' .This 'ा' is also often misplaced in the previous or next syllable. There is often confusion between च and व, ध and थ, ट and ठ, ड and ढ, त and न, प and य, म and स, च्छ and त्थ, ट्ट and ट्ठ, ड्ड and ड्ढ, and त्त and त्र.

I have not also included in this work a critical edition of the commentary of Prabhānanda on the *JDSH*, because I had access to two versions of this commentary only: one of the printed edition Ed1 and one of the Ms. LD2. I only used the Ms. version of LD2 as a corrective on the printed edition of Ed1.

2 Text and translation

। श्रीहरिभद्रसूरिविरचिता ।

। जम्बूद्वीपसंग्रहणी ।

। श्रीप्रभानन्दसूरिविरचितवृत्तिसहिता ।

śrī-Haribhadra-sūri-viracitā

Jambūdvīpasaṃgrahaṇī

śrī-Prabhānanda-sūri-viracita-vṛtti-sahitā

Summary of Jambūdvīpa

composed by the venerable Haribhadra Sūri

with a commentary composed by the venerable

Prabhānanda Sūri

नत्वा श्रीवीरजिनं संदर्शितविश्वविश्ववस्तुचयम्।
श्रीक्षेत्रसंग्रहण्या वृत्तिं कुर्वे यथाशक्ति ॥

natvā śrī-vīra-jinaṃ saṃdarśita-viśva-viśva-vastu-cayam;
śrī-Kṣetrasaṃgrahaṇyā vṛttiṃ kurve yathā-śakti.

Paying homage to the Jina, the magnificent hero, who understands the whole of reality, I compose a commentary on the venerable *Kṣetrasaṃgrahaṇī*[1] to the utmost of my powers.

दत्तैकान्तवादिसंदोहापारसादानां गिरास्वर्गापगानादानुवादानां श्रीहरिभद्रसूरिपादानां कृतेर्व्याचिख्यासायां मादृशस्याल्पमेधसः को ऽवकासः तथाप्यर्थनिपुणप्रकरणरागात् स्वशक्तिमजानानो ऽप्युपचक्रमे ॥

dattaikānta-vādi-saṃdohāpāra-sādānāṃ girā-svargāpagā-nādānuvādānāṃ śrī-haribhadra-sūri-pādānāṃ kṛter vyācikhyāsāyāṃ mādṛśasyālpa-medhasaḥ ko 'vakāsaḥ? tathāpy artha-nipuṇa-prakaraṇa-rāgāt sva-śaktim ajānāno 'py upacakrame.

Is it appropriate for a man of little understanding like me to try to comment upon the [literary] product of the verses of the venerable Haribhadra Sūri, being the ultimate ruin of the mass of 'respected' absolutists[2] and resounding jubilantly like the

---

[1] For the alternative names of the *JDSH*, see 'Introduction', pp. 22-23.

[2] Anekāntavāda, 'Non-Absolutism', or 'Relativism' is the corner stone of Jaina philosophy. Anekāntavāda originally centres around four ontological doctrines, viz. that any real object (*vastu*) is, in an ontological perspective, existent and non-existent (*sat* & *asat*), eternal

heavenly Gaṅgā[1]? Nonetheless, though I do not consider my own capacities [very high], I have started [this commentary] out of enthusiasm for a treatise [so] perfect in content.

---

and non-eternal (*nitya* & *anitya*), universal and particular (*sāmānya* & *viśeṣa*), and describable and indescribable (*abhilāpya* & *anabhilāpya*). According to the Jainas, other philosophical systems like Buddhism, Nyāya, Vedānta, etc. adhere in some way or other to one of the alternatives exclusively (*ekānta*) and hence do so erroneously. In that sense, the Jainas called their philosophical opponents '*ekānta-vādins*' or 'absolutists'. For details, see e.g. Mookerjee, S.: *The Jaina Philosophy of Non-absolutism; A Critical Study of Anekantavada*, 2nd ed. Delhi: Motilal Banarsidass, 1978, and Matilal, B.K.: *The Central Philosophy of Jainism (Anekantavada)*, Ahmedabad: L.D. Institute of Indology (L.D. series, 79), 1981. The word 'respected' is, of course, used ironically here.

[1] *girā-svargāpagā-nāda-anuvādānām*, lit. 'resounding (like) the roaring of the heavenly river (viz. the Gaṅgā) with praise'. The word '*girā*' is the instrumental singular of *gir* 'praise' used in compound as i.e. also in *girā-vṛdh* 'delighting in or thriving by praise'.

SŪTRA 1

इह तावत् सूत्रकारः प्रथमं चतुरतिशयस्वरूपभगवन्नमस्कारमङ्गलाभिधायिकां शिष्टोपदिष्टमार्गानुसरणार्थमाद्यगाथामाह -

iha tāvat sūtra-kāraḥ prathamaṃ catur-atiśaya-svarūpa-bhagavan-namaskāra-maṅgalābhidhāyikāṃ śiṣṭopadiṣṭa-mārgānusaraṇārtham ādya-gāthām āha -

Now at the start the author of the manual puts forward the first verse that, in order to follow the procedure of instruction, expresses the greeting formula to the Lord whose essence consists of the four superior qualities[1]:

नमिय[2] जिणं सव्वन्नुं[3], जय[4]पुज्जं[5] जय[6]गुरुं[7] महावीरं[8] ।
जंबूदीव[1]पयत्थे[2], वुच्छं[3] सुत्ता[4] सपर[5]हेउं[6] ॥ १ ॥

---

[1] As it appears from the commentary, the four *atiśayas* of Lord Mahāvīra are 1. that He is a victor (*jina*) of the passions, etc., 2. that He is omniscient (*sarva-jña* and *sarva-darśin*), 3. that He is an object of universal reverence (*jagat-pūjya*) and, 4. that He is a universal teacher (*jagad-guru*).

[2] नमिअं LD2. नमियु Bhog4. नमिऊण Bhog6. नमिअ Bhog15.

[3] Bhog6 reads जितमोहं and omits सव्वन्नुं. सव्वन्नूं LD2. सव्वनुं Bhog2 & 13. सवन्नु Bhog4, 7, 10 & 15. सवन्नू Bhog8, 16 & 17. सव्वनं LD1 & Bhog12.

[4] जग Ed1, 2 & 3, Bhog9, 10, 13 & 14.

[5] पूज्जं Bhog7.

[6] जग Ed1, 2 & 3, LD1, Brd1, 2 & 3, Bhog1, 7, 9, 10, 11, 13, 14, 15, 16. Both जग and जय are attested Pkt. forms for Skt. जगत्. I have consistently opted for जय.

[7] गुरु LD1, Brd1, Bhog6, 7, 10, 12, 13 & 16. गुरूं Brd2. गुरू Bhog4, 15 & 17.

[8] महाविरं Brd2. माहाविरं Bhog2. माहावीरं Bhog4 & 17.

namiẏa jiṇaṃ savvȧnnuṃ, jaẏa-pujjaṃ jaẏa-guruṃ mahāvīraṃ;
jaṃbūdīva-paẏatthe, vucchaṃ suttā sa-para-heuṃ. 1.

(नत्वा जिनं सर्वज्ञं जगत्पूज्यं जगद्गुरुं महावीरम्। जम्बूद्वीपपदार्थान् वक्ष्ये सूत्रात्स्वपरहेतोः ॥ १ ॥ *natvā jinaṃ sarva-jñaṃ jagat-pūjyaṃ jagad-guruṃ mahāvīram; jambūdvīpa-padārthān vakṣye sūtrāt sva-para-hetoḥ. 1.*)

1. Paying homage to Mahāvīra, the Victor, omniscient, object of universal reverence and universal teacher, I will explain the elements of Jambūdvīpa based on authoritative manual[s[7]], for my own sake and for the sake of others.

COMMENTARY

नमिय जिण^इत्यादि - महावीरं नत्वा जम्बूद्वीपपदार्थान् वक्ष्ये इति सम्बन्धः। तत्र कर्मविदारणादिगुणाद्वीरः। उक्तं च -

"विदारयति यत्कर्म, तपसा च विराजते।

---

[1] जम्बूद्दीव Ed1, 2 & 3, LD2, Brd1, Tueb, Bhog12, 16 & 17. जम्बूदिव Brd2. जम्बुदिव Bhog2. जम्बुद्दीव Bhog4, 5 & 7. जम्बुदीव Bhog13 & 14. जम्बूदीवि Bhog15. जम्बूदीव is the regular Pkt. form for Skt. जम्बूद्वीप.

[2] ययत्ते Bhog12.

[3] बुच्छं Bhog8.

[4] सुता LD1, Brd2 & 3, Bhog10 & 13. ससूत्ता Bhog2. सुत्तं Bhog6.

[5] सयर Brd2. सुपडि Bhog6. सपरे Bhog17.

[6] हेऊ Ed2 & 3, Bhog1, 9, 10, 13, 14 & 17. हेओं LD1. हेउ LD2, Bhog7, 15 & 16. हेओ Bhog6. Note that ***-uṃ*** is, in fact, the ending of the accusative singular.

[7] The commentary mentions the *Jambūdvīpaprajñapti* and the *Kṣetrasamāsa* with an 'etc.' (*ādi*) added.

तपोवीर्येण युक्तश्च, तस्माद्वीर इति स्मृतः ॥ १ ॥"[1]

ततो महांश्चासौ वीरश्च महावीरश्चरमतीर्थंकरः, तं नत्वा प्रणम्य, किंविशिष्टमित्याह, रागादीनष्टादशान्तरङ्गारीन् जयत्यभिभवतीति जिनस्तं तथोक्ततं, इत्यनेनापायापगमातिशयो ऽपायरूपान्तरारिक्षयात्। तथा सर्वज्ञं, सर्वं जीवाजीवगतिस्थित्यादिकं जानाति वेत्तीति सर्वज्ञः, तं तथाविधं, इह ज्ञानग्रहणेन दर्शनमपि गृहीतं तेन सर्वदर्शिनमित्यपि प्रत्येतव्यं, तन्नान्तरीयकत्वात्, एतेन तु ज्ञानातिशयः सूचितः। तथा जगत्पूज्यं, अत्र जगच्छब्देन भिन्नग्रन्थिकभव्यसंज्ञिपर्याप्तपञ्चेन्द्रियग्रहः, ततो जगतः पूज्यो ऽर्चनीयो जगत्पूज्यं तथाप्रकारं, अनेन तु विशेषणेन पूजातिशयः। पुनः कीदृशं? जगद्गुरुं, इह जगच्छब्देन चतुर्दशरज्ज्वात्मकलोकपरिग्रहः, ततो जगच्चराचरं गृणाति कथयति जगद्गुरुः, तम् अनेकद्वीपसागर-सुरालयनैरयिकालयादिपूर्णजगद्वक्तारमित्यर्थो, मूककेवलिनो हि सर्वज्ञाः सर्वदर्शिनो ऽपि वचनसामर्थ्याभावान्न विश्वस्वरूपं निरूपयितुमलम्भूष्णवो भवन्त्यनेन तद्व्यय(व?)च्छेदाद्वचनातिशयः प्रत्यपादि। एवं गाथार्द्धेन भगवन्नमस्काररूपं मङ्गलमुक्तं, अपरार्द्धे तु अभिधेयादीनाह - **जंबुद्दीवपयत्थि**^इति, जम्बूवृक्षविशेषस्तेन उपलक्षितो द्वीपो जम्बूद्वीप, उत्तरकुरुक्षेत्रे हि नीलवद्वर्षधरमाल्यवद्वक्षस्कारशीतानदीनां बहुमध्यदेशभागे बहुतद्वृक्षलक्षलक्षितो जम्बूवृक्षो ऽस्ति, तन्नाम्नायं जम्बूद्वीपः। उक्तं च **भागवत्यङ्गे** -

> **"से केणट्ठेणं भंते, एवं वुच्चइ जंबूद्दीवे दीवे? गोयमा, जंबूद्दीवेणं दीवे मंदरस्स पव्वयस्स**[2] **उत्तरेणं लवणस्स दाहिणेणं जाव तत्थ बहवे जंबूरुका जंबूवन्ना जाव उवसोहेमाणा चिट्ठंति, से तेणट्ठेणं गोयमा, एवं वुच्चइ जंबूद्दीवे दीवे"**[3]

---

[1] Origin of quotation untraced.

[2] For **पव्वयस्य** of Ed1.

[3] स केनार्थेन भदन्त! एवमुच्यते, जम्बूद्वीपो द्वीपः? गौतम, जम्बूद्वीपो ननु द्वीपो मन्दरस्य पर्वतस्योत्तरेण लवणस्य दक्षिणेण यावत् तत्र बहवो जम्बूवृक्षा जम्बूवर्णा यावद् उपशोभमानास् तिष्ठन्ति, स तेनार्थेन गौतम! एवमुच्यते जम्बूद्वीपो द्वीपः ॥ Quotation from the *Bhagavaī* according to the *vṛtti* but I could not trace it there.

इति तत्र पदार्थाः क्षेत्रपर्वतनदीवनादयो ऽभिधेयस्तुरूपाः, तान्, किं करिष्यामि? इत्याह, वुच्छं वक्ष्याम्यभिधास्यामि, इहाऽस्मदर्थक्रियायोगात्सूत्रे ऽनुक्तो ऽप्यहमित्यात्मनिर्देशो ज्ञातव्यो, जम्बूद्वीपपदार्थान् वक्ष्यामि, अनेन त्वभिधेयं निगदिततं, न भगवतो ऽतिशायिज्ञानमन्तरेण चक्षुरगोचरैतावत्क्षेत्र-स्वरूपप्ररूपणप्रवीणतास्तीत्यादि परप्रश्ननिराकरणायाह - **सुत्त**^इति सूत्रं सिद्धान्तो गणधरादिरचितजम्बूद्वीपप्रज्ञप्तिक्षेत्रसमासादि तस्मात्, न स्वमत्यनुसारेण। किमर्थमेतावान् प्रयासः क्रियते? इत्याह - **सपरहेउ**^इति, स्व आत्मा परो ऽन्यस्तयोर्हेतुर्निमित्तं तदर्थमित्यर्थ, एतेन सम्बन्धो ऽभिहितः, स च स्वपरभेदाद् द्विधा, पुनरेकैको ऽनन्तरपरंपरभेदाद् द्विधा, तत्रान्तरः कर्तुर्भव्यसत्त्वानुग्रहः[1], परस्य श्रोतुस्त्वेतदर्थावगमो जम्बूद्वीप-विचारज्ञानरूपः, परंपरस्तु द्वयोरपि परमपदावाप्तिरिति। अभिधानं तूत्तरत्र गाथायां स्वयमेव सूत्रकारो भणिष्यति ॥ १ ॥

namiya jiṇa^*ity ādi - mahāvīraṃ natvā jambūdvīpa-padārthān vakṣye iti sambandhaḥ. tatra karma-vidāraṇādi-guṇād vīraḥ. uktaṃ ca -*

"vidārayati yat karma, tapasā ca virājate;
tapo-vīryeṇa yuktaś ca, tasmād vīra iti smṛtaḥ. 1".

tato mahāṃś cāsau vīraś ca mahāvīraś carama-tīrthaṅkaraḥ, taṃ natvā praṇamya, kiṃ viśiṣṭam ity āha, rāgādīn aṣṭādaśāntaraṅgārīn jayaty abhibhavatīti jinaḥ, taṃ tathoktaṃ, ity anenāpāyāpagamātiśayo 'pāya-rūpāntarāri-kṣayāt. tathā sarva-jñaṃ, sarvaṃ jīvājīva-gati-sthity-ādikaṃ jānāti vettīti sarva-jñaḥ, taṃ tathā-vidhaṃ, iha jñāna-grahaṇena darśanam api gṛhītaṃ tena sarva-darśinam ity api pratyetavyaṃ, tan-nāntarīyakatvāt, etena tu jñānātiśayaḥ sūcitaḥ. tathā jagat-pūjyaṃ, atra jagac-chabdena bhinna-granthika-bhavya-saṃjñi-paryāpta-pañcendriya-grahaḥ, tato jagataḥ pūjyo 'rcanīyo jagat-pūjyas taṃ tathā-prakāraṃ,

---

[1] For सत्वानुग्रहः of Ed1.

anena tu viśeṣaṇena pūjātiśayaḥ. punaḥ kīdṛśaṃ? jagad-guruṃ, iha jagac-chabdena catur-daśa-rajjv-ātmaka-loka-parigrahaḥ, tato jagac-carācaraṃ gṛṇāti kathayati jagad-guruḥ, tam aneka-dvīpa-sāgara-surālaya-nairayikālayādi-pūrṇa-jagad-vaktāram ity artho, mūka-kevalino hi sarva-jñāḥ sarva-darśino 'pi vacana-sāmarthyābhāvān na viśva-svarūpaṃ nirūpayitum alambhūṣṇavo bhavanty, anena tad-vyaya(va?)-cchedād vacanātiśayaḥ pratyapādi. evaṃ gāthārdhena bhagavan-namaskāra-rūpaṃ maṅgalam uktaṃ. aparārdhe tu abhidheyādīn āha - ***jaṃbuddīva-payatthi^****iti, jambūr vṛkṣa-viśeṣaḥ, tena upalakṣito dvīpo jambūdvīpa, uttarakuru-kṣetre hi nīlavad-varṣadhara-mālyavad-vakṣaskāra-śītā-nadīnāṃ bahu-madhya-deśa-bhāge bahu-tad-vṛkṣa-lakṣa-lakṣito jambū-vṛkṣo 'sti, tan-nāmnāyaṃ jambūdvīpaḥ. uktaṃ ca bhāgavaty-aṅge:*

> "***se keṇaṭṭheṇaṃ bhaṃte, evaṃ vuccaï jaṃbūddīve dīve? goyamā, jaṃbūddīveṇaṃ dīve maṃdarassa pavvayassa uttareṇaṃ lavaṇassa dāhiṇeṇaṃ jāva tattha bahave jaṃbū-rukā jaṃbū-vannā jāva uvasohemāṇā ciṭṭhaṃti, se teṇaṭṭheṇaṃ goyamā, evaṃ vuccaï jaṃbūddīve dīve***"[1]

iti tatra padārthāḥ kṣetra-parvata-nadī-vanādayo 'bhidheyas tu rūpāḥ, tān, kiṃ kariṣyāmi? ity āha - ***vucchaṃ*** *vakṣyāmy abhidhāsyāmi, ihāsmad-arthakriyā-yogāt sūtre 'nukto 'py aham ity ātma-nirdeśo jñātavyo, jambūdvīpa-padārthān vakṣyāmy, anena tv abhidheyaṃ nigaditam. na bhagavato*

---

[1] Origin of quotation untraced. Chāyā: *sa kenārthena bhadanta! evam ucyate, jambūdvīpo dvīpaḥ? gautama, jambūdvīpo nanu dvīpo mandarasya parvatasyottareṇaṃ lavaṇasya dakṣiṇeṇaṃ yāvat tatra bahavo jambū-vṛkṣā jambū-varṇā yāvad upaśobhamānās tiṣṭhanti, sa tenārthena gautama! evam ucyate jambūdvīpo dvīpaḥ.*

'tiśāyi-jñānam antareṇa cakṣur-agocaraitāvat kṣetra-svarūpa-prarūpaṇa-pravīṇatāstīty ādi para-praśna-nirākaraṇāyāha - **sutta**^*iti sūtraṃ siddhānto gaṇadharādi-racita-jambūdvīpa-prajñapti-kṣetrasamāsa^ādi tasmāt, na sva-maty-anusāreṇa. kim artham etāvān prayāsaḥ kriyate? ity āha -* **sa-para-heu**^*iti, sva ātmā paro 'nyas tayor hetur nimittaṃ tad-artham ity artha, etena sambandho 'bhihitaḥ, sa ca sva-para-bhedād dvidhā, punar ekaiko 'nantara-paraṃpara-bhedād dvidhā, tatrāntaraḥ kartur bhavya-sattvānugrahaḥ, parasya śrotus tv etad-arthāvagamo jambūdvīpa-vicāra-jñāna-rūpaḥ, param-paras tu dvayor api parama-padāv āptir ity, abhidhānaṃ tūttaratra gāthāyāṃ svayam eva sūtra-kāro bhaṇiṣyati. 1.*

1. '***namiya jiṇa***', etc. The [basic] construction [of the sentence] is: Paying homage to Mahāvīra, I will explain the elements of Jambūdvīpa. A victor here arises through the qualities of throwing off karma, etc. It is said:

> "*It is taught that he who throws off karma through penance, prevails. Committed to penance and vigorous exertion, that is how he becomes a victor.*"

[The word] 'Mahāvīra (Great Hero)' [is made up of] '*mahā* (great)' and '*vīra* (hero)'. [Mahāvīra is] the last Ford-maker. Paying homage to Him means saluting Him. [The author] specifies His nature.[1] A Jina (victor) is someone who conquers or subdues the eighteen inner enemies, viz. passion, etc.[2] To

---

[1] Lit. '[The author] explains how He is qualified'.

[2] Reference is made to the eighteen kinds of sin (*pāpa*) here called the 'inner enemies' (*antar-aṅga-ari*): 1. harming life (*jīva-hiṃsā*), 2. untruthfulness (*asatya*), 3. dishonesty (*adattādāna*), 4. unchastity (*abrahmacarya*), 5. excessive love for one's own possessions or

Him so described [homage is paid]. This means that He stands above death and destruction because He has destroyed the inner enemies in the form of death. Next[1] [there is the word] '*sarva-jñaṃ* (omniscient)'. An omniscient being knows or understands all modes and states of existence, etc. of the sentient and non-sentient. He [viz. Mahāvīra] is of such a kind. Here one must also understand that He has complete comprehension, because comprehension is obtained when knowledge is acquired since [comprehension] is inherent in that [viz. knowledge]. With this [the quality of His] superior knowledge is indicated. Next [there is the expression] '*jagat-pūjyaṃ* (object of universal reverence)'. Here the word '*jagat* (world)' implies the [mass of] the intelligent fully developed five-sensed beings as can be found [as described] in different treatises[2]. So, '*jagat-pūjyaṃ*' [means] 'object of reverence or

---

covetousness (*parigraha*), 6. anger (*krodha*), 7. conceit (*māna*), 8. illusion (*māyā*), 9. avarice (*lobha*), 10. over-fondness for persons or things (*rāga*), 11. hatred or envy (*dveṣa*), 12. quarrelsomeness (*kleśa*), 13. slander (*abhyākhyāna*), 14. tale-bearing or calumny (*paiśunya*), 15. blaming or finding fault in others (*nindā*), 16. indulgment or lack of self-control (*rati*), 17. hypocrisy (*māyā-mṛṣā*), and 18. taking or believing in false truths (*mithyā-darśana śalya*). See Stevenson, 1970 [1915], pp. 116*ff.*

[1] '*tathā*' is often used in the commentary starting a new sentence in order to indicate that an explanation already started is continued, in the sense of 'Even so ..., Next ..., And ..., etc.'.

[2] *bhinna-granthika-bhavya-*, lit. 'present in different treatises'. I take *granthika* to mean *grantha*. The Jaina Canon categorizes living beings according to the number of their senses (*indriya*), their development and the possession of intelligence (*saṃjñin* or *asaṃjñin*). The five senses are sensation or touch, taste, smell, vision and hearing. Living

worship for the world'. He [viz. Mahāvīra] is of such a kind. With this specification, [His] excellence as an object of veneration [is indicated]. How is He furthermore? [He is] a universal teacher. Here the word '*jagat* (universe)' implies the [whole] world characterised by the fourteen *rajjus*.[1] So, a universal teacher instructs or teaches[2] the aggregate of all things created in the universe, animate or not. He is the teacher of the entire universe, the many continents and oceans, the abodes of the gods and of the denizens of hell, etc. This is the meaning [of this clause]. However, omniscient beings and likewise beings with complete comprehension are silent Kevalins. They are not able to describe the nature of the whole universe since they do not have the capacity to speak. With this, because [He] is excluded from this[3], [His] excellence in teaching is acknowledged. So, in the [first] half of the verse the benediction is expressed as homage to the Lord. In the latter half [verse the author] gives the contents, etc.: ***'jaṃbuddīva-paẏatthe'***. A Jambū is a particular kind of tree.

---

beings possess one, two, three, four or five senses. They are either undeveloped or not fully developed (*aparyāpta*) or fully developed (*paryāpta*).

[1] See Fig. 1, p. 266.

[2] The verb '*gṛṇāti*' here derives from the root *gṝ*. meaning 'to announce, to proclaim, to relate, etc.' but also 'to teach in verses'.

[3] The clause '*tad-vyaya(va?)-cchedāt*' is puzzling. The *tad-vyacchedāt* of LD2 is impossible. Either we read '*tad-vyaya-cchedāt*': 'because [in case of Mahāvīra] there is absence of disappearance of that [capacity to speak]', or we amend to '*tad-vyavacchedāt*': 'because [in case of Mahāvīra] there is absence of this [incapacity to speak]'. Both interpretations amount, of course, to the same: Mahāvīra is not an ordinary Kevalin since He preserves the capacity to speak and teach.

Jambūdvīpa is the island (*dvīpa*) characterised by that [tree]. For, in the land of Uttarakuru, exactly in the middle, between the Nīlavat World Mountain range, the Mālyavat Vakṣaskāra mountain range and the Śītā river there is a Jambū tree characterised by many lakhs [more] of these trees.[1] This Jambū-isle (Jambūdvīpa) is named after that. In the *Bhagavatī Aṅga* it is stated:

> *"Why is it, Reverend, that this island is called Jambūdvīpa? Well, Gautama, Jambūdvīpa is an island where, north of Mount Mandara and south of the Lavaṇa Ocean, so many Jambū trees, viz. [trees] of the Jambū species, grow in such a lustre [that it is named after that]. That is why this island is called Jambūdvīpa, Gautama!"*

The elements [mentioned] here are the topics to be explained, viz. the continents, the mountains, the rivers, the forests, etc. These [elements will be explained]. [The author] declares what he will do: '***vuccham***' or, 'I will explain' [or] 'explicate'. Since it was intended to be useful for himself, [the author] has

---

[1] This Jambū tree, named 'Sudarśanā', is located in the centre of the eastern half of Uttarakuru with the Nīla(vat) mountains in the north, the round Mālyavat Vakṣaskāra mountains in the east, and the Śītā river in the west. It stands on a platform (*jambūpīṭha*) and is eight *yojanas* high. Its root is made of diamond, its stem and branches of gold and its leafs of beryl. It has fragrant blossoms looking like gems and its fruits are like ambrosia. On its four raised main branches, there are palaces and on top of its stem, there is a temple (*siddhāyatana*). Here the god Anādṛta, a descendant of the Garuḍas, dwells. This central Jambū tree is surrounded by other trees of the same kind but half its size, which, in turn, are surrounded by other Jambū trees, etc. For a full description, see Prabhānanda's commentary on verse 10 & 11 and Kirfel, pp. 234-235.

not expressed the word 'I' in his manual. So the reference to the person [of the author] himself must be conjectured. [He says] 'I will explain the elements of Jambūdvīpa'. With this, the contents are defined. Except for the extraordinary knowledge of the Lord, there is not that much skill available in expounding the essentials of the world. Therefore, in order to ward off criticisms from opponents, [the author] states: '***sutta***'. A *sūtra* (manual) is an authoritative treatise like the *Jambūdvīpaprajñapti*, the *Kṣetrasamāsa*, etc., composed by the Gaṇadharas, etc. [The author composes his manual] based on that, not according to his own ideas. Why does [the author] make such an effort? He says: '***sa-para-heu***'. This means: myself is I, the other is another person, a reason (*hetu*) is a purpose, for the sake (*-hetoḥ*) of these. Herewith the construction [of the sentence] is described. This [purpose] is twofold since distinction is made between one's own person and other persons. It is again twofold because distinction [is made] between each [of the two sides] individually and both mutually. In this case, the author obtains future wisdom for his individual person while the other [party], viz. the audience, obtains understanding of its meaning in the form of deliberate knowledge of Jambūdvīpa. Finally, both together obtain spiritual perfection. In the next verse, the author of the manual will give the contents for himself only.

SŪTRA 2

इदानीमभिधेयरूपदशद्वारपुरःसरं[1] कविः प्रकरणाभिधानमाह -
idānīm abhidheya-rūpa-daśa-dvāra-puraḥsaraṃ kaviḥ pra-karaṇa-abhidhānam āha -
Now the poet gives the contents of his treatise by means of ten topics[2] forming its subject matter:

खंडा[3] १ जोयण[4] २ वासा ३, पव्वय[5] ४ कूडा ५ य तित्थ[6] ६ सेढीओ[7] ७ ।
विजय[8] ८ द्दह[9] ९ सलिलाओ[10] १०, पिंडेसिं[11] होइ[12] संघयणी[13] ॥ २ ॥[14]

---

[1] For पुरस्सरं.
[2] *dvāra*, lit. 'door' and so also 'entry', here in the sense of 'topic'.
[3] खडा Bhog15.
[4] जोअण LD2.
[5] पवय Bhog10.
[6] तिथ Brd3.
[7] सेढीआ/सेढीउ(?) Bhog6 & 15. सेढीउं Brd2.
[8] विजया Bhog5 & 12.
[9] दह Ed1, LD2, Brd2 & 3, Bhog1, 4, 5, 6, 8, 12 & 15. Only द्दह is metrically correct.
[10] सलीलाओ Brd2. सलीलाउ Brd3. सलिलाओ/सलिलाउ(?) Bhog6, 8, 15 & 17.
[11] पिण्डेसि LD1 & Bhog10. पिडेसि Bhog2. पिण्डसिं Bhog12. पिंडेंसि Bhog15. पिंदिंसिं Bhog17.
[12] होई LD1, Brd3, Bhog7 & 16. होय Bhog6, 9, 11, 13, 14 & 17.
[13] संगहणी Tueb & Bhog12. संघयणि Bhog2. संगयणी Bhog5.
[14] In all mss. the topics are numbered. The three printed sources omit the numbering. Bhog15 introduces this verse with द्वारगाथा. This is the first verse of *sū.* 125 of the *Jambūdvīpaprajñapti* (*JDP*, ed. Jhaveri, p. 425): **खंडा १ जोअण २ वासा ३, पव्वय ४ कूडा ५ य तित्थ ६ सेढीओ ७ । विजय ८ द्दह ९ सलिलाओ १०, पिंडेए होइ संगहणी ॥ २ ॥.**

khaṃḍā 1 joẏaṇa 2 vāsā 3, pavvaẏa 4 kūḍā 5 ẏa tittha 6 seḍhīo 7;
vijaẏa 8 ddaha 9 salilāo 10, piṃḍ'-esiṃ[1] hoi saṃghaẏaṇī. 2.

(खण्डानि योजनवर्षाणि पर्वतकूटाश्च तीर्थश्रेणयः[2] । विजयह्रदसलिलाः पिण्ड ए(ते)षां भवति संग्रहणी ॥ २ ॥ *khaṇḍāni yojana-varṣāṇi parvata-kūṭāś ca tīrtha-śreṇayaḥ; vijaya-hrada[3]-salilāḥ piṇḍa e(te)ṣāṃ bhavati saṃgrahaṇī[4]. 2.*)

2. The (1) sectors, the (2) yojanas and the (3) continents, the (4) World Mountain ranges and the (5) peaks, the (6) fortresses and the (7) rows [of abodes], the (8) provinces, the (9) mountain lakes and the (10) rivers, [the description of] the sum total of these [constitute] the '*Saṃgrahaṇī* (Summary)'.

COMMENTARY

खंडा^इति[5] - तत्र खण्डानि विस्तारेण भरतप्रमाणानि, योजनानि घनीकृतरूपाणि, वर्षाणि भरतक्षेत्रादीनि, पर्वता वैताढ्यादयः, कूटानि वैताढ्यादिपर्वतशिखरःस्थितानि शृङ्गरूपाणि सिद्धायतनकूटादीनि, तीर्थानि मागधादीनि, श्रेणयो दीर्घवैताढ्येषु पार्श्वद्वये ऽपि विद्याधरनगराभियोगिक-देवनिवासश्रेणयो, विजयाः कच्छादयो, ह्रदाः पद्मादयो महाह्रदाः, सलिला गङ्गाद्या महानद्यः। इह समास एवं कर्त्तव्यो योजनानि च वर्षाणि च

[1] Pkt. *piṃḍ'-esiṃ* is an irregular sandhi form of *piṃḍo* + *esiṃ* or in chāyā *piṇḍa eṣām*.

[2] For श्रेणी = **सेढि** < *सेट्ठि for *सिट्ठि < श्लिष्टि. See Pischel, §66.

[3] For ह्रद > **द्रह** or **दह**. See Pischel, §354.

[4] For संग्रहणी = **संघयणी** < *संघतनी. See Pischel, §267.

[5] **खंडेत्ति** is missing in Ed1.

योजनवर्षाणि प्राकृतत्वाल्लिङ्गव्यत्यय, एवमग्रे ऽपि, नवरतं, तीर्थानि च श्रेणयश्च तास्तीर्थश्रेणयः,

"स्त्रीपुंनपुंसकानां सहवचने स्यात्परं लिङ्गं"[1]

इति वचनात्, स्त्रीत्वमेवमग्रे ऽपि विज्ञेयतं, **पिंडेसिं होइ संघयणि**^इति। एषां दशानां वर्णनीय[2]पदार्थानां पिण्डः समवायः संग्रहणिर्भवति, पिण्डशब्दः समूहे ऽप्यस्ति[3], यदाह हैमानेकार्थः -

"पिण्डो वृन्दे जपापुष्पे गोले वोले[4] ऽङ्गसिह्लयोर्"[5]

इति। एतानि खण्डादीनि दशापि परमार्थतः क्षेत्रमेव, तत एवं निरुक्तिः, क्षेत्रं जम्बूद्वीपलक्षणं सङ्गृह्यत उपादीयते ऽनयेति क्षेत्रसंग्रहणिरवयवे समुदायोपचारात्। इमानि दश द्वाराण्यत्र प्रकरणे ऽभिधास्यन्त इति॥ २॥

khaṃḍā^*iti - tatra khaṇḍāni vistāreṇa bharata-pramāṇāni, yojanāni ghanī-kṛta-rūpāṇi, varṣāṇi bharata-kṣetrādīni, parvatā vaitāḍhyādayaḥ, kūṭāni vaitāḍhyādi-parvata-śikharaḥ-sthitāni śṛṅga-rūpāṇi siddhāyatana-kūṭādīni, tīrthāni māgadhādīni, śreṇayo dīrgha-vaitāḍhyeṣu pārśva-dvaye 'pi vidyādhara-nagarābhiyogika-deva-nivāsa-śreṇayo, vijayāḥ kacchādayo, hradāḥ padmādayo mahā-hradāḥ, salilā gaṅgādyā mahā-nadyaḥ. iha samāsa evaṃ kartavyo yojanāni ca varṣāṇi ca yojana-varṣāṇi prākṛtatvāl liṅga-vyatyaya, evam agre 'pi, navaraṃ, tīrthāni ca śreṇayaś ca tās tīrtha-śreṇayaḥ,*

"strī-puṃ-napuṃsakānāṃ saha-vacane syāt paraṃ liṅgaṃ"

iti vacanāt[1]*, strītvam evam agre 'pi vijñeyam.* ***piṃḍ'-esiṃ hoi saṃghayaṇī***^*iti. eṣāṃ daśānāṃ varṇanīya-padārthānāṃ*

---

[1] Origin of this *vacana* or *vyākaraṇa* untraced.

[2] Ed1 वणनीय.

[3] Ed1 असि.

[4] Ed1 बोले.

[5] Origin of quotation untraced.

piṇḍaḥ samavāyaḥ saṃgrahaṇir bhavati, piṇḍa-śabdaḥ samūhe 'py asti, yad āha haimānekārthaḥ -

"piṇḍo vṛnde japā-puṣpe gole vole 'ṅga-sihlayor"[2]

iti. etāni khaṇḍādīni daśāpi paramārthataḥ kṣetram eva, tata evaṃ niruktiḥ, kṣetraṃ jambūdvīpa-lakṣaṇaṃ saṃgṛhyata upādīyate 'nayeti kṣetra-saṃgrahaṇir avayave samudāyopacārāt. imāni daśa dvārāṇy atra prakaraṇe 'bhidhāsyanta iti. 2.

2. '***khaṃḍā***' [etc.]. Among these [ten topics], sectors have the width of Bharata[3]. Yojanas [here] have a squared form[4]. The continents are the regions of Bharata, etc. The mountain ranges are the Vaitāḍhya[5], etc. The mountain peaks, the Siddhāyatana peak, etc.[6], are located on the top of the Vaitāḍhya, etc. mountains [and] have the form of a horn. The fortresses are Māgadha[7], etc. The rows are the series of abodes of the

---

[1] Origin of this rule untraced.

[2] *sihla* = *ṣilha*. Origin of this metaphor untraced.

[3] A *khaṇḍa* or sector measures $526\,{}^{6}/_{19}$ *yojanas* in width or ${}^{1,00,000}/_{190}$. See Kirfel, p. 215.

[4] Here in the *JDSH* a *yojana* is also treated as a superficial measure, viz. as a square *yojana*.

[5] Vaitāḍhya = Vijayārdha.

[6] The Vaitāḍhya mountains, which with its magnificent terraces and groves are a playground for the gods, have nine mountain peaks: 1. Siddhāyatana, 2. Dakṣiṇārdhabharata, 3. Khaṇḍaprapāta(guhā), 4. Māṇibhadra, 5. Vaitāḍhya, 6. Pūrṇabhadra, 7. Tamisra(guhā), 8. Uttarārdhabharata, and 9. Vaiśramaṇa. See Kirfel, p. 224*ff.*

[7] Bharata, Airāvata and all Vijayas in Mahāvideha have three Tīrthas or fortresses at their ocean shores or riversides: Māgadhatīrtha, Prabhāsatīrtha and Varadāmatīrtha. See Kirfel, p. 227.

Ābhiyogika[1] gods in the Vidyādhara cities on both sides of the long Vaitāḍhya mountains. The provinces are Kaccha, etc. The lakes are the great [mountain] lakes [viz.] Padma, etc. The waters are the great rivers [like] the Gaṅgā, etc. Here the compound has to be analysed in the following manner: '*yojanāni*' and '*varṣāṇi*' constitute '*yojana-varṣāṇi*'[2]. Since this is Prākrit there is a change of gender [in '*varṣa*'] [3], but only at the beginning [of a compound], not elsewhere.[4] According to the rule that "*feminin, masculine and neuter can change gender in a compound word*", the feminine gender must be understood [here] in the beginning.[5] **'piṃḍesiṃ hoi saṃghayaṇī** [description of] the sum total of these [constitutes] the '*Saṃgrahaṇī*'.' The sum total or the collection

---

[1] The Ābhiyogika (or Ābhiyogya; see Kirfel, p. 224 & Deleu, 1976, p. 220) gods are lit. the 'servants' of the Indras.

[2] As a *dvandva* compound.

[3] The word '*varṣa*' is masculine in Skt. (although in older Indo-Aryan also neuter). The commentator considers it as neuter in gender. Therefore, we have '*varṣāni*' in his commentary, although we read '***vāsā***' and not '***vāsāiṃ***' in Pkt.

[4] Just as it is the case in Indian mathematics where the first number of a compound figure is the one most to the right, in verbal compounds the first word is what is considered to be the last one.

[5] This sentence is puzzling. Pkt. '***vāsā***', as used here in verse 2, must be plural, either of the masculine or feminine gender. Prabhānanda considers it as feminine. Skt. '*varṣa*' and Pkt. '***vāsa, varisa***', however, are masculine, or neuter when used in the sense of a division of the earth (as in '*bharata-varṣa*', hence '*bharata-varṣāni*' in the chāyā). Skt. '*varṣā*' and Pkt. '***vāsā, varisā***' are feminine but this only in the sense of rain.

of these ten elements to be explained is the 'Summary'. The expression '*piṇḍa* (sum total)' is also used in the sense of 'essence'[1] as is [exemplified] in the several meanings of '*haima*'[2] [or] as it is said:

> "*In a heap of flowers of the China rose [or] in a ball of gum myrrh there is a collection of their parts as well as [they contain] their own 'incense'*"[3].

These ten [elements], the sectors, etc., ultimately [constitute] the world. Hence the etymological interpretation of the word: the world (*kṣetra*) named 'the Isle of the rose-apple tree (*jambūdvīpa*)' is summarily described or summed up by this [*Saṃgrahaṇī*]. Hence [also the alternative title] 'Summary (*saṃgrahaṇi*) of the world (*kṣetra*)', used as a *pars pro toto*[4]. These ten topics will be explained in this work here.

---

[1] The word '*samūha*' means 'sum, totality' as well as 'essence'.

[2] The word '*haima*' means 'covered with snow' as well as 'consisting or made of gold'.

[3] The 'essence' of the Japā flower or China rose is its incense or, as one of the definitions of 'essence' goes: " ... what emits or diffuses a fragrant odour". The fact that the words '*japā*' and '*piṇḍa*' are both used for the China rose may have some special significance in this context.

[4] The word '*kṣetra*' means, strictly speaking, a region, continent (= *varṣa*) or land, but it is also used the denote Jambūdvīpa in general.

SŪTRA 3

अथ यथोद्देशस्तथा निर्देश इति न्यायमाश्रित्य प्रथमं गाथात्रयेण खण्डान्याह -
atha yathoddeśas tathā nirdeśa iti nyāyam āśritya prathamaṃ gāthā-trayeṇa khaṇḍāny āha -
Next, relying on the rule that an explanation has to follow the order of the enumeration, in the third verse [the author] treats the sectors first:

नउय[1]सयं[2] खंडाणं[3], भरहपमाणेण[4] भाइए[5] लक्खे[6] ।
अहवा नउय[7]सय[8]गुणं[9], भरहपमाणं[10] हवइ[11] लक्खं[12] ॥ ३ ॥[1]

---

[1] णउअ Ed2 & Ed3. नओय LD. नउअ LD2, Bhog4, 7, 9, 10. नउअ/नओअ(?) Bhog13 & 14. नउय (standard Pkt. नउइ) probably from *नवत for नवति.

[2] सयं १९० Bhog1, 2, 5, 10 & 14. सय १९० Bhog9 & 13. सया १९० Bhog6. नउसअय Bhog16. नउयसय Bhog17.

LD1 and Brd1, 2 & 3 have additionally दारं (< Skt. द्वारं) at the beginning of the verse. Ed2 & 3: णउअ. LD2: नउअ.

[3] खण्डाण Bhog12. संखण्डाण Bhog15.

[4] पमाणेण/यमाणेण(?) LD2, Brd1 and Bhog15. पर(?)माणेण Bhog6. प्पमाणेण Bhog7 & 16.

[5] भाईए LD1 & Bhog17. भाइए लक्खे is replaced by जम्बूदीवंसि in Bhog6.

[6] लक्खे १९० Tueb.

[7] णउअ Ed2 & 3. नओय LD1. नउअ Tueb, Bhog4, 7, 10, 13, 14, 15 & 16. नउअ/नओअ(?) Bhog9.

[8] सयं Brd2 & 3, Bhog7 & 16.

[9] गुणे १९० Bhog2. गुणे Bhog5 & 12. गुंणं Bhog7 & 14. गुंण Bhog16.

[10] पमाणे LD2, Bhog5, 12 & 15. पमाण Brd3, Bhog9 & 10. प्पमाणं Bhog7 & 16. पमाणं/पमाणो(?) Brd1. Bhog2 omits णं.

[11] हवई LD1. Brd3 omits व.

[12] लक्ख Bhog15.

naüẏa-saẏaṃ khaṃḍāṇaṃ, bharaha-pamāṇeṇa bhāie lakkhe;
ahavā naüẏa-saẏa-guṇaṃ, bharaha-pamāṇaṃ havaï lakkhaṃ. 3.

(नवति(त्यधिक)शतं खण्डानां भरतप्रमाणेन भाजिते लक्षे। अथवा नवतिशतगुणं भरतप्रमाणं भवति लक्षम् ॥ ३॥ *navati(ty-adhika)-śataṃ khaṇḍānāṃ bharata-pramāṇena bhājite lakṣe; athavā navati-śata-guṇaṃ bharata-pramāṇaṃ bhavati lakṣam. 3.*)

3. When [the diameter of Jambūdvīpa, viz. one] lakh [of *yojanas*] is divided with Bharata as [standard] measure, one hundred and ninety sectors are obtained. In other words, one hundred and ninety times the measure of Bharata is one lakh [of *yojanas*].

COMMENTARY

नउयसय^इति - समस्तमपि जम्बूद्वीपं नवत्युत्तरं शतं खण्डानां भणिष्यमाणप्रकारेण भवतीति शेषः। क्षेत्रपर्वतविस्तारमाश्रित्य खण्डानि ज्ञातव्यानि न पुनर्दीर्घत्वेन, यतः - धनुष्पृष्ठाकारत्वादाद्यं भरतक्षेत्रं लघीयस्ततः पराणि क्रमेण दीर्घतराणि यावन्महाविदेहो मध्यविभागे योजनलक्षदैर्घ्यः। कियत्प्रमाणानि खण्डानि भवन्ति? इत्याह **भरहपमाणेण**^इत्यादि, भरतं प्रथमं वर्षं तस्य प्रमाणं मानं षड्विंशत्यधिकपञ्चयोजनशतानि सयोजनैकोनविंशषड्भागानि, तेन भाजिते

[1] Verse 3 is introduced with दारं in LD1, Brd1, 2 & 3, Bhog7, 10, 11, 15, 16 & 17, with दारगाहा in Bhog2, with दाराणि in Bhog5 & 12, and with द्वारं in Bhog9, 13 & 14.
Bhog6 has for the second half of the verse: भरहप्पमाणेण विंहत्ते काउउभयत्थ कलागुणणं ॥

भागे हृते सति यल्लभ्यते तत्समानि खण्डानि भवन्ति। तद्यथा - जम्बूद्वीपविष्कम्भो योजनलक्षं, एक एककस्तदग्रे पञ्च शून्यानि ध्रियन्ते १०००००, एष भाज्यराशिः। भरतमानं तु प्राक् कथितं ५२६ योजन, कला ६, अयं च भागहारः, ततो लब्धं नवत्युत्तरं शतं १९०, एतानि सर्वजम्बूद्वीपखण्डानि, पुनर्विधानान्तरेण खण्डानयनायोपायमाह - अहवा^इत्यादि, अथवा प्रकारान्तरेण भरतप्रमाणमुक्तस्वरूपं नवत्यधिकेन शतेन गुणितं जम्बूद्वीपविष्कम्भमानं लक्षयोजनरूपं भवति। तथाहि - भरतमानं ५२६ यो. कला ६, एष मूलराशिर्, नवत्युत्तरं शतं च १९० गुणकारः, ततो गुणिते लब्धं योजनानि लक्षं १०००००, एतत्पुनर्जंबूद्वीपमानमिति ॥ ३ ॥

***naüya-saya**^iti - samastam api jambūdvīpaṃ navaty-uttaraṃ śataṃ khaṇḍānāṃ bhaṇiṣyamāṇa-prakāreṇa bhavatīti śeṣaḥ. kṣetra-parvata-vistāram āśritya khaṇḍāni jñātavyāni na punar dīrghatvena, yataḥ - dhanuṣ-pṛṣṭhākāratvād ādyaṃ bharata-kṣetraṃ laghīyaḥ, tataḥ parāṇi krameṇa dīrghatarāṇi yāvan mahāvideho madhya-vibhāge yojana-lakṣa-dairghyaḥ. kiyat-pramāṇāni khaṇḍāni bhavanti? ity āha **bharaha-pamāṇeṇa**^ity ādi, bharataṃ prathamaṃ varṣaṃ, tasya pramāṇaṃ mānaṃ ṣaḍ-viṃśaty-adhika-pañca-yojana-śatāni sa-yojanaikona-viṃśa-ṣaḍ-bhāgāni, tena bhājite bhāge hṛte sati yal labhyate tat samāni khaṇḍāni bhavanti. tad yathā: jambūdvīpa-viṣkambho yojana-lakṣaṃ, eka ekakas tad-agre pañca śūnyāni dhriyante 100,000, eṣa bhājya-rāśiḥ, bharata-mānaṃ tu prāk kathitaṃ 526 yojana, kalā 6, ayaṃ ca bhāga-hāraḥ, tato labdhaṃ navaty-uttaraṃ śataṃ 190, etāni sarva-jambūdvīpa-khaṇḍāni, punar vidhānāntareṇa khaṇḍānayanāyopāyam āha - **ahavā**^ity ādy, athavā prakārāṇtareṇa bharata-pramāṇam ukta-svarūpaṃ navaty-adhikena śatena guṇitaṃ jambūdvīpa-viṣkambha-mānaṃ lakṣa-yojana-rūpaṃ bhavati. tathā hi: bharata-mānaṃ 526 yo.*

kalā 6, eṣa mūla-rāśir, navaty-uttaraṃ śataṃ ca 190 guṇa-kāraḥ, tato guṇite labdhaṃ yojanāni lakṣaṃ 100,000, etat punar jambūdvīpa-mānam iti. 3.

3. '***naüẏa-saẏa***' [etc.]. To this must be added that, in a way that will be explained [below], Jambūdvīpa contains one hundred and ninety sectors in total.[1] Sectors should be reckoned with relation to the width of the continents and mountain ranges, not by [their] length. Therefore, because it has the form of a bow[2] the continent of Bharata is the smallest. From there the others enlarge gradually until Mahāvideha [is reached], that in its middle part has a width of one lakh of *yojanas*. As to the question of the size of the sectors, [the author] answers: '***bharaha-pamāṇeṇa***' (the measure of Bharata), etc. Bharata is the first continent. Its measure or size is five hundred and twenty-six *yojanas* plus six nineteenths of one *yojana*. So, when [the whole of Jambūdvīpa] is divided into parts or portions [of 526 $^{6}/_{19}$ *yojanas*], what is obtained are sectors of the same size. Therefore, the diameter of Jambūdvīpa is one lakh *yojanas*. There is one single number one to start with and five zeros are added. This is a divisible number. Now, the size of Bharata already spoken of is 526

---

[1] The Pkt. text reads '***naüẏa-saẏaṃ***'. This could be interpreted as simply '*navati-śatam*' or just 'ninety hundred - 9,000'. We should however understand '*navaty-**adika**-śatam*' or '*navaty-**uttaraṃ** śatam*': hundred **plus** ninety.

[2] Lit. 'the back of a bow'.

yojanas and 6 fractions[1]. This is the divisor. Hence, one hundred and ninety [*yojanas*] - 190 - are obtained. These are all the sectors of Jambūdvīpa. Again, [the author] explains a means to calculate the [amount of] sectors in another manner: '***ahavā***', etc. Alternatively or, in another manner, the size of Bharata as already explained, multiplied with one hundred and ninety results in one lakh of *yojanas*, being the size of the diameter of Jambūdvīpa. For, the size of Bharata is 526 *yojanas* and 6 fractions. This is a cardinal number. Moreover, one hundred and ninety - 190 - is the multiplier. Hence, when multiplied, we obtain one lakh - 100,000. This is, again, the measure of [the diameter of] Jambūdvīpa.

[1] A *kalā* is a small part of anything, any single part or portion of a whole, esp. a sixteenth part. In this case it cannot be a sixteenth part since 100,000 divided by 190 is 526.3157, etc. or 526 and $^{6}/_{19}$.

SŪTRAS 4 & 5

पुनर्मुग्धावबोधनार्थं वर्षाणि वर्षधरांश्चाश्रित्य तृतीयं प्रकारमाह -
punar mugdhāvabodhanārthaṃ varṣāṇi varṣa-dharāṃś cāśritya tṛtīyaṃ prakāram āha -
Next, in order to instruct the ignorant, [the author] explains [the topic of the sectors] in a third manner based on the continents and the World Mountain ranges[1]:

अहवेग[2]खंड[3] भरहे[4], दो हिमवंते[5] य[6] हेमवइ[7] चउरो[8]।
अट्ठ[9] महाहिमवंते[10], सोलस[11] खंडाइ[12] हरिवासे[13] ॥ ४ ॥

---

[1] *varṣa-dhara = varṣa-dhara-parvata*, lit. 'the mountains supporting the continents'.

[2] अहविग Ed3, LD1 & 2, Bhog4, 7, 8, 9, 10, 11, 13, 16 & 17. अहविग is metrically impossible. अहविगह Brd1. अहवेगं Brd2 & 3. अहविइग Bhog1. अट्ठिंग(?) Bhog15.

[3] खण्डे Ed3, Bhog4. खण्डं LD1 & 2, Brd1, Bhog9 & 13.

[4] भरहखण्डं Bhog5. भरहखंद १ Bhog12. भरहे १ Tueb, Bhog2.

[5] हिमवते Bhog9. हिमवत्ते Bhog15.

[6] अ Ed2, LD1 & 2, Brd2 & 3, Bhog4, 7 & 16. य or अ omitted by Ed3 & Bhog2. य २ Tueb & Bhog2.

[7] Brd1, 2 & 3, Bhog1, 7, 11, 15, 16 & 17 have हि in stead of हे. हिमवई Bhog17. हीमवई LD1. हेमवईअ LD2. हेमवय Bhog2 & Bhog5.

[8] चऊरो LD1. चउरो ४ Tueb, Bhog2 & 5.

[9] अट्ठ ८ Bhog5.

[10] हिमवंते ८ Tueb, Bhog2 & 12. हिमवंत्त Bhog7. हिमवंत्ते Bhog15.

[11] सोलस्य(?) LD2. सोलस १६ Bhog5. सोलस्स Bhog6 & 12.

[12] Ed1, 2 & 3, Brd2, Bhog1, 8, 9, 12, 13, 15 & 16 have खण्डाइं but this is metrically impossible. खंदाई LD1 & Brd3. खण्डाउ Bhog6. ख is sometimes written as ष.

[13] हरिवासे १६ Tueb & Bhog2. हिरवासे Bhog10. हरिवासो Bhog12. हहरिवासे Bhog13.

बत्तीसं[1] पुण[2] निसढे[3], मिलिया[4] तेसट्ठि[5] बीय[6]पासेवि[7] ।
चउ[8]सट्ठी[9] उ[10] विदेहे[11], ति[12]रासि[13]पिंडे[14] उ[15] णउय[16]सयं[17] ॥ ५ ॥

ahav'-ega-khaṃḍa bharahe, do himavaṃte ẏa hemavaï caüro;
aṭṭha mahāhimavaṃte, solasa khaṃḍāi harivāse. 4.
battīsaṃ puṇa nisaḍhe, miliẏā tesaṭṭhi bīẏa-pāse vi;

---

[1] बतिसं Brd2. वत्तीसं Bhog12. बत्तिसं Bhog15 & 16.
[2] पूण LD1. पुणं Bhog4.
[3] निसद्ढे Ed1, Bhog8, 9 & 14. निसद्ढे ३२ Bhog12. निसढे ३२ Tueb & Bhog2. स omitted in Bhog5.
[4] मिलिआ Bhog10.
[5] तेसट्ठी Ed3, Brd2 & Bhog14. तेसट्ठि ३६ Tueb, Bhog2, 5 & 12. तेरस्सढि(?) Bhog6.
[6] वीय Brd2 & Bhog1. बिइय Bhog5. विईय Bhog12. बिय Bhog15.
[7] वी LD1 & 2, Brd2 & 3, Bhog1 & 10. ऽवि Ed2. वि ३६ Tueb & Bhog2. पि Bhog8 & 9.
[8] चऊ LD1. चओ(?) Bhog9.
[9] सट्ठि Bhog7, 8, 9, 10, 12, 13 & 16. सिट्ठि Bhog2. सवि Bhog15.
[10] ओ Ed3, LD1, Brd1 & 2, Bhog1, 2, 4, 7, 9, 11, 12, 13, 14, 16 & 17. उ is often mistaken for ओ.
[11] विदेहे ३४ Tueb, Bhog2, 5 & 12. विदेहिं Bhog13.
[12] ते Bhog4 & 6.
[13] राशि LD1, Brd2 & 3, Bhog16. रासी Bhog14.
[14] पिण्डेण LD1, Bhog1, 7, 11 & 17. पिण्डेणन Bhog1. पीडे Bhog2. षंदेण Brd2 & 3. पिण्डेहिं Ed3. पिण्डें Bhog9 & 10. पिण्डेंण Bhog16. पिंदि Bhog13.
[15] Omit उ: Ed3, LD1, Brd2 & 3, Bhog7, 11, 16 & 17. Have य or अ (= च) in stead of उ (= तु): Tueb, Bhog5, 6, 9, 10, 12, 13 & 14. उं Bhog8. उ and following न interchanged in Bhog1.
[16] णउअ Ed2, Bhog4, 7 & 16. नउय LD2, Brd1 & 2, Tueb, Bhog5, 6, 8, 11, 12 & 17. नउअ Bhog10, 13 & 14. नओ(?)य LD1. नओ(?)अ Bhog9.
[17] सय Bhog1 & 11. सयं १९० Tueb, Bhog5 & 6.

caüsaṭṭhī u videhe, ti-rāsi-piṃḍe u ṇaüya-sayaṃ. 5.

(अथवैकखण्डं भरते द्वौ हिमवन्ते च हैमवति चत्वारि। अष्टो महाहिमवन्ते षोडश खण्डानि हरिवषम्॥ ४॥ द्वात्रिंशत् पुनर्निषेधे मिलितास्त्रि-षष्टिर्द्वितीयपार्श्वे ऽपि। चतुःषष्टिस्तु विदेहे, त्रिराशिपिण्डे तु नवति-(त्यधिक)शतम्॥ ५॥ *athavaika-khaṇḍaṃ bharate dvau himavante ca haimavate catvāri; aṣṭau mahā-himavante ṣoḍaśa khaṇḍāni hari-varṣam. 4. dvātriṃśat punar niṣedhe militās triṣaṣṭir dvitīya-pārśve 'pi; catuḥ-ṣaṣṭis tu videhe tri-rāśi-piṇḍe tu navati(ty-adhika)śatam. 5.*)

4-5. Or, there is one sector in Bharata, two in Himavanta and four in Haimavata. In Mahāhimavanta, there are eight sectors and sixteen in Harivarṣa. Further, thirty-two in Niṣadha [while] sixty-three are found on the other side. Sixty-four are in Videha. Therefore, in total there are one hundred [and] ninety [sectors].

COMMENTARY

अहव^इत्यादि[1] - अथवेति विकल्पान्तरे, भरतनाम्नि क्षेत्रे[2] एकमेकसंख्याकं खण्डं भवतीत्यादि, शेषो ऽध्याहार्यः, खण्डप्रमाणत्वात्तस्य। यदुक्तं -

"पंच सये छव्वीसे, छच्च कला वित्थडं भरहवासं।"[3]

---

[1] LD2 adds 'बत्तीसमिति'.

[2] LD has 'भरते, भरतनाम्नि क्षेत्रे ...': in Bharata, in the continent named Bharata ...

[3] बृहत्क्षेत्रसमास २९ (*BKSJ*, p. 62), fully:
पंच सए छव्वीसे, छच्च कला वित्थडं भरहवासं।
दस सय बावन्नहिया, बारस य कलाओ हिमवंते॥

इति, तथा **दो हिमवंति**^इति[1] - हिमवति[2] वर्षधरे द्वे द्विसंख्ये खण्डे भवतः। यतो भरतक्षेत्रात् पराणि वर्षधरवर्षाणि क्रमेण द्विगुणद्विगुणविस्ताराणि। तदुक्तं

"भरहेरवयप्पभिई, दुगुणा दुगुणा य होइ विक्खंभो[3]**।**
वासावासहराणं, जाव य वासं विदेहं ति ॥ १ ॥"[4]

तथा **हेमवइ चउरो**^इति - हैमवते द्वितीये क्षेत्रे चत्वारि चतुःसंख्याकानि खण्डानि। **अट्ठ**^इत्यादि - महाहिमवति द्वितीये वर्षधरे ऽष्टौ खण्डानि। हरिवर्षे तृतीये क्षेत्रे षोडश खण्डानि। तथा **बत्तीसम्**^इति - निषेधे तृतीयवर्षधरे पुनर्द्वात्रिंशत् खण्डानि भवन्तीति सर्वत्र सम्बध्यते। इति महाविदेहव्यतिरिक्तेषु दक्षिणदिग्वर्त्तिषु वर्षवर्षधरेषु सर्वमीलने त्रिषष्टिखण्डानि जातानि। इदानीमुत्तरदिग्व्यवस्थिततद्क्षेत्रवर्षधरखण्डानि निरूपयति - **मिलिया**^इत्यादि, एवमेव मिलितानि समुदितानि त्रिषष्टिः खण्डानि द्वितीयपार्श्वे ऽपि भवेयुस्तद्यथा - एकं खण्डमैरवते, द्वे शिखरिगिरौ, चत्वारि हैरण्यवतक्षेत्रे, अष्टौ रुक्मिपर्वते, षोडश रम्यकक्षेत्रे, द्वात्रिंशत्तु नीलवति वर्षधर इति। **चउसट्ठी**^इत्यादि - इह पदैकदेशे ऽपि पदसमुदायोपचाराद्विदेह इति महाविदेहे सर्ववर्षवर्षधरमध्यवर्त्तिनि क्षेत्रे चतुःषष्टिः खण्डानि भवन्ति। एतावता सर्वसंख्यया किं जातमित्याह - **तिरासि**^इत्यादि त्रयश्च ते राशयश्च त्रिराशयस्तेषां पिण्डः समूहः, यद्वा त्रयाणां राशीनां समाहारस्त्रिराशिस्तस्य

(पञ्चशतानि षट्विंशति [अधिकानि] षट् च कला विस्तृतं भरतवर्षम्। दश शतानि द्विपञ्चाशदधिकानि द्वादश च कला हिमवति ॥ २९ ॥).

[1] Read हिमवंते.

[2] LD2: हेमवति.

[3] Ed1: विक्खंभे.

[4] बृहत्क्षेत्रसमास २७ (*BKSJ*, p. 60):
भरहेरवयप्पभिइ, दुगुणा दुगुणो उ होइ विक्खंभो।
वासावासहराणं, जाव य वासं विदेह त्ति ॥ २७ ॥
(भरतैरावतप्रभृति द्विगुणो द्विगुणस्तु भवति विष्कम्भः। वर्षवर्षधारणं यावच्च वर्षं विदेह इति ॥ २७ ॥).

पिण्डस्तस्मिन्, तुः पुनरर्थे, नवत्यधिकं शतं खण्डानि स्युरिति गाथाद्वयार्थः ॥ ४-५ ॥

ahavā*^ity ādi - athaveti vikalpāntare, bharata-nāmni kṣetre ekam eka-saṃkhyākaṃ khaṇḍaṃ bhavatīty ādi, śeṣo 'dhyāhāryaḥ, khaṇḍa-pramāṇatvāt tasya. yad uktaṃ:*

"paṃca-saẏe chavvīse, chac ca kalā vitthaḍaṃ bharaha-vāsaṃ*"[1]*

iti. tathā ***do himavaṃte****^iti - himavati varṣa-dhare dve dvi-saṃkhye khaṇḍe bhavataḥ. yato bharata-kṣetrāt parāṇi varṣa-dhara-varṣāṇi krameṇa dviguṇa-dviguṇa-vistārāṇi. tad uktaṃ:*

"bharaḥ'-eravaẏa-ppabhiī, du-guṇā du-guṇā ẏa hoi vikkhaṃbhe;

vāsā-vāsa-harāṇaṃ, jāva ẏa vāsaṃ videhaṃ ti. 1*"[2].*

tathā ***hemavaï caüro****^iti - haimavate dvitīye kṣetre catvāri catuḥ-saṃkhyākāni khaṇḍāni.* ***aṭṭha****^ity ādi - mahāhimavati dvitīye varṣa-dhare 'ṣṭau khaṇḍāni. harivarṣe tṛtīye kṣetre ṣoḍaśa khaṇḍāni. tathā* ***battīsam*** *iti - niṣedhe tṛtīya-varṣa-dhare punar dvātriṃśat khaṇḍāni bhavantīti sarvatra sambadhyate. iti mahāvideha-vyatirikteṣu dakṣiṇa-dig-vartiṣu*

---

[1] *BKSJ*, verse 29, p. 62, fully:

paṃca-sae chavvīse, chac ca kalā vitthaḍaṃ bharaha-vāsam;
dasa saẏa bāvann'ahiẏā, bārasa ẏa kalāo himavante. 29.

(*pañca-śatāni ṣaṭ-viṃśati(-adhikāni) ṣac ca kalā vistṛtaṃ bharata-varṣam; daśa śatāni dvi-pañcāśad-adhikāni dvādaśa ca kalā himavati. 29.*)

[2] *BKSJ*, verse 27, p. 60:

bharaḥ'-Eravaẏa-ppabhii, du-guṇā du-guṇo u hoi vikkhaṃbho;
vāsa-vāsa-harāṇaṃ, jāva ẏa vāsaṃ videha tti. 27.

(*bharatairāvata-prabhṛti dvi-guṇo dvi-guṇas tu bhavati viṣkambhaḥ; varṣa-varṣa-dhāraṇaṃ yāvac ca varṣaṃ videha iti. 27.*)

varṣa-varṣa-dhareṣu sarva-mīlane tri-ṣaṣṭi-khaṇḍāni jātāni. idānīm uttara-dig-vyavasthita-tad-kṣetra-varṣa-dhara-khaṇḍāni nirūpayati: ***miliyā'***^*ity ādi, evam eva militāni samuditāni tri-ṣaṣṭiḥ khaṇḍāni dvitīya-pārśve 'pi bhaveyuḥ, tad yathā: ekaṃ khaṇḍam airavate, dve śikhari-girau, catvāri hairaṇyavata-kṣetre, aṣṭau rukmi-parvate, ṣoḍaśa ramyaka-kṣetre, dvātriṃśat tu nīlavati varṣa-dhara iti.* ***caüsaṭṭhī'***^*ity ādi - iha padaika-deśe 'pi pada-samudāyopacārād videha iti mahāvidehe sarva-varṣa-varṣa-dhara-madhya-vartini kṣetre catuḥṣaṣṭiḥ khaṇḍāni bhavanti. etāvatā sarva-saṃkhyayā kiṃ jātam ity āha -* ***tirāsi'***^*ity ādi, trayaś ca te rāśayaś ca tri-rāśayas teṣāṃ piṇḍaḥ samūho, yadvā trayāṇāṃ rāśīnāṃ samāhāras tri-rāśis tasya piṇḍaḥ, tasmin, tuḥ punar arthe, navaty-adhikaṃ śataṃ khaṇḍāni syur iti gāthā-dvayārthaḥ. 4-5.*

4-5. '***ahavā***', etc. [The word] '*athavā* (otherwise)' [is used to indicate] an alternative. In the land named Bharata there is one, i.e. amounting to one, sector, etc. The [size of] the rest [of the continents and World Mountain ranges] has to be supplied based on the measure of the sector of that [continent]. It is said:

> *"The continent of Bharata has a size of five hundred twenty-six and six fractions [526 $^{6}/_{19}$]"*[1].

Next '***do himavaṃti***'. In the World Mountain range of Himavat there are two, i.e. the number of two, sectors. From

[1] *BKSJ*, verse 29, p. 62, translated in full: "The continent of Bharata has a size of five hundred twenty-six and six fractions. Himavat [measures] one thousand fifty-two and twelve fractions".

there on, from the continent of Bharata onwards, the other World Mountain ranges and continents are successively doubled in size. It is said:

> "*Starting from Bharata and Airāvata onwards the width is doubled each time, continent and World Mountain range, the one after the other, until the continent of Videha [is reached]*".

Next '***hemavaï caüro***'. In Haimavata, the second continent, there are four, i.e. amounting to four sectors. [Next] '***aṭṭha***' etc. In Mahāhimavat, the second World Mountain range, there are eight sectors. In Harivarṣa, the third continent, there are sixteen sectors. Next '***battīsaṃ***', etc. In Niṣadha, the third World Mountain range, there are thirty-two sectors. All are connected in the same manner. So, when all continents and World Mountain ranges located in the southern region except Mahāvideha are reckoned together, sixty-three sectors are obtained. Now the sectors of the World Mountain ranges and their continents located in the northern region are considered: '***miliyā***', etc. In exactly the same manner sixty-three sectors can be reckoned or considered in the second hemisphere also, viz. one sector in Airavata[1], two in the Śikharin mountain range, four in the continent of Hairaṇyavata, eight in the Rukmin mountain range, sixteen in the continent of Ramyaka and thirty-two in the Nīlavat World Mountain range. [Next] '***caüsaṭṭhī***', etc. In Mahāvideha - or in Videha [as it is called] here because it is used as an abbreviation[2] - the continent lying in the middle of all World Mountain ranges and continents,

[1] For Airāvata.

[2] *padaika-deśe 'pi pada-samudāyopacārāt*, lit. 'because one single word can be used for a collection of words'.

there are sixty-four sectors. [The author] explains how such a total number is produced: ‘***tirasi***’, etc. ‘Three’ and ‘figures’ [make up] ‘three figures’. The collection or aggregate of these or the sum of three figures is the ‘sum of three’. In that [collection is meant here]. The word ‘*tu* (however)’ is used in the sense of ‘*punar* (again)’. [So, in total] there must be one hundred and ninety sectors. This is the meaning of the two verses.

SŪTRA 6

अथ जम्बूद्वीपे योजनपरिमाणानि खण्डानि कियन्ति भवन्ति? इत्यादिकं घनीकृतयोजनद्वारं गाथापञ्चकेनाह -
atha jambūdvīpe yojana-parimāṇāni khaṇḍāni kiyanti bhavanti? ity ādikaṃ ghanī-kṛta-yojana-dvāraṃ gāthā-pañcakenāha -
Next, in the fifth verse [the author] treats the topic of the square *yojanas*, starting with the question how many sectors Jambūdvīpa contains, measured in *yojanas*, etc.:

जोयण[1]परिमाणाइं[2], समचउरंसाइ[3] इत्थ[4] खण्डाइं[5] ।
लक्खस्स[6] य परिहीए[7], तप्पाय[8] गुणे[9] य[10] हुंतेव[11] ॥ ६ ॥[12]

---

[1] जोअण LD1 & Tueb.
[2] परिमाणइं Ed3 & LD1. परिमाणाइ LD2 & Brd2, परिमाणाई Brd3, Bhog12 & Bhog13, परिमाणांइं Bhog2 & 11.
[3] Only Brd1 & 2, Bhog4, 10, 12 & 13 have the metrically correct चउरंसाइ. चतुरंसाइं Ed1. चउरंसाइं Ed2 & 3, LD2, Tueb, Bhog1, 2, 5, 6, 8, 9, 11, 14, 15 & 16. चतुरंसाई Brd3. चोरंसाइं LD1. चउरंसांइं Bhog7. चउरांसाइं Bhog17.
[4] इथ Brd3. ईत्थ Bhog7.
[5] खण्डाइ Brd2. खण्डाओ(?) Bhog6. खण्डाई Bhog12.
[6] लखस्स Brd2, Bhog4 & 13. लक्खसु(?) LD1. लखस Bhog12.
[7] परिहिए Brd2 & 3, Bhog2, 9, 10, 13, 14 & 15. परिहीरं(?) Bhog6.
[8] तंप्पाय Brd3. तप्पये Bhog9.
[9] गुणेण Ed2, Bhog12. गूंणे LD1. गुंणि Bhog14.
[10] Ed1 suggests ते for य. Bhog12 omits य.
[11] हुंतेवं LD1, Brd1, Bhog1, 5, 6, 8, 11, 12, 15 & 16. हुंतेव १५००० Tueb.
[12] Verse 6 begins with दारं १ or २(?) in Bhog2 & 5, with द्वारं १ or २(?) in Bhog12 & 14, with द्वारं in Bhog9, with दारं in Bhog10, and with द्वार २ in Bhog15.

joẏaṇa-parimāṇāiṃ, sama-caüraṃsāiṃ ittha khaṃḍāiṃ;
lakkhassa ẏa parihīe, tap-pāẏa-guṇe ẏa huṃt'-eva. 6.

(योजनप्रमाणानि समचतुरस्राण्यत्र खण्डानि। लक्षस्य च परिधेस्तत्पादगुणिते च भवन्त्येव॥ ६॥ *yojana-pramāṇāni sama-caturasrāṇy atra khaṇḍāni; lakṣasya ca paridhes tat-pāda-guṇite ca bhavanty eva. 6.)*

6. Sectors are congruent squares here with the size of one *yojana*. [Take a circle] of one lakh [*yojanaṣ* in diameter] and multiply the circumference with the quadrant of that [diameter]. Exactly [that many square *yojanas*] constitute [the surface area of Jambūdvīpa][1].

COMMENTARY

जोयण^इति - खण्डप्रमाणमजानानं शिष्यं प्रति गुरुस्तत्प्रमाणमाचष्टे - अत्रास्मिन् जम्बूद्वीपे प्रक्रान्तप्रकरणे वा घनीकृतयोजनपरिमाणानि समचतुरस्राणि[2] खण्डानि योजनानि भण्यन्ते। समास्तुल्यप्रमाणाश्चत्वारो ऽस्राः कोटयो येषां तानि तथोक्तानि। तथाहि, कल्पनाय किल कश्चिद् देवः सकलमपि जम्बूद्वीपं योजनप्रमाणेष्टिकाचितं करोति, प्रतरविस्तारेण तत्प्रमाणा यावन्तीष्टका भवन्ति तावन्त्येव योजनखण्डानि भवेयुः। तदानयनाय करणमाह - **लक्खस्स**^इत्यादि, लक्षस्येति योजनलक्षणप्रमाणं वृत्तक्षेत्रं तस्य परिधिर्बाह्यपरिमण्डलं भणिष्यमाणप्रमाणं तस्य **तप्पायगुणे**^इति[3], तस्य लक्षस्य यः पादश्चतुर्थो ऽशः पञ्चविंशतिसहस्ररूपस्तेन गुणो गुणकारस्तस्मिन्

---

[1] Therefore, the surface area of a circle is the circumference multiplied by one quarter of the diameter.

[2] समचतुरस्राणां Ed1.

[3] **तप्पायगुं त्ति** Ed1.

कृते सति, चः समुच्चये, किं भवतीत्याह - य हुंति^इति[1] प्राकृतत्वाल्लिङ्गव्यत्ययः। ततस्तानि योजनपरिमाणानि खण्डानि भवन्ति संपद्यन्ते। तथाहि लक्षस्य परिधौ पञ्चविंशत्या सहस्रैर्गुणिते वांछिताङ्को लभ्यत इति भावः, स चोत्तरत्र प्रपञ्चेन भणिष्यति ॥ ६ ॥

joẏaṇa^-itti *- khaṇḍa-pramāṇam ajānānaṃ śiṣyaṃ prati gurus tat-pramāṇam ācaṣṭe: atrāsmin jambūdvīpe prakrānta-prakaraṇe vā ghanī-kṛta-yojana-parimāṇāni sama-caturasrāṇi khaṇḍāni yojanāni bhaṇyante. samās tulya-pramāṇāś catvāro 'srāḥ koṭayo yeṣāṃ tāni tathoktāni. tathā hi, kalpanāya kila kaścid devaḥ sakalam api jambūdvīpaṃ yojana-pramāṇeṣṭikā-citaṃ karoti, pratara-vistāreṇa tat-pramāṇā yāvantīṣṭakā bhavanti tāvanty eva yojana-khaṇḍāni bhaveyuḥ. tad-ānayanāya karaṇam āha -* ***lakkhassa****^ity ādi, lakṣasyeti yojana-lakṣaṇa-pramāṇaṃ vṛtta-kṣetraṃ tasya paridhir bāhya-parimaṇḍalaṃ bhaṇiṣyamāṇa-pramāṇaṃ tasya* ***tap-pāẏa-guṇe****^iti, tasya lakṣasya yaḥ pādaś caturtho 'ṃśaḥ pañca-viṃśati-sahasra-rūpas tena guṇo guṇa-kāras tasmin kṛte sati, caḥ samuccaye, kiṃ bhavatīty āha -* ***ẏa huṃti****^iti, prākṛtatvāl liṅga-vyatyayaḥ. tatas tāni yojana-parimāṇāni khaṇḍāni bhavanti sampadyante. tathā hi lakṣasya paridhau pañca-viṃśatyā sahasrair guṇite vāñchitāṅko labhyata iti bhāvaḥ, sa cottaratra prapañcena bhaṇiṣyati. 6.*

6. '***joẏaṇa***' [etc.]. The teacher in front of his pupil who does not know the measure of a sector explains its size. Here in Jambūdvīpa or here in the treatise in question congruent squares with the size of one square *yojana* are called sectors [or simply] *yojanas*. The [forms] of the same size, possessing

[1] तेहुंति त्ति Ed1.

the same four corners or angles, are defined as such. For, suppose a god constructs the whole of Jambūdvīpa as a heap of bricks of the size of one *yojana*. As many bricks there are of that size spread out all over, exactly that many sectors of one [square] *yojana* there would be. [The author] explains the way to calculate this: '***lakkhassa***', etc. or '*lakṣasya*'. [Take] a circular field measuring one lakh of *yojanas*. [Then take] the circumference or the outer perimeter of that. [Take] the measure mentioned, [and] the '***tap-pāẏa-guṇa***' of that, viz. the quadrant or the fourth part of that, being twenty-five thousand. [Take] the coefficient of that as the multiplier. When this is done - '*ca* (and)[1]' is used in conjunctive sense - what do we have? [The author] says: '***te***[2] ***huṃti***'. There is a change of gender [here] since this is Prākrit. Therefore, these sectors are measured out or assessed in [square] *yojanas*. For, the sense is: when the circumference is multiplied with twenty-five thousand lakhs, the required number is obtained. This will be explained in detail below.

---

[1] **ẏa** in the Pkt. text.

[2] The Pkt. '***te***' found in the commentary is absent in the basic text. It stands for Skt. '*khaṇḍāṇi*' that explains the subsequent remark since '***te***' is a nominative masculine plural, while '*khaṇḍāni*' is a nominative neuter plural.

SŪTRA 7

अधुना यदुक्तं लखस्स य परिहीए^इति परिधेर्नापकीर्तनं तस्यानयनाय करणगाथामाह - विक्खंभ^इति।
adhunā yad uktaṃ ***lakhassa ẏa parihīe****^iti paridher nāpakīrtanaṃ tasyānayanāya karaṇa-gāthām āha* ***vikkhaṃbha****^iti.*
Now, [since] in the expression ‘***lakhassa ẏa parihīe***’[1] the [actual size of the] circumference is not mentioned, [the author] formulates the verse in which the way to calculate it is given: ‘***vikkhaṃbha***’ [etc.]:

विक्खंभ[2]वग्ग[3]दह[4]गुण[5],करणी[6] वट्टस्स[7] परिरओ[8] होइ[9]।
विक्खंभ[10]पाय[11]गुणिओ[12], परिरओ[13] तस्स[14] गणिय[1] पयं[2] ॥ ७ ॥[3]

---

[1] See *sū.* 6, pp. 57*ff.*
[2] विक्खभ LD1.
[3] वगा LD1, Bhog15 & 17.
[4] हद Bhog15.
[5] गूंण LD1. गुणं Bhog4.
[6] करिणी Ed1, 2 & 3, LD2, Brd1 & 3, Bhog9, 14 & 15. करिणि Bhog2. करणि Bhog4. करणं Bhog5 & 12.
[7] वटस्स LD1. वट्टंस Brd2 & 3, Bhog8. वटस Bhog6.
[8] परिरउ Bhog6, 8 & 12. परिरी Bhog9. परिरो Bhog10. परिसे Bhog15.
[9] होई. LD1, Brd3, Bhog2, 6, 11, 13 & 17. सोऊ Bhog5. हीइ Bhog9. सोइ Bhog12. होइं Bhog15.
[10] विक्खभ Brd2. विखंभ Bhog17.
[11] पायं Bhog12.
[12] गुणीओ Brd2 & 3, Bhog1, 6, 8, 9, 10, 13, 14 & 16. गुंणी LD1. गुणिउ Bhog15. गुणीउ Bhog17.
[13] परिरउ Bhog15 & 17.
[14] तस Bhog17.

vikkhaṃbha-vagga-daha-guṇa,-kariṇī vaṭṭassa parirao hoi; vikkhaṃbha-pāẏa-guṇio, parirao tassa gaṇiẏa-paẏaṃ. 7.

(विष्कम्भवर्गदशगुणकरणी वृत्तस्य परिरयो भवति। विष्कम्भपादगुणितः परिरयस्तस्य गुणितपदम्॥ ७॥ *viṣkambha-varga-daśa-guṇa-karaṇī vṛttasya parirayo bhavati; viṣkambha-pāda-guṇitaḥ parirayas tasya gaṇita-padam. 7.*)

7. The circumference of a circle is the square root of ten times the square of the diameter. Its surface area is the circumference multiplied with a quarter of the diameter.

COMMENTARY

विक्खंभ^इति - इह जम्बूद्वीपपरिधिना प्रयोजनं, स च वेदिकाशिरःकट-कजालकबाह्यदिग्भागवर्त्ती ग्राह्यो, ऽतो मूले द्वादशयोजनानि पृथुला वेदिका तस्याश्च मध्यान्यष्टौ योजनानि जम्बूद्वीपमध्ये[4] ज्ञातव्यानि, योजनचतुष्टयमानो बाह्यप्रदेशो लवणसमुद्रमध्ये गण्यते विष्कम्भ^इत्यादि विष्कम्भो विस्तारस्तस्य वर्गस्तावतैव गुणनं, यथा चत्वारश्चतुर्भिर्गुणिताः षोडश भवन्तीत्यादि स च दशगुणो दशकेन गुणितस्तस्य करणिर्विषमसमेत्यादिना वर्गमूलानयनतं. एवं कृते किं भवति? इत्याह - वट्टस्स^त्यादि, वृत्तस्य वर्त्तुलक्षेत्रस्य परिरयः परिधिर्भवति स्यात्। विष्कम्भस्य पादेन चतुर्थांशेन

[1] गणिअ LD2. गणीय Bhog16. गंणीयं Bhog17.

[2] पय LD1, Bhog6, 9 & 15. प is written twice in Bhog10 and omitted in Bhog12.

[3] This is the same as verse 7 of Chapter I of the बृहत्क्षेत्रसमास. The metre, however, is defective in the 4th foot of the second halve verse where a short syllable is missing.

[4] Ed1: जम्बूद्वीपे.

गुणितः सन् परिरयो गणितपदं भवति। किञ्च सर्ववृत्तक्षेत्राणां परिधिगणितपदयोरानयनायायमेव करणविधिरिति गाथाक्षरार्थः। भावार्थस्त्वयं यथा - जम्बूद्वीपस्य विष्कम्भो योजनलक्षमानः, तत एको न्यस्यते तदग्रे, पञ्च शून्यानि १०००००, तस्य वर्गो विधीयते एककस्याग्रे दशशून्यानि १०००००००००० पुनर्दशगुणने एकशून्यवृद्धिः १००००००००००० एतस्य राशेर्मूलमेतदार्याद्वयानुसारेणानेतव्यं, यथा -

"विषमात्पदतस्त्यक्त्वा वर्गस्थानच्युतेन मूलेन।
द्विगुणेन भजेच्छेषं लब्धं, विनिवेशयेत् पंक्त्याम्॥ १॥
तद्वर्गं संशोध्य द्विगुणीकुर्वीत पूर्ववल्लब्धतं।
उत्सार्य ततो विभजेत्, शेषं द्विगुणं कृतं दलयेत्॥ २॥"[1]

ततो लब्धाङ्कस्य छेदराशिः, षट् लक्षाणि, द्वात्रिंशत्सहस्राणि, चत्वारि शतानि, सप्तचत्वारिंशदधिकानि ६३२४४७, एतानि च प्रान्तवर्त्तिसप्तकं मुक्त्वा सर्वाण्यर्द्धीक्रियन्ते ततो जातानि त्रीणि लक्षाणि षोडश सहस्राणि द्वे शते सप्तविंशत्यधिके ३१६२२७, शेषमुपरीदमुद्धरति चत्वारि लक्षाणि, चतुरशीतिसहस्राणि, चत्वारि शतानि, एकसप्तत्यर्गलानि ४८४४७१, अमूनि च योजनानि, गव्यूतं योजनस्य चतुर्थांशः, ततश्चतुर्भिर्गुणितानि जाता एकोनविंशतिर्लक्षाः, सप्तत्रिंशत्सहस्रा, अष्टौ शतानि, चतुरशीति युतानि गव्यूतानां १९३७८८४, ततश्छेदराशिना षड्लक्षादिना नवरमन्तयसप्तकमपि द्विगुणं कृत्वा भागे हृते लब्धं गव्यूतत्रितयं, शेषमिदमुपरिष्टात्तिष्ठति, चत्वारिंशत्सहस्राणि, पञ्चशतानि, द्वाविंशत्यधिकानि ४०५२२, एकेन गव्यूतेन धनुःसहस्रद्वयं भवति, तावता च गव्यूतरूप उद्धरितराशिर्गुण्यते, तद्यथाग्रे शून्यत्रयं दत्वा मूलराशिर्द्विगुणो विधीयते, जाता अष्टौ कोटयो दशलक्षाश्चतुश्चत्वारिंशत् सहस्राः ८१०४४०००, पूर्वोक्तच्छेदराशिना भागो ह्रियते लब्धमष्टाविंशत्यधिकं धनुःशतं १२८, शेषमिदमुपरिधनूरूपं तिष्ठति। एकोननवतिः सहस्राण्यष्टाशीत्यधिकान्यष्टौ शतानि ८९८८८, ततो ऽङ्गुलानयनाय षण्णवत्या एकस्य गुणकारे दत्ते जातानि षडशीतिलक्षाण्येकोनत्रिंशत्सहस्राणि द्वे शते ऽष्टचत्वारिंशदधिके ८६२९२४८ प्राक्तनरीत्या छेदराशिमधो विहाय भागे हृते लब्धानि त्रयोदशाङ्गुलानि १३,

---

[1] Quotation untraced, but also found in the commentary on the बृहत्क्षेत्रसमास (*BKSJ*, verse 7, p. 30).

उपरीदमवशिष्यते, चत्वारि लक्षाणि, सप्त सहस्राणि, षट्चत्वारिंशदधिकानि त्रीणि शतानि ४०७३४६, अर्द्धांगुलानयनाय एष राशिर्द्विगुणीक्रियते, जातान्यष्टौ लक्षाणि, चतुर्दश सहस्राणि, षट्शतानि, द्विनवत्यर्गलानि ८१४६९२, प्राक्तनेन च्छेदराशिना भक्ते लब्धमर्द्धमङ्गुलं, शेषमुद्धरति, एका लक्ष, द्व्यशीतिः सहस्राणि, द्वे शते अष्टात्रिंशदधिके १८२२३८, एष जम्बूद्वीपस्य परिधिरिति ॥ ७ ॥

vikkhaṃbha*^*iti* - *iha jambūdvīpa-paridhinā prayojanaṃ, sa ca vedikā-śiraḥ-kaṭaka-jālaka-bāhya-dig-bhāga-vartī grāhyo, 'to mūle dvādaśa-yojanāni pṛthulā vedikā tasyāś ca madhyāny aṣṭau yojanāni jambūdvīpa-madhye jñātavyāni, yojana-catuṣṭaya-māno bāhya-pradeśo lavaṇa-samudra-madhye gaṇyate viṣkambha*[1]*^ity ādi viṣkambho vistāras tasya vargas tāvataiva guṇanaṃ, yathā catvāraś caturbhir guṇitāḥ ṣoḍaśa bhavantīty ādi sa ca daśa-guṇo daśakena guṇitas tasya karaṇir viṣama-samety ādinā varga-mūlānayanaṃ, evaṃ kṛte kiṃ bhavati? ity āha* - ***vaṭṭassa^*ity ādi, vṛttasya vartula-kṣetrasya parirayaḥ*[2] *paridhir bhavati syāt. viṣkambhasya pādena caturthāṃśena guṇitaḥ san parirayo gaṇita-padaṃ bhavati. kiñca sarva-vṛtta-kṣetrāṇāṃ paridhi-gaṇita-padayor*

[1] Originally, this must have been a reference to the Pkt. word occurring in the verse. So, most probably '***vikkhaṃbha***' for '*viṣkambha*'.

[2] ***pariraẏa*** is attested as a Pkt. word, not as a Skt. word, although the *Pāia-sadda-mahaṇṇavo*, H.T. Seṭh (1963) gives the Skt. chāyā as *pariraya*. It is a synonym of *parinidhi*. **pariraya* probably derives from **pari-ri*. or *-rī*. The root *ri./rī.* means 'to let go', etc. Compare this with *rīti* derived from *ri./rī.* in the sense of 'course, line, boundary', etc. **pari-raya* would then mean something like 'the boundary around something' or 'perimeter'.

ānayanāyāyam eva karaṇa-vidhir iti gāthākṣarārthaḥ. bhāvārthas tv ayaṃ yathā: jambūdvīpasya viṣkambho yojana-lakṣa-mānaḥ, tata eko nyasyate tad-agre, pañca śūnyāni: 100000, tasya vargo vidhīyate ekakasyāgre daśa-śūnyāni 10000000000 punar daśa-guṇane eka-śūnya-vṛddhiḥ 100000000000 etasya rāśer mūlam etad āryādvaya^anusāreṇānetavyaṃ, yathā:

"viṣamāt padatas tyaktvā varga-sthāna-cyutena mūlena;
dvi-guṇena bhajec cheṣaṃ labdhaṃ viniveśayet paṅktyām. 1.

tad-vargaṃ saṃśodhya dvi-guṇī-kurvīta pūrva-val labdhaṃ;
utsārya tato vibhajet śeṣaṃ dvi-guṇaṃ kṛtaṃ dalayet. 2."

tato labdhāṅkasya cheda-rāśiḥ, ṣaṭ lakṣāṇi, dvātriṃśat-sahasrāṇi, catvāri śatāni, sapta-catvāriṃśad-adhikāni: 632447, etāni ca prānta-varti-saptakaṃ muktvā sarvāṇy ardhī-kriyante tato jātāni trīṇi lakṣāṇi ṣoḍaśa sahasrāṇi dve śate sapta-viṃśaty-adhike: 316227, śeṣam uparīdam uddharati catvāri lakṣāṇi, catur-aśīti-sahasrāṇi, catvāri śatāni, eka-saptaty argalāni: 484471, amūni ca yojanāni, gavyūtaṃ yojanasya caturthāṃśaḥ, tataś caturbhir guṇitāni jātā ekona-viṃśatir lakṣāḥ, sapta-triṃśat-sahasrā, aṣṭau śatāni, catur-aśīti yutāni gavyūtānāṃ 1937884, tataś cheda-rāśinā ṣaḍ-lakṣādinā navaram antya-saptakam api dvi-guṇaṃ kṛtvā bhāge hṛte labdhaṃ gavyūta-tritayaṃ, śeṣam idam upariṣṭāt tiṣṭhati, catvāriṃśat-sahasrāṇi, pañca-śatāni, dvāviṃśaty-adhikāni 40522, ekena gavyūtena dhanuḥ-sahasra-dvayaṃ bhavati, tāvatā ca gavyūta-rūpa uddharita[1]-rāśir guṇyate, tad yathāgre śūnya-trayaṃ datvā mūla-rāśir dvi-guṇo vidhīyate, jātā aṣṭau koṭayo daśa-lakṣāś catuścatvāriṃśat sahasrāḥ 81044000,

---

[1] = *uddhārita.*

pūrvokta-ccheda-rāśinā bhāgo hriyate labdham aṣṭāviṃśaty-adhikaṃ dhanuḥ-śataṃ 128, śeṣam idam upari dhanū-rūpaṃ tiṣṭhati. ekona-navatiḥ sahasrāṇy aṣṭāśīty-adhikāny aṣṭau śatāni 89888, tato 'ṅgulānayanāya ṣaṇ-ṇavatyā ekasya guṇa-kāre datte jātāni ṣaḍaśīti-lakṣāṇy ekonatriṃśatsahasrāṇi dve śate 'ṣṭa-catvāriṃśad-adhike 8629248 prāktana-rītyā cheda-rāśim adho vihāya bhāge hṛte labdhāni trayodaśāṅgulāni 13, uparīdam avaśiṣyate, catvāri lakṣāṇi, sapta sahasrāṇi, ṣaṭ-catvāriṃśad-adhikāni trīṇi śatāni 407346, ardhāṅgulā-nayanāya eṣa rāśir dvi-guṇī-kriyate, jātāny aṣṭau lakṣāṇi, catur-daśa sahasrāṇi, ṣaṭ-śatāni, dvi-navaty-argalāni 814692, prāktanena ccheda-rāśinā bhakte labdham ardham aṅgulaṃ, śeṣam uddharati, ekā lakṣa, dvy-aśītiḥ sahasrāṇi, dve śate aṣṭātriṃśad-adhike 182238, eṣa jambūdvīpasya paridhir iti. 7.

7. '***vikkhaṃbha***' [etc.]. Here the subject is the wall around Jambūdvīpa. Moreover, this [wall] must be conceived as surrounded at the outside by a lattice and it has a balcony[1] on top. At the base [this wall] is twelve *yojanas* [wide]. The balcony is [four *yojanas*] wide and its average width must be reckoned as eight *yojanas* inside Jambūdvīpa.[2] [Now, in order

[1] In the *Jainendra Siddhānta Kośa* (J. Varṇī, 1970), Part III, p. 601 a *vedikā* is described as a wall that stands on the outskirts of mountains, rivers, islands, etc. Their occurrence in the world is widespread (पर्वत नदी द्वीप आदिको घेरे रहनेवाली दीवारको वेदिका कहत हैं। लोकमें इन्का अवस्थान व विस्तार।).

[2] This wall (also called a '*jagatī*', see Kirfel, p. 214) looks like a rampart around a city. It is eight *yojanas* high and four at the top. It is made of diamond. The lattice around it (*jāla-kaṭaka*, ibid. = *kaṭaka-*

to calculate its circumference] imagine an outer region in the middle of the Lavaṇa Ocean measuring four *yojanas.*[1] [First] '*viṣkambha*', etc. '*viṣkambha* (diameter)' means 'width'. [Take] the square of that. At this point [make] the multiplication, viz. four multiplied with four is sixteen, etc. '*daśa-guṇa* (ten times)' means 'multiplied with ten'. [Carry out] that operation. [Calculate] the square root with the even-and-uneven [method], etc.[2] When this is done, what do we have? [The author] says: '***vaṭṭassa*** (of a circle)', etc.[3] A wall can enclose a circle or a round space. The circumference being multiplied with a quarter or fourth part of the diameter is the surface area.[4] The general meaning of the verse is: this is the formula to calculate the circumference and surface area of all circular fields. The particular meaning, however, is this: the diameter of Jambūdvīpa is one lakh of *yojanas*. So [the number] one is put down in the front, [then] five zeros: 100,000. The square of that is formed: one single number one

---

jālaka) consists of gems. It is $^1/_2$ *yojana* high and 500 *dhanus* broad. The circular lotus balcony on top of this wall (*padma-vara-vedikā*, ibid.) has the same measures. On this balcony, there are lovely gardens.

[1] Prabhānanda is using an example to explain how the circumference and the surface area of a circle are calculated. He holds an imaginary circle of four leagues in diameter before the reader or listener, situated somewhere out in the vast plain of the Lavaṇa Ocean.

[2] This will be explained below.

[3] If d is the diameter of a circle and $d = 4$ *yojanas*, then the formula to calculate the circumference is $\sqrt{10d^2}$ or in this case 12,64 *yojanas*. This calculation is correct if we keep in mind that for the Jainas the value of $\pi = \sqrt{10}$ or 3,16, etc.

[4] Or, if C is the circumference of a circle, then the formula to calculate the surface area is $C\,^d/_4$. This is again correct if $\pi = \sqrt{10}$ or 3,16, etc.

in front and ten zeros: 10,000,000,000. When multiplied again with ten, one zero is added: 100,000,000,000. [Calculate] the base or root of that. This to be calculated according to [the method of] Āryādvaya[1], viz.

> "*After having subtracted of the odd place, divide by twice the root extracted from the place of the square. The result obtained should be put down in the line. The square of that, double [this]. After having subtracted, with the number of the following odd place added [and] after having moved the result as before, then divide. Double the result. The result should be halved.*"[2]

---

[1] Āryādvaya = Āryabhaṭa I (not Āryabhaṭa II). See Datta & Singh (1962[3]), p. 170*ff.* Compare also with the calculation as described in the commentary of Siddhasena Gaṇi on the *Tattvārthādhigamasūtra* (ref. found in Datta & Singh, idem, p. 171, thanks to the suggestion of Dr. Jean-Michel Delire). The complete calculation is given in 'Appendix 1'.

[2] Let us take the number 196 as an example. This example and the graphic presentation of it are based on the edition and translation by François Patte of the *Līlāvatī* of Bhāskara with the commentaries of Gaṅgādhara and Sūryadāsa (ref. communicated by Dr. J-M. Delire). First the odd (*viṣama*, *v*) and even (*sama*, *s*) places have to be determined, starting from the first number which, in Indian mathematics, is the one most to the right:

←		
1	9	6
viṣama	*sama*	*viṣama*

---

v		*S*		*v*		
	196		96		16	
$1^2 =$	1	$2 \times \boxed{4} =$	8	$4^2 =$	16	
	096		16		00	
2				28		$\sqrt{196} = 28 \div 2 =$ 14

Now we have the verses of the *JDSH* in which the algorithm is explained:

viṣamāt padatas tyaktvā varga-sthāna-cyutena mūlena;
dvi-guṇena bhajec cheṣaṃ labdhaṃ viniveśayet paṅktyām. 1.
tad-vargaṃ saṃśodhya dvi-guṇī-kurvīta pūrva-val labdhaṃ;
utsārya tato vibhajet śeṣaṃ dvi-guṇaṃ kṛtaṃ dalayet. 2.

I have arranged a part of the second verse in a slightly different manner in order to try to make sense of the algorithm: *tad-vargaṃ* ***dvi-guṇī-kurvīta saṃśodhya*** *pūrva-val labdhaṃ.* Analysis:

(1) *viṣamāt padatas tyaktvā:* After having subtracted [the root] of the [last] odd place [from the last odd place]: $\sqrt{1} = 1$, $1 - 1 = 0$,

(2) *varga-sthāna-cyutena mūlena dvi-guṇena bhajet:* divide [the following even place] by twice the root extracted from the place of the square: $9 \div (1 \times 2) = 4$.

(3) *śeṣaṃ labdhaṃ viniveśayet paṅktyām:* The result obtained [viz. of the doubling of the root, 2] should be put down in the line [of the result, here the last row below].

(4) *tad-vargaṃ:* [Take] the square of that: $2^2 = \boxed{4}$.

(5) *dvi-guṇī-kurvīta:* Double [this]: $4 \times 2 = 8$.

(6) *saṃśodhya:* After having subtracted: $9 - 8 = 1$, with the number 6 of the following odd place added = 16,

Accordingly, the number of the divisor is obtained: six lakhs, thirty-two thousand, four hundred and forty-seven or 632,447[1]. All these [numbers], setting aside the [number] seven occurring at the end, are divided by two. Then three lakhs, sixteen thousand two hundred and twenty-seven occur: 316,22-7. This result is placed on top. The four lakhs, eighty-four thousand, four hundred and seventy-one or 484,471, is taken up again [in order to continue the approximation procedure][2]. These are *yojanas*. A *gavyūta* is one fourth of a *yojana*. So, multiplied with four, nineteen lakhs plus thirty-seven thousand, eight hundred and eighty-four *gavyūtas*: 1,937,884 are obtained. Then, with the divisor of six lakhs, etc. [viz. the 632,447 mentioned higher up] but only with the last seven multiplied by two added [viz. 632,454[3]], when the fraction is obtained, three *gavyūtas* result. This is placed on top. [Next, we have] forty thousand, five hundred and twenty-two:

---

(7) *pūrva-val labdham utsārya:* [and] after having moved the result [viz. 16, to the next column] as [done] before [with the number 96],

(8) *tato vibhajet:* then divide [this result by 4 which is the square root of $16 = 4^2$]: $16 \div 4 = 4$.

(9) *śeṣaṃ dvi-guṇaṃ:* Double the result (in the sense of '*śeṣaṃ dvi-guṇī-kurvīta*'): 4 x 2 = 8 [and put it in the line of the result: 28 is obtained].

(10) *kṛtaṃ dalayet:* The result should be halved [in order to obtain the outcome]: $28 \div 2 = 14$.

[1] This number corresponds with step E of the calculation as presented in 'Appendix 1'.

[2] See step **F** in 'Appendix 1', p. 278.

[3] This divisor of 632,454 will be used in the remaining part of the calculation, obviously in order to round off the calculation.

40,522.[1] One *gavyūta* is two thousand *dhanus*. So far, the extricated root is calculated in the form of *gavyūtas*. [Now it will be calculated in *dhanus*], viz. first three zeros are put down, then multiplied by two. The result is eight crores, ten lakhs and forty-four thousand: 81,044,000 [*dhanus*]. This is divided by the divisor previously mentioned [viz. 632,454]. One hundred and twenty-eight *dhanus* are obtained: 128. This result is put on top in the form of *dhanus*. [Then we have] eighty-nine thousand, eight hundred and eighty-eight, 89,888. Then in order to calculate in *aṅgulas*, when ninety-six [*aṅgulas*] for one [*dhanus*] are taken, eighty-six lakhs, twenty-nine thousand, two hundred and forty-eight, 8,629,248 [*aṅgulas*] are obtained. Following the previous method, the denominator [viz. 632,454] is placed below [and] when divided thirteen, 13 *aṅgulas* are obtained. This [result] is put as remainder on top. Four lakhs, seven thousand, three hundred and forty-six: 407,346 [remains]. In order to reckon in half *aṅgulas*, this number is doubled. The result is eight lakhs, fourteen thousand, and six hundred and ninety-two: 814,692. When divided with the previous denominator one-half *aṅgula* is obtained. The result is put on top. [This yields] one lakh, eighty-two thousand, two hundred and thirty-eight: 182,238 [as remainder]. This is the [calculation of the] circumference of Jambūdvīpa [with 316,227 *yojanas*, 3 *gavyūtas*, 128 *dhanus*, 13 *aṅgulas* and 1 half *aṅgula* as outcome].

---

[1] See step **G** in 'Appendix 1', p. 278.

SŪTRA 8

अमुमेवार्थं स्पष्टतरमाह -
amum evārthaṃ spaṣṭataram āha -
[The author] states the matter more explicitly:

परिही[1] तिलक्ख[2] सोलस[3],सहस्स[4] दो[5] य[6] सय[7] सत्त[8]वीस[9]हिया[10] ।
कोसतिगट्ठा[11]वीसं[12], धणु[13]सय[14] तेरङ्गुल[15]द्ध[16]हियं[17] ॥ ८ ॥

---

[1] परिहि Ed3, Bhog2, 4, 7, 9, 10, 14 & 17. परीहा Bhog6. परही Bhog16.
[2] क्ख omitted in Bhog2. तिलक्खा Bhog5. तिलख Bhog6 & 10.
[3] सोलस्स Brd2 & 3, Bhog1, 7, 9 & 16. स omitted in Bhog6. सहस्ससोलदो... Bhog12. सोलअ Bhog13.
[4] सहस Bhog8 & 10. सयस्स Bhog17.
[5] दो omitted in Brd3.
[6] य omitted in LD1 & 2, Bhog6, 8, 10 & 12. In LD1, this is corrected in the margin. इ for य in Bhog1, 7, 11 & 16. ई in Bhog15.
[7] सय omitted in LD1 & Bhog17.
[8] सत Brd3 & Bhog1. सभ Bhog13. सत्ता Bhog15.
[9] विस Brd2 & Bhog13. विसा Bhog4.
[10] हीया LD1, Brd2 & 3, Tueb हिआ LD2. हिया ३१८२२७ Bhog2. हियाओ Bhog6. हीआ Bhog15.
[11] तिगमट्ठा Ed3. तिगट्ठ Bhog1. तीग३अट्ठा Bhog2. Bhog4 has तिगंट्ठा and adds ३१६२२७ कोओ ४१२८ अं १३१ after तिगं. तिगसट्ठ Bhog5. तीयअट्ठ Bhog6. तिगअट्ठा Bhog9, 10 & 13. तिगअट्ठ Bhog12. तिगअवा(?) Bhog15. तिगऽट्ठा Bhog16.
[12] विसं Brd2. वीस Bhog1 & 15.
[13] धणुं Bhog4, 10, 12 & 13.
[14] सयं LD2 & Bhog8. सय १२७ Bhog2.
[15] तेरंगुरि(?)हील Bhog8. तेरगुल Bhog10 & 14.
[16] द्धती Bhog2. द्धम Bhog6. द(?) Bhog12. ध Bhog15.
[17] हिअं Ed1. हिय LD1, Bhog9 & 13. हियं १३ Bhog2.

parihī ti-lakkha solasa,-sahassa do ẏa saẏa satta-vīsa-hiẏā; kosa-tig'*[1]*-aṭṭhā-vīsaṃ, dhaṇu-saẏa ter'-aṃgul'-addha-hiẏaṃ. 8.

(परिधिस्त्रिलक्षाः षोडषसहस्रा द्वे च शते सप्तविंशत्यधिके। क्रोशत्रयमष्टाविंशं धनुःशतं त्रयोदशाङ्गुलमर्द्धाधिकम्॥ ८॥ *paridhis tri-lakṣāḥ ṣoḍaṣa-sahasrā dve ca śate sapta-viṃśaty-adhike; krośa-trayam aṣṭā-viṃśaṃ dhanuḥ-śataṃ, trayodaśāṅgulam ardhādhikam. 8.*)

8. The circumference [of Jambūdvīpa] is three lakhs, sixteen thousand and two hundred and twenty-seven [*yojanas*], three *krośas*, one hundred and twenty-eight *dhanus*, thirteen and a half *aṅgulas*.

COMMENTARY

परिही^इति - योजनानां तिस्रो लक्षाः, षोडश सहस्रा, द्वे शते सप्तविंशत्यधिके, क्रोशत्रयमष्टाविंशं, धनुःशतं, त्रयोदशाङ्गुलान्यर्द्धं चाङ्गुलं साधिकं जम्बूद्वीपस्य परिधिः परिक्षेपो भवति। इहाधिकग्रहणादेका यूका लिक्षा चैका लभ्यत इत्यादि विशेषार्थिना स्वयमेवाभ्यूह्यं, सूत्रकारेणोपेक्षितत्वान्मयापि न लिखितमिति॥ ८॥

parihī*^iti - yojanānāṃ tisro lakṣāḥ, ṣoḍaśa sahasrā, dve śate sapta-viṃśaty-adhike, krośa-trayaṃ, aṣṭā-viṃśaṃ dhanuḥ-śataṃ, trayo-daśāṅgulāny ardhaṃ cāṅgulaṃ sādhikaṃ jambūdvīpasya paridhiḥ parikṣepo bhavati. ihādhika-grahaṇād ekā yūkā likṣā caikā labhyata ity ādi viśeṣārthinā svayam evābhyūhyaṃ, sūtra-kāreṇopekṣitatvān mayāpi na likhitam iti. 8.*

---

[1] **triga** < *trika*.

8. '**parihī**' [etc.]. The circumference [or] perimeter of Jambūdvīpa is three lakhs, sixteen thousand, two hundred and twenty-seven *yojanas*, three *krośas*, one hundred and twenty-eight *dhanus*, thirteen and a half *aṅgulas* and [somewhat] more.[1] The word '*adhika* (more)' here implies one *yūkā* and one *likṣā*[2]. Who desires to know the details can make the calculation himself.[3] Since it is left out by the author of the manual, I do not mention it also.

---

[1] See Kirfel, p. 124: '... 316227 Yojana, 3 Gāvyuta, 128 Dhanus und noch etwas mehr als $13^{1}/_{3}$ Aṅgula.' Note that the *JDSH* here ends with $^{1}/_{2}$ in stead of $^{1}/_{3}$. Note also that a *krośa* is the same as a *gavyūta*.

[2] Lit. 'an egg of a louse'. For the Jaina linear measures, see Kirfel, p. 337.

[3] The diameter of Jambūdvīpa is 100,000 *yojanas*. The value of π as calculated by the Jainas is $\sqrt{10}$ or 3,16227, etc.

SŪTRAS 9 & 10

अधुना जम्बूद्वीपस्य गणितपदे कृते यत्संपद्यते तदभिधित्सुराह -
adhunā jambūdvīpasya gaṇita-pade kṛte yat sampadyate tad abhidhitsur āha -
Now that the surface area of Jambūdvīpa has been treated [the author], wishing to explain what this amounts to, explicates:

सत्तेव[1] य[2] कोडि[3]सया[4], नउआ[5] छप्पन्न[6] सय[7]सहस्साइं[8] ।
चउ[9]णउयं[10] च सहस्सा[11], सयं[12] दिवड्ढं[13] च[14] साहीयं[15] ॥ ९ ॥[16]
गाउयमेगं[1] पनरस[2], धणू[3]सया[4] तह[5] धणूणि[6] पन्न[7]रस[8] ।[9]

---

[1] सतेव Brd2, Bhog2 & 12. सत्तिव Bhog9.
[2] LD1, Brd2 & 3, Bhog1, 6 & 15 omit य.
[3] कोडी LD1, Brd2 & 3, Bhog1.
[4] शया Bhog9 & 13. ससय Bhog10.
[5] नओया LD1. नउया Brd1, 2 & 3, Tueb, Bhog1, 5, 8 & 7.
[6] छपन्न LD1, 2(?), Brd1. छप्पण्ण Bhog2. च्छप्पन्न Bhog10. छप्पण Bhog12. छप्पन्नंच Bhog15. छप्पान Bhog17.
[7] सये Bhog16.
[8] सहस्साइ Brd2, Bhog5 & 15. सहस्साय Bhog9 & 10. सहस्सायं Bhog12. सहस्साये Bhog14. सहस्साई Bhog17.
[9] चओ LD1, Bhog9 & 13.
[10] णंओयं LD1. णवइं Bhog5. णऊयं Bhog7 & 16. णओयं Bhog9 & 13. णवइ Bhog12. णसयं Bhog17. उ omitted in Bhog8, 10 & 15.
[11] हस्सा omitted in Brd2.
[12] सय Brd2 & 3.
[13] दीवड्ढं Bhog1. द्विवड्ढं Bhog2. दिवढं Bhog15.
[14] च ७९०५३८४१५० Bhog2.
[15] साहियं Ed2 & 3, Brd2 & 3, Bhog4, 7, 10, 11, 13, 14, 15 & 16. साहीय LD1. साहीअं LD2. साहिय Bhog2.
[16] Bhog6 omits this verse.

सट्ठिं[10] च[11] अङ्गुलाइं[12], जंबुद्दीवस्स[13] गणिय[14]पयं[15] ॥ १० ॥[16]

satt'-eva ẏa koḍi-saẏā, naüā chap-panna saẏa-sahassāiṃ;
caü-ṇaüẏaṃ ca sahassā, saẏaṃ divaḍḍhaṃ ca sāhīẏaṃ. 9.
gāüẏam egaṃ pana-rasa, dhaṇū-saẏā taha dhaṇūṇi panna-rasa;
saṭṭhiṃ ca aṃgulāiṃ, jaṃbuddīvassa gaṇiẏa-paẏaṃ. 10.

(सप्तैव च कोटिशतानि नवतिः षट्पञ्चाशच्छतसहस्राणि। चतुर्नवति च सहस्राणि शतं द्वितीयार्द्धं च साधिकम्॥ ९॥ गव्यूतमेकं पञ्चदश धनुशतानि

---

[1] गाउअमेगं Ed3, LD2, Bhog10, 15 & 16. गाओअमे LD1, गाऊअमे Bhog7. गाऊयमे Bhog17.

[2] पाणरस LD1, Brd2 & 3, Bhog7 & 17. [प]न्नरस्स Bhog6. पण्णरस Bhog16.

[3] धणु Ed3, LD2, Brd1 & 3, Bhog2(?), 5, 6, 8, 10, 11, 12 & 14. धणूं Brd2. धणुं Bhog13.

[4] स्सया Bhog5.

[5] तहय Bhog8.

[6] धणुणि Brd3, Bhog6, 10, 11 & 14. धणूंणि Bhog4. धणुंणि Bhog12.

[7] पन्नं LD1. पन Brd2 & Bhog4. पण्ण Bhog7 & 16. पणBhog15 & 17.

[8] रस १५१५ Bhog2. रसं Bhog5, 7, 8, 11, 12, 16 & 17.

[9] गाउयमेगं प is missing in Bhog6.

[10] सट्ठिं Ed2. सट्ठि LD1, Brd2 & 3, Bhog2 & 14.

[11] य Bhog2. च/व(?) Bhog12. चउ Bhog15.

[12] अंगुलाइ Brd2, Bhog1, Bhog13. अंगुलाई Brd3, Bhog17. अंगुलाइं ३० Bhog2. अंगुलांइं Bhog16.

[13] जम्बूद्दीवस्स Ed1, LD2, Brd1, Bhog4, 5, 9, 10, 11 & 12. जम्बूदीवस्स in Ed2, LD1, Bhog1, 2, 6, 8 & 17 is metrically possible. जम्बीदीवस Brd2 & 3.

[14] गणीय LD1, Brd2, Bhog16. य omitted in Bhog6 & 12.

[15] पय Brd2, Bhog9. पयः Bhog13.

[16] In Bhog8, this is verse 11.

तथा धनूंसि पञ्चदश। षष्टिश्चाङ्गुलानि जम्बूद्वीपस्य गणितपदम्॥ १०॥
saptaiva ca koṭi-śatāni navatiḥ ṣaṭ-pañcāśac chata-sahasrāṇi catur-navati ca sahasrāṇi śataṃ dvitīyārdhaṃ ca sādhikam. 9. gavyūtam ekaṃ pañca-daśa dhanu-śatāni tathā dhanūṃsi pañca-daśa; ṣaṣṭiś cāṅgulāni jambūdvīpasya gaṇita-padam. 10.)

9-10. The surface area of Jambūdvīpa is seven hundred and ninety crores, fifty-six hundred thousand and ninety-four thousand, one hundred, and half of the second [*yojanas*] increased with one *gavyūta*, fifteen hundred *dhanus*, fifteen *dhanus* and sixty *aṅgulas*.

COMMENTARY

सत्तेव य^इति - **गाउय^इति**[1] - एवो ऽवधारणे - सप्तकोटिशतानि नवतिकोटयः षट्पञ्चाशल्लक्षाणि चतुर्णवतिसहस्राणि, द्वितीयार्द्धं शत च द्वितीयं शतमर्द्धं यत्र तत् द्वितीयार्द्धं सार्द्धं शतमित्यर्थः। चः समुच्चये। कीदृशमित्याह - साधिकमधिकेन सहिततं, आधिक्यमेवाविष्करोति, **गाउय^इति** - एकमेकसंख्याकं गव्यूतं क्रोशं, पञ्चदशधनुःशतानि पञ्चदशोत्तराणीत्यर्थः। चः समुच्चयार्थः स च भिन्नक्रमः, तत एवं योज्यते, षष्टिरङ्गुलानि च, जम्बूद्वीपस्य गणितपदं भवतीति शेषः। इदमुक्तं भवति, यदि समचतुरस्राणि समस्तजम्बूद्वीपस्य योजनप्रमाणानि खण्डानि क्रियन्ते तदा यथोक्तसंख्यानि गव्यूताद्यधिकानि भवन्ति। तद्यथा, जम्बूद्वीपस्य परिधिर्योजनानां तिस्रो लक्षाः षोडश सहस्राणि सप्तविंशशतद्वयाधिकानीत्येवंरूपः पञ्चविंशत्या सहस्रैर्गुणनीयः, ततो भवन्ति सप्तकोटीशतानि नवतिः कोटयः षट्पञ्चाशल्लक्षाणि पञ्चसप्ततिः सहस्राणि ७९०५६७५०००, पुनर्गव्यूतत्रितयं पञ्चविंशत्या सहस्रैर्गुणितं जातानि पञ्चसप्ततिः सहस्राणि क्रोशानां ७५०००, एषां चतुर्भिर्भागे हृते लब्धा अष्टादश सहस्राः सप्तशती पञ्चाशदधिका

[1] Ed1 omits गाउयेत्ति.

योजनानां १८७५०, एष एकराशिर्मूलराशौ[1] मीलनीयः, ततो ऽष्टाविंशं धनुःशतं पञ्चविंशत्या सहस्रैर् गुणनीयं जातानि द्वात्रिंशद्धनुषां लक्षाणि ३२०००००, अष्टभिर्धनुःसहस्रैर्योजनं भवतीति कृत्वा तदानयनायाष्टभिरेव सहस्रैर्भागो ह्रियते, लब्धाश्चत्वारो योजनशताः ४००, एते ऽपि मूलराशिमध्ये प्रक्षेप्तव्याः, ततः सार्धत्रयोदशाङ्गुलेषु पञ्चविंशत्यैव सहस्रैर्गुणितेषु लब्धानि त्रीणि लक्षाणि सप्तत्रिंशत्सहस्राणि पंचशताधिकानि ३३७५००, एषां धनुरानयनार्थं षण्णवत्या भागो ह्रियते, जातानि त्रीणि धनुःसहस्राणि पंचदशोत्तरपंचशताधिकानि ३५१५, षष्टिरङ्गुलानि चोपरिष्टात्। पुनर्गव्यूतानयनाय धनुःसहस्रद्वयेन भागे हृते लब्धं गव्यूतमेकतं, अधस्तादुद्धरितानि पंचदश शतानि पंचदशोत्तराणि धनुषां १५१५। सर्वांकमीलने जातानि सप्त कोटीशतानि, नवतिकोटयः, षट्पंचाशल्लक्षाणि, चतुर्नवतिः सहस्राणि, सार्धशताधिकानि समचतुरस्राणां योजनप्रमाणखण्डानां, तथैकं गव्यूतं पंचदशोत्तराणि पंचधनुःशतानि षष्टिरङ्गुलानि च, ७९०५६९४१५०, गव्यू. १ धनुः १५१५ अङ्गुल ६०, इति सर्वजम्बूद्वीपगणितपदं प्रपंचितं तत्प्रपंचितेन समर्थितं द्वितीयं योजनद्वारम्॥ ९-१० ॥

satt'-eva ẏa^iti* - *gāuẏa^iti *- evo 'vadhāraṇe - sapta-koṭi-śatāni navati-koṭayaḥ ṣaṭ-pañcāśal-lakṣāṇi catur-ṇavati-sahasrāṇi, dvitīyārdhaṃ śata ca dvitīyaṃ śatam ardhaṃ yatra tat dvitīyārdhaṃ sārdhaṃ śatam ity arthaḥ. caḥ samuccaye. kīdṛśam ity āha - sādhikam adhikena sahitaṃ, ādhikyam evāviṣkaroti,* ***gāüẏa^iti*** *- ekam eka-saṃkhyākaṃ gavyūtaṃ krośaṃ, pañca-daśa-dhanuḥ-śatāni pañca-daśottarāṇīty arthaḥ. caḥ samuccayārthaḥ sa ca bhinna-kramaḥ, tata evaṃ yojyate, ṣaṣṭir aṅgulāni ca, jambūdvīpasya gaṇita-padaṃ bhavatīti śeṣaḥ. idam uktaṃ bhavati, yadi sama-caturasrāṇi samasta-jambūdvīpasya yojana-pramāṇāni khaṇḍāni kriyante*

---

[1] For एषो ऽकराशिर्मूलराशौ.

tadā yathokta-saṃkhyāni gavyūtādy-adhikāni bhavanti. tad yathā, jambūdvīpasya paridhir yojanānāṃ tisro lakṣāḥ ṣoḍaśa sahasrāṇi saptāviṃśa-śata-dvayādhikānīty evaṃ-rūpaḥ pañca-viṃśatyā sahasrair guṇanīyaḥ, tato bhavanti sapta-koṭī-śatāni navatiḥ koṭayaḥ ṣaṭ-pañcāśal-lakṣāṇi pañca-saptatiḥ sahasrāṇi 7905675000, punar gavyūta-tritayaṃ pañca-viṃśatyā sahasrair guṇitaṃ jātāni pañca-saptatiḥ sahasrāṇi krośānāṃ 75000, eṣāṃ caturbhir bhāge hṛte labdhā aṣṭādaśa sahasrāḥ sapta-śatī pañcāśad-adhikā yojanānāṃ 18750, eṣa eka-rāśir mūla-rāśau mīlanīyaḥ, tato 'ṣṭāviṃśaṃ dhanuḥ-śataṃ pañca-viṃśatyā sahasrair guṇanīyaṃ jātāni dvātriṃśad-dhanuṣāṃ lakṣāṇi 3200000, aṣṭabhir dhanuḥ-sahasrair yojanaṃ bhavatīti kṛtvā tad-ānayanāyāṣṭabhir eva sahasrair bhāgo hriyate, labdhāś catvāro yojana-śatāḥ 400, ete 'pi mūla-rāśi-madhye prakṣeptavyāḥ, tataḥ sārdha-trayodaśāṅguleṣu pañca-viṃśatyaiva sahasrair guṇiteṣu labdhāni trīṇi lakṣāṇi sapta-triṃśat-sahasrāṇi pañca-śatādhikāni 337500, eṣāṃ dhanur-ānayanārthaṃ ṣaṇ-ṇavatyā bhāgo hriyate, jātāni trīṇi dhanuḥ-sahasrāṇi pañca-daśottara-pañca-śatādhikāni 3515, ṣaṣṭir aṅgulāni copariṣṭāt. punar gavyūtānayanāya dhanuḥ-sahasra-dvayena bhāge hṛte labdhaṃ gavyūtam ekam, adhastād uddharitāni pañca-daśa śatāni pañca-daśottarāṇi dhanuṣāṃ 1515. sarvāṅka-mīlane jātāni sapta koṭī-śatāni, navati-koṭayaḥ, ṣaṭ-pañcāśal-lakṣāṇi, catur-navatiḥ sahasrāṇi, sārdha-śatādhikāni sama-caturasrāṇāṃ yojana-pramāṇa-khaṇḍānāṃ, tathaikaṃ gavyūtaṃ pañca-daśottarāṇi pañca-dhanuḥ-śatāni ṣaṣṭir aṅgulāni ca, 7905694150, gavyū. 1 dhanuḥ 1515 aṅgula 60, iti sarva-jambūdvīpa-gaṇita-padaṃ prapañcitaṃ tat-prapañcitena samarthitaṃ dvitīyaṃ yojana-dvāram. 9-10.

9-10. ***'satt'-eva ẏa'***, ***'gāuẏa'*** [etc.]. The meaning is as follows. [The word] '*eva* (only)' is used in restrictive sense. Seven hundred crores, ninety crores, fifty-six lakhs, ninety-four thousand, the second half and hundred is the second hundred [and] half, so that [we have] hundred and the half of the second or, one hundred and a half.[1] [The word] '*ca*' is used in conjunctive sense. [The author] explains in which [sense]: '*sādhikam* (increased)' which means '*adhikena sahitaṃ* (joined with more)'. [The author] imparts how much more: ***'gāuẏa'***: one, amounting to one *gavyūta* or *krośa*, fifteen hundred and fifteen *dhanus*. So far the meaning. [The word] '*ca*' is used in conjunctive sense, but it is not in the correct place[2]. So it should be arranged as follows: '*ṣaṣṭir aṅgulāni ca*' (and sixty *aṅgulas*)[3]. The rest [of the sentence is]: the surface area of Jambūdvīpa. It is said that if the sectors of the whole of Jambūdvīpa are construed as congruent squares with the size of one *yojana*, then there are the numbers as expressed [above] plus one *gavyūta*, etc. Namely, the circumference of

---

[1] So we have in succession:

7,000,000,000	
900,000,000	
5,600,000	
94,000	
150	
7,905,694,150	square *yojanas*

[2] Lit. 'out of order or out of place, displaced'.

[3] Instead of '*ṣaṣṭiś cāṅgulāni*'.

Jambūdvīpa is three lakhs, sixteen thousand and two hundred and twenty-seven [*yojanas*], which has to be multiplied with twenty-five thousand. Therefore, there are seven hundred and nine crores, fifty-six lakh and seventy-five thousand: 7,905,675,000 [square *yojanas*]. Further, three *gavyūtas* multiplied with twenty-five thousand results in seventy-five thousand *krośas*: 75,000. When this is divided by four, we obtain eighteen thousand seven hundred and fifty *yojanas*: 18,750. This same figure[1] must be included in the basic row of numbers.[2] Considering that one *yojana* is equal to eight thousand *dhanus*, in order to calculate this number [in *yojanas*, 3,200,000 *dhanus*] are divided by eight thousand. The result is four hundred *yojanas*: 400. This [number] also has to be added to the basic row of numbers. Next, when thirteen and a half *aṅgulas* are multiplied with twenty-five thousand, the result is three lakhs thirty-seven thousand and five hundred: 337,500. In order to calculate this in *dhanus*, divide this by ninety-six. The result is three thousand five hundred and fifteen *dhanus*: 3,515, with a remainder of sixty *aṅgulas*. Then, in order to calculate in *gavyūtas*, when divided by two thousand *dhanus* the result is round down on one *gavyūta* fifteen hundred plus fifteen *dhanus*: 1,515. When all numerical figures are brought together we have seven hundred crores, ninety crores, fifty-six lakhs, ninety-four thousand one hundred and a half square sections of the size of one *yojana* plus one *gavyūta*, fifteen hundred and fifteen *dhanus* and sixty *aṅgulas*: 7,905,694,150 - 1 *gavyū*. - 1515 *dhanus* - 60 *aṅgulas*. In this manner, the

---

[1] *eka-rāśi*.

[2] *mūla-rāśi*, viz. the original row of numbers constituting the result of the root extraction.

surface area of the whole of Jambūdvīpa is treated at length and this treatment the second topic of the *yojanas* has been considered.

SŪTRAS 11 & 12

संप्रति क्रमायातं तृतीयं क्षेत्रद्वारं गाथायाः प्रथमपादेनाह -
samprati kramāyātaṃ tṛtīyaṃ kṣetra-dvāraṃ gāthāyāḥ prathama-pādenāha-
Now, proceeding in regular order, in the first quarter of the [next] verse [the author] treats the third entry, the continents.[1]

अथ पुनरक्षरार्थो भणिष्यते, तत्र व्याख्यायमानक्रमागतं चतुर्थं पर्वतद्वारमाह -
atha punar akṣarārtho bhaṇiṣyate, tatra vyākhyāyamāna-kramāgataṃ caturthaṃ parvata-dvāram āha -

Again, [the author] will explain the literal meaning [first]. Then he treats the fourth topic of the mountains, describing them in due order:

भरहाइ[2] सत्त[3]वासा[4], वियड्ढ[5] चउ[1] चउर[2]तीस[3] वट्टियरे[4]।

---

[1] It is important to note that in Ed1 this introductory sentence and the commentary that follows are brought under the verses 9 and 10 that treat the surface area of Jambūdvīpa. This commentary however begins with 'भरहाइ' etc. This and the contents of the commentary clearly show that it belongs to verse 11. However, for the sake of clarity I have kept the two versions of the commentaries on verse 11 as distinct entities.

[2] भरहाइं LD1, Bhog4, 5 & 13. भरहाई Brd3, Bhog6, 7, 12 & 17.

[3] सत Brd2. सन्न/सत्त(?) Bhog6 & 9. साया Bhog8.

[4] खित्ताणां विजयाणं in stead of भरहाइ सत्तवासा in Ed1, Ed2. वासा ७ Tueb. वां(?)सा Bhog1. चासा Bhog6. Bhog2, 5 & 7 have दारं ३ here, द्वा ३ Bhog12, द्वार Bhog15, द्वारं ३ Bhog16.

[5] There is some confusion here. The regular Pkt. form is वेअड्ढ (Skt. वैताढ्य). वे is shortened to वि metri causa. But only Ed2, 3 & 16 with certainty and Bhog10, 12, 13, 14 & 15 possibly have वियड्ढ. The

सोलस[5] वक्खा[6]रगिरी[7], दो चित्त[8]विचित्त[9] दो[10] जमगा[11] ॥ ११ ॥[12]
दोसय[13] कणय[14]गिरीणं[15], चउ[16] गयदंता[17] य[18] तह[1] सुमेरू[2] य[3] ।

---

difference between ड्ढ and ट्ठ is not always clear. वियट्ठ Ed1, LD2 (with अ for य), Brd3, Tueb, Bhog1, 2(with वि omitted), 4, 5 (with वे for वि), 7, 8, 9, 11 & 17. वियट्ट LD1. वियठ Brd2.

[1] चओ LD1. चउ ४ Bhog2 & 12. चउ २ Bhog13 & 17, here meaning चउ used twice in succession.

[2] र omitted in LD2, Bhog1, 5, 8 & 12. चओर LD1. चउ omitted in Bhog6 with the three following syllables unreadable.

[3] तिंस Ed2 & 3. तिस Bhog2, 7, 10, 14 & 15. त्तास Bhog8.

[4] वट्टयरे LD2. वेयड्ढा(?) ३४ Bhog2. वटियरे Bhog6. वटि(?)यरे Bhog10 & 12. वट्टियरे ३४ Bhog8. वढीयरे Bhog17.

[5] सोलस्स Bhog6. सोलस १६ Bhog8. स omitted in Bhog12.

[6] खा with र omitted in LD1. र omitted in Brd3. खार Brd2, Bhog2, 8, 10 & 17.

[7] Ed1, Brd1, Tueb, Bhog5 (with १६ added), 9, 11, 12, 15 & 16 have the metrically correct गिरी. गिरि Ed2 & 3, LD1, Brd3, Bhog2 (with १६ added), 4, 6, 7, 8, 10, 13, 14 & 17. गिरीओ LD2. गीरि Brd2, गीरी Bhog1.

[8] चित Brd2, Bhog15.

[9] विचित Brd2, Bhog15. विचित्त २ Bhog5, 8 & 12. विचीत्त २ Bhog2. विवि(?)त्त Bhog11.

[10] दो omitted in Bhog6.

[11] जमग्गा LD1, Brd2 & 3, Bhog9. जगमा LD2. जमगा २ Bhog2, 5 & 8.

[12] This is verse 12 in Bhog8. In Bhog2 & 5 verse 11 begins with दारं २. Bhog7 simply has दारं, Bhog12 द्वा २, Bhog15 द्वार.

[13] दे(?)सय Bhog11. दोशय Bhog6.

[14] य is missing in Bhog5. कणग Bhog6 & 12.

[15] गिरिणं Brd2, Bhog10, 14, 15 & 17. गिरिणा २०० Bhog2. गिरीणं २०० Bhog5, 8 & 13.

[16] चऊ LD1. चौ Bhog17.

[17] गजदंता Bhog2 & 4.

[18] य is missing in Ed3. य ४ Bhog2 & 8.

छव्वासहरा[4] पिंडे[5], एगुण[6]सत्तरि[7] सया[8] दुन्नि[9] ॥ १२ ॥[10]

bharahāi sapta vāsā, viẏaḍḍha caü caüra-ʾtīsa vaṭṭ'-iẏare;
solasa vakkhāra-girī, do citta-vicitta do jamagā. 11.
do saẏa kaṇaẏa-girīṇaṃ, caü gaẏa-daṃtā ẏa taha sumerū ẏa;
chav-vāsa-harā piṃḍe, eg'-uṇa-sattari saẏā dunni. 12.

(भरतादीनि सप्त वर्षाणि वैताढ्याश्चत्वारश्चतुस्त्रिंशद् वृत्तेतराः। षोडश वक्षस्कारगिरयो द्वौ चित्रविचित्रौ द्वौ यमकौ॥ ११॥ द्वे शते काञ्चनगिरीणां चत्वारो गजदन्ताश्च तथा सुमेरुश्च। षड्वर्षधराः पिण्ड एकोनसप्तति(त्यधिके) शते द्वे॥ १२॥ *bharatādīni sapta varṣāṇi vaitāḍhyāś catvāraś catus-triṃśad vṛttetarāḥ; ṣoḍaśa vakṣaskāra-girayo dvau citra-vicitrau dvau Yamakau. 11. dve śate kāñcana-girīṇāṃ catvāro gaja-dantāś ca tathā sumeruś ca; ṣaḍ-varṣa-dharāḥ, piṇḍa ekona-saptati(tyadhike) śate dve. 12.*)

11-12. The seven world continents are Bharata, etc. [They contain] four round Vaitāḍhya [mountains], thirty-four

---

[1] तहय Bhog5.

[2] सुमेरु Ed2 & 3, LD1, Brd3, Bhog1, 4(?), 6, 8, 9, 13, 14 & 15. सूमेरु Bhog10. सूमेरू Bhog17. तहयमेरु Bhog12.

[3] अ Ed2, LD1 & 2, Bhog13. य १ Bhog2. वं Bhog17.

[4] छवासहरा Ed1, 2 & 3, Bhog6, 9, 10, 12 & 14. छवासहरा ६ Bhog2. छव्व(?)सिहरी Bhog5. छव्वासहरी Bhog15. छव्वासाहरा Bhog17.

[5] पिडे LD1, Brd3, Bhog15. पीडे Bhog2. पिण्डें Bhog10.

[6] एगूंण LD1. एगुंण Bhog13 & 16. एगूण LD2. एगुणे Brd1. इगुण Bhog14.

[7] सत्तरी Ed1, Bhog1. सत्तर Tueb, Bhog4, 9 & 10. सिंतरी Bhog2. हत्तर Bhog5 & 6. हत्तरि Bhog12.

[8] संया Bhog2.

[9] दुन्निः Ed1. दुन्नी Ed2. दुनि Brd2. दुन्नि २६९ Tueb, Bhog5 & 8. दुनी २६९ Bhog2. दुण्णि Bhog12. दूनि Bhog7.

[10] In Bhog8 this is verse 13.

others [viz. straight ones], sixteen Vakṣaskāra mountains, the couple Citra and Vicitra, two Yamaka mountains, two centuries of Kāñcana mountains and four Gajadantas and so also the magnificent Meru. [Finally] there are six World Mountain ranges. [So] there are two hundred and sixty-nine [mountains] in all.

COMMENTARY

भरहाइ^इति - वर्षाणि क्षेत्राणि मनुष्यनिवासस्थानानीत्यर्थः, तानि कियत्संख्यानि? किंनामानि च भवन्ति इत्याह, सत्त त्ति सप्तसंख्यानि नामतस्तु भरतादीनि, आदिशब्दाद्धेमवतहरिवर्षमहाविदेहरम्यक[है]रण्यकवतानां ग्रहः, तथा वर्षशब्दो नपुंसकलिङ्गः पुंस्त्वे प्रयुक्तो ऽपि प्राकृतत्वात् न दोषाय, 'लिङ्गं व्यभिचार्यपि' इति वचनात्, अमूनि च सर्वक्षेत्राणि स्वाधिष्ठातृदैवतसमाननामानि। तथाहि - भरताधिपतिर्यो यो देव उत्पद्यते तं तं तत्सामानिकाद्या देवा 'भरत' इत्याह्वयन्ति, ततस्तन्नाम्ना तदधिष्ठितं क्षेत्रमपि भरतमिति कथ्यते। तथाचागमः -

"से केणट्ठेणं भंते भरहे वासे इति? गोयमा, भरहे देवे महड्ढीए, महज्जुए जाव पलिओवमट्ठिइए परिवसइ, से एएणट्ठेणं गोयमा, एवं वुच्चइ भरहे वासे।"[1]

इति एवं हैमवतादिष्वपि भावनीयमिति संक्षेपार्थः। विस्तरार्थस्त्वयं - सर्वद्वीपसमुद्राणां मध्ये परिपूर्णचन्द्रमण्डलसंस्थानः सर्वतो लक्षयोजनमानो जम्बूद्वीपो ऽस्ति, स चैकयावज्रमय्याष्टयोजनोच्छ्रयया मूलमध्योपरितनविभागेषु क्रमेण द्वादशाष्टचतुर्योजन-विस्तारया वेदिकया सर्वतो वेष्टितो ऽस्ति। यदागमः -

---

[1] Quotation untraced. Chāyā: स केनार्थेन भदन्त, भरतो वर्ष इत? गौतम, भरतो देवो महर्द्धिको महाद्युतो यावत पल्योपमस्थितिकः परिवसति, स एतेनार्थेन गौतम, एवमुच्यते भरतः वर्षः॥

"से णं जंबूद्दीवे एगा जगईए, सव्वओ समंता सपरिक्खित्ते सा णं जगई अट्ठजोअणां उड्ढं उच्चत्तेणं, मूले बारसजोयणाइं विक्खंभेणं, मज्झे अट्ठजोअणाइं विक्खंभेणं, उवरिं चत्तारि जोअणाइं विक्खंभेणं, मूले वित्थिन्ना, मज्झे संखित्ता, उवरिं तणुआ, गोपुच्छसंठाणसंठिया, सव्ववइरामया अच्छा सण्हा, जाव पडिरूवा"[1]

इति। तस्याश्चोपरिष्टादर्द्धयोजनोच्चः पञ्चधनुःशतविस्तीर्णो गवाक्षकटकः, तथा तस्या एव बहुदेशमध्यभागे गवाक्षकटकप्रमाणोच्छ्रायदैर्घ्या परिक्षेपेण जगतीसमाना, नानारत्ननिर्माणा विविधपद्ममंडिता, पद्मवरवेदिकास्ति। यदुक्तं राजप्रश्नीयोपाङ्गे -

"से केणठ्ठेणं भंते! एवं वुच्चइ, पउमवरवेइया? गोयमा पउमवरवेइया णां तत्थ तत्थ देसे तहिं तहिं वेइयासु, वेइयाबाहासु य, वेइयाफलएसु य, वेइयापुडंतरेसु य, खंभेसु, खंभबाहासु, खंभफलएसु, खंभपुडंतरेसु, सूईसु, सूईमुहेसु, सूईफलएसु, सूईपुडंतरेसु, पक्खेसु, पक्खबाहासु, पक्खफलएसु, पक्खपुडंतरेसु, बहुयाइं, पउमाइं, कुमुयाइं, नलिणाइं, सुभगाइं, सोगंधियाइं, पुंडरीयाइं, सयवत्ताइं, सहस्सवत्ताइं, सव्वरयणामयाइं, अच्छाइं, पडिरूवाइं, महयावासिक्कयछत्तसमाणाइं, पण्णत्ताइं, समणाउसो, से एणं अट्ठेणं गोयमा, एवं वुच्चइ पउमवरवेइया"[2]

---

[1] This is part of *sū.* 124 of the *Jīvājīvābhigama* as published by Shāha Naginbhai Ghelābhāi Javeri, Śreṣṭhi Devacandra Lālbhāī Jainapustakoddhāre Granthāṅkaḥ 50, Bombay, 1919: (... जंबुद्दीवे) ... से णं एक्काए जगतीए सव्वतो समंता संपरिक्खित्ते॥ सा णं जगती अट्ठ जोयणाइं उड्ढं उच्चत्तेणं मूले बारस जोयणाइं विक्खंभेणं मज्झे अट्ठ जोयणाइं विक्खंभेणं उप्पिं चत्तारिं जोयणाइं विक्खंभेणं मूले विच्छिण्णा मज्झे संखित्ता उप्पिं तणुया गोपुच्चसंठाणसंठिता सव्ववइरामई अच्छा सण्ह ... (ज़ाव) ... पडिरूवे. छाया: (... जम्बूद्वीपः) ... सा खलु एकया जगत्या सर्वतः समन्तात संपरिक्षिप्तः॥ सा खलु जगतय अष्टयोजनान्य ऊर्ध्वम उच्चत्वेन, मूले द्वादशयोजनानि विष्खम्भेण, मध्ये ऽष्टयोजननि विष्खम्भेण, उपरि चत्त्वारि योजनानि विष्खमभेण, मूले विस्तीर्णा, मध्ये संक्षिप्ता, उपरि तनुका, गोपुच्छसंस्थानसंस्थिता, सटर्ववज्रमय्य अच्छा श्लक्ष्णा, ... (यावत्) ... प्रतिरूपः॥.

[2] This a part of *sū.* 9 of the *Rājapraśnīyasūtra*, Jaina-Śāstroddhāra-Samiti ed. (with Skt. commentary by Pūjyaśrī Ghāsīlālji and with Hindī and Gujaratī translation), Rajkot, 1965, Vol. I, p. 459: से केणठ्ठेणं भंते!

इति। तस्याः पार्श्वद्वये ऽपि द्वौ वनखण्डौ वेदिकामानदैर्घ्यौ विद्येते, नवरं विस्तारेणाभ्यन्तरः सार्द्धधनुःशतद्वयोनयोजनयुग्मप्रमाणो, बाह्यस्तु वनखण्डो ऽर्द्धाष्टमधनुःशतहीन-योजनयुग्ममानो, यतस्तत्रान्यान्यप्यभ्यन्तरात् वनखण्डादधिकानि पञ्चधनुःशतानि जालकटकेनावरुद्धानि, परं श्रीमलयगिरिपादैर्नैतद्विवक्षितं, द्वयोरपि वनखण्डयोरेकमेव मानमुक्तं, तत्त्वं तु बहुश्रुता विदन्ति। तस्यां च वेदिकायां मेरुपर्वतात्पञ्चचत्वारिंशद्योजन-सहस्राणि दक्षिणस्यां दिश्यतिगत्य अष्टयोजनोच्छ्रायं चतुर्योजनविस्तारं प्रत्येकमेकैकक्रोशविस्तारया द्वारशाखया कलितं, ततः सामस्त्येन सार्द्धयोजनचतुष्टयविस्तारं वैडूर्यमयाभ्यां कपाटाभ्यां वज्रमय्या परिधिया निर्जटिततं, अनेकसामानिकसुरादिदेवाग्रमहिष्यादिदेवीकृतसेवार्द्ध-पल्योपमायुर्वैजयन्तदेवाधिष्ठितं वे(वै) जयन्ताभिधानं द्वारमस्ति। तथा अमुतो द्वारात् उदीच्यां हिमवन्तं पूर्वापरयोस्तु लवणोदन्वन्तं यावद्गतं भरतनामकं विजयक्षेत्रं तच्च बहुमध्यदेशभागे पूर्वापरयोर्लवणसमुद्रप्राप्तेन पञ्चाशद्योजनविस्तीर्णेन तदर्द्धोच्चेन रजतमयेन वैताढ्यपर्वतेन द्विधा कृतं, तेन दक्षिणभरतार्द्धमुत्तरभरतार्द्धं चेति भण्यते। हिमवत्पर्वतोर्ध्वतलस्थितात् पद्मह्रदान्निर्गताभ्यां प्रथमं पूर्वापरयोर्गत्वा स्वस्वनामधेयकूटादावृत्य दक्षिणां दिशमनुश्रित्य विजयाढ्यपर्वतं विभिद्य दक्षिणलवणोदधिं प्रविष्टाभ्यां

एवं वुच्चइ - पउमवरवेइया - पउमवरवेइया? गोयमा! पउमवरवेइयाएणां तत्थ तत्थ तहिं तहि देसे वेइयासु य वेइयाफलएसु य वेइयापुडंतरेसु य खंभेसु य खंभबाहासु य खंभसीसेसु खंभपुडंतरेसु सूईसु सूईमुखेसु सूईफलएसु सूईपुडंतरेसु पक्खेसु पक्खबाहासु पक्खपेरंमतेसु पक्खपुडंतरेसु, बहुयाइं उप्पलाइं पउमाइं कुसुमाइं णलिणाइं सुभगाइं सोगंधियाइं पुंडरीयाइं महापुंडरीयाइं सयवत्ताइं सहस्सवत्ताइं सव्वरयणामयाइं अच्छाइं जाव पडिरूवाइ महयावासिक्कछत्तसमाणाइं पण्णत्ताइं समणाउसो! से एएणं अट्ठेणं गोयमा! पउमवरवेइया - पउमवरवेइया. छाया: अथ केनार्थेन भदन्त! एवमुच्यते - पद्मवरवेदिका पद्मवरवेदिका? गौतम! पद्मवरवेदिकायाः खलु तत्र तत्र तस्मिन् तस्मिन् देशे वेदिकासु वेदिकाबाहुषु च वेदिकाफलकेषु च वेदिकापुटान्तरेषु च स्तम्भेषु च स्तम्भबाहुषु च स्तम्भशिरस्सु स्तम्भपुटान्तरेषु सूचिषु सूचीमुखेषु सूचीपुटान्तरेषु पक्षेषु पक्षबाहुषु पक्षपर्यन्तेषु पक्षपुटान्तरेषु बहुकानि उत्पलानि पद्मानि कुमुदानि नलिनानि सुभगानि सौगन्धिकानि पुण्डरीकाणि महापुण्डरीकाणि शतपत्राणि सहस्रपत्राणि सर्वरत्नमयानि अच्छानि यावत् प्रतिरूपाणि महावार्षिकछत्रसमानानि प्रज्ञप्तानि श्रमणायुष्मन् तत् एतेनार्थेन गौतम! पद्मवरवेदिका - पद्मवरवेदिका॥.

गङ्गासिन्धुभ्यां तच्च कृतषट्खण्डं, तत्र च प्राणिप्राणव्यपरोपणप्रवणान्तःकरण-म्लेच्छव्याप्तत्वादनार्याणि पञ्च खण्डानि। एकं च वैताढ्यात् दक्षिणस्यां दिशि एकादशकलाधिकं चतुर्दशोत्तरं योजनशतमतिगत्यनव-योजनविस्तीर्णया द्वासशयोजनदीर्घया अयोध्यया नगर्या विराजितं, गङ्गासिन्धुवैताढ्यदक्षिण-समुद्राणां मध्यस्थितं जिनचक्रयर्द्धचक्रिप्रमुखोत्तमपुरुषाध्यासितमार्यं। उक्तं च - "आर्यावर्त्तो जन्मभूमिर्जिनचक्रयर्द्धचक्रिणाम्"[1] इति। तथा वैताढ्ये ऽपाच्यां तमिस्रा गुहास्ति, सा च द्वादशयोजनायामा पञ्चाशद्योजनदैर्घ्या कृतकृतमालदेवनिवासा वेजयन्तसमानद्वारा, तस्याश्च बहुमध्यदेशे द्वियोजनान्तराले प्रत्येकं त्रियोजनविस्तारे उन्मग्नजलानिमग्नजले नद्यौ स्तः। एवं प्राच्यां नृत्तमालदेवाधिष्ठिता खण्डप्रपातगुहा। तस्य च गिरेर्मूलाद्दशयोजनान्युत्प्लुत्य वेदिकावनखण्डमंडितं पर्वतप्रमाणदैर्घं प्रत्येकं दशदशयोजनविस्तारं विद्याधरनगरश्रेणिद्वयं विद्यते, किञ्च दक्षिणदिग्वर्त्तिन्यां श्रेणौ सुप्रजोभिर्जनपदैर्विराजितानिरथनूपुरचक्रवालपुरःसराणि पञ्चाशद्विद्याधर-नगराणि उत्तरश्रेणौ तु गगनवल्लभादीनि षष्टिः पुराणि, तेषु धरणेंद्रप्रकाशिताष्टाचत्वारिंशत्सहस्रमहाविद्याप्रसादोपनतप्रकम्रसमस्तमनोरथार्थि तथिपदार्थसमासादितपरमानंदसंदोहा, गगनगमनसामर्थ्यसमन्विता विद्याधराः सुखमासते। पुनर्दशयोजनान्युपरिष्टादारुह्य विद्याधरश्रेणिसमा ऽविषमोन्नतभूमिरिंद्राभियोगिकदेवकृतनिवासा श्रेणिद्वयी समस्ति। ततो ऽपि पञ्चसु योजनेषूपरि दशयोजनानि विस्तीर्णं, वेदिकावनखण्डमनोहरतं, अनल्पकल्पवासिदेवक्रीडायोग्यं स्थानमास्ते। तत्र सपादशतयोजनोच्छ्रयाणि तावन्मूलविस्ताराणि उपरिष्टात् सार्द्धद्वादशक्रोशायामानि नव कूटानि। तथाहि, सिद्धायतन १ दक्षिणार्द्धभरत २ खण्डप्रपात ३ मणिभद्र ४ विजयाढ्य ५ पूर्णभद्र ६ तमिस्रागुह ७ उत्तरार्द्धभरत ८ वैश्रमण ९ नामानि, तेषु माणिभद्रविजाढ्य-पूर्णभद्रकूटानि हिरण्यमयानि, अपराणि षट्रत्नमयानि, प्रथमे पूर्वदिग्वर्त्तिनि (कूटे) क्रोशदैर्घ्यं क्रोशार्द्धविस्तीर्णं चत्वारिंशदर्गलचतुर्दशधनुःशतोच्छ्रायं सिद्धायतनं, तस्मिन् पञ्चधनुः शतोच्चानि तदर्द्धविस्ताराणि त्रीणि द्वाराणि तिसृषु दिक्षु। तद्यथा - प्राच्यां प्रथमं द्वारं, द्वितीयं दक्षिणस्यां, तृतीयमुदीच्यां, प्रतीच्यां तु न किंचिदिति। किञ्च सर्वेषु सिद्धायतनेषु प्रासादेषु च जम्बूद्वीपमध्ये ऽयमेव द्वारदिग्विभागः, तस्य हि बहुमध्यदेशे

[1] Quotation untraced.

क्रोशचतुर्थांशायामविष्कम्भा तदर्द्धपृथुला मणिपीठिका, तस्या उपरि पञ्चधनुःशतायामविस्तारस्तदधिकोच्छ्रायो देवच्छन्दकस्तत्राष्टोत्तरं शतं प्रतिमाः, ता हि जघन्यतः सप्तहस्तप्रमाणा उत्कर्षतः पञ्चधनुःशतोच्चा ऋषभवर्द्धमानचंद्राननवारिषेणाख्याः सन्ति। पूर्णकलशनागदन्त-शालभंजिकाजालकटकादिरचनाविशेषाः सर्वचैत्येषु ज्ञेयाः। ततः परं भरतार्द्धकूटं, तत्र भरतदेवस्य सिद्धायतनप्रमाणः प्रासादः। खण्डप्रपाततमिस्रागुहयोर्नृत्तमालकृतमालौ देवौ, अन्येषु पञ्चसु स्वनामानो देवाः प्रासादेषु विलसन्ति। तथा हिमवन्नितम्बे दक्षिणदिशि मूले द्वादश योजनानि उपरि चत्वारि विस्तीर्णो ऽष्टयोजनोच्छ्रय ऋषभदेवनिवासो रत्नमय ऋषभकूटनामा पर्वतो ऽस्ति। स च 'भूमिकूट' इति इह प्रकरणे प्रसिद्धः। चक्री षट्खण्डां वसुन्धरां विजित्यास्मिन् स्वनाम लिखति। भरतमुत्तरेण पूर्वापरयोर्लवणसमुद्रं प्राप्तो भरताद् द्विगुणविस्तारो योजनशतोच्छ्रयो हेममयो हिमवान् वर्षधरस्तदुपरि बहुमध्यदेशभागो योजनसहस्रदैर्घ्यस्तदर्द्धविस्तरो दशयोजनावगाढो जलपूर्णः पद्महदस्तस्य रजतमयं कूलं, वज्रमयपाषाणाश्चतुर्दिशिमणिसोपानाः, तन्मध्ये योजनायामविस्तारम-र्द्धयोजनपिण्डं दशयोजनोच्चनालं गव्यूतद्वयं जलादुपरि स्थितं पद्मं विद्यते, वज्रमयं तस्य मूलमरिष्टमयः कन्दः। वैडूर्यमयो नालः बाह्यपत्राणि च, मध्यानि तु जम्बूनदमयानि, कनकमयीकर्णिका, स्वर्णमयानि केसराणि, विविधमणिमयं पुष्करं, सा च कर्णिका द्विगव्यूतप्रमाणा पृथुला त्वेकं गव्यूतं, तस्या उपरि पीठिकादेवच्छन्दकादियुतं श्रीदेवीभवनतं, एतादृशेनार्द्धप्रमाणेन कमलानामष्टशतेन वृतं, तत्र श्रीदेव्या आभरणानि, तद्बाह्येषु वायव्यौदीच्यैशानेषु दिग्भागेषु चत्वारि कमलसहस्राणि ४०००, तेषु तावन्तम् एव सामानिका देवा देव्यो वा। पूर्वस्यां दिशि चतुर्षु पद्मेषु चतसृणां महामंत्रिसदृशीनां स्थानानि, आग्नेय्यामष्टसु पद्मसहस्रेषु श्रीदेव्या अभ्यन्तरायां पर्षदि देवानामष्टौ सहस्राः ८०००, दक्षिणस्यां दिशि दशसु पद्मसहस्रेषु १००००, तावन्त एव मध्यपर्षदि मित्रस्थानीया देवाः। नैर्ऋत्यां द्वादशसु पद्मसहस्रेषु १२०००, तावन्त एव किङ्करस्थानीयाः सुराः बाह्यपर्षदि। पश्चिमायां सप्तसु पद्मेषु सप्तानामनीकाधिपतीनामाश्रयाः, तथा चतसृषु दिक्षु पूर्वादिकासु षोडशसु पद्मसहस्रेषु १६००० आत्मरक्षकदेवानां स्थानानि, एतद्वेष्टनकत्रयं मध्यं। अपरे ऽपि बाह्याः त्रयः परिरयाः, तेष्वभ्यन्तरे परिक्षेपे द्वात्रिंशल्लक्षाणि ३२०००००, मध्यमे चत्वारिंशच्छतसहस्राणि ४००००००, अष्टाचत्वारिंशल्लक्षाणि

४८००००० पद्मानां बाह्ये भवन्ति। एवं सर्वाग्रेण एका कोटी विंशतिलक्षाणि पञ्चाशत्सहस्राणि विंशत्यधिकमेकं शतं च १२०५०१२० पद्महृदे पद्मानि। महापद्मादिष्वप्येषैवकमलानां संख्येति, तस्मात्तु ह्रदात् पूर्वद्वारतोरणात् पञ्चयोजनशतानि पूर्वस्यां पूर्वतोपरि गत्वा गङ्गावर्त्तकूटादावर्त्त्य दक्षिणाभिमुखं पञ्चयोजनशतानि, त्रयोविंशानि साधिकाध्युष्टकलायुतान्यतिक्रम्य द्विगव्यूतदीर्घान्मकरमुखान्निःसृत्य गङ्गाप्रपातकुण्डे निपतति। तच्च कुण्डं षष्टियोजनायामविस्तारमुपरिष्टात्, अधस्तु दशयोजनन्यूनं दशयोजनावगाढं वज्रमयतलं त्रिद्वारतोरणसोपानादियुतं, तन्मध्ये गङ्गाद्वीपो ऽष्टयोजनायामविष्कम्भो गव्यूतद्वयं जलादुपरि गतः, तन्मध्ये भवनं, तत्र पीठिकायां गङ्गादेव्याः शय्येति। ततो दक्षिणतोरणाद्विनिर्गत्य विजयाढ्यपर्वतं जगतीं च विभिद्य चतुर्दशनदीसहस्रपरीता जलधिं प्रविशेष गङ्गा। तस्या ह्रदाद् विनिर्गमे मकरमुखे कुण्डात्प्रवाहे च सक्रोशानि षट् योजनानि विस्तारः क्रोशार्द्धमुद्वेधः मुखप्रस्तारः प्रवाहाद् दशगुणः। उक्तं च -

"जो जीसे वित्थारो, सलिलाए होइ आढवंतीए।
सो दसहिं पडिपुन्नो मुहवित्थारो मुणेयव्वो ॥ १ ॥"[1]

उद्वेधस्तु सर्वत्र प्रस्तारात्पञ्चाशत्तमो भागः। यत उक्तं -

"जो जत्थ उ वित्थारो, सलिलाए होइ जंबुदीवंमि।
पन्नासइमं भागं, तस्सुव्वेहं वियाणाहि ॥ १ ॥"[2]

तथाऽस्या अपि द्वे तटे वेदिकावनखण्डवती, न चैतद्याद्दच्छिकतं, यदागमः -

"गङ्गा णं महानई उभओ [...] पासेहिं दोहि य पउमवरवेइयाहिं दोहि य वणसंडेहिं संपरिखित्ता।"[3]

---

[1] बृहत्क्षेत्रसमास, verse 227 (*BKSJ*, p. 225):
यो यस्या विस्तारः सलिलाया भवत्यारभमाणायाः।
स दशभिः प्रत्युत्पन्नो मुखविस्तारो ज्ञातव्यः ॥ २२७ ॥

[2] बृहत्क्षेत्रसमास, verse 228 (*BKSJ*, p. 225):
ये यत्र तु विस्तारः सलिलाया भवति जम्बूद्वीपे।
पञ्चाशत्तमं भागं तस्योद्वेधं विजानीहि ॥ २२८ ॥

[3] गङ्गा ननु महानदी उभयः [...] पार्श्वैर् द्वे च पद्मवरवेदिकाभिर् द्वे च वनसंदेहैः संपरिक्षिप्ता ॥ Quotation untraced.

एवं पश्चिमतोरणद्वारान्निर्गता सिन्धवावर्त्तकूटादावर्त्य विवृतमुखाकारात् नालान्निपत्य सिन्धुदेवीनिवासं कुण्डं मध्येकृत्य तथैव जलधिं गता सिन्धुनदी। तथोत्तरतोरणाद्विनिर्गता गङ्गाद्विगुणमानपरिवारा स्वनामकुण्डे निपत्य शब्दापातिनं गव्यूतद्वयेनास्पृशन्ती हैमवतं क्षेत्रं मध्येकृत्यापरोदधिं गता रोहितांशा। हिमवति सर्वरत्नमयान्येकादश कूटानि। तद्यथा - सिद्धायतन १ क्षुल्लहिमवत् २ भरत ३ इला ४ गङ्गा ५ श्री ६ रोहितांशा ७ सिन्धु ८ सुरा(देवी) ९ हैमवत १० वैश्रमणाख्यानि ११ तेषां मूलविस्तार उच्चत्वं च पञ्चयोजनशतानि, शिखरविस्तारस्तु तदर्धमानः, प्रथमकूटे (क्षुल्लनाम्नि) सिद्धायतनं पञ्चाशद्योजनानि दीर्घं तदर्धं पृथुलं षट्त्रिंशद्योजनोच्छ्रयं, तस्मिन् त्रीणि द्वाराणि, तेषामायामो ऽष्टौ योजनानि, तदर्धं विष्कम्भः, अष्टयोजनायामविष्कम्भा तस्य मध्ये मणिपीठिका; सा च चत्वारि योजनानि पृथुला, तदुपरि देवच्छन्दकस्तत्प्रमाणः आयामोच्छ्रायाभ्यां किंचिदधिकः। तत्र प्रतिमा यथा वैताढ्याद्यकूटे प्रोक्ताः। शेषेसु दशसु कूटेषु सार्धद्वाषष्टियोजनोच्छ्रायाः सक्रोशैकत्रिंशद्योजनविस्ताराः सिंहासनादियुक्ताः प्रासादाः सन्ति। हिमवन्महाहिमवतोरन्तराले भरताच्चतुर्गुणविस्तारं पूर्वापरयोर्लवणसमुद्रं प्राप्तं स्वनामदेवाधिष्ठायकं दशविधकल्पपादप-प्रभावोपढौकिताभिलषिताहारनेपथ्यभरणशयनीयावासादिलालितवपुर्भिर्युगलिकैर्विराजितं हैमवतनामकं क्षेत्रमस्ति। तत्र ते युगलधर्मिणश्चतुःषष्टिपृष्ठकरण्डभ्राजितमेकगव्यूतोच्चं चतुर्थभक्तान्ते कृतमनोऽभिलषिताहारं रोगजराप[1]मृत्युदुःखदौर्मनस्यादिरहितमेकपल्योपमायुर्देहं दधानाः, पर्यंते एकोनाशीतिदिनान्यपत्यानि पालयित्वा स्वस्य समस्थितिष्वल्पस्थितिषु वा देवेषूत्पद्यन्ते। अत्र च केचिदेतेषां चणकबदरामलकप्रमितमाहारमेकद्वित्रिगव्यूतप्रमाणशरीराणां क्रमेण, अपरे चाष्टादशव्यञ्जनाकुलां रसवतीं भोजनतयाभिदधति। तन्न सकर्णानां कर्णमवतंसयति, यतः शर्कराजित्वररसा पृथ्वी कल्पवृक्षाणां फलानि च तेषामाहारतयोपयुज्यन्ते। आह चागमः -

"पुढवी पुप्फफलाहारा, ते णं मणुआ पन्नत्ता।"[2]

---

[1] जराप from Skt. जरात्व (= वृद्धत्व) in the sense of the Hindi बुढ़ापा.

[2] This is part of *sū.* 111 of the जम्बूद्वीपप्रज्ञप्ति ed. Shāha Naginbhai Ghelābhāi Javeri, Śreṣṭhi Devacandra Lālbhāī Jainapustakoddhāre

तत्र च सिंहव्याघ्रसर्पबिडालादयो दुष्टतिर्यंचो ऽपि क्षेत्रस्वाभाव्यान्मिथो हिंस्यहिंसक-भाववर्जिताः प्रतनुकषायतयावतिष्ठन्ते। अतस्तद्भाव-भावितत्वादपि देवगतिमेवाश्नुवते। दंशमशकयूकामत्कुणप्रमुखाः शरीरसंतापकारिणः क्षुद्रजन्तवस्तु मूलतो ऽपि न भवन्ति। कालस्तत्र सुषमदुषमारूप एक एव। तन्मध्ये पञ्चवर्णरत्नमयः सर्वतः सहस्रयोजनप्रमाणः पल्याकाराः शब्दापाती वृत्तवैताढ्यपर्वतो, ये ऽमुं रजतमयमभिदधति, तेषां जम्बूद्वीपप्रज्ञप्त्या सह विरोधः। तत्र ह्येवमुक्तं -

"कहि णं भंते हेमवए वासे सद्दावईनामं वट्टवेयड्ढपव्वए पन्नत्ते? गोयमा रोहियाए महानईए, पच्चच्छिमेणं रोहिअंसाए महानए पुरच्छिमेणं हेमवयवासस्स बहुमज्झदेसभागे इत्थणं सद्दावई नामं वट्टवेयड्ढे पव्वए पन्नत्ते, एगं जोयणसहस्सं उड्ढं उच्चत्तेणं, अढ्ढाइयाइं जोयणसयाइं उव्वेहेणं, सव्वत्थसमे, पल्लगसंठाणसंथिए, एगं जोयणसहस्सं आयामविक्खंभेणं तिन्नि जोयणसहस्साइं एगं च बावट्ठंजोयणसयं (३१६२) किंचि विसेआहियं परिक्खेवेणं सव्वरयणामए अच्छे इत्यादि।"[1]

Granthāṅkaḥ 50, Bombay, 1919, p. 150. The full sentence reads: **ते णं भंते मणुया! किमाहारमाहारेंति? गोयमा! पुढविफुप्फफलाहारा ते मणुयगणा पण्णत्ता समणाउसो!** छाया: ते खलु भदन्त मनुजाः! किमाहारमाहारन्ति गौतम! पृथिवीपुष्पफलाहारास्ते मनुजगणाः प्रज्ञप्ताः श्रमणायुष्मन्! The quotation also occurs verbatim in the *JDP*, *sū.* 22, ed. Javeri, p. 117: पुढवीफुप्फफलाहारा ते मणुआ पण्णत्ता ..., with reference to the *Jīvābhigamasūtram* (ed. Shāha Naginbhai Ghelābhāi Javeri, 1919) by Śanticandra, commentator on the *JDP*.

[1] जम्बूद्वीपप्रज्ञप्ति, सू. ७७, ed. Shāha Naginbhai Ghelābhāi Javeri, Śreṣṭhi Devacandra Lālbhāī Jainapustakoddhāre Granthāṅkaḥ 50, Bombay, 1919: **कहि णं भन्ते! हेमवए वासे सद्दावई णामं वट्टवेअद्धपव्वए पण्णत्ते? गोयमा! रोहिआए महाणईए पच्चच्छिमेणं रोहिअंसाए महाणईए पुरत्थिमेणं हेमवयवासस्स बहुमज्झदेसभाए एत्थ णं सद्दावए णामं वट्टवेअद्धपव्वए पण्णत्ते एगं जोअणसहस्सं उद्धं उच्चत्तेणं अद्धाइज्जाइं जोअणसयाइं उव्वेहेणं सव्वत्थसमे पल्लगसंठाणसंथिए एगं जोअणसहस्सं आयामविक्खंभेणं तिण्णि जोअणसहस्साइं एगं च बावत्थं जोअणसयं किंचिविसेसाहिअं परिक्खेवेणं पण्णत्ते, सव्वरयणामए अच्छे। ...** छाया: कुत्र ननु भदन्त! हैमवतवर्षे शब्दापाती नाम्ना वृत्तवैताढ्यपर्वतः प्रज्ञप्तः? गौतम! रोहितामहानद्याः पश्चिमेन

उमास्वातिवाचको ऽप्येवमेवाह तथा च तद्वाक्यं -

"वृत्तो विविधरत्नमयः सर्वतः साहसरः शब्दापातिगिरिरिति ।"[1]

अत एतद्वर्णके यत्क्षेत्रसमासे 'रययमया' इत्युक्तं, तन्न संवादीति[2], किन्तु 'रयणमया' इति संवादी पाठ इति तथा तदुपरि स्वाभिधानदेवभवनं हिमवत्कूटप्रासादसदृशं। तदुत्तरो हैमवतक्षेत्राद् द्विगुणविस्तारो ऽर्जुनमयो योजनशतद्वयोच्चो महाहिमवान्, तत्र बहुमध्ये पद्महृदाद् द्विगुणायामविष्कम्भो महापद्महृदः कृतह्रीदेवीनिवासः। पद्मानि पद्महृदसंख्या(संनिभा)न्यत्र, एतद्दक्षिणतोरणान्निःसृत्य पञ्चकलाधिकानि पञ्चोत्तराणि षोडशयोजनशतानि पर्वतमुल्लंघ्य रोहितादेव्यधिष्ठिते गङ्गाप्रतापकुण्डाद् द्विगुणायामविष्कम्भे दशयोजनोद्वेधे रोहिताप्रतापकुण्डे निपत्य शब्दापातिनं चतुर्थांशेन परिधाय गव्यूतद्वयेनास्पृशन्त्यष्टाविंशत्या नदीसहस्रैः समं रोहितांशासमविस्तारा रोहिता पूर्वोदधिं प्राविशत्। तथोत्तरद्वारान्निर्गत्य प्रवाहे पंचविंशतियोजनायामा मुखे तु दशगुणविस्तारा स्वनाम्नि कुण्डे निपत्य एकयोजनास्पृष्टगन्धापातिका प्रवाहे मुखे च क्रमेणार्द्धपञ्चयोजनोद्वेधा षट्पञ्चाशन्नदीसहस्रसहिता हरिकान्ता पश्चिमोदधिं गता। तस्मिन् पर्वते ऽष्टौ कूटानि, तद्यथा सिद्धायतन १ महाहिमवत् २ हैमवत ३ रोहिता ४ ह्री ५ हरिकान्ता ६ हरित् ७ वैडूर्य ८ नामानि, हिमवत्कूटतुल्यानि स्वनामधेयदैवतानि। तस्मादुत्तरस्यां दिशि हरिवर्षं क्षेत्रं तत्र युगलिनः प्रागुक्तयुगलिकेभ्यो द्विगुणविशेषणाः केवलं कृतचतुःषष्टिदिनापत्यपालनाः षष्ठप्रान्ते विहिताहाराश्च, तस्य बहुमध्यदेशभागे ऽरुणदेववसतिः शब्दापातिविशिष्टो गन्धापाती। कालस्तु तत्र सुषमारूपः सदैव। तदुत्तरो हरिवर्षक्षेत्राद् द्विगुणविस्तारश्चतुःशत-

---

रोहितांशा महानद्याः पूर्वेण हैमवतवर्षस्य बहुमध्यदेशभागे तत्र ननु शब्दापाती नाम्ना वृत्तवैताढ्यपर्वतः प्रज्ञप्तः, एकं योजनसहस्रम् ऊर्ध्वोच्चत्वेन अर्धतृतीयानि योजनशतानि उद्वेधेन सर्वत्र समः पल्यङ्कसंस्थानसंस्थितः एकं योजनसहस्रम् आयामविष्कम्भाभ्यां त्रीणि योजनसहस्राणि एकं च द्वाषष्ट्यधिकं योजनशतं किञ्चिद्विशेषेण परिक्षेपेण प्रज्ञप्तं सर्वात्मना रत्नमयः आच्छः, ... Also quoted in the commentary on the बृहत्क्षेत्रसमास, verse 173 (*BKSJ*, p. 178).

[1] जम्बूद्वीप्समास of उमास्वाति (*JDSU*, p. 8, line 4). The sentence in full reads: तन्मध्ये वृत्तो विविधरत्नमयः सर्वतः साहस्रः शब्दापाती गिरिः ।.

[2] For संवावदीति of Ed1.

योजनोच्छ्रयस्तपनीयमयो निषधगिरिः, तदुपरि महापद्माद् द्विगुणायाम विष्कम्भो दशयोजनावगाढः पद्महृदविशिष्टपद्मपूर्णः कृतधृतिदेवीनिवासः तिगिंछिहृदः, तद्दक्षिणादिग्भागे सैककलानि सप्तसहस्राणि चत्वारि शतानि एकविंशानि योजनानां पर्वतमुल्लंघ्य स्वनामकुण्डं मध्येकृत्य हरिकान्तावत् केवलं पूर्वोदधिं गता हरित्सलिला। उत्तरेण शीतोदा निर्गता, तस्याः प्रवाहो जिह्वका च पञ्चाशद्योजनानि, हरिन्नदीकुण्डाद् द्विगुणकुण्डा, निषध १ देवकुरु २ सूर्य ३ सुलस ४ विद्युत्प्रभ ४ हृदान् विभिद्य चतुरशीत्या नदीसहस्रैरन्विता, भद्रशालवन-मध्यप्रवृत्ता, योजनद्वयान्तरे मन्दरमलगन्ती, अपरदिगभिमुखं विद्युत्प्रभविदारिकापरविदेहं द्विधा विधाय एकैकस्माद्विजयादष्टाविंशति नदीसहस्रानुगता, जयन्तद्वारादधो जगतीं विदार्य पञ्चशतयोजनायामा, दशयोजनोद्वेधा, पश्चिमजलधिं (जलधिमधि)गता। तस्मिन् पर्वते नव कूटानि, तद्यथा - सिद्धायतन १ निषध २ हरिवर्ष ३ प्राग्विदेह ४ हरित् ५ धृति ६ शीतोदा ७ अपरविदेह ८ रुचका ९ भिधानानि हिमवत्कूटसदृशानि। निषधादुत्तरो वैडूर्यमयस्तिगिंछि-प्रतिच्छन्दः केशरिहृदमध्यो नीलवान् वर्षधरः, तत्र नव कूटानि, तथाहि - सिद्धायतन १ नील २ प्राग्विदेह ३ शीता ४ कीर्त्ति ५ नारी ६ अपरविदेह ७ रम्यक ८ उपदर्शन ९ कूटाख्यानि निषधकूटमानामि। ततः केसरिहृदाद् दक्षिणदिशि सैककलानि सप्तयोजनसहस्राणि चत्वारि शतान्येकविंशत्यधिकानि पर्वताधित्यकामुल्लंघ्य, स्वनामदैवतकुण्डं मध्येकृत्य, नील १ उत्तरकुरु २ चंद्र ३ एरवत ४ माल्यवत् ५ हृदान् विभिद्य, भद्रशालसत्क [सक्त?[1]]-चतुरशीतिनदीसहस्रपरीता, माल्यवद्विदेहविजय द्वारच्छेदिनी, पूर्वोदधिं गता शीता, शेषं शीतोदावत्। निषधनीलवदन्तरा महाविदेहो लक्षयोजनानि तस्य मध्यदैर्घ्यं विष्कम्भस्तु निषधाद् द्विगुणः। तन्मध्ये सहस्रयोजनावगाढो नवनवतियोजनसहस्रोच्चः भूमितले दशसहस्रविस्तार उपरि सहस्रयोजनायामः रत्नमध्यः स्वर्णमयो मेरुगिरिः। तदुपत्यकायां पूर्वापरयोर्द्वाविंशतियोजनसहस्रायामं उत्तरदक्षिणयोस्तु प्रत्येकं सार्द्धयोजनशतद्वयविस्तारं, नानावृक्षकलितं, भद्रशालवनं। तन्मध्ये मेरुपर्वतात् पञ्चाशता योजनैर्हिमवत्सिद्धायतन-प्रमाणानि चतुर्दिश्यानि

---

[1] Also LD2 has the enigmatic स्त्क. Maybe it is a wrong reading for सक्त: mfn. clinging or adhering to, sticking in (with loc. or comp.), belonging to (with gen.).

चत्वारि सिद्धायतनानि। तावतैव विदिक्षु पञ्चशत्पञ्चाशद्योजनायामास्तदर्द्धविष्कम्भो दशदशयोजनावगाढाश्चतस्रश्चतस्रो वाप्यः। तन्नामानि यथा - पद्म १ पद्मप्रभा २ कुमुदा ३ कुमुदप्रभा ४, उत्पलगुल्मा १ नलिनी २ उत्पला ३ उत्पलोज्ज्वला ४, भृङ्गा १ भृङ्गनिभा २ अञ्जना ३ कज्जलप्रभा ४, श्रीकन्ता १ श्रीमहिता २ श्रीचंद्रा ३ श्रीनिलयाः ४, पूर्वोत्तरक्रमाद-वगन्तव्याः, तन्मध्ये प्रासादाः पञ्चशत योजनोच्चास्तदर्द्धविस्ताराः सिंहासनरुचिराश्चत्वारः, तेषु दाक्षिणात्यौ सौधर्मेंद्रस्य, औदीच्यौ त्वीशानेन्द्रस्य। शीताशीतोदयोर्नद्योः कूलद्वये ऽपि द्वौ द्वौ कूटपर्वतौ दिग्गजनामानौ, तन्नामानि शीतानद्या उत्तरदिग्भागाद्दक्षिणावर्त्तनेन गण्यानि, तानि चेमानि पद्मोत्तर १ नील २ सुहस्त ३ अञ्जन ४ कुमुद ५ पलाश ६ अवतंस ७ रोचन ८ इति एते कूटगिरयः स्वनामदेवाः। ततो मेरुमूलादुत्पत्य योजनानां पञ्चशत्या नन्दनं वनं। तत्र दिक्षु चतसृष्वपि हिमवत्कूटसमानि चत्वारि सिद्धायतनानि, विदिक्षु प्राग्वत् प्रासादान्विताः पुष्करिण्यः, तथाहि - नन्दो त्तरा १ नन्दा २ सुनन्दा ३ नन्दिवर्द्धना ४, नन्दिषेणा १ अमोघा २ गोस्तूपा ३ सुदर्श ना ४, भद्रा १ विशाला २ कुमुदा ३ पुंडरीकिणी ४, विजया १ वेजयन्ती २ जयन्ती ३ अपराजिता ४। अस्यां मेखलायामष्टौ दिक्कुमारिणां कूटानि, तथाहि - नन्दन १ मन्दर २ निषध ३ हैमवत ४ रजत ५ रुचक ६ सागरचित्र ७ वज्र ८ नामानि। एतेष्वष्टौ दिक्कुमार्यो ऽवतिष्ठन्ते, ताश्चेमाः - मेघङ्करा १ मेघवती २ सुमेघा ३ मेघमालिनी ४ सुवत्सा ५ वत्समित्रा ६ वारिषेणा ७ बलाहका ८ इति। एता देव्यो जिनजन्मनि मेघवर्षां विदधति। तथेशानकोणे सहस्र-योजनोच्छ्रायविस्तारमुपरिष्टादर्द्धायामं बलकूटं स्वनामदेवतं, तच्च पञ्च-योजनशतानि नन्दनवनाद्बहिर्निःसृतं। उक्तं च -

"**नंदणवणरुंभेत्ता, पंचसए जोयणाइं नीसरिउं;**
आयासे[1] **पंचसए, रुंभेत्ता ठाइ बलकूडे ॥ १ ॥**"[2]

---

[1] For incorrect **आयामे**, see note below.

[2] बृहत्क्षेत्रसमास, verse 258 (*BKSJ*, p. 225):
नंदणवनरुंधित्ता, पंचसए जोयनाइं नीसरिउं।
आयासे पंच सए, रुंभित्ता भाई बलकूडो ॥ १५८ ॥

ततो द्विषष्टिसहस्राणि पञ्चशताधिकानि योजनानामुपरिष्टादारुह्य सौमनसं वनं नन्दनवनसदृशं, केवलं कूटानि तत्र न सन्ति। वाप्यो यथा - सुमनाः १ सौमनसा २ सौमनान्ता ३ मनोरमा ४, उत्तरकुरु १ देवकुरु २ वीरसेना ३ सरस्वती ४, विशाला १ माघभद्रा २ अभयसेना ३ रोहिणी ४, भद्रोत्तरा १ भद्रा २ सुभद्रा ३ भद्रवती ४। सेषं तथैव। ततः षट्त्रिंशत्सहस्राणि योजनानामुपरि गत्वा सौमनसविशिष्टं पण्डकवनं, तद्विस्तारः सहस्रं योजनानि, बहुमध्यदेशभागे चूला चास्य, सा उपर्यधो द्वादशचतुर्योजनायामा चत्वारिंशद्योजनोच्चा वैडूर्यमयी, तस्य उपरि सिद्धायतनं विजयार्द्धसदृशं मध्ये वनं, विदिक्षु षोडश पुष्करिण्यः, तद्यथा - पुण्ड्रा १ पुण्ड्रप्रभा २ सुरक्ता ३ रक्तवती ४, क्षीररसा १ इक्षुरसा २ अमृतरसा ३ वारुणी ४, शंखोत्तरा १ शंखा २ शंखावर्त्ता ३ बलाहका ४, पुष्पोत्तरा १ पुष्पवती २ सुपुष्पा ३ पुष्पमालिनी ४। प्रासादाः सिद्धायतनानि च प्राग्वत्। वनान्ते चतसृषु दिक्षु एकैका जिनाभिषेकशिला, तद्यथा - प्राच्यां पाण्डुशिला १, दक्षिणस्यामतिपाण्डुशिला २, अपाच्यां रक्तशिला ३, उत्तरायामतिरक्तशिला ४ इति। ताश्च सर्वार्द्धचंद्रसंस्थानसंस्थिताः पञ्चयोजनशतायामास्तदर्द्धविस्ताराश्चतुर् योजनोत्सेधा अर्जुनकनकनिर्माणाः, तासु पाण्डुकम्बलारक्तकम्बलयोरुपरि द्वे सिंहासने, शेषयोस्त्वेकैकं, सिंहासनानां च सर्वेषामायामो विष्कम्भश्च पञ्चधनुःशतानि, तदर्द्धं पृथुत्वं प्राच्यापाच्येषु विजयोद्भवा जिना अभिषिच्यन्ते। इतरयोस्तु भरतैरवतोत्पन्नास्तीर्थंकरा इति। तथा चतसृष्वपि मेरोर्विदिक्षु गजदन्ताकारवक्षस्कारनामानः पर्वताः सन्ति। इदमुक्तं भवति, यथा गजस्य दन्ता मूले स्थूलास्ततः क्रमेण हीयमाना यावदन्ते सूक्ष्माः, एवमेते ऽपि, आदौ निषधनीलवन्तौ निकषा चतुर्योजनशतोच्चाः पञ्चयोजनशतविस्ताराः, तत उच्चत्वे क्रमेण वर्द्धमाना विस्तारे तु हीयमानास्तुरगकन्धराकृतयो यावन्मेरुसम(याः?)[1]। पञ्चयोजनशतान्युच्चा अङ्गुलासंख्येयभागविस्तारा भवन्ति। ते चामी - आग्नेय्यां रजतमयः सप्तकूटपरिष्कृतः सौमनसः १ नैर्ऋत्यां तपनीयमयो नवकूटान्वितो विद्युत्प्रभः २ वायव्यां हिरण्मयः सप्तकूटो गन्धमादनः ३ एशान्यां वैडूर्यमयो

(नन्दनवनं रुध्वा पञ्चशतानि [पञ्चशतं] योजनानि निःसृत्य। आकाशे पञ्चशतानि [पञ्चशतं] रुध्वा भाति [तिष्ठति] बलकूटः॥ १५८॥)

[1] In the sense of 'समीपे', Ed1, p. 23, note.

नवकूटांकितो माल्यवान् ४ प्रत्येकमेतेषां त्रिंशद्योजनसहस्राणि नवोत्तरं शतद्वयं कलाषट्कं चायामः। सर्वेषु प्रथमे प्रथमे कूटे सिद्धायतनं, कूटानि चामूनि हिमवत्कूटप्रमाणानि, एतेषां नामानि मेरुदिग्विभागाद् गणनीयानि, तथाहि - सौमनसे वक्षस्कारगिरौ सिद्धायतन १ सौमनस २ मङ्गलापाति ३ देवकुरु ४ विमल ५ कञ्चन ६ वशिष्टानि ७। पञ्चमषष्ठयोस्तोयधाराविचित्रदेवते। तथा विद्युत्प्रभे - सिद्धायतन १ विद्युत्प्रभ २ देवकुरु ३ पद्म ४ कनक ५ स्वस्तिक ६ शीतोदा ७ सदाजल ८ हरि ९ नामानि, कनकस्वस्तिककूटयोः पुष्पमाल-अनिन्दितदेवते। तथा गन्धमादने - सिद्ध १ गन्धमादन २ गन्धलावत् ३ उत्तरकुरु ४ स्फाटिक ५ लोहित ६ आनन्दानि ७। पञ्चमषष्ठयोर्भोगङ्कराभोगवत्यौ देव्यौ। तथा मालवति - सिद्ध १ माल्यवत् २ उत्तरकुरु ३ कच्छ ४ सागर ५ रजत ६ शीता ७ पूर्णभद्र ८ हरित्सहानि ९, सागर रजतयोस्सुभोगाभोगमालिन्यौ देव्यौ। शेषाणि स्वनामतुल्यदैवतानि। एतेषु हरिस्स[1]हरिकूटे सहस्रयोजनोच्छ्रायायामे उपरिष्टात्तु पञ्चयोजन शतविस्तारे, शेषाणि प्राक्कथितप्रमाणानि। मन्दरगन्धमादननीलवन्माल्यवतां मध्ये उत्तरकुरुक्षेत्रं, तच्चैकादशयोजनसहस्राणि द्विचत्वारिंशान्यष्टौ शतानि च कलाद्वयाधिकानि विस्तीर्णं, तत्र मिथुनधर्माणो युगलिनस्त्रिगव्यूतोच्चा अष्टमभक्तावसान-कृताहारास्त्रिपल्यपरमायुषः षडधिकार्द्धतृतीयशत-पृष्टकरण्डकांकिततनवः सुषमसुषमाकालम-नुभवन्तः कल्पद्रुफलसंतुष्टा एकोनपञ्चाशद्दिनान्यपत्यानि पर्यंते प्रतिपाल्य सुखमृत्यवो देवेषूत्पद्यन्ते। अथ शीतायाः प्राच्यामपाच्यां च नीलवतस्तु याम्यायामष्टौ शतानि चतुस्त्रिंशानि यादृशैः सप्तभिर्योजनं भवति तादृशांश्चतुरो भागांश्चातिक्रम्य द्वौ यमकपर्वतौ, तयोर्मूलविस्तार उच्चत्वं च सहस्रं योजनानि, उपरि तदर्द्धविस्तारः, तयोरुपरि कनकमयौ प्रासादौ, हिमवद्वत् तावति च। दक्षिणदिशि नीलाद्या ह्रदाः। उक्तं च -

"जावइयंमि पमाणंमि, हुंति जमगा नीलवंताओ।
तावइयमंतरं खलु, जमग दहाणं दहाणं च॥ १॥"[2]

---

[1] For हरित्स of Ed1.

[2] Quotation untraced but also quoted in the commentary on verse 271 of the बृहत्क्षेत्रसमास (*BKSJ*, p. 265):
जावइयम्मि पमाणम्मि, होंति जमगा नीलवंता उ।

ते च उदग्दक्षिणयोर्दीर्घाः पूर्वापरयोस्तु विस्तीर्णाः पद्महृदप्रमाणाः स्वनामदेवनिवासाः, तेषां प्रागपरयोर्दिशोरेकैकस्य दश दश काञ्चनगिरयः स्वनामदेववसतयः, तेषां उच्चत्वं मूलविस्तारश्च शतं शतं योजनानि, उपरि तु पञ्चाशद्योजनानि, परस्परं शिखरव्यवधानं शतं शतं योजनानां, मूले तु नास्त्यन्तरं। तथा शीतायाः प्राच्यां पञ्चशतयोजनायामविस्तारमभ्यन्तरे द्वादशयोजनपृथुलं क्रमेण हीयमानं यावदन्ते ऽर्द्धयोजनमानं जम्बूनदमयं जम्बूपीठमस्ति, तच्च द्विगव्यूतोच्चया पञ्चधनुःशतविस्तीर्णया पद्मवरवेदिकया परिक्षिप्तं, तस्य चतुसृष्वपि दिक्षु द्विक्रोशोच्छ्रयाणि तदर्द्धविस्ताराणि ध्वजतोरणवन्दनमालाविभासितानि चत्वारि द्वाराणि। तथा च बहुमध्ये चतुर्योजनोच्छ्रया अष्टयोजनायामा मणिपीठिका, तस्या उपरिष्टाद् जम्बूवृक्षः, स चाष्टयोजनविष्कम्भोच्छ्रयः वज्रमयमूलः, तस्यावगाहः स्कन्धश्च द्वे योजने, षड्योजनदैर्घ्याः शाखास्ताश्च सौवर्णाः, स्कन्धः पत्राणि च वैडूर्यमयानि, प्रवालमयाः पल्लवाः, रत्नमयानि फलानि। प्राच्ये शाले[1] भवनं, तत्र मणिपीठिकायामनादृतदेवस्थानं, शेषेषु प्रासादाः, मध्ये सिद्धायतनं, सर्वाणि विजयार्द्धप्रमाणानि, तत्परिवेष्टने ऽष्टोत्तरं शतं जम्बूनां, परिवारजम्बूसंख्या पद्महृदवत्, तदधिपतिरनादृतो देवः, ततः पञ्चाशतं योजनान्यतिगम्य प्रथमवनखण्डे चतसृषु दिक्षु भवनानि, विदिक्षु चतसृणां पुष्करिणीनां मध्ये प्रासादाः, भवनप्रासादमध्ये ऽष्टौ कूटानि ऋषभकूटप्रमाणानि जम्बूनदानि, तेषु सिद्धायतनानि शालिवनपूर्वोत्तरादिप्रासादेषु सिंहासनानि। मन्दराद्दक्षिणे देवकुरुः। निषधोत्तरौ चित्रविचित्रौ यमकवत्, हृदास्तु निषधादयः, तदपरार्द्धे ग[I?]रुडावासः शाल्मलितरुः जम्बवा सदृशवर्णकः। प्रागपरयोर्द्वात्रिंशद्विजयाः। तथाहि - प्राग्विदेहः शीतया अपरविदेहस्तु शीतोदया द्विधाकृतः। पुनरेकैको विभागश्चतुर्भिर्वक्षस्कारैः तिसृभिस्तिसृभिश्चान्तर्नदीभिरन्तरा निपत्याष्टधा कृतः, ततो ऽष्टभिश्चत्वारो गुणिता जाता यथोक्तसंख्या विजयाः, तथा दाक्षिणात्या गङ्गासिन्धुभ्यां

तावइयमन्तरं खलु, जमग दहाणं दहाणं च ॥ २७१ ॥
(छाया: यावति प्रमाणे भवन्ति यमका नीलवन्तादयः। तावति अन्तरं खलु यमकाभ्यां दक्षिणं दक्षिणं च ॥)

[1] Variant: शाख्यायां.

नदीभ्यातं, औदीच्यास्तु रक्तारक्तोदाभ्यां विभज्य त्रिधाकृताः। पुनः प्रतिविजयं वैताढ्येन निपत्य षट् खण्डानि कृतानि। उक्तं च -

"विजयं पडिवेयड्ढो, गङ्गासिन्धुसमा डु डुन्नि[1] नई।
तेहिं कया छखंडा, विदेह बत्तीस विजयाणं॥ १॥"[2]

तत्रैकस्य विजयस्यायामः षोडशयोजनसहस्राणि द्विचत्वारिंशान्यष्टौ शतानि कलाद्वयाधिकानि, तथा विस्तारो द्वात्रिंशतिशतानि त्रयोदशोत्तराण्यर्द्धगव्यूतानि निषधनीलवतोर्नितम्बे प्रतिविजयमेकैकमृषभकूटं, शीताशीतोदयोर्गंगा-सिन्धुसङ्गमे क्रमेण मागधप्रभासौ तीर्थे, वरदामतीर्थं तु तयोर्बहुमध्यदेशभाग इति। इह भद्रशालमुखवनयोर्मध्ये चत्वारो वक्षस्कारास्तदन्तरे तिस्रो नद्यः, तासामन्तराले ऽष्टौ विजयाः, सर्वे ऽपि चतुर्भिर्गुणिता जातान्यष्टौ वनानि, षोडश वक्षस्काराः, द्वादशान्तर्नद्यो, द्वात्रिंशद्विजयाः। प्रतिविजयं च द्वे द्वे महानद्यौ, निषधसविधवर्तिकुण्डाद्विनिर्गते गङ्गासिन्धुनाम्न्यौ, केवलमौदीच्येषु षोडशसु विजयेषु माल्य(नील?)[3]वदुपकण्ठस्थितकुण्डान्निःसृते नामतो रक्तारक्तवत्यौ विद्येते। तत्र वक्षस्काराणां नामानि यथा - चित्र १ पद्म २ नलिन ३ एकशैलाः ४, त्रिकूट १ वैश्रमण २ सुदर्शन ३ अञ्जनाः ४, अङ्कवत् १ पद्मवत् २ आशीविष ३ सुखावहाः ४, चन्द्र १ सूर्य २ नाग ३ देवगिरयः ४ इति। प्रतिवक्षस्कारं चत्वारि चत्वारि कूटानि सिद्धायतन १ स्वनाम २ पूर्वविजय ३ अपरविजयाख्यानि। तथान्तर्नद्यः कुण्डनिर्गमाः कुण्डमध्यद्वीपाः स्वनामदेवीवसतयः शीताशीतोदानुगमिन्यः प्रत्येकं पञ्चविंशत्यधिकशत-योजनविस्तारा दशगव्यूतावगाहाः, ताश्च द्वादश नामतो यथा - ग्राह[ा]वती १ ह्रद[ा]वती २ वेगवती ३, तप्तजला १ मत्तजला २ उन्मत्तजलाः ३, क्षीरोदा १ सिंहस्रोता २ ऽन्तर्वाहिन्यः ३, ऊर्मिमालिनी १ गम्भीरमालिनी २ फेनमालिन्य ३ इति। विजया यथा - कच्छ १ सुकच्छ २ महाकच्छ ३ कच्छवत् ४ आवर्त ५ मङ्गलावर्त ६ पुष्कर ७ पुष्करवन्तः ८, वच्छ १ सुवच्छ २ महावच्छ ३ वच्छवत् ४ रम्य ५ रम्यक ६ रमणीय ७ मङ्गलवन्तः ८, पद्म १ सुपद्म २ महापद्म ३ पद्मवत् ४ शङ्ख ५ कुमुद ६ नलिनि ७ सलिलवन्तः ८, वप्र १ सुवप्र २ महावप्र ३

---

[1] For दु दुन्नि.

[2] छाया: विजयं प्रति वैताढ्यो गङ्गासिन्धुसमे द्वे द्वे नद्यौ। ताभ्यां कृताः षट्खण्डा विदेहे द्वात्रिंशद्विजयाणाम्॥ Origin of quotation untraced.

[3] In this context, माल्यवत must be a mistake.

वप्रवत् ४ वल्गु ५ सुवल्गु ६ गण्डिल ७ गण्डिलवन्तः ८, गिरिभिर्नदीभिश्च विभक्ताः। प्रतिविजयं चैकैका नगरी, तद्यथा - क्षेमा १ क्षेमपुरी २ अरिष्टा ३ अरिष्टवती ४ खड्गी ५ अञ्जूषा ६ औषधी ७ पुण्डरीकिण्यः ८, सुषीमा १ कुण्डला २ अपराजिता ३ प्रभाकरी ४ अङ्कवती ५ पद्मावती ६ शुभा ७ रत्नसञ्चयाः ८, अश्वपुरी १ सिंहपुरी २ महापुरी ३ विजयपुरी ४ राज्या ५ विराज्या ६ अशोका ७ वीतशोका ८, विजया १ वैजयन्ती २ जयन्ती ३ अपराजिता ४ चक्रपुरी ५ खड्गपुरी ६ अवध्या ७ अयोध्या ८, एताः सर्वाः पुर्यो भरतायोध्याप्रतिकृतय इति। इह वक्षस्कारान्तर्नदीविजयपुरीणां सर्वेषां गणनाक्रमो माल्यवद्वक्षस्काराद-वगन्तव्यः। तथा विजयादीनां वैताढ्येषु प्रत्येकं पार्श्वद्वये ऽपि पञ्चपञ्चाशत्पञ्चपञ्चाशन्नगराणि सन्ति, यतो नितम्बद्वयमपि समानदैर्घ्यं, भरतैरावतयोस्तु धनुष्पृष्ठाकारत्वान्मध्यबाह्ययोः पार्श्वयोर्महदन्तरमतः तत्रैकस्यां दिशि पञ्चाशदन्यस्यां तु षष्टिः सजनपदानि पुराणीति। नीलवतः परतो रम्यकं क्षेत्रं हरिवर्षवत् केवलं, नाम्ना माल्यवानिह वृत्तवैताढ्यः, ततः परो महाहिमवत्प्रतिच्छायो रुक्मी शैलः, तदुपरि बुद्धिदेवीनिवासो महापद्मप्रतिरूपो महापुण्डरीको ह्रदः, कूटान्यष्टावत्र तानि चामूनि सिद्ध १ रुक्म २ रम्यक ३ नरकान्त ४ बुद्धि ५ रौप्य ६ हैरण्यवत ७ मणिकाञ्चन ८ नामानि। तत्र दक्षिणानरकान्तापूर्वगाहरिकान्तावत्, रूप्यकूलोत्तराऽपरदिग्गामिनी रोहितावत्। तदन्तरं हैरण्यवतक्षेत्रं हैमवतप्रख्यं नवरं, तन्मध्ये नामतो विकटापाती वृत्तवैताढ्यः प्रभासदेवाधिवासः, किं च सर्वे ऽपि वृत्तवैताढ्या एकप्रमाणवर्णाः। तदुपरि स्वर्णमयः शिखरिवर्षधर लक्ष्मीनिवासः पद्मविशिष्टः पुण्डरीको ह्रदस् तत्र, तस्माद् दक्षिणां दिशमाश्रित्य रोहितांशासदृशी सुवर्णकूला, रक्तारक्तवत्यौ तूत्तरगे गङ्गासिन्धू इव प्रमाणतः। तदुपरिष्टाच्चैकादशकूटानि, तद्यथा - सिद्धायतन १ शिखरि २ हैरण्यवत ३ सुरादेवी ४ रक्ता ५ लक्ष्मी ६ सुवर्णा ७ रक्तोदा ८ गन्धापाति ९ एरवत १० तिगिंछि ११ संज्ञानि हिमवतकूटसदृंशि। सर्वक्षेत्राणामुत्तरदिगवस्थितं भरतप्रतिकलमैरवतं, वैताढ्यस्तु व्यत्ययनगरसंख्य इति। तथाऽस्माज्जम्बूद्वीपादसंख्येषु द्वीपसमुद्रेष्वतिक्रान्तेषु कश्चिद् जम्बूद्वीपाभिधानो द्वीपो ऽस्ति, तस्मिन् सर्वे विजयादिद्वारवर्षधरपर्वतकूट-नदीह्रदवृक्षविजयाद्यधिष्ठातृणां देवानां राजधान्यः सन्ति। उक्तं च जम्बूद्वीपप्रज्ञप्तौ -

"रायहाणीओ जंबूद्दीवे मंदरस्स पव्वयस्स दाहिणेणं तिरियमसंखिज्जे दीवसमुद्दे वीइवइत्ता अन्नंमि जंबूद्दीवे बारसजोयणसहस्साइं उगाहेत्ता इत्थणं रायहाणीओ भाणियव्वाओ।"[1]
तासां विशेषवर्णनं क्षेत्रसमासबृहद्वृत्तेरवसेयमिति समस्तप्रकरणसमुदायार्थः [॥ ११, १२ ॥]

bharahāi^*iti - varṣāṇi kṣetrāṇi manuṣya-nivāsa-sthānānīty arthaḥ, tāni kiyat saṃkhyāni? kiṃ nāmāni ca bhavanti ity āha,* **satta**^*iti sapta-saṃkhyāni nāmatas tu bharatādīni, ādi-śabdād dhemavata-harivarṣa-mahāvideha-ramyaka- hairaṇyaka ^airavatānāṃ grahaḥ, tathā varṣa-śabdo na-puṃsaka-liṅgaḥ puṃstve prayukto 'pi prākṛtatvāt na doṣāya, 'liṅgaṃ vyabhicāry api' iti vacanāt, amūni ca sarva-kṣetrāṇi svādhiṣṭhātṛ-daivata-samāna-nāmāni. tathā hi: bharatādhipatir yo yo deva utpadyate taṃ taṃ tat-sāmānikādyā devā 'bharata' ity āhrayanti, tatas tan-nāmnā tad-adhiṣṭhitaṃ kṣetram api 'bharatam' iti kathyate. tathā ca^āgamaḥ:*

---

[1] जम्बूद्वीपप्रज्ञप्ति, सू. १४ (ed. Javeri, 1920, p. 82). छाया: राजधानी जम्बूद्वीपे मन्दरस्य पर्वतस्य दक्षिणेन तिर्यकसंख्येये द्वीपसमुद्रे व्यतिक्रम्य अन्यस्मिञ् जम्बूद्वीपे द्वादशयोजनसहस्राणि अवगाह्य अत्र ननु राजधानी भणितव्या. The sentence replenished is: कहि णं भंते! दाहिणड्ढभरहकूडस्स देवस्स दाहिणड्ढ[भरह]ा णामं रायहाणी पण्णत्ता?, गो. ! मंदरस्स पव्वतस्स दक्खिणेणं तिरियमसंखेज्जदीवसमुद्दे वीईवइत्ता अयण्णं जंबुद्दीवे दीवे दक्खिणेणं बारस जोयणसहस्साइं ओगाहित्ता एत्थ णं दाहिणड्ढभरहकूडस्स देवस्स दाहिणड्ढभरहा णामं रायहाणी भणिअव्वा ... छाया: कुत्र ननु भन्ते! दक्षिणार्धभरतकूटस्य देवस्य दक्षिणार्धा नाम्ना रजधानी प्रज्ञप्ता?, गौतम! मन्दरस्य पर्वतस्य दक्षिणेन तिर्यकसंख्येयद्वीपसमुद्रे व्यतिक्रम्य अन्यस्मिञ् जम्बूद्वीपे द्वीपे दक्षिणेन द्वादशयोजनसहस्राणि अवगाह्य अत्र ननु दक्षिणार्धभरतकूटस्य देवस्य दक्षिणार्धभरता नाम्ना राजधानी भणितव्या ...

> **"se keṇaṭṭheṇaṃ bhaṃte, bharahe vāse iti? goẏamā, bharahe deve mahaḍḍhīe mahajjue jāva paliovamaṭṭhiie parivasaï, se eeṇaṭṭheṇaṃ goẏamā evaṃ vuccaï bharahe vāse"**[1]

iti evaṃ haimavatādiṣv api bhāvanīyam iti saṃkṣepārthaḥ. vistarārthas tv ayaṃ - sarva-dvīpa-samudrāṇāṃ madhye paripūrṇa-candra-maṇḍala-saṃsthānaḥ sarvato lakṣa-yojana-māno jambūdvīpo 'sti, sa caikayā vajra-mayyāṣṭa-yojanocchrayayā mūla-madhyoparitana-vibhāgeṣu krameṇa dvādaśāṣṭa-catur-yojana-vistārayā vedikayā sarvato veṣṭito 'sti. yad āgamaḥ:

> **"se ṇaṃ jaṃbūddīve egā jagaīe, savvao samaṃtā saparikkhitte sā ṇaṃ jagaī aṭṭha-joaṇāiṃ uḍḍhaṃ uccatteṇaṃ, mūle bārasa-joẏaṇāïṃ vikkhaṃbheṇaṃ, majjhe aṭṭha-joaṇāïṃ vikkhaṃbheṇaṃ, uvariṃ cattāri joaṇāiṃ vikkhaṃbheṇaṃ, mūle vitthinnā, majjhe saṃkhittā, uvariṃ taṇuā, gopuccha-saṃṭhāṇa-saṃṭhiẏā, savva-vaïrā-maẏā acchā saṇhā, jāp(v?)a vaḍirūvā"**[2]

---

[1] Quotation untraced. Chāyā: *sa kenārthena bhadanta, bharato varṣa iti? gautama, bharato devo maha-rddhiko mahā-dyuto yāvat palyopama-sthitikaḥ parivasati, sa etenārthena, gautama, evam ucyate bharato varṣaḥ.*

[2] Part of *sū.* 124 of the *Jīvājīvābhigamasūtra* as published by Shāha Naginbhai Ghelābhāi Javeri, Śreṣṭhi Devacandra Lālbhāī Jainapustakoddhāre granthāṅkaḥ 50, Bombay, 1919: ***(... jaṃbuddīve) ... se ṇaṃ ekkāe jagatīe savvato samaṃtā saṃparikkhitte. sā ṇaṃ jagatī aṭṭha joyaṇāiṃ uḍḍhaṃ uccatteṇaṃ, mūle bārasa joyaṇāiṃ vikkhaṃbheṇaṃ, majjhe aṭṭha joyaṇāiṃ vikkhaṃbheṇaṃ, uppiṃ cattāri joyaṇāiṃ vikkhaṃbheṇaṃ, mūle vicciṇṇā, majjhe saṃkhittā, uppiṃ taṇuyā, gopuccha-saṃṭhāṇa-saṃṭhitā, savva-vaïrā-maī acchā saṇha ... (jāva) ... paḍirūve.*** Chāyā: *(... jambūdvīpaḥ) ... sā khalu ekayā*

iti. tasyāś copariṣṭād ardha-yojanoccaḥ pañca-dhanuḥ-śata-vistīrṇo gavākṣa-kaṭakaḥ, tathā tasyā eva bahu-deśa-madhya-bhāge gavākṣa-kaṭaka-pramāṇocchrāya-dairghyā parikṣepeṇa jagatī-samānā nānā-ratna-nirmāṇā, vividha-padma-maṇḍitā, padma-vara-vedikāsti. yad uktaṃ Rājapraśnīyopāṅge -

"se keṇaṭṭheṇaṃ bhaṃte! evaṃ vuccaï, paüma-vara-veiẏā? goẏamā paüma-vara-veiẏā ṇaṃ tattha tattha dese tahiṃ tahiṃ veiẏāsu, veiẏā-bāhāsu ẏa, veiẏā-phalaesu ẏa, veiẏā-puḍaṃtaresu ẏa, khaṃbhesu, khaṃbha-bāhāsu, khaṃbha-phalaesu, khaṃbha-puḍaṃtaresu, sūīsu, sūī-muhesu, sūī-phalaesu, sūī-puḍaṃtaresu, pakkhesu, pakkha-bāhāsu, pakkha-phalaesu, pakkha-puḍaṃtaresu, bahuẏāiṃ, paümāiṃ, kumuẏāiṃ, naliṇāiṃ, subhagāiṃ, sogaṃdhiẏāiṃ, puṃḍarīẏāiṃ, saẏa-vattāiṃ, sahassa-vattāiṃ, savva-raẏaṇā-maẏāiṃ, acchāiṃ, paḍirūvāiṃ, mahaẏāvāsikkaẏachattasamāṇāiṃ, paṇṇattāiṃ, samaṇāuso, se eṇam aṭṭheṇaṃ goẏamā, evaṃ vuccaï paüma-vara-veiẏā"[1]

---

jagatyā sarvataḥ samantāt saṃparikṣiptaḥ. sā khalu jagaty aṣṭa-yojanāny ūrdhvam uccatvena, mūle dvādaśa-yojanāni viṣkambheṇa, madhye 'ṣṭa-yojanāni viṣkambheṇa, upari cattvāri yojanāni viṣkambheṇa, mūle vistīrṇā, madhye saṃkṣiptā, upari tanukā, gopuccha-saṃsthāna-saṃsthitā, sarva-vajra-mayy acchā ślakṣṇā, ... (yāvat) ... pratirūpaḥ. The same, in a very similar wording, can be found in the *Jambūdvīpaprajñapti* as published by Shāha Naginbhai Ghelābhāi Javeri, Śreṣṭhi Devacandra Lālbhāī Jainapustakoddhāre granthāṅkaḥ 52, Boṃbay, 1920, *sū.* 4, p. 19.

[1] *Rājapraśnīyasūtra*, Jaina-Śāstroddhāra-Samiti ed. (with Skt. commentary by Pūjyaśrī Ghāsīlālјī and with Hindī and Gujaratī translation), Rajkot, 1965, Vol. I, *sū.* 70, p. 459: ***se keṇaṭṭheṇaṃ bhaṃte! evaṃ vuccaï-paümavaraveiẏā? goẏamā!***

iti. tasyāḥ pārśva-dvaye 'pi dvau vana-khaṇḍau vedikā-māna-dairghyau vidyete, navaraṃ vistāreṇābhyantaraḥ sārdha-dhanuḥ-śata-dvayona-yojana-yugma-pramāṇo, bāhyas tu vana-khaṇḍo 'rdhāṣṭama-dhanuḥ-śata-hīna-yojana-yugma-māno, yatas tatrānyāny apy abhyantarāt vana-khaṇḍād adhikāni pañca-dhanuḥ-śatāni jāla-kaṭakenāvaruddhāni, paraṃ śrī-malayagiri-pādair naitad vivakṣitaṃ, dvayor api vana-khaṇḍayor ekam eva mānam uktaṃ, tattvaṃ tu bahu-śrutā vidanti. tasyāṃ ca vedikāyāṃ meru-parvatāt pañca-catvāriṃśad-yojanasahasrāṇi dakṣiṇasyāṃ diśy atigatya aṣṭa-

---

paümavaraveiẏāeṇaṃ tattha tattha tahiṃ tahi dese veiẏāsu ẏa veiẏāphalaesu ẏa veiẏāpuḍaṃtaresu ẏa khaṃbhesu ẏa khaṃbhabāhāsu ẏa khaṃbhasīsesu khaṃbhapuḍaṃtaresu sūīsu sūī-mukhesu sūīphalaesu sūīpuḍaṃtaresu pakkhesu pakkhabāhāsu pakkhaperaṃtesu pakkhapuḍaṃtaresu bahuẏāiṃ uppalāiṃ paümāiṃ kumuẏāiṃ, ṇaliṇāiṃ subhagāiṃ, sogaṃdhiẏāi puṃḍarīẏāiṃ mahāpuṃḍarīẏāiṃ saẏavattāiṃ sahassavattāiṃ savvaraẏaṇāmaẏāiṃ, acchāiṃ jāva paḍirūvāiṃ mahaẏāvāsikkachattasamāṇāiṃ paṇṇattāiṃ samaṇāuso! se eeṇam aṭṭheṇaṃ goẏamā! paümavaraveiẏā-paüma-vara-veiẏā. Chāyā: *atha kenārthena bhadanta! evam ucyate: padma-vara-vedikā padma-vara-vedikā? gautama! padma-vara-vedikāyāḥ khalu tatra tatra tasmin tasmin deśe vedikāsu vedikā-bāhuṣu ca vedikā-phalakeṣu ca vedikā-puṭāntareṣu ca stambheṣu ca stambha-bāhuṣu ca stambha-śirassu stambha-puṭāntareṣu sūciṣu sūcī-mukheṣu sūcī-puṭāntareṣu pakṣeṣu pakṣa-bāhuṣu pakṣa-paryanteṣu pakṣa-puṭāntareṣu bahukāni utpalāni padmāni kumudāni nalināni subhagāni saugandhikāni puṇḍarīkāṇi mahā-puṇḍarīkāṇi śata-patrāṇi sahasra-patrāṇi sarva-ratna-mayāni acchāni yāvat pratirūpāṇi mahā-vārṣika-chattra-samānāni prajñaptāni śramaṇāyuṣman tat etenārthena gautama. evam ucyate padma-vara-vedikā padma-vara-vedikā.* The same is found in the *Jīvājīvābhigama*, *sū.* 125 (pub. by Shāha Naginbhai Ghelābhāi Javeri, Bombay, 1919, p. 179).

yojanocchrāyaṃ catur-yojana-vistāraṃ pratyekam ekaika-krośa-vistārayā dvāra-śākhayā kalitaṃ, tataḥ sāmastyena sārdha-yojana-catuṣṭaya-vistāraṃ vaiḍūrya-mayābhyāṃ kapāṭābhyāṃ vajra-mayyā paridhiyā nirjaṭitaṃ, aneka-sāmānika- surādi- devāgra- mahiṣy- ādi- devī- kṛta- sevārdha-palyopamāyur-vaijayanta- devādhiṣṭhitaṃ ve(vai?) jayantābhidhānaṃ dvāram asti. tathā amuto dvārāt udīcyāṃ himavantaṃ pūrvāparayos tu lavaṇodanvantaṃ yāvad gataṃ bharata-nāmakaṃ vijaya-kṣetraṃ tac ca bahu-madhya-deśa-bhāge pūrvāparayor lavaṇa-samudra-prāptena pañcāśad-yojana-vistīrṇena tad-ardhoccena rajata-mayena vaitāḍhya-parvatena dvidhā kṛtaṃ, tena dakṣiṇa-bharatārdham uttara-bharatārdhaṃ ceti bhaṇyate. himavat-parvatordhva-tala-sthitāt padma-hradān nirgatābhyāṃ prathamaṃ pūrvāparayor gatvā sva-svanāma-dheya-kūṭād āvṛtya dakṣiṇāṃ diśam anuśritya vijayāḍhya-parvataṃ vibhidya dakṣiṇa-lavaṇodadhiṃ praviṣṭābhyāṃ gaṅgā-sindhubhyāṃ tac ca kṛta-ṣaṭ-khaṇḍaṃ, tatra ca prāṇi-prāṇa-vyaparopaṇa-pravaṇāntaḥ-karaṇa-mleccha-vyāptatvād anāryāṇi pañca khaṇḍāni. ekaṃ ca vaitāḍhyāt dakṣiṇasyāṃ diśi ekādaśa-kalādhikaṃ caturdaśottaraṃ yojana-śataṁ atigatya nava-yojana-vistīrṇayā dvāsaśa-yojana-dīrghayā ayodhyayā nagaryā virājitaṃ, gaṅgā-sindhu-vaitāḍhya-dakṣiṇa-samudrāṇāṃ madhya-sthitaṃ jina-cakry-ardha-cakri-pramukhottama-puruṣādhyāsitam āryaṃ. uktaṃ ca -

"āryāvarto janma-bhūmir jina-cakry-ardha-cakriṇām"[1]

iti. tathā vaitāḍhye 'pācyāṃ tamisrā guhāsti, sā ca dvādaśa-yojanāyāmā pañcāśad-yojana-dairghyā kṛta-kṛtamāla-deva-

---

[1] Quotation untraced.

nivāsā ve(ai?)jayanta-samāna-dvārā, tasyāś ca bahu-madhya-deśe dvi-yojanāntarāle pratyekaṃ tri-yojana-vistāre unmagnajalā-nimagnajale nadyau staḥ. evaṃ prācyāṃ nṛtta-māla-devādhiṣṭhitā khaṇḍa-prapāta-guhā. tasya ca girer mūlād daśa-yojanāny utplutya vedikā-vana-khaṇḍa-maṇḍitaṃ parvata-pramāṇa-dairghaṃ pratyekaṃ daśa-daśa-yojana-vistāraṃ vidyādhara-nagara-śreṇi-dvayaṃ vidyate, kiñca dakṣiṇa-dig-vartinyāṃ śreṇau suprajo(a?)bhir jana-padair virājitāni rathanūpuracakravāla-puraḥsarāṇi pañcāśad-vidyādhara-nagarāṇi, uttara-śreṇau tu gaganavallabhādīni ṣaṣṭiḥ purāṇi, teṣu dharaṇendra-prakāśitāṣṭācatvāriṃśat-sahasra- mahāvidyā- prasādopanata- prakamra- samasta-manorathātithi-padārtha-samāsādita-paramānanda-saṃdohā, gagana-gamana-sāmarthya-samanvitā vidyādharāḥ sukham āsate. punar daśa-yojanāny upariṣṭād āruhya vidyādhara-śreṇi-samāviṣamonnata-bhūmir indrābhiyogika-deva-kṛta-nivāsā śreṇi-dvayī samasti. tato 'pi pañcasu yojaneṣūpari daśa-yojanāni vistīrṇaṃ, vedikā-vana-khaṇḍa-manoharaṃ, analpa-kalpavāsi-deva-krīḍā-yogyaṃ sthānam āste. tatra sa-pāda-śata-yojanocchrayāṇi tāvan mūla-vistārāṇi upariṣṭāt sārdha-dvādaśa-krośāyāmāni nava kūṭāni. tathā hi, siddhāyatana 1 dakṣiṇārdhabharata 2 khaṇḍaprapāta 3 maṇibhadra 4 vijayāḍhya 5 pūrṇabhadra 6 tamisrāguha 7 uttarārdhabharata 8 vaiśramaṇa 9 nāmāni, teṣu māṇibhadra-vijayāḍhya-pūrṇabhadra-kūṭāni hiraṇya-mayāny, aparāṇi ṣaṭ-ratna-mayāni, prathame pūrva-dig-vartini kūṭe krośa-dairghyaṃ krośārdha-vistīrṇaṃ catvāriṃśad-argala-caturdaśa-dhanuḥ-śatocchrāyaṃ siddhāyatanaṃ, tasmin pañca-dhanuḥ-śatoccāni tad-ardha-vistārāṇi trīṇi dvārāṇi tisṛṣu dikṣu. tad yathā - prācyāṃ prathamaṃ dvāraṃ, dvitīyaṃ dakṣiṇasyāṃ, tṛtīyam udīcyāṃ, pratīcyāṃ tu na kiñcid iti. kiṃ ca sarveṣu siddhāyataneṣu prāsādeṣu ca jambūdvīpa-madhye 'yam eva dvāra-dig-vibhāgaḥ, tasya hi bahu-madhya-deśe krośa-caturthāṃśāyāma-viṣkambhā tad-ardha-pṛthulā maṇi-pīṭhikā, tasyā upari pañca-dhanuḥ-śatāyāma-vistāras tad-adhikocchrāyo devacchandakaḥ, tatrāṣṭottaraṃ śataṃ pratimāḥ, tā hi jaghanyataḥ sapta-hasta-pramāṇā utkarṣataḥ pañca-dhanuḥ-śatoccā ṛṣabha-vardhamāna-candrānana-vāriṣeṇākhyāḥ santi. pūrṇa-kalaśa-nāga-danta-śāla-bhañjikā-jālakaṭakādi-racanā-viśeṣāḥ sarva-caityeṣu jñeyāḥ. tataḥ paraṃ bharatārdha-kūṭaṃ, tatra bharata-devasya siddhāyatana-pramāṇaḥ prāsādaḥ, khaṇḍaprapāta-tamisrāguhayor nṛtamāla-kṛtamālau devau, anyeṣu pañcasu sva-nāmāno devāḥ prāsādeṣu vilasanti. tathā himavan-nitambe dakṣiṇa-diśi mūle dvādaśa yojanāni upari catvāri vistīrṇo 'ṣṭa-yojanocchraya ṛṣabha-deva-nivāso ratna-maya ṛṣabha-kūṭa-nāmā parvato 'sti. sa ca 'bhūmikūṭa' iti iha prakaraṇe prasiddhaś, cakrī ṣaṭ-khaṇḍāṃ vasundharāṃ vijityāsmin sva-nāma likhati. bharatam uttareṇa pūrvāparayor lavaṇa-samudraṃ prāpto bharatād dvi-guṇa-vistāro yojana-śatocchrayo hema-mayo himavān varṣa-dharaḥ, tad-upari bahu-madhya-deśa-bhāgo yojana-sahasra-dairghyas tad-ardha-vistaro daśa-yojanāvagāḍho jala-pūrṇaḥ padma-hradaḥ, tasya rajata-mayaṃ kūlaṃ, vajra-maya-pāṣāṇāś catur-diśi maṇi-sopānāḥ, tan-madhye yojanāyāma-vistāram ardha-yojana-piṇḍaṃ daśa-yojanocca-nālaṃ gavyūta-dvayaṃ jalād upari sthitaṃ padmaṃ vidyate, vajra-mayaṃ tasya mūlam ariṣṭa-mayaḥ kandaḥ, vaiḍūrya-mayo nālaḥ bāhya-patrāṇi ca, madhyāni tu jambū-nada-mayāni, kanaka-mayī karṇikā, svarṇa-mayāni kesarāṇi, vividha-maṇi-mayaṃ puṣkaraṃ, sā ca karṇikā dvi-gavyūta-pramāṇā pṛthulā tv ekaṃ gavyūtaṃ, tasyā upari pīṭhikā-devacchandakādi-yutaṃ śrī-

devī-bhavanaṃ, etādṛśenārdha-pramāṇena kamalānām aṣṭa-śatena vṛtaṃ, tatra śrī-devyā ābharaṇāni, tad-bāhyeṣu vāyavy-audīcyaiśāneṣu dig-bhāgeṣu catvāri kamala-sahasrāṇi 4000, teṣu tāvantam eva sāmānikā devā devyo vā. pūrvasyāṃ diśi caturṣu padmeṣu catasṛṇāṃ mahāmantri-sadṛśīnāṃ sthānāni, āgneyyām aṣṭasu padma-sahasreṣu śrī-devyā abhyantarāyāṃ parṣadi devānām aṣṭau sahasrāḥ 8000, dakṣiṇasyāṃ diśi daśasu padma-sahasreṣu 10000, tāvanta eva madhya-parṣadi mitrasthānīyā devāḥ, nairṛtyāṃ dvādaśasu padma-sahasreṣu 12000, tāvanta eva kiṃkara-sthānīyāḥ surāḥ bāhya-parṣadi. paścimāyāṃ saptasu padmeṣu saptānām anīkādhipatīnām āśrayāḥ, tathā catasṛṣu dikṣu pūrvādikāsu ṣoḍaśasu padma-sahasreṣu - 16000 - ātma-rakṣaka-devānāṃ sthānāni, etad veṣṭanaka-trayaṃ madhyam. apare 'pi bāhyās trayaḥ parirayāḥ, teṣv abhyantare parikṣepe dvātriṃśal-lakṣāṇi 3200000, madhyame catvāriṃśac-chata-sahasrāṇi 4000000, aṣṭācatvāriṃśal-lakṣāṇi 4800000 padmānāṃ bāhye bhavanti. evaṃ sarvāgreṇa ekā koṭī, viṃśati-lakṣāṇi, pañcāśat-sahasrāṇi, viṃśaty-adhikam ekaṃ śataṃ ca 12050120 padma-hrade padmāni. mahā-padmādiṣv apy eṣaiva kamalānāṃ saṃkhyeti. tasmāt tu hradāt pūrva-dvāra-toraṇāt pañca-yojana-śatāni pūrvasyāṃ pūrvatopari gatvā gaṅgāvarta-kūṭād āvartya dakṣiṇābhimukhaṃ pañca-yojana-śatāni, trayoviṃśāni sādhikādhyuṣṭa-kalā-yutāny atikramya dvi-gavyūta-dīrghān makara-mukhān niḥsṛtya gaṅgā-prapāta-kuṇḍe nipatati. tac ca kuṇḍaṃ ṣaṣṭi-yojanāyāma-vistāram upariṣṭāt, adhas tu daśa-yojana-nyūnaṃ daśa-yojanāvagāḍhaṃ vajra-maya-talaṃ tri-dvāra-toraṇa-sopānādi-yutaṃ, tan-madhye gaṅgā-dvīpo 'ṣṭa-yojanāyāma-viṣkambho gavyūta-dvayaṃ jalād upari gataḥ, tan-madhye bhavanaṃ, tatra pīṭhikāyāṃ gaṅgā-devyāḥ śayyeti. tato dakṣiṇa-toraṇād vinirgatya vijayāḍhya-parvataṃ jagatīṃ ca vibhidya catur-daśa-nadī-sahasra-parītā jaladhiṃ praviśeṣa gaṅgā. tasyā hradād vinirgame makara-mukhe kuṇḍāt pravāhe ca sa-krośāni ṣaṭ yojanāni vistāraḥ krośārdham udvedhaḥ[1] *mukha-prastāraḥ pravāhād daśa-guṇaḥ. uktaṃ ca:*

"jo jīse vitthāro salilāe hoi āḍhavaṃtīe;
so dasahiṃ paḍipunno muha-vitthāro muṇeẏavvo. 1"[2]

udvedhas tu sarvatra prastārāt pañcāśattamo bhāgaḥ. yata uktaṃ:

"jo jattha u vitthāro, salilāe hoi jaṃbudīvaṃmi;
pannāsaïmaṃ bhāgaṃ, tass' uvvehaṃ viẏāṇāhi. 1"[3]

tathāsyā api dve taṭe vedikā-vana-khaṇḍa-vatī, na caitad yādṛcchikaṃ. yad āgamaḥ -

"gaṃgā ṇaṃ mahānaï(ī?) ubhao [...] pāsehiṃ dohi ẏa paüma-vara-veiẏāhiṃ dohi ẏa vaṇa-saṃḍehiṃ saṃparikhittā."[4]

evaṃ paścima-toraṇa-dvārān nirgatā sindhv-āvarta-kūṭād āvartya vivṛta-mukhākārān nālān nipatya sindhu-devī-nivāsaṃ kuṇḍaṃ madhye-kṛtya tathaiva jaladhiṃ gatā sindhu-nadī.

---

[1] The word *udvedha* derives from *ud + vyadh.* (from whence *udviddha* 'tossed upwards, high'). Hence *udvedha* is used in the sense of 'height'.

[2] *BKSJ*, verse 227, p. 225:
yo yasyā vistāraḥ salilāyā bhavaty ārabhamāṇāyāḥ;
sa daśabhiḥ pratyutpanno mukha-vistāro jñātavyaḥ.

[3] *BKSJ*, verse 227, p. 225:
yo yatra tu vistāraḥ salilāyā bhavati jambūdvīpe;
pañcāsattamaṃ bhāgaṃ tasyodvedhaṃ vijānīhi.

[4] Quotation untraced. Chāyā: *gaṅgā nanu mahā-nady ubhayaḥ [...] pārśvair dve ca padma-vara-vedikābhir dve ca vana-saṃdehaiḥ saṃparikṣiptā.*

tathottara-toraṇād vinirgatā gaṅgā-dviguṇa-māna-parivārā sva-nāma-kuṇḍe nipatya śabdāpātinaṃ gavyūta-dvayenāspṛśantī haimavataṃ kṣetraṃ madhye-kṛtyāparodadhiṃ gatā rohitāṃśā. himavati sarva-ratna-mayāny ekādaśa kūṭāni. tad yathā: siddhāyatana 1 kṣullahimavat 2 bharata 3 ilā 4 gaṅgā 5 śrī 6 rohitāṃśā 7 sindhu 8 surā(-devī) 9 haimavata 10 vaiśramaṇākhyāni 11 teṣāṃ mūla-vistāra uccatvaṃ ca pañca-yojana-jatāni, śikhara-vistāras tu tad-ardha-mānaḥ, prathama-kūṭe siddhāyatanaṃ pañcāśad-yojanāni dīrghaṃ tad-ardhaṃ pṛthulaṃ ṣaṭ-triṃśad-yojanocchrayaṃ, tasmin trīṇi dvārāṇi, teṣām āyāmo 'ṣṭau yojanāni, tad-ardhaṃ viṣkambhaḥ, aṣṭa-yojanāyāma-viṣkambhā tasya madhye maṇi-pīṭhikā, sā ca catvāri yojanāni pṛthulā, tad-upari devaccandakas tat-pramāṇaḥ āyāmocchrāyābhāṃ kiñcid adhikaḥ. tatra pratimā yathā vaitāḍhyādya-kūṭe proktāḥ. śeṣeṣu daśaṣu kūṭeṣu sārdha-dvāṣaṣṭi-yojanocchrāyāḥ sa-krośaika-triṃśad-yojana-vistārāḥ siṃhāsanādi-yuktāḥ prāsādāḥ santi. himavan-mahāhimavator antarāle bharatāc catur-guṇa-vistāraṃ pūrvāparayor lavaṇa-samudraṃ prāptaṃ sva-nāma-devādhiṣṭhāyakaṃ daśa-vidha-kalpa-pādapa-prabhāvo-paḍhaukitābhilaṣitāhāra-nepathya-bharaṇa-śayanīyāvāsādi-lālita-vapurbhir yugalikair virājitaṃ haimavata-nāmakaṃ kṣetram asti. tatra te yugala-dharmiṇaś catuḥ-ṣaṣṭi-pṛṣṭha-karaṇḍa-bhrājitam eka-gavyūtoccaṃ caturtha-bhaktānte kṛtamano 'bhilaṣitāhāraṃ roga-jarā(pa?)-mṛtyu-duḥkha-daurmanasyādi-rahitam eka-palyopamāyur dehaṃ dadhānāḥ, paryante ekonāśīti-dināny apatyāni pālayitvā svasya sama-sthitiṣv alpa-sthitiṣu vā deveṣūtpadyante. atra ca kecid eteṣāṃ caṇaka-badarāmalaka-pramitam āhāram eka-dvi-tri-gavyūta-pramāṇa-śarīrāṇāṃ krameṇa, apare cāṣṭā-daśa-vyañjanākulāṃ rasavatīṃ bhojanatayābhidadhati. tan na sa-karṇānāṃ karṇam avataṃsayati, yataḥ śarkarā-jitvara-rasā pṛthvī kalpa-vṛkṣāṇāṃ phalāni ca teṣām āhāratayopayujyante. āha ca^āgamaḥ:

"***puḍhavī puppha-phalāhārā, te ṇaṃ maṇuā pannattā.***" [1]

tatra ca siṃha-vyāghra-sarpa-biḍālādayo duṣṭa-tiryañco 'pi kṣetra-svābhāvyān mitho-hiṃsya-hiṃsaka-bhāva-varjitāḥ pratanu-kaṣāyatayāvatiṣṭhante. atas tad-bhāva-bhāvitatvād api deva-gatim evāśnuvate. daṃśa-maśaka-yūkā-matkuṇa-pramukhāḥ śarīra-saṃtāpa-kāriṇaḥ kṣudra-jantavas tu mūlato 'pi na bhavanti. kālas tatra suṣama-duṣamā-rūpa eka eva. tan-madhye pañca-varṇa-ratna-mayaḥ sarvataḥ sahasra-yojana-pramāṇaḥ palyākārāḥ śabdāpātī vṛtta-vaitāḍhya-parvataḥ, ye 'muṃ rajata-mayam abhidadhati, teṣāṃ jambūdvīpa-prajñaptyā saha virodhaḥ. tatra hy evam uktaṃ:

"***kahi ṇaṃ bhaṃte hemavae vāse saddāvaī nāmaṃ vaṭṭa-veẏaḍḍha-pavvae pannatte? goẏamā rohiẏāe mahā-naīe paccacchimeṇaṃ rohiaṃsāe mahā-naīe, puracchimeṇaṃ hemavaẏa-vāsassa bahu-majjha-desa-bhāge ittha ṇaṃ saddāvaī nāmaṃ vaṭṭa-veẏaḍḍhe pavvae pannatte, egaṃ joẏaṇa-sahassaṃ uḍḍhaṃ uccatteṇaṃ, aḍhḍhāiẏāiṃ joẏaṇa-saẏāiṃ uvveheṇaṃ, savvattha same, pallaga-saṇṭhāṇa-santhie, egaṃ joẏaṇa-sahassam āẏāma-***

---

[1] This occurs in *sū.* 111 of the *Jīvājīvābhigama*. The full sentence reads: ***te ṇaṃ bhaṃte! maṇuẏā kim āhāram āhāreṃti? goẏamā! puḍhavi-phuppha-phalāhārā te maṇuẏa-gaṇā paṇṇattā samaṇuso!*** Chāyā: *te khalu bhadanta! manujāḥ kim āhāram āhāranti? gautama! pṛthivī-puṣpa-phalāhārās te manuja-gaṇāḥ prajñaptāḥ śramaṇāyuṣman!* It also occurs verbatim in the *JDP*, *sū.* 22, ed. Javeri, p. 117: ***puḍhavī-phuppha-phalāhārā te maṇuā paṇṇattā ...***

vikkhaṃbheṇaṃ tiṇni joẏaṇa-sahassāim egaṃ ca bāvaṭṭhaṃ joẏaṇa-saẏaṃ (3162) kiṃci-viseāhiẏaṃ parikkheveṇaṃ savva-raẏaṇā-mae acche ity ādi".[1]

Umāsvāti-vācako 'py evam evāha tathā ca tad-vākyaṃ

"vṛtto vividha-ratna-mayaḥ sarvataḥ sāhasaraḥ śabdāpāti-giriḥ."[2]

iti, ata etad varṇake yat kṣetra-samāse ***raẏaẏa-maẏā****^ity uktaṃ, tan na saṃvādīti, kintu* ***raẏaṇa-maẏā****^iti saṃvādī pāṭha iti. tathā tad-upari svābhidhāna-deva-bhavanaṃ himavat-kūṭa-prāsāda-sadṛśaṃ. tad-uttaro haimavata-kṣetrād dvi-guṇa-vistāro 'rjuna-mayo yojana-śata-dvayocco mahāhimavān,*

---

[1] *Jambūdvīpaprajñapti, sū.* 77, ed. Javeri, p. 299: ***kahi ṇaṃ bhante! hemavae vāse saddāvaī ṇāmaṃ vaṭṭa-veaddha-pavvae paṇṇatte? goyamā! rohiāe mahā-ṇaīe paccacchimeṇaṃ rohiaṃsāe mahā-ṇaīe puratthimeṇaṃ hemavaya-vāsassa bahu-majjha-desa-bhāe ettha ṇaṃ saddāvae ṇāmaṃ vaṭṭa-veaddha-pavvae paṇṇatte, egaṃ joaṇa-sahassa uddhaṃ uccatteṇaṃ addhāijjāiṃ joaṇa-sayāim uvveheṇaṃ savvattha same pallaga-saṃṭhāṇa-saṃthie egaṃ joaṇa-sahassaṃ āyāma-vikkhaṃbheṇaṃ tiṇṇi joaṇa-sahassāiṃ egaṃ ca bāvatthaṃ joaṇa-sayaṃ kiñci visesāhiaṃ parikkheveṇaṃ paṇṇatte, savva-rayaṇā-mae acche, ...*** Chāyā: *kutra nanu bhadanta! haimavata-varṣe śabdāpātī nāmnā vṛtta-vaitāḍhya-parvataḥ prajñaptaḥ? gautama! rohitā-mahā-nadyāḥ paścimena rohitāṃśā mahā-nadyāḥ pūrveṇa haimavata-varṣasya bahu-madhya-deśa-bhāge tatra nanu śabdāpātī nāmnā vṛtta-vaitāḍhya-parvataḥ prajñaptaḥ, ekaṃ yojana-sahasram ūrdhvoccatvena ardha-tṛtīyāni yojana-śatāny uddvedhena sarvatra samaḥ palyaṅka-saṃsthāna-saṃsthita ekaṃ yojana-sahasram āyāma-viṣkambhābhyāṃ trīṇi yojana-sahasrāṇi ekaṃ ca dvāṣaṣṭy-adhikaṃ yojana-śataṃ kiñcid-viśeṣeṇa parikṣepeṇa prajñaptaṃ sarvātmanā ratna-mayaḥ acchaḥ, ...*

[2] *JDSU*, p. 8, line 4: "*[tan-madye] vṛtto vividha-ratna-mayaḥ sarvataḥ sāhasraḥ śabdāpātī giriḥ.*

tatra bahu-madhye padma-hradād dvi-guṇāyāma-viṣkambho mahā-padma-hradaḥ kṛta-hrī-devī-nivāsaḥ, padmāni padma-hrada-saṃkhyā(saṃnibhā)ny atra,. etad-dakṣiṇa-toraṇān niḥsṛtya pañca-kalādhikāni pañcottarāṇi ṣoḍaśa-yojana-śatāni parvatam ullaṅghya rohitā-devy-adhiṣṭhite gaṅgā-pratāpa-kuṇḍād dvi-guṇāyāma-viṣkambhe daśa-yojanodvedhe rohitā-pratāpa-kuṇḍe nipatya śabdāpātinaṃ caturthāṃśena paridhāya gavyūta-dvayenāspṛśanty aṣṭāviṃśatyā nadī-sahasraiḥ samaṃ rohitāṃśā-sama-vistārā rohitā pūrvodadhiṃ prāviśat. tathottara-dvārān nirgatya pravāhe pañca-viṃśati-yojanāyāmā mukhe tu daśa-guṇa-vistārā sva-nāmni kuṇḍe nipatya eka-yojanāspṛṣṭa-gandhāpātikā pravāhe mukhe ca krameṇārdha-pañca-yojanodvedhā ṣaṭ-pañcāśan-nadī-sahasra-sahitā harikāntā paścimodadhiṃ gatā. tasmin parvate 'ṣṭau kūṭāni, tad yathā siddhāyatana 1 mahāhimavat 2 haimavata 3 rohitā 4 hrī 5 harikāntā 6 harit 7 vaiḍūrya 8 nāmāni, himavat-kūṭa-tulyāni sva-nāma-dheya-daivatāni. tasmād uttarasyāṃ diśi hari-varṣaṃ kṣetraṃ tatra yugalinaḥ prāg-ukta-yugalikebhyo dvi-guṇa-viśeṣaṇāḥ kevalaṃ kṛta-catuḥ-ṣaṣṭi-dināpatya-pālanāḥ ṣaṣṭha-prānte vihitāhārāś ca, tasya bahu-madhya-deśa-bhāge 'ruṇa-deva-vasatiḥ śabdāpāti-viśiṣṭo gandhāpātī. kālas tu tatra suṣamā-rūpaḥ sadaiva. tad-uttaro hari-varṣa-kṣetrād dvi-guṇa-vistāraś catuḥ-śata-yojanocchrayas tapanīya-mayo niṣadha-giriḥ, tad-upari mahā-padmāt dvi-guṇāyāma-viṣkambho daśa-yojanāvagāḍhaḥ padma-hrada-viśiṣṭa-padma-pūrṇaḥ kṛta-dhṛti-devī-nivāsas tigiñchi-hradaḥ, tad-dakṣiṇa-dig-bhāge saika-kalāni sapta-sahasrāṇi catvāri śatāni eka-viṃśāni yojanānāṃ parvatam ullaṅghya sva-nāma-kuṇḍaṃ madhya-kṛtya harikāntā-vat kevalaṃ pūrvodadhiṃ gatā harit-salilā. uttareṇa śītodā nirgatā, tasyāḥ pravāho jihvikā ca pañcāśad-yojanāni, harin-

nadī-kuṇḍād dvi-guṇa-kuṇḍā, niṣadha 1 devakuru 2 sūrya 3 sulasa 4 vidyutprabha 5 hradān vibhidya catur-aśītyā nadī-sahasrair anvitā, bhadraśāla-vana-madhya-pravṛttā, yojana-dvayāntare mandaram alagantī, apara-dig-abhimukhaṃ vidyutprabha-vidārikāpara-videhaṃ dvidhā vidhāya ekaikasmād vijayād aṣṭāviṃśati-nadī-sahasrānugatā, jayanta-dvārād adho jagatīṃ vidārya pañca-śata-yojanāyāmā, daśa-yojanodvedhā, paścima-jaladhiṃ (-jaladhim adhi)gatā. tasmin parvate nava kūṭāni, tad yathā: siddhāyatana 1 niṣadha 2 harivarṣa 3 prāgvideha 4 harit 5 dhṛti 6 śītodā 7 aparavideha 8 rucaka 9 abhidhānāni himavat-kūṭa-sadṛśāni. niṣadhād uttaro vaiḍūrya-mayas tigiñchi-praticchandaḥ keśari-hrada-madhyo nīlavān varṣa-dharaḥ, tatra nava kūṭāni, tathā hi: siddhāyatana- nīla- prāgvideha- śītā- kīrti- nārī- aparavideha-ramyaka-upadarśana-kūṭākhyāni niṣadha-kūṭa-mānāmi. tataḥ kesari-hradād dakṣiṇa-diśi saika-kalāni sapta-yojanasahasrāṇi catvāri śatāny eka-viṃśaty-adhikāni parvatādhityakām ullaṅghya, sva-nāma-daivata-kuṇḍaṃ madhye-kṛtya, nīla-uttarakuru-candra-eravata-mālyavat-hradān vibhidya, bhadraśāla-pada-catur-aśīti-nadī-sahasra-parītā, mālyavad-videha-vijaya-dvāra-cchedinī, pūrvodadhiṃ gatā śītā, śeṣaṃ śītodā-vat. niṣadha-nīlavad-antarā mahāvideho lakṣa-yojanāni tasya madhya-dairghyaṃ viṣkambhas tu niṣadhād dvi-guṇaḥ. tan-madhye sahasra-yojanāvagāḍho nava-navati-yojanasahasroccaḥ bhūmi-tale daśa-sahasra-vistāraḥ upari sahasra-yojanāyāmaḥ ratna-madhyaḥ svarṇa-mayo meru-giriḥ. tad-upatyakāyāṃ pūrvāparayor dvāviṃśati-yojanasahasrāyāmam uttara-dakṣiṇayos tu pratyekaṃ sārdha-yojana-śata-dvaya-vistāraṃ, nānā-vṛkṣa-kalitaṃ, bhadraśāla-vanaṃ. tan-madhye meru-parvatāt pañcāśatā yojanair himavat-siddhāyatana-pramāṇāni catur-diśyāni catvāri siddhāyatanāni. tāvataiva vidikṣu pañca-śat-pañcāśad-yojanāyāmās tad-ardha-viṣkambho daśa-daśa-yojanāvagāḍhāś catasraś catasro vāpyaḥ. tan-nāmāni yathā: padma 1 padmaprabhā 2 kumudā 3 kumudaprabhā 4, utpalagulmā 1 nalinī 2 utpalā 3 utpalojjvalā 4, bhṛṅgā 1 bhṛṅganibhā 2 añjanā 3 kajjalaprabhā 4, śrīkantā 1 śrīmahitā 2 śrīcandrā 3 śrīnilayāḥ 4, pūrvottara-kramād avagantavyāḥ, tan-madhye prāsādāḥ pañca-śata-yojanoccās tad-ardha-vistārāḥ siṃhāsana-rucirāś catvāraḥ, teṣu dākṣiṇāt yau saudharmyendrasya, audīcyau tv īśānendrasya. śītā-śītodayor nadyoḥ kūla-dvaye 'pi dvau dvau kūṭa-parvatau diggaja-nāmānau, tan-nāmāni śītā-nadyā uttara-dig-bhāgād dakṣiṇāvartanena gaṇyāni, tāni cemāni padmottara-nīla-suhasta-añjana-kumuda-palāśa-avataṃsa-rocana-iti ete kūṭa-girayaḥ sva-nāma-devāḥ. tato meru-mūlād utpatya yojanānāṃ pañca-śatyā nandanaṃ vanaṃ. tatra dikṣu catasṛṣv api himavat-kūṭa-samāni catvāri siddhāyatanāni, vidikṣu prāgvat prāsādānvitāḥ puṣkariṇyaḥ, tathā hi: nandottarā 1 nandā 2 sunandā 3 nandivardhanā 4, nandiṣeṇā 1 amoghā 2 gostūpā 3 sudarśanā 4, bhadrā 1 viśālā 2 kumudā 3 pundarīkiṇī 4, vijayā 1 vejayantī 2 jayantī 3 aparājitā 4. asyāṃ mekhalāyām aṣṭau dik-kumāriṇāṃ kūṭāni, tathā hi: nandana 1 mandara 2 niṣadha 3 haimavata 4 rajata 5 rucaka 6 sāgaracitra 7 vajra 8 nāmāni. eteṣv aṣṭau dik-kumāryo 'vatiṣthante, tāś cemāḥ: meghaṃkarā 1 meghavatī 2 sumeghā 3 meghamālinī 4 suvatsā 5 vatsamitrā 6 vāriṣeṇā 7 balāhakā 8 iti. etā devyo jina-janmani megha-varṣā vidadhati. tatheśāna-koṇe sahasra-yojanocchrāya-vistāram upariṣṭād ardhāyāmaṃ bala-kūṭaṃ sva-nāma-daivataṃ, tac ca pañca-yojana-śatāni nandana-vanād bahir niḥsṛtaṃ. uktaṃ ca:

"***nandaṇa-vaṇa-ruṃbhettā, paṃca-sae joyaṇāiṃ nīsariuṃ;***

āyāme paṃca-sae, ruṃbhettā ṭhāi bala-kūḍe. 1"[1]
tato dvi-ṣaṣṭi-sahasrāṇi pañca-śatādhikāni yojanānām upariṣṭād āruhya saumanasaṃ vanaṃ nandana-vana-sadṛśaṃ, kevalaṃ kūṭāni tatra na santi. vāpyo yathā: sumanāḥ 1 saumanasā 2 saumanāntā 3 manoramā 4, uttarakuru 1 devakuru 2 vīrasenā 3 sarasvatī 4, viśālā 1 māghabhadrā 2 abhayasenā 3 rohiṇī 4, bhadrottarā 1bhadrā 2 subhadrā 3 bhadravatī 4. śeṣaṃ tathaiva. tataḥ ṣaṭ-triṃśat-sahasrāṇi yojanānām upari gatvā saumanasa-viśiṣṭaṃ paṇḍaka-vanaṃ, tad-vistāraḥ sahasraṃ yojanāni, bahu-madhya-deśa-bhāge cūlā cāsya, sā upary adho dvādaśa-catur-yojanāyāmā catvāriṃśad-yojanoccā vaiḍūrya-mayī, tasya upari siddhāyatanaṃ vijayārdha-sadṛśaṃ madhye vanaṃ, vidikṣu ṣoḍaśa puṣkariṇyaḥ, tad yathā: puṇḍrā 1 puṇḍraprabhā 2 suraktā 3 raktavatī 4, kṣīrarasā 1 ikṣurasā 2 amṛtarasā 3 vāruṇī 4, śaṅkhottarā 1 śaṅkhā 2 śaṅkhāvartā 3 balāhakā 4, puṣpottarā 1 puṣpavatī 2 supuṣpā 3 puṣpamālinī 4. prāsādāḥ siddhāyatanāni ca prāg-vat. vanānte catasṛṣu dikṣu ekaikā jinābhiṣeka-śilā, tad yathā: prācyāṃ pāṇḍu-śilā 1, dakṣiṇasyām atipāṇḍu-śilā 2, apācyāṃ rakta-śilā 3, uttarāyām atirakta-śilā 4 iti. tāś ca sarvārdha-candra-saṃsthāna-saṃsthitāḥ pañca-yojana-śatāyāmās tad-ardha-vistārāś catur-yojanotsedhāḥ arjuna-kanaka-nirmāṇāḥ, tāsu pāṇḍu-kambalā-rakta-kambalayor upari dve siṃhāsane, śeṣayos tv ekaikaṃ,

---

[1] *BKSJ*, verse 158, p. 168:
nandaṇa-vana[ṃ] rundhittā, pañca-sae joyanāiṃ nīsariuṃ;
āyāse pañca sae, rumbhittā bhāī balakūḍo. 158.
(*nandana-vanaṃ rudhvā pañca-śatāni [pañca-sataṃ] yojanāni niḥsṛtya; ākāśe pañca-śatāni [pañca-sataṃ] rudhvā bhāti [tiṣṭhati] balakūṭam. 158.*)

siṃhāsanānāṃ ca sarveṣām āyāmo viṣkambhaś ca pañca-dhanuḥ-śatāni, tad-ardhaṃ pṛthutvaṃ prācyāpācyeṣu vijayodbhavā jinā abhiṣicyante. itarayos tu bharata-airavatotpannās tīrthaṅkarā iti. tathā catasṛṣv api meror vidikṣu gaja-dantākāra-vakṣaskāra-nāmānaḥ parvatāḥ santi. idam uktaṃ bhavati, yathā gajasya dantā mūle sthūlās tataḥ krameṇa hīyamānā yāvad ante sūkṣmāḥ, evam ete 'pi, ādau niṣadha-nīlavantau nikaṣā catur-yojana-śatoccāḥ pañca-yojana-śata-vistārāḥ, tata uccatve krameṇa vardhamānā vistāre tu hīyamānās turaga-kandharākṛtayo yāvan meru-samayāḥ. pañca-yojana-śatāny uccā aṅgulāsaṃkhyeya-bhāga-vistārā bhavanti. te cāmī - āgneyyāṃ rajata-mayaḥ sapta-kūṭa-pariṣkṛtaḥ saumanasaḥ 1 nairṛtyāṃ tapanīya-mayo nava-kūṭānvito vidyutprabhaḥ 2 vāyavyāṃ hiraṇ-mayaḥ sapta-kūṭo gandhamādanaḥ 3 eśānyāṃ vaiḍūrya-mayo nava-kūṭāṅkito mālyavān 4 pratyekam eteṣāṃ triṃśad-yojanasahasrāṇi navottaraṃ śata-dvayaṃ kalā-ṣaṭkaṃ cāyāmaḥ, sarveṣu prathame prathame kūṭe siddhāyatanaṃ, kūṭāni cāmūni himavat-kūṭa-pramāṇāni, eteṣāṃ nāmāni meru-dig-vibhāgād gaṇanīyāni, tathā hi: saumanase vakṣaskāra-girau siddhāyatana 1 saumanasa 2 maṅgalāpāti 3 devakuru 4 vimala 5 kañcana 6 vaśiṣṭāni 7. pañcama-ṣaṣṭhayos toyadhārā-vicitra-devate. tathā vidyutprabhe: siddhāyatana 1 vidyutprabha 2 devakuru 3 padma 4 kanaka 5 svastika 6 śītodā 7 sadājala 8 hari 9 nāmāni, kanaka-svastika-kūṭayoḥ puṣpamālā-anindita-devate. tathā gandhamādane: siddha 1 gandhamādana 2 gandhalāvat 3 uttarakuru 4 sphāṭika 5 lohita 6 ānandāni 7. pañcama-ṣaṣṭhayor bhogaṃkarā-bhogavatyau devyau. tathā mālavati: siddha 1 mālyavat 2 uttarakuru 3 kaccha 4 sāgara 5 rajata 6 śītā 7 pūrṇabhadra 8 haritsahāni 9, sāgara-rajatayos subhogā-bhogamālinyau devyau. śeṣāṇi sva-nāma-tulya-daivatāni. eteṣu haritsaha-hari-kūṭe sahasra-yojanocchrāyāyāme upariṣṭāt tu pañca-yojana-śata-vistāre, śeṣāṇi prāk-kathita-pramāṇāni. mandara-gandhamādana-nīlavan-mālyavatāṃ madhye uttarakuru-kṣetraṃ, tac caikādaśa-yojanasahasrāṇi dvi-catvāriṃśāny aṣṭau śatāni ca kalā-dvayādhikāni vistīrṇaṃ, tatra mithuna-dharmāṇo yugalinas tri-gavyūtoccā aṣṭama-bha[u?]ktāvasāna-kṛtāhārās tri-palya-paramāyuṣaḥ ṣaḍ-adhikārdha-tṛtīya-śata-pṛṣṭa-karaṇḍakāṅkita-tanavaḥ suṣama-suṣamā-kālam[1] *anubhavantaḥ kalpa-dru-phala-saṃtuṣṭā ekona-pañcāśad-dināny apatyāni paryante pratipālya sukha-mṛtyavo deveṣūtpadyante. atha śītāyāḥ prācyām apācyāṃ ca nīlavatas tu yāmyāyām aṣṭau śatāni catus-triṃśāni yādṛśaiḥ saptabhir yojanaṃ bhavati tādṛśāṃś caturo bhāgāṃś cātikramya dvau yamaka-parvatau, tayor mūla-vistāra uccatvaṃ ca sahasraṃ yojanāni, upari tad-ardha-vistāraḥ, tayor upari kanaka-mayau prāsādau, himavad-vat tāvati ca. dakṣiṇa-diśi nīlādyā hradāḥ. uktaṃ ca:*

> ***"jāvaïyaṃmi pamāṇaṃmi, huṃti jamagā nīlavaṃtāo;***
> ***tāvaïyam aṃtaraṃ khalu, jamaga dahāṇaṃ dahāṇaṃ ca .1."***[2]

te ca udag-dakṣiṇayor dīrghāḥ pūrvāparayos tu vistīrṇāḥ padma-hrada-pramāṇāḥ sva-nāma-deva-nivāsāḥ, teṣāṃ prāg-

---

[1] Probably *ākāla* for *kāla*.

[2] Origin of quotation untraced but it also occurs in the commentary on verse 271 of the *BKSJ*, p. 265:

jāvaïyammi pamāṇammi, hoṃti jamagā nīlavaṃtā u;
tāvaïyamantaraṃ khalu, jamaga dahāṇaṃ dahāṇaṃ ca .271.

(Chāyā: *yāvati pramāṇe bhavanti yamakā nīlavantādayaḥ; tāvati antaraṃ khalu, yamakābhyāṃ dakṣiṇaṃ dakṣiṇaṃ ca.*).

aparayor diśor ekaikasya daśa daśa kāñcana-girayaḥ sva-nāma-deva-vasatayaḥ, teṣām uccatvaṃ mūla-vistāraś ca śataṃ śataṃ yojanāni, upari tu pañcāśad-yojanāni, parasparaṃ śikhara-vyavadhānaṃ śataṃ śataṃ yojanānāṃ, mūle tu nāsty antaraṃ. tathā śītāyāḥ prācyāṃ pañca-śata-yojanāyāma-vistāram abhyantare dvādaśa-yojana-pṛthulaṃ krameṇa hīyamānaṃ yāvad ante 'rdha-yojana-mānaṃ jambū-nada-mayaṃ jambū-pīṭham asti, tac ca dvi-gavyūtoccayā pañca-dhanuḥ-śata-vistīrṇayā padma-vara-vedikayā parikṣiptaṃ, tasya catusṛṣv api dikṣu dvi-krośocchrayāṇi tad-ardha-vistārāṇi dhvaja-toraṇa-vandana-mālā-vibhāsitāni catvāri dvārāṇi. tathā ca bahu-madhye catur-yojanocchrayā aṣṭa-yojanāyāmā maṇi-pīṭhikā, tasyā upariṣṭād jambū-vṛkṣaḥ, sa cāṣṭa-yojana-viṣkambhocchrayaḥ vajra-maya-mūlaḥ, tasya avagāhaḥ skandhaś ca dve yojane, ṣaḍ-yojana-dairghyāḥ śākhās tāś ca sauvarṇāḥ, skandhaḥ patrāṇi ca vaiḍūrya-mayāni, pravāla-mayāḥ pallavāḥ, ratna-mayāni phalāni. prācye śāle[1] *bhavanaṃ, tatra maṇi-pīṭhikāyām anādṛta-deva-sthānaṃ, śeṣeṣu prāsādāḥ, madhye siddhāyatanaṃ, sarvāṇi vijayārdha-pramāṇāni, tat-pariveṣṭane 'ṣṭottaraṃ śataṃ jambūnāṃ, parivāra-jambū-saṃkhyā padma-hrada-vat, etad-adhipatir anādṛto devaḥ, tataḥ pañcāśataṃ yojanāny atigamya prathama-vana-khaṇḍe catasṛṣu dikṣu bhavanāni, vidikṣu catasṛṇāṃ puṣkariṇīnāṃ madhye prāsādāḥ, bhavana-prāsāda-madhye 'ṣṭau kūṭāni ṛṣabha-kūṭa-pramāṇāni jambū-nadāni, teṣu siddhāyatanāni, śāli-vana-pūrvottarādi-prāsādeṣu siṃhāsanāni. mandarād dakṣiṇe devakuruḥ, niṣadhottarau citra-vicitrau Yamaka-vat, hradās tu niṣadhādayaḥ, tad-*

[1] Variant reading: *śākhyāyāṃ*.

aparārdhe ga[ā?]ruḍāvāsaḥ śālmali-taruḥ jambvā sadṛśa-varṇakaḥ. prāg-aparayor dvātriṃśad-vijayāḥ. tathā hi: prāg-videhaḥ śītayā apara-videhas tu śītodayā dvidhā-kṛtaḥ, punar ekaiko vibhāgaś caturbhir vakṣaskārais tisṛbhis tisṛbhiś cāntar-nadībhir antarā nipatyāṣṭadhā-kṛtaḥ, tato 'ṣṭabhiś catvāro guṇitā jātā yathokta-ntkhyā vijayāḥ, tathā dākṣiṇātyā gaṅgā-sindhubhyāṃ nadībhyāṃ, audīcyās tu raktā-raktodābhyāṃ vibhajya tridhā-kṛtāḥ. punaḥ prati vijayaṃ vaitāḍhyena nipatya ṣaṭ khaṇḍāni kṛtāni. uktaṃ ca:

"***vijayaṃ paḍi veyaḍḍho, gaṃgā-siṃdhu-samā du dunni naī;***
tehiṃ kayā cha-khandā, videha battīsa vijayāṇaṃ. 1."[1]

tatraikasya vijayasyāyāmaḥ ṣoḍaśa-yojanasahasrāṇi dvi-catvāriṃśāny aṣṭau śatāni kalā-dvayādhikāni, tathā vistāro dvātriṃśati-śatāni trayodaśottarāṇy ardha-gavyūtāni niṣadha-nīlavator nitambe prativijayam ekaikam ṛṣabha-kūṭaṃ, śītā-śītodayor gaṅgā-sindhu-ntgame krameṇa māgadha-prabhāsau tīrthe, varadāma-tīrthaṃ tu tayor bahu-madhya-deśa-bhāga iti. iha bhadraśāla-mukha-vanayor madhye catvāro vakṣaskārās tad-antare tisro nadyaḥ, tāsām antarāle 'ṣṭau vijayāḥ, sarve 'pi caturbhir guṇitā jātāny aṣṭau vanāni, ṣoḍaśa vakṣaskārāḥ, dvādaśāntar-nadyo dvātriṃśad-vijayāḥ. prati-vijayaṃ ca dve dve mahā-nadyau, niṣadha-savidha-varti-kuṇḍād vinirgate gaṅgā-sindhu-nāmnyau, kevalam audīcyeṣu ṣoḍaśasu vijayeṣu mālya(nīla?)vad-upakaṇṭha-sthita-kuṇḍāt niḥsṛte nāmato raktārakta(ā)vatyau saritau vidyete. tatra vakṣaskārāṇāṃ nāmāni - yathā citra 1 padma 2 nalina 3

---

[1] *vijayaṃ prati vaitāḍhyo, gaṅgā-sindhu-same dve dve nadyau; tābhyāṃ kṛtāḥ ṣaṭ-khaṇḍā, videhe dvātriṃśad vijayānāṃ.* Origin of quotation untraced.

ekaśailāḥ 4, trikūṭa 1 vaiśramaṇa 2 sudarśana 3 añjanāḥ 4, aṅkavat 1 padmavat 2 āśīviṣa 3 sukhāvahāḥ 4, candra 1 sūrya 2 nāga 3 devagirayaḥ 4 iti. prati-vakṣaskāraṃ catvāri catvāri kūṭāni siddhāyatana 1 svanāma 2 pūrva-vijaya 3 apara-vijayākhyāni. tathāntar-nadyaḥ kuṇḍa-nirgamāḥ kuṇḍa-madhya-dvīpāḥ svanāma-devī-vasatayaḥ śītā-śītodānugaminyaḥ pratyekaṃ pañca-viṃśaty-adhika-śata-yojana-vistārā daśa-gavyūtāvagāhāḥ, tāś ca dvādaśa nāmato yathā: grāha[ā]vatī 1 hradava[ā]tī 2 vegavatī 3, taptajalā 1 mattajalā 2 unmattajalāḥ 3, kṣīrodā 1 siṃhasrotā 2 antarvāhinyaḥ 3, ūrmimālinī 1 gambhīramālinī 2 phenamālinyaḥ 3 iti. vijayā yathā - kaccha 1 sukaccha 2 mahākaccha 3 kacchavat 4 āvarta 5 maṅgalāvarta 6 puṣkara 7 puṣkaravantaḥ 8, vaccha 1 suvaccha 2 mahāvaccha 3 vacchavat 4 ramya 5 ramyaka 6 ramaṇīya 7 maṅgalavantaḥ 8, padma 1 supadma 2 mahāpadma 3 padmavat 4 śaṅkha 5 kumuda 6 nalini 7 salilavantaḥ 8, vapra 1 suvapra 2 mahāvapra 3 vapravat 4 valgu 5 suvalgu 6 gaṇḍila 7 gaṇḍilavantaḥ 8, giribhir nadībhiś ca vibhaktāḥ. prati-vijayaṃ caikaikā nagarī, tad yathā - kṣemā 1 kṣemapurī 2 ariṣṭā 3 ariṣṭavatī 4 khaḍgī 5 mañjūṣā 6 auṣadhī 7 puṇḍarīkiṇyaḥ 8, susīmā 1 kuṇḍalā 2 aparājitā 3 prabhākarī 4 aṅkavatī 5 padmāvatī 6 śubhā 7 ratnasañcayāḥ 8, aśvapurī 1 siṃhapurī 2 mahāpurī 3 vijayapurī 4 rājyā 5 virājyā 6 aśokā 7 vītaśokā 8, vijayā 1 vaijayantī 2 jayantī 3 aparājitā 4 cakrapurī 5 khaḍgapurī 6 avadhyā 7 ayodhyā 8, etāḥ sarvāḥ puryo bharata-ayodhyā-pratikṛtaya iti. iha vakṣaskārāntarnadī-vijaya-purīṇāṃ sarveṣāṃ gaṇanākramo mālyavad-vakṣaskārād avagantavyaḥ. tathā vijayādīnāṃ vaitāḍhyeṣu pratyekaṃ pārśva-dvaye 'pi pañca-pañcāśat-pañca-pañcāśan nagarāṇi santi, yato nitamba-dvayam api samāna-dairghyaṃ, bharata-airāvatayos tu dhanuṣ-pṛṣṭhākāratvān madhya-bāhyayoḥ pārśvayor mahad-antaraṃ, ataḥ tatraikasyāṃ diśi pañcāśad anyasyāṃ tu ṣaṣṭiḥ sajana-padāni purāṇīti. nīlavataḥ parato ramyakaṃ kṣetraṃ harivarṣa-vat kevalaṃ, nāmnā mālyavān iha vṛtta-vaitāḍhyaḥ. tataḥ paro mahāhimavat-praticchāyo rukmī śailaḥ, tad-upari buddhi-devī-nivāso mahāpadma-pratirūpo mahāpuṇḍarīko hradaḥ, kūṭāny aṣṭāv atra tāni cāmūni siddha 1 rukma 2 ramyaka 3 narakānta 4 buddhi 5 raupya 6 hairaṇyavata 7 maṇikāñcana 8 nāmāni. tatra dakṣiṇā narakāntā pūrva-gā harikāntā-vat, rūpya-kūlottarāpara-dig-gāminī rohitā-vat. tad-antaraṃ hairaṇyavata-kṣetraṃ haimavata-prakhyaṃ navaraṃ, tan-madhye nāmato vikaṭāpātī vṛtta-vaitāḍhyaḥ prabhāsa-devādhivāsaḥ, kiñca sarve 'pi vṛtta-vaitāḍhyā eka-pramāṇa-varṇāḥ. tad-upari svarṇa-mayaḥ śikhari-varṣadhara lakṣmī-nivāsaḥ padma-viśiṣṭaḥ puṇḍarīko hradas tatra, tasmād dakṣiṇāṃ diśam āśritya rohitāṃśā-sadṛśī suvarṇakūlā, raktā-raktavatyau tūttara-ge gaṅgā-sindhū iva pramāṇataḥ. tad-upariṣṭāc caikādaśa-kūṭāni, tad yathā: siddhāyatana 1 śikhari 2 hairaṇyavata 3 surādevī 4 raktā 5 lakṣmī 6 suvarṇā 7 raktodā 8 gandhāpāti 9 ẹravata 10 tigiñchi 11 saṃjñāni himavata-kūṭa-saṃdṛśi. sarva-kṣetrāṇām uttara-dig-avasthitaṃ bharata-pratikalam airavataṃ, vaitāḍhyas tu vyatyaya-nagara-saṃkhya iti. tathāsmāj jambūdvīpād asaṃkhyeṣu dvīpa-samudreṣv atikrānteṣu kaścid jambūdvīpābhidhāno dvīpo 'sti, tasmin sarve vijayādi-dvāra-varṣadhara-parvata-kūṭa-nadī-hrada-vṛkṣa-vijayādy-adhiṣṭhātṝṇāṃ devānāṃ rāja-dhānyaḥ santi. uktaṃ ca Jambūdvīpaprajñaptau:

"rāẏahāṇīo jaṃbūddīve mandarassa pavvaẏassa dāhiṇeṇaṃ tiriẏaṃ asaṃkhijje dīva-samudde vīivaïttā

annaṃmi jaṃbūddīve bārasa-joyaṇa-sahassāiṃ ugāhettā itthaṇaṃ rāyahāṇīo bhāṇiyavvāo." [1]

tāsāṃ viśeṣa-varṇanaṃ kṣetrasamāsa-bṛhad-vṛtter avaseyam iti samasta-prakaraṇa-samudāyārthaḥ.

'***Bharahāi***' [etc.]. The meaning is as follows. The continents [or] the [world] regions are places inhabited by human beings. [The author] explains how many there number and what their names are: '***satta*** (seven)'. There are seven [continents], namely Bharata, etc. The word 'etc.' comprises Hemavata, Harivarṣa, Mahāvideha, Ramyaka, Hairaṇyaka, and Airavata. The word '*varṣa* (continent)' is neuter. Although it is connected with the masculine gender, this is not a mistake since this is Prākrit, [viz.] according to the rule that gender is

---

[1] *JDP sū.* 14, ed. Javeri, p. 82. Chāyā: *rāja-dhānī jambūdvīpe mandarasya parvatasya dakṣiṇena tiryak asaṃkhyeye dvīpa-samudre vyatikramya anyasmin jambūdvīpe dvādaśa-yojana-sahasrāṇi avagāhya atra nanu rāja-dhānī bhaṇitavyā*. The sentence replenished is: ***kahi ṇaṃ bhaṃte! dāhiṇaḍḍhabharaha-kūḍassa devassa dāhiṇaḍḍh[a-bharah]ā ṇāmaṃ rāyahāṇī paṇṇattā?, go.! maṃdarassa pavvatassa dakkhiṇeṇaṃ tiriyam asaṃkhejjadīvasamudde vīīvaittā ayaṇṇaṃ jaṃbuddīve dīve dakkhiṇeṇaṃ bārasa joyaṇa-sahassāiṃ ogāhittā ettha ṇaṃ dāhiṇaḍḍhabharaha-kūḍassa devassa dāhiṇaḍḍhabharahā ṇāmaṃ rāyahāṇī bhaṇiavvā ...*** Chāyā: ***kutra nanu bhante! dakṣiṇārdhabharata-kūṭasya devasya dakṣiṇārdha[-bharah]ā nāmnā rajadhānī prajñaptā?, gautama! mandarasya parvatasya dakṣiṇena tiryak asaṅkhyeya-dvīpa-samudre vyatikramya anyasmiñ jambūdvīpe dvīpe dakṣiṇena dvādaśa-yojana-sahasrāṇi avagāhya atra nanu dakṣiṇārdhabharata-kūṭasya devasya dakṣiṇārdhabharatā nāmnā rājadhānī bhaṇitavyā ...***

variable also.[1] All [world] continents have a name that is the same as their own presiding tutelary godhead. For, gods of similar rank and dignity, etc. call every god that rules over Bharata 'Bharata'. Therefore, the land reigned by him is also named after him: 'Bharata'. Moreover, relating to this the Canon [says]:

> "*Why is it, Reverend, that Bharata is called a continent? Gautama, Bharata is divine, magnificent and great since it occupies an immense territory. That is why Bharata is called a continent, Gautama*!".

The same applies to [the other continents] Haimavata, etc. This is the condensed meaning. The full meaning, however, is as follows. Jambūdvīpa, [situated] in the centre of all islands and oceans [and] looking like the disk of the full moon, measures one lakh *yojanas* [in diameter] all over. It is enclosed everywhere by one single wall[2], made of diamonds, eight *yojanas* high. Its width gradually [decreases] at the base, middle and upper parts [from] twelve to eight and to four *yojanas*. As the Canon [puts it]:

> "*There is one single wall [around] Jambūdvīpa. Everywhere, on all sides, this wall is closed. It is eight yojanas high or tall, at the base twelve yojanas broad, in the middle eight yojanas broad and at the top four yojanas broad. at the base it is wide, in the middle thin and the top very slender. It is formed like a cow's tail. It is completely made of diamond, pure and polished like a statue.*"

On top of that there is a lattice railing, half a *yojana* high and five hundred *dhanus* wide. Right in the middle of this [wall]

---

[1] See Pischel, R. (1973[1900]), §356*ff.*

[2] *vedikā* or *jagatī*. For a description of this wall, see Kirfel, p. 214.

there is precious lotus pavilion all around like a terrace with the [same] measure as the lattice railing in height and width, fashioned of a variety of precious stones and adorned with various sorts of lotuses. As it is saíd in the *Rājapraśnīya Upāṅga*:

> "*What does it mean, Lord, when a precious lotus pavilion is called a 'precious lotus pavilion'? Gautama, a precious lotus pavilion is known to have on its balconies, on the posts of its balconies, on the slabs of its balconies and on the hollow spaces of its balconies, on its pillars, on the flat sides of its pillars, on the top of its pillars, on the hollow sides of its pillars, on its railings, on the apexes of its railings, in the hollows of its railings, on its flanks, on the flat sides of its flanks, on the round sides of its flanks and on the hollow sides of its flanks masses of lotuses, delicate, fragrant, of night and day, blue and white, huge, with hundreds of petals, all made of jewels and beautiful, like pictures resembling large rain parasols. You, O monk, this is what is meant when a precious lotus pavilion is called a 'precious lotus pavilion'*".

On both sides of this [lotus pavilion] two groves with the same length as the pavilion are found, only that the inner [grove] is two *yojanas* minus two hundred *dhanus* wide, while the outer grove one *yojana* minus eight hundred and a half *dhanus*, because it is five hundred *dhanus* more confined by the lattice than the inner grove[1]. On the other hand, this is not expressly

[1] Lit. 'because there are more obstacles (*avaruddhāni*)'. The translation is very tentative here.

stated in the verses of the venerable Malayagiri[1]. It is also said that both groves have exactly the same size. All the same, [only] the very learned know the truth. On this wall, forty-five thousand *yojanas* away from Mount Meru in southern direction, there is a tower named Vaijayanta, eight *yojanas* high, each one [of its sides] four *yojanas* wide[2] [and] furnished with a door post one crore wide. Therefore, in total its width is four times one plus a half *yojanas*.[3] It is provided with a wall made of diamond with two gates made of beryl. It is the home of the Vaijayanta gods who live up to one *palyopama* and a half[4], the foremost of the multitudes of the Sāmānikasura, etc. gods and they are serving the goddess Mahiṣī, etc.[5] Next, from this tower onwards reaching up to the Himavanta Mountains in the north and to the Salt Ocean in the East and West, the *vijaya* continent[6] named Bharata [lies]. This [continent] is divided in its centre into two [parts] by the Vaitāḍhya mountain range

---

[1] Malayagiri composed a commentary on the *Kṣetrasamāsa* of Jinabhadra (also named *Bṛhatkṣetrasamāsa*). Haribhadra Sūri wrote a *vṛtti* on the same text in Saṃ. 1185 (*Jainendra Siddhānta Kośa,* J. Varṇī, 1970, p. 98).

[2] See Kirfel, p. 214. See also Fig. 6, p. 271.

[3] A *krośa* being $^1/_4$ of a *yojana.*

[4] One *palyopama* (Pkt. **paliovama**) is the time that passes when a container of 1 *yojana* in diameter and height, densely filled with fine hairs that grow in 7 days, is completely empty when every 100 years one tiny hair is taken out. See Kirfel, p. 339.

[5] A detailed description of the towers is given in the *Jivājīvābhigamasūtra, sū.* n° 492-630.

[6] Lit. a region of 'conquest'. A *vijaya* is a region that is conquered by a Cakravartin. In this sense it is also a province or district. Bharata has six of such provinces.

that reaches up to the Salt Ocean in the East and the West. It is fifty *yojanas* wide and half of that high[1] [and] is made of silver. That is the reason way they speak of Dakṣiṇabharatārdha (Southern Half-Bharata) and Uttara-bharatārdha (Northern Half-Bharata).[2] This [continent of Bharata] is divided into six parts by the Gaṅgā and the Sindhu.[3] [Both rivers] arise out of Lake Padma situated on the plateau on top of the Himavat Mountains. First they run to the East and the West [when they] appear out of the peaks bearing the same names. Then they flow southwards crossing the Vijayāḍhya[4] Mountains and reach the Salt Ocean in the South. Among these sectors, five are destitute of Āryas because they are occupied by barbarians who have their hearts and minds set on the destruction of life.[5] One [sector] is '*ārya* (noble)'. [This *ārya* sector] is crowned with the city of Ayodhyā, nine *yojanas* wide, and twelve *yojanas* long. [Ayodhyā] lies one hundred fourteen and eleven nineteenths [114 $^{11}/_{19}$] *yojanas* south of the Vaitāḍhya Mountains right in the centre amid the Gaṅgā, the

---

[1] In cross-section, the Vaitāḍhya mountain range looks like a three layered structure (See Fig. 12, p. 277) of which the lowest, middle and highest sections are 50, 30 and 10 *yojanas* broad and 10, 10, and 5 *yojanas* high. Its foundation reaches $6^{1}/_{4}$ *yojanas* underneath the surface of the earth. See Kirfel, p. 223.

[2] Both parts are 238 $^{3}/_{19}$ broad. Ibid.

[3] See Fig. 6, p. 271.

[4] The name 'Vijayāḍhya' is clearly a mix of 'Vijayārdha' and 'Vaitāḍhya'. Ibid.

[5] See Fig. 6, p. 271.

Sindhu and the ocean.[1] It is inhabited by superior folk headed by perfect and semi-perfect world rulers[2]. It is said:

"*Āryāvarta is the native place of the perfect world rulers and the semi-perfect world rulers*".[3]

Next, in the west of the Vaitāḍhya Mountains there is a cave [called] Tamisrā[4]. This [cave], twelve *yojanas* wide and fifty *yojanas* long, is the abode of the Kṛtamāla[5] gods and it has the same [kind of] gates as [fort] Vaijayanta. Right in the middle of it, two *yojanas* from each other, there are two rivers, the

---

[1] Kirfel (p. 225) identifies the Vaitāḍhya mountain range with the Himālayas.

[2] A *cakravartin* or *cakrin* is a world ruler. In every world period or during every full turn of the wheel of time twenty-four *cakra-vartins* appear, twelve in the upward half cycle (*utsarpiṇī*) and twelve in the downward half cycle (*avasarpiṇī*). Their life histories are all more or less the same. Thanks to their power and cunning, but also by means of magical jewels (*ratna*), they conquer a huge realm. These jewels are fourteen in number in case of a 'full' *cakra-vartin*, here called '*jina-cakrin*', and seven in case of a 'half (*ardha*)' *cakra-vartin*. For details, see Jozef Deleu (1976): *Die mythologie des jinismus*; entry 'Cakravartin', pp. 230-231.

[3] For a description and a list of Ārya and Mleccha peoples inhabiting Bharata, see Kirfel, pp. 225-227.

[4] Also Tamiśraguhā and Pkt. Tamisaguhā, lit. the 'dark one'. See Kirfel, p. 221. The Sindhu passes the Vaitāḍhya mountains through this tunnel-cave. The entrance in the north and the exit in the south of the Vaitāḍhya mountains have gates similar to those of the Vaijayanta fort (See Fig 6, p. 271). Both are 8 *yojanas* high and 4 *yojanas* deep and broad. See Kirfel, p. 223.

[5] Pkt. Kayamāla. See Kirfel, p. 223.

Unmagnajalā and the Nimagnajalā[1] each three *yojanas* wide.[2] The Khaṇḍaprapāta[3] cave, dwelling of the Nṛtamāla[4] gods [situated in] in the East [of the Vaitāḍhyas] is similar. Ten *yojanas* upwards from the foot of this mountain, all along the mountain range, the double row of the Vidyādhara cities is situated. [These rows] are each ten *yojanas* wide [and] are adorned with clusters of terraces and woods. In the southern row there are fifty Vidyādhara cities starting with Rathanūpuracakravāla[5]. In the northern row, on the other hand, there are sixty cities, Gaganavallabha, etc.[6] There the Vidyādharas[7] live happily, enjoying supreme bliss, all [their] wishes and desires fulfilled by the favour of the forty-eight magical skills promulgated by Dharaṇendra[8] and [also] possessing the capacity to move through the sky. Rising ten *yojanas* there are again two rows with flat as well as elevated

---

[1] Lit. the 'emerged' or 'emerging', and the 'submerged' or 'submerging' rivers respectively.

[2] According to Kirfel (p. 223) the Unmagnajalā and Nimagnajalā are 12 *yojanas* long and 3 *yojanas* wide. He adds that the *Trailokyadīpikā* locates both rivers in the Khaṇḍaprapāta cave where they are only 2 *yojanas* long and broad. There they discharge into the Gaṅgā (Id.).

[3] Pkt. Khaṇḍappavāya (See Kirfel, p. 221), lit. the 'sector-cascade'. The Gaṅgā passes the Vaitāḍhya mountains through this cave.

[4] Pkt. Naṭṭamāla. See Kirfel, p. 223.

[5] Pkt. Rahaneuracakkavāla. Id.

[6] For the Digambara list of the Vidyādhara cities based on the *Trailokyadīpikā*, see Kirfel, pp. 223-224. For the Śvetāmbara list based on the *Paümacariya*, see his 'Nachtrag', pp. 329-330.

[7] See J. Deleu (1976): *Die mythologie des jinismus*, p 279.

[8] Dharaṇendra is a southern Indra associated with the Nāgakumāras. See Kirfel, p. 263 & Deleu, Id., pp. 234 and 279.

grounds like the Vidyādhara rows. [Here] the Indrābhiyogika gods have settled.[1] Five *yojanas* higher up from there, ten *yojanas* wide, there is an abode, lovely with its groves and pavilions, which is used by the numerous Kalpavāsin[2] gods for their amorous sports. There are nine peaks there, six [*yojanas*] and a quarter high, as much in diameter at the base [and] twelve and a half *krośas* at the top.[3] [Their] names are [from East to West]: 1. Siddhāyatana, 2. Dakṣiṇārdhabharata, 3. Khaṇḍaprapāta, 4. Maṇibhadra, 5. Vijayāḍhya, 6. Pūrṇabhadra, 7. Tamisrāguha, 8. Uttarārdhabharata and 9. Vaiśramaṇa.[4] Among these, the Māṇibhadra, Vijayāḍhya, and Pūrṇabhadra peaks are made of gold. The others are made of six [kinds of] jewels. The Jina temple (*siddhāyatana*) on the first peak located in the East is one *krośa* long, half a *krośa* wide and fourteen hundred and forty *dhanus* high[5]. In there, there are three gates at three sides, five *dhanus* high, and half that size

---

[1] Besides the Ābhiyogika (or Ābhiyogya, Pkt. Ābhioga) gods of the Indras (of the Īśānas as well according to the *Trailokyadīpikā*) also the Lokapāla gods dwell here. See Kirfel, p. 224.

[2] The heavens from Saudharma as far as Acyuta are called Kalpa. Their inhabitants are named '*kalpopanna*'. See Kirfel, pp. 291*ff.* These must be the same as the '*kalpa-vāsin*' mentioned here.

[3] This agrees with the measures given by Kirfel, p. 224: $^{25}/_{4}$ *yojanas* high, as wide at the base, $^{25}/_{8}$ (= 3 $^{1}/_{8}$) *yojanas* or 12 $^{1}/_{2}$ *krośas* (or *gavyūtas*) wide at the top.

[4] Also: 1. Pkt. Siddhāẏaẏaṇa, 2. Pkt. Dāhiṇaḍḍhaharaha, 3. Khaṇḍaprapātaguhā, Pkt. Khaṇḍappavāẏaguhā, 4. Pkt. Māṇibbadda, 5. Vaitāḍhya, Vijayārdha, Pkt. Veaḍḍha, 6. Pkt. Puṇṇabhadda, 7. Tamiśra, Tamisra(guhā), Pkt. Tamisaguhā, 8. Pkt. Uttaraḍḍhabharaha, 9. Vaiśravaṇa, Pkt. Vesamaṇa. See Kirfel, p. 224.

[5] Or, "... etwas weniger als $^{1}/_{2}$ Krośa hoch, ... ", see Kirfel, p. 225.

wide, viz. the first gate in the east, the second in the south, and the third in the north. In the west, there is none. Moreover, the same spatial distribution of gates applies for all temples and palaces in Jambūdvīpa. Right in the middle of this [temple], there is a jewel pedestal, half a *krośa* long and wide and one-half of that thick. On top of that, there is a *devacchandaka*[1], five hundred *dhanus* long and wide and something more than that high. On that, there are one hundred and eight statues. Their size ranges from seven *hastas* to five hundred *dhanus* and represent Ṛṣabha, Vardhamāna, Candrānana and Vāriṣeṇa.[2] One should know that in all sanctuaries there are exquisite arrangements of round pinnacles, elephant's tusks, images made of *śāla* wood, lattices, etc. Next, there is the Bharatārdha peak. On that the palace of king Bharata [lies]. It has the same size as the *siddhāyatana* temple. In the Khaṇḍaprapāta and Tamisrāguhā [passages], the gods Nṛtamāla and Kṛtamāla [dwell][3]. In the palaces on the other five [peaks][4] gods bearing the same name [as the peaks] dally. Next, south of the slopes of Himavat there is a mountain

[1] A kind of altar according to Kirfel, p. 225.

[2] See Kirfel, ibid.

[3] Under the Vaitāḍhya (Veaḍḍha) or Vijayārdha mountains in the east and in the west the Gaṅgā and Sindhu flow through two elongated passages or tunnels (*guhā*), the Khaṇḍaprapāta and the Tamisrā (Tamiśrā) respectively. Both are 50 *yojanas* long, 12 wide and 8 high. In the Tamisrā two tributaries join the Sindhu: east the Unmagnajalā and west the Nirmagnajalā. See Kirfel, p. 223.

[4] Viz. the Maṇibhadra, Vijayāḍhya, Pūrṇabhadra, Uttarārdhabharata and Vaiśramaṇa peaks.

named Ṛṣabhakūṭa.[1] It is twelve *yojanas* wide at the base, four at the top, [and] eight *yojanas* high. It is the abode of the god Ṛṣabha [and] it is made of jewels. In the treatise here[2], it is known as 'Bhūmikūṭa'. When a world ruler conquers a kingdom with six regions[3], he writes his name on it[4]. North of Bharata, in the east and west touching the Salt Ocean the continental mountain range of Himavat [lies]. It is double the size of Bharata, one hundred *yojanas* high [and] is made of gold. On top of it, in the central part, Lake Padma [lies]. It is one thousand *yojanas* broad, its length half of that, ten *yojanas* deep and filled with water. Its banks are made of silver. The crystal stairs at its four sides [are covered with] stones made of diamond. In the middle of it, a lotus is found. It is one *yojana* in diameter. Its stalk is one-half *yojana* in diameter and ten *yojanas* high [and] towers two *gavyūtas* above the water. Its root is made of diamond, its bulb of *ariṣṭa*[5] [and] its stalk and outer leaves of beryl. Its inner [leaves] are made of *jambūnada*[6], its seed vessel of gold, its stamens of gold and its flower of various sorts of gems. This seed vessel measures two *gavyūtas* while it is one *gavyūta* thick. On it the goddess Śrī[7] [dwells]. It is provided with a pedestal, a *devacchandaka*[8] etc.

---

[1] The Ṛṣabha peak lies right in the middle of the northern *khaṇḍa* of Bharata. See Kirfel, p. 225.

[2] It is not clear which *prakaraṇa* is meant here.

[3] Viz. Bharata.

[4] Viz. he gives his own name to it.

[5] Lit. 'unhurt', a kind of jewel.

[6] Gold according to Kirfel, p. 219.

[7] Pkt. Siri.

[8] See p. 131.

[and] is encircled by hundred and eight lotuses that are so that they are half the size [of the central lotus]. On these the ornaments of the goddess Śrī are [kept]. Outside them, in the northwestern, northern, and northeastern regions there are four thousand [other] lotuses - 4,000. On these as many Sāmānika[1] gods and goddesses [dwell]. In the eastern region on four lotuses, the four worthy Mahāmantrin [gods] dwell. In the southeast on eight thousand lotuses the eight thousand - 8,000 - gods in the inner assembly of the goddess Śrī [live].[2] In the southern region on ten thousand lotuses - 10,000 - as many Mitrasthānīya gods [dwell] in the middle assembly.[3] In the south-west on twelve thousand lotuses - 12,000 - as many Kiṃkarasthānīya gods [reside] in the outer assembly.[4] In the west, on seven lotuses, the seven Anīkādhipati [gods] have their seat. In the four cardinal regions of the east, etc., on sixteen thousand lotuses - 16,000 - [as many] Ātmarakṣaka gods reside. This is the three-fold inner ring. In the west, also there are three outer rings [of lotuses]. In these, there are thirty-two lakh - 3,200,000 - of lotuses in the inner circle, forty hundred thousand - 4,000,000 - in the middle and forty-eight hundred thousand - 4,800,000 - in the outer. Therefore, in total there are one crore, twenty lakh, fifty thousand, and one hundred and twenty lotuses - 12,050,120 - in Lake Padma. Also in [the lakes] Mahāpadma, etc. there is the same amount of lotuses. [Emerging] from this lake out of the eastern portal, flowing eastward for five hundred *yojanas*, turning

---

[1] Lit. ' of equal rank or dignity'.

[2] These are the Abhyantarapāriṣadya gods. See Kirfel, p. 219.

[3] Or the Madyapāriṣadya deities. Ibid.

[4] Or the Bāhyapāriṣadya gods. Ibid.

away from the Gaṅgāvarta peak[1] in southern direction, crossing five hundred and twenty-three plus three and a half nineteenths *yutas*[2] [in total] towards the South and emerging from the two *gavyūta* long mouth of Makara[3], [the Gaṅgā] plunges into Gaṅgā-cascade-basin (Gaṅgaprapātakuṇḍa). This basin is sixty *yojanas* long and broad on the surface. At the bottom, however, it ten *yojanas* less. It is ten *yojanas* deep, its base is made of diamond, and it has three arched doorways, stairs, etc. In the middle of it [lies] the isle of Gaṅgā (Gaṅgādvīpa), eight *yojanas* in diameter, rising two *gavyūtas* above water[level]. In the middle of it, there is a mansion. There, on a pedestal, is the seat of the goddess Gaṅgā. Then, flowing out of the southern portal towards the Vijayāḍhya Mountains and breaking through the wall around Jambūdvīpa, the Gaṅgā enters the ocean[4], [on its way] filled by fourteen thousand tributaries. When she comes out her lake, at the Makara mouth and where she leaves her basin she is six *yojanas* plus one *krośa* broad and one half *krośa* deep [while] her estuary is ten times [the size of] her source.[5] It is said:

---

[1] Gaṅgāvarta is the name of a city of the Vidyādharas (See Kirfel, p. 330). Here, however, it must be identified with the Gaṅgā-kūṭa on Himavat (Id., p. 218).

[2] = 4 *hastas*.

[3] Makara: a kind of sea-monster, sometimes identified as a crocodile, a shark, a dolphin, etc. It is regarded as a symbol of the 9th Arhat of the present Avasarpiṇī and is represented as an ornament on gates or on headdresses.

[4] Near to the Māgadha fort (Māgadhatīrtha; see Kirfel, p. 221).

[5] Or 6 $^1/_4$ *yojanas* broad and $^1/_2$ *yojana* deep, and 62 $^1/_2$ *yojanas* broad and 1 $^1/_2$ *yojanas* deep respectively. Ibid.

"Whatever the width of a river where she starts, the width of her mouth is reckoned ten times [that size]".

Whatever, the depth is one-fiftieth part of the width all over since it is said :

"Whatever and wherever the width of a river in Jambūdvīpa, know the depth to be its fiftieth part".

Both her shores [are covered with] clusters of pavilions and groves. This is not [stated] just like that, because the Canon says:

"The Gaṅgā is a main river [...]. Both its banks are richly endowed with pavilions and groves.".

In like manner the Sindhu emerges from the western portal [of Lake Padma], deviates before the Sindhvāvarta peak[1], falls down from a tube in the form of an open mouth [and] cleaves through the basin [of the Sindhu waterfall][2], abode of the goddess Sindhu and likewise reaches the ocean[3]. The Rohitāṃśā emerges from the northern portal [of Lake Padma]. She is twice as long as the Gaṅgā. She falls down into a basin of the same name[4], [then] touches the Śabdāpātin with [a distance of] two *gavyūtas*[5], divides the continent of Haimavata in two [parts and] enters the ocean in the West. On Himavat there are eleven peaks made of several [kinds of] jewels. Their names are: 1. Siddhāyatana, 2. Kṣullahimavat, 3. Bharata, 4. Ilā, 5. Gaṅgā, 6. Śrī, 7. Rohitāṃśā, 8. Sindhu, 9. Surā, 10.

---

[1] Lit. the 'peak of the Sindhu whirlpool'. Ibid.

[2] Viz. the Sindhuprapātakuṇḍa. Ibid.

[3] Close to the Prabhāsa fort (Prabhāsatīrtha; Ibid.).

[4] Viz. the Rohitāṃśāprapātakuṇḍa.

[5] This means that the Rohitāṃśā turns away to the west $^1/_2$ *yojana* before reaching Mount Śabdāpāti. See Kirfel, p. 221.

Haimavata and 11. Vaiśramaṇa.[1] Their width[2] at the base and their height are five hundred *yojanas*. Their width at the top is half that size. On the first peak, there is a *siddhāyatana* temple, fifty *yojanas* long, half of that broad and thirty-six *yojanas* high. It has three gates. These are eight *yojanas* long and half of that broad. In the middle, it has a pedestal of jewels, eight *yojanas* wide and broad. This [pedestal] is four *yojanas* thick. On top of that, there is a *devacchandaka*[3], its height a bit more than its length and width.[4] The idols in there are said to be similar [to those] on the first Vaitāḍhya peak.[5] On the other ten peaks there are palaces, sixty-two *yojanas* and a half high, thirty-one *yojanas* and one *krośa* wide, and furnished with a lion-throne. In the region between Himavat and Mahāhimavat the continent named Haimavata [lies], four times the width of Bharata, in the east and west bordering the Salt Ocean, [and] bearing the name of its tutelary deity. It is ruled by twins taking food as they please, put at their disposal by the magical powers of ten kinds of wishing trees, wearing ornaments, their bodies cherished by [comfortable] beds and houses.[6] There

---

[1] Or, 1. Siddhakūṭa, 2. Himavatk° or Himavantak°, 3. Pkt. Bharahak°, 4. Ilādevīk°, 5. Gaṅgādevīk°, 6. Pkt. Sirik°, 7. Pkt. Rohiaṃsak°, 8. Sindhudevīk°, 9. Surādevīk°, 10. Pkt. Hemavaẏak° and 11. Pkt. Vesamaṇak°. See Kirfel, pp. 217-218.

[2] Or diameter, since they are envisaged as an oblate cone.

[3] See p. 131.

[4] Viz. 500 *dhanus* long and wide and a bit more in height. See Kirfel, p. 225.

[5] See p. 131.

[6] For a description of these twins (*yugalika* = *yugala*), a boy and a girl, and the ten kinds of wishing trees (*kalpa-pādaka* = *kalpa-taru* = *kalpa-vṛkṣa*), see Stevenson (1970[1915]), p. 273*ff.*

these [beings] live according the law of twin-couples. They have a body adorned with sixty-four ribs. They are one *gavyūta* in size and take [all] food they like at the end of [every] fourth meal[1]. [Their body] is free from disease, old age, death, suffering and sorrow [and] lives one *palyopama*. At the end [of their lives], having protected [their] offspring for seventy-nine days, they are born [again] as gods of the same or lesser status as their own. Some of them here have a body gradually one, two or three *gavyūtas* in size, [as] their food is restricted to *caṇaka*, *badara* or *āmalaka*[2]. Others are said to enjoy food full of eighteen condiments. In addition, of those having ears, this ear is not ringed[3] because (?)[4] the earth has a taste that surpasses sugar (*śarkarājitvara*) and they consume fruits of wishing trees as their food. The Canon says:

> "... *these people are known to have earth, flowers and fruits as their food ....!*"[5]

There are also found malignant animals [like] lions, tigers, snakes, cats, etc. that, owing to the idiosyncrasy of the

---

[1] i.e. at the evening of every 2nd day.

[2] *caṇaka*: the chickpea, *badara*: the edible fruit of the jujube, *āmalaka*: the fruit of the *Emblic myrobalan*.

[3] Or, decorated.

[4] The use of *yatas* here is problematic.

[5] *Jīvājīvābhigama*, *sū.* 111, in full: "Indeed, Lord, these people, what is their food? What do they eat? Gautama, these people are known to have earth, flowers and fruits as their food, O monk!". Further in *sū.* 111 it is said that this earth tastes like sugar (गुड़ - *guṛa*). Also in the *JDP*, *sū.* 22, ed. Javeri, p. 117. Here the taste of the earth is compared with खण्ड - *khaṇḍa* and मत्स्यंडिका - *matsyaṃḍikā*, sugar and the juice of sugarcane. Mention of people feeding on earth is also found in Jñānamatī, Ā., 1985, p. 51, with reference to the *Tiloẏapaṇṇati*, verse 455.

continent, [live] together without violence[1] because there is very little passion. Consequently, because of the inherent inevitability of that [state], they obtain rebirth as a god. Also grovelling creatures [like] gadflies, mosquitoes, bugs, etc. that cause pain to the body are absent. Time is uniformly *suṣama-duṣama* there. In the centre of that, the round Vaitāḍhya mountain Śabdāpāti is located. It is cylindrical in shape, is made of five-coloured gems, and is one thousand *yojanas* in size everywhere.[2] Some say that it is made of silver. Their [view, however] is contradicted by the *Jambūdvīpaprajñapti*. Therein is said that:

> "*Where, O Lord, in the Haimavata cotinent is the round Vaitāḍhya mountain named Śabdāpāti considered to be [located]? Gautama, west of the great Rohitā River and east of the great Rohitāṃśā River, right in the central part of the Haimavata continent, there exactly the round Vaitāḍhya mountain named Śabdāpāti is considered to be [located]. It is one thousand yojanas high and two hundred and a half yojanas deep. It is the same all over, having the form and shape of a cylinder. It is one thousand yojanas broad and wide and its circumference is reckonend to be a bit more than three thousand plus one hundred and sixty-two yojanas. It is magnificent [and] made of jewels...*".[3]

---

[1] *mitho-hiṃsya-hiṃsaka-bhāva*, lit. 'the state of being mutual victim of violence and perpetrator of violence'

[2] The Śabdāpāti is 1,000 *yojanas* high and its diameter is also 1,000 *yojanas*. Its root is 250 *yojanas* buried in the surface of the earth and its circumference is a bit more than 3,162 *yojanas*. See Kirfel, p. 228.

[3] *JDP*, *sū.* 77, ed. Javeri, p. 299.

In addition, the Master Umāsvāti expresses himself in exactly the same manner. Accordingly, his statement is that

"Mount Śabdāpāti is round, is made of different kinds of gems [and] is thousand [yojanas] everywhere".

Then there is what is stated in a section in the *Kṣetrasamāsa*: "***raẏaẏa-maẏā***". This is not correct [since] "***raẏaṇa-maẏā***" is the correct reading. Next, on top of that there is a divine residence of the same name similar to the palaces on the peaks of Himavat.[1] North of that Mahāhimavat [lies], double the size of Haimavata, made of silver [and] two hundred *yojanas* high. There, right in the middle Lake Mahāpadma [is located], [it's] length and breath double the size of Lake Padma, made the abode of the goddess Hrī[2]. It contains the same amount of lotuses as Lake Padma. The Rohitā emerges from the southern portal of this [Lake Mahāpadma]. She crosses the [Mahāhimavat] Mountains sixteen hundred *yojanas* plus five and five nineteenths [1,605 $^5/_{19}$, in southern direction and] plunges into the basin of the Rohitā cascade, residence of the goddess Rohitā, ten *yojanas* deep, its breath and width double that of the basin of the Gaṅgā falls. [Then] she encircles the Śabdāpāti for one fourth [of a *yojana*] at a distance of two *gavyūtas*. Having the same length as the Rohitāṃśā, she discharges into ocean in the east joined by twenty-eight thousand tributaries. The Harikāntā comes out of the northern portal [of Lake Mahāpadma]. She is twenty-five *yojanas* broad at the source [and] ten times that amount wide at [her] mouth. She falls down into a basin of the same name, [then encircles]

---

1 Here the god Śabdāpāti resides (Svāti according to the *Jambūdvīpasamāsa* and *Lokaprakāśa*, see Kirfel, ibid).

2 Pkt. Hiri or Hirī.

the Gandhāpāti(ka), surrounding it over [a distance of] one *yojana*. She is one half and five *yojanas* deep at the source and mouth respectively and enters the ocean in the west joined by fifty-six thousand tributaries. On this mountain range, there are eight peaks, namely 1. Siddhāyatana, 2. Mahāhimavat, 3. Haimavata, 4. Rohitā, 5. Hrī, 6. Harikāntā, 7. Harit and 8. Vaiḍūrya. The gods [residing there] have the same names [as these peaks], just like [it is the case with] the peaks on Himavat. From there, in northern direction, the continent of Harivarṣa [lies]. The twins over there are as the twins mentioned earlier[1] but doubly so qualified[2]. They are nourishing their offspring during sixty-four days [and] their food is supplied at the end of [every] sixth [meal][3]. In the very centre of it, [Mount] Gandhāpāti[4] [lies], abode of the god Aruṇa, qualified like [Mount] Śabdāpāti. Time, however, is always *suṣama* here. North of that the Niṣadha Mountains [lie], twice the width of the continent of Harivarṣa, four hundred *yojanas* high [and] made of gold, On top of these, in length and width twice the size Mahāpadma, ten *yojanas* deep, Lake Tigiñchi [is located], filled with the [same amount of] lotuses that qualify Lake Padma, made the residence of the goddess Dhṛti[5]. In the southern part of that [Niṣadha range] the Harit river [first] flows through the mountains for seven

---

[1] See p. 137.

[2] All numbers and sizes in Harivarṣa are twice those of Haimavata. See Kirfel, p. 228.

[3] I.e., the meal eaten at the end of a fast of three days. See Monier-Williams, p. 1110.

[4] Elsewhere Vikaṭāpāti, Pkt. Viadāvaī. See Kirfel, p. 228.

[5] Pkt. Dhii or Dhiī.

thousand, four hundred and twenty-one and one nineteenth *yojanas*. [Then] she [plunges] into a basin of the same name, splits [Harivarṣa] in two just like the Harikāntā [and] reaches the ocean in the East. The Śītodā arises in the North [of the Niṣadha range]. Her source and mouth are fifty *yojanas*.[1] Her basin is twice the size of the basin of the Harit river. She runs through the lakes 1. Niṣadha, 2. Devakuru, 3. Sūrya, 4 Sulasa and 5. Vidyutprabha[2]. She is joined by eighty-four thousand tributaries. She proceeds through the centre of the heart of the forest of Bhadraśāla [and] evades[3] Mount Mandara. Turning westward she cuts through the Vidyutprabha [Vakṣāra mountain range], divides West-Videha in two [and], joined by twenty-eight thousand tributaries from every province in turn, she runs underneath the earth below Jayanta tower. Five hundred *yojanas* wide and ten *yojanas* deep at her mouth she reaches the ocean in the west. On this [Niṣadha] mountain range, there are nine peaks similar to the peaks on Himavat. Their names are: 1. Siddhāyatana, 2. Niṣadha[4], 3. Harivarṣa[5], 4. Prāgvideha[6], 5. Harit[1], 6. Dhṛti[2], 7. Śītodā[3], 8. Aparavideha[4]

---

[1] This cannot be correct since the mouth of all great rivers (*mahā-nadī*) is ten times the size of their source. This applies also to the Śītodā: fifty *yojanas* at the source and five hundred *yojanas* at the mouth. See Kirfel, p. 222.

[2] The lakes Niṣadha (Pkt. Nisaha), Devakuru, Sūrya (Pkt. Sūra, Savitṛ in the *Trailokyadīpikā*), Sulasa and Vidyutprabha (Pkt. Vijjuppabha) are located in Devakuru. See Kirfel, p. 236.

[3] *alagantī*: 'not adhering', viz. encircling from afar.

[4] Pkt. Nisaḍha.

[5] Pkt. Harivāsa.

[6] Also Pūrvavideha, Pkt. Puvvavideha. See Kirfel, p. 218.

and 9. Rucaka[5]. North of Niṣadha the World Mountain range of Nīlavat [lies], made of beryl. In the middle of it Lake Keśari [is located], counter image of Lake Tigiñchi. There are nine peaks there with the [same] size as [those on] Niṣadha, namely Siddhāyatana, Nīla, Prāgvideha[6], Śītā[7], Kīrti[8], Nārī[9], Aparavideha[10], Ramyaka[11] and Upadarśana[12]. Further, from Lake Keśari the Śītā flows through the mountain plateau [of Nīlavat] for seven thousand, four hundred twenty-one and one nineteenth *yojanas*. She [plunges] into the basin of the deity of the same name, divides [Mahāvideha] in two [and] runs through the lakes Nīla[13], Uttarakuru, Candra[14], Eravata[15], and Mālyavat[16]. She [crosses] the forest of Bhadraśāla, passes through the Mālyavat [Vakṣaskāra mountains], Videha, and the Vijaya tower [and] reaches the ocean in the east. The rest [of the description] is like [in case of] the Śītodā. In between

---

[1] Also Hari (ibid.)·

[2] Pkt. Dhiī.

[3] Pkt. Sīoā or Sītodā.

[4] Pkt. Avaravideha.

[5] Pkt. Ruaga.

[6] Also Pūrvavideha (ibid.).

[7] Pkt. Sīā or Sītā.

[8] Pkt. Kitti.

[9] Also Narikāntā or Narakāntā (ibid.)

[10] Pkt. Avaravideha.

[11] Pkt. Rammaga.

[12] Also Adarśaka (ibid.). Pkt. Uvadaṃsaṇa.

[13] Pkt. Nīlavanta. See Kirfel, p. 236.

[14] Pkt. Canda.

[15] Or: Airāvata, Pkt. Erāvaẏa. Ibid.

[16] Pkt. Mālavanta.

Niṣadha and Nīlavat Mahāvideha [lies]. It is one lakh *yojanas* long and double the size of Niṣadha broad[1]. In the middle of that Mount Meru [rises] ninety-nine thousand *yojanas* high [with its root] thousand *yojanas* deep. It is ten thousand [*yojanas*] in diameter at ground level [and] thousand [*yojanas*] in diameter at the upper side. [Meru] is made of gold with precious stones in the middle.[2] In the lowlands at its foot the forest of Bhadraśāla [lies], in the east and west twenty-two thousand *yojanas* wide and in the north and south each two hundred and fifty broad. It consists of various kinds of trees. In the middle of it, at the four main points of the compass, fifty *yojanas* from Mount Meru, there are four *siddhāyatana* [temples] of the [same] size as the *siddhāyatana* temples of Himavat. To the same extent, there are four ponds each in the intermediate points of the compass, each fifty *yojanas* long, half of this wide and [again] each ten *yojanas* deep. Their names, to be taken successively from east to west, are 1. Padma, 2. Padmaprabhā, 3. Kumudā and 4. Kumudaprabhā; 1. Utpalagulmā, 2. Nalinī, 3. Utpalā and 4. Utpalojjvalā; 1. Bhṛṅgā, 2. Bhṛṅganibhā, 3. Añjanā and 4. Kajjalaprabhā; 1. Śrīkantā, 2. Śrīmahitā, 3. Śrīcandrā and 4. Śrīnilayā.[3] Amid

---

[1] Viz. $33{,}684^{4}/_{19}$ *yojana*. See Kirfel, p. 229.

[2] In Kirfel (p. 229) Mount Meru is described as consisting of three parts: the base made of earth, stone, diamond and pebbles, the middle part of *aṅka* (a kind of metal), crystal, silver and gold (according to the *Trailokyadīpikā*: *ratna*) and the upper part of gold. The top or *cūlikā* is made of beryl.

[3] The order given in Kirfel (p. 230) is slightly different: viz. in the northeast: 1. Padma (Pkt. Paümā), 2. Padmaprabhā (Pkt. Paümappabhā), 3. Kumudā and 4. Kumudaprabhā (Pkt. Kumudappabhā); in the

these [four groups of lakes] there are four palaces, five hundred *yojanas* high and half of that broad and wide, with magnificent *siṃhāsana* thrones. Those in the south[1] belong to the Saudharmya lords[2], those in the north[3] to the Īśāna lords. On both banks of the rivers Śītā and Śītodā, two by two, there are two mountain peaks called the Diggajas[4] (the Mountains of the Elephants of the quarters). Their names must be considered turning to the south from the northern direction of the river Śītā onwards. They are the Padmottara, Nīla, Suhasta, Añjana, Kumuda, Palāśa, Avataṃsa and Rocana.[5] Their tutelary gods have the same names. Five hundred *yojanas* above the base of Meru the forest of Nandana[6] [lies]. There, in the four cardinal regions there are also four *siddhāyatana* temples similar to

---

southeast: 1. Utpalagulmā (Pkt. Uppalagummā), 2. Nalinī, 3. Utpalā (Pkt. Uppalā) and 4. Utpalojjvalā (Pkt. Uppalujjalā); in the southwest: 1. Bhṛṅgā (Pkt. Bhiṃgā), 2. Bhṛṅganibhā (Pkt. Bhiṃganibhā), 3. Añjanā and 4. Añjanaprabhā (Pkt. Aṃjanappabhā) in stead of Kajjalaprabhā (Pkt. Kajjlappabhā); in the northwest: 1. Śrīkantā (Pkt. Sirikantā), 2. Śrīcandrā (Pkt. Siricaṃdā), 3. Śrīmahitā (Pkt. Sirimahiā) and 4. Śrīnilayā (Pkt. Siriṇilayā).

[1] In the southeast and southwest.

[2] The Śakra lords according to Kirfel, p. 230.

[3] In the northeast and northwest.

[4] Elsewhere called Dighastikūṭa (Pkt. Disāhatthikūḍa). See Kirfel, p. 230.

[5] The Padmottara (Pkt. Paümuttara), Nīla or Nīlavat (Pkt. Nīlavanta), Suhasti (Pkt. Suhatthi), Añjana(giri), Kumuda, Palāśa (Pkt. Palāsa), Vaḍaṃśa (Pkt. Vaḍi(ṃ)sa or Vataṃsa) and Rocana (Pkt. Roaṇa) according to Kirfel, p. 230.

[6] Pkt. Nandaṇa. It has the form of a ring, 500 *yojanas* broad. See Kirfel, p 230.

[those on] the peaks of Himavat. In the intermediate regions, there are lotus lakes with palaces, viz. 1. Nandottarā, 2. Nandā, 3. Sunandā and 4. Nandivardhanā; 1. Nandiṣeṇā, 2. Amoghā, 3. Gostūpā and 4. Sudarśanā; 1. Bhadrā, 2. Viśālā, 3. Kumudā and 4. Puṇḍarīkiṇī; 1. Vijayā, 2. Vejayantī, 3. Jayantī and 4. Aparājitā.[1] On the slope [of Mount Meru, in the forest of Nandana lie] the eight peaks of the Dikkumārī[2], namely 1. Nandana, 2. Mandara, 3. Niṣadha, 4. Haimavata, 5. Rajata, 6. Rucaka, 7. Sāgaracitra and 8. Vajra.[3] On these eight [peaks] the Dikkumārī reside. They are the 1. Meghaṃkarā, 2. Meghavatī, 3. Sumeghā, 4. Meghamālinī, 5. Suvatsā, 6. Vatsamitrā, 7. Vāriṣeṇā and 8. Balāhakā.[4] These goddesses produce torrential rains when a Jina is born. Then, in the northeastern point of compass[5], Balakūṭa [lies]. It has the same

---

[1] Nandottarā, Nandā, Sunandā and Nandivardhanā or Vardhanā in the northeast; Nandiṣeṇā, Amoghā, Gostūpā and Sudarśanā in the southeast; Bhadrā, Viśālā, Kumudā and Puṇḍarīkiṇī in the southwest; Vijayā, Vejayantī or Vaijayantī, Jayantī and Aparājitā in the northwest. The *Jambūdvīpasamāsa* and *Lokaprakāśa* place Aparājitā before Jayantī. See Kirfel, p. 231.

[2] Lit. 'lords of the celestial regions'.

[3] 1. Nandana, 2. Mandara, 3. Niṣadha (Pkt. Nisaha), 4. Haimavata (Pkt. Hemavaẏa), 5. Rajata (Pkt. Raẏaẏa), 6. Rucaka (Pkt. Ruaga), 7. Sāgaracitra and 8. Vajra (Pkt. Vaïra). See Kirfel, p. 231.

[4] 1. Meghaṃkarā (Pkt. Mehaṃkarā), 2. Meghavatī (Pkt. Mehāvaī), 3. Sumeghā (Pkt. Sumehā), 4. Meghamālinī (Pkt. Mehamālinī), 5. Suvatsā or Suvacchā, 6. Vatsamitrā or Vacchamitrā, 7. Vāriṣeṇā or Vajrasenā (Pkt. Vaïraseṇā) and 8. Balāhakā (Pkt. Balāhaẏā). See Kirfel, p. 231.

[5] In the northwest outside the eight peaks of the Dikkumārī goddesses according to Kirfel, p. 232. But the *aiśāna* direction (lit. 'relating to belonging to Śiva') is the Northeast.

name as its god. Its height and diameter are one thousand *yojanas* [while] half that size at the top. It stretches five hundred *yojanas* outside Nandana forest. It is said:

"*Reaching out of Nandana forest, five hundred yojanas further, five hundred yojanas in the air, Balakūṭa stands*".[1]

Rising up sixty-two thousand and five hundred *yojanas* from there[2] Saumanasa forest [lies], similar to Nandana forest except that there are no peaks. The lotus lakes [here] are 1. Sumanā[3], 2. Saumanasā, 3. Saumanāntā[4] and 4. Manoramā; 1. Uttarakuru, 2. Devakuru, 3. Vīrasenā and 4. Sarasvatī; 1. Viśālā, 2. Māghabhadrā, 3. Abhayasenā and 4. Rohiṇī; 1. Bhadrottarā, 2. Bhadrā, 3. Subhadrā and 4. Bhadravatī[5].[6] The rest is the same [as Nandana forest].[7] Moving thirty-six thousand *yojanas* upwards from there Paṇḍaka[8] forest [lies][9], qualified [like] Saumanasa. It is one thousand *yojanas* wide and in the middle of it the crest[10] [of Mount Meru stands]. This

---

[1] This is a strange, if not awkward, position for a mountain, its base half on the platform of Nadana forest and half pending in the air.

[2] Viz. on the next terrace.

[3] Sumanas. See Kirfel, p. 232.

[4] Saumanāṃśā. Ibid.

[5] Bhadrāvatī. Ibid.

[6] Sumanā, Saumanasā, Saumanāntā and Manoramā in the northeast; Uttarakuru, Devakuru, Vīrasenā and Sarasvatī in the southeast; Viśālā, Māghabhadrā, Abhayasenā and Rohiṇī in the southwest; Bhadrottarā, Bhadrā, Subhadrā and Bhadravatī in the northwest.

[7] Viz. the palaces inside the lotus lakes of Saumanasa forest. They are the same as in the other forests. See Kirfel, ibid.

[8] Pkt. Paṇḍaga or Pāṇḍaga.

[9] Viz. on the terrace on top of Mount Meru.

[10] *cūlā = cūlikā*. See Kirfel, pp. 232-233.

[crest] is twelve and four *yojanas* at the base and the top [respectively and] is made of beryl. On its top there is a temple similar to [the one on] Vijayārdha. There is a forest in the middle. In the intermediate compass regions, there are sixteen lotus lakes, viz. 1. Puṇḍrā, 2. Puṇḍraprabhā, 3. Suraktā and 4. Raktavatī[1]; 1. Kṣīrarasā, 2. Ikṣurasā, 3. Amṛtarasā and 4. Vāruṇī; 1. Śaṅkhottarā, 2. Śaṅkhā, 3. Śaṅkhāvartā and 4. Balāhakā; 1. Puṣpottarā, 2. Puṣpavatī, 3. Supuṣpā and 4. Puṣpamālinī.[2] The palaces and temples are as [described] before. In every of the four cardinal regions at the edges of the forest, there is a *jinābhiṣeka* stone[3], viz. 1. Pāṇḍuśilā in the east, 2. Atipāṇḍuśilā in the south, 3. Raktaśilā in the west, 4. Atiraktaśilā in the north.[4] These [stones] are lying in the position of a half moon. They are five hundred *yojanas* long, half of that broad and four *yojanas* high. They are made of silver and gold.[5] Among these, on top of the Pāṇḍukambalā and Raktakambalā there are two thrones. On the two others, there is only one. The length and width of all these thrones

---

[1] Raktāvatī. Ibid.

[2] Puṇḍrā, Puṇḍraprabhā, Suraktā and Raktavatī in the north-east; Kṣīrarasā, Ikṣurasā, Amṛtarasā and Vāruṇī in the southeast; Śaṅkhottarā, Śaṅkhā, Śaṅkhāvarttā and Balāhakā in the southwest; Puṣpottarā, Puṣpavatī, Supuṣpā and Puṣpamālinī in the northwest.

[3] Lit. 'inauguration of a Jina or Victor'.

[4] According to Kirfel, p. 232: Pāṇḍu (Pkt. Paṇḍu, *Sthānāṅga*: Pāṇḍukambalā) in the east, Pāṇḍukambalā (*Sthānāṅga* & *Jambūdvīpasamāsa*: Atipāṇḍukambalā) in the south, Raktā (Pkt. Rattā, Sthānāṅga: Raktakambalā) in the west and Raktakambalā (*Sthānāṅga* & *Jambūdvīpasamāsa*: Atiraktakambalā) in the north.

[5] The stones in the east and west are made of gold while those in the south and north of silver. See Kirfel, p. 233.

[measures] five hundred *dhanus*. Their height is half of that. On the southern and northern [thrones] the Jinas coming from the Provinces are consecrated[1], while on the other two [thrones] the Tīrthaṅkaras originating from Bharata and Airavata [are consecrated]. Next, at the four intermediate regions of Meru there are mountain ranges in the form of an elephant's tusk, named Vakṣaskāra[2]. It is said that these [mountain ranges] resemble the tusks of an elephant, thick at the base, then gradually decreasing until at the end they become narrow. At the beginning, they converge with the Niṣadha and Nīlavat [World Mountain ranges]. There they are four hundred *yojanas* high and five hundred *yojanas* broad. Then they increase gradually in height while they decrease in width like the head of a horse, until they meet with Meru. [There] they are five hundred *yojanas* high and an innumerable [small] part of an *aṅgula* wide. They are 1. Saumanasa in the southeast, made of silver and furnished with seven peaks, 2. Vidyutprabha in the south-west, made of purified gold and endowed with nine peaks, 3. Gandhamādana in the north-west, made of gold, with seven peaks, and 4. Mālyavat in the northeast, made of beryl and marked with nine peaks. Each of them is thirty thousand, two hundred and nine plus six nineteenths [30,209 $^{6}/_{19}$ *yojanas*] long[3]. On all [these four Vakṣaskāra mountain ranges], there is a temple on every first

---

[1] This does not agree with what Kirfel (p. 233) writes: "Wie im *Jambūdvīpasamāsa* noch zugefügt wird, findet hier die Weihe der südlichen und nördlichen Tīrthakara statt."

[2] Or Vakṣāra, Pkt. Vakkhāra.

[3] *kalā*: a small part of anything, any single part or portion of a whole, esp. a sixteenth part. With the Jainas a *kalā* is $^{1}/_{19}$. See Kirfel, p. 233.

peak. These peaks have the same measures as [those] of Himavat. Their names as enumerated from the point of Meru onwards are on the Saumanasa Vakṣaskāra Mountains: 1. Siddhāyatana[1], 2. Saumanasa, 3. Maṅgalāpāti, 4. Devakuru, 5. Vimala, 6. Kañcana and 7. Vaśiṣṭa. On the fifth and the sixth [peak], the Toyadhārā and Vicitra gods [dwell].[2] Then, on the Vidyutprabha [we have the peaks] named 1. Siddhāyatana[3], 2. Vidyutprabha, 3. Devakuru, 4. Padma, 5. Kanaka, 6. Svastika, 7. Śītodā, 8. Sadājala[4] and 9. Hari. On the Kanaka and Svastika peaks, the Puṣpamālā and Anindita gods [dwell].[5] Even so on the Gandhamādana [we find] the 1. Siddha, 2. Gandhamādana, 3. Gandhalāvat[6], 4. Uttarakuru, 5. Sphāṭika[7], 6. Lohita[8] and 7. Ānanda. On the fifth and the sixth the Bhogaṃkarā and Bhogavatī gods live. Next [we have the peaks] on Mālavat: 1. Siddha, 2. Mālyavat, 3. Uttarakuru, 4. Kaccha, 5. Sāgara, 6. Rajata, 7. Śītā, 8. Pūrṇabhadra and 9. Haritsaha. On Sāgara and Rajata, the Subhogā[9] and Bhogamālinī gods [reside]. The rest

---

[1] Or simply Siddha. See Kirfel, p. 233.

[2] The fifth and sixth peak are the Vimala and Kañcana. According to the *Stānāṅga* these mountains are the residence of the Suvatsā and Vatsamitra gods. The *JDSU* agrees with the *JDSH* on this point. See Kirfel, p. 234.

[3] Or again simply Siddha. See Kirfel, p. 233.

[4] Also Śatajvala. See Kirfel, p. 234.

[5] According to the *Sthānāṅga* on these mountains the Vāriṣeṇā and Balāhakā gods have their residence. Again the *JDSU* agrees with the *JDSH* on this point. See Kirfel, p. 234.

[6] Also Gandhelavat or Gandhilāvatī. See Kirfel, p. 233.

[7] Also Sphaṭika (ibid.).

[8] Also Lohitākṣa (ibid.).

[9] Or simply Bhogā (Kirfel, p. 234).

[of the peaks are inhabited by] gods of the same name. Among these, the Haritsaha and Hari peaks are one thousand *yojanas* high and broad [at the base] while five hundred *yojanas* broad at the top. The rest have dimensions that are already described.[1] In between Mandara, Gandhamādana, Nīlavat, and Mālyavat the land of Uttarakuru [lies]. It is eleven thousand, eight hundred and forty-two plus two-nineteenths [11,842 $^{2}/_{19}$] *yojanas* broad. Its inhabitants live as twins[2] according to the law of couples[3]. They are three *gavyūtas* in length, take food prepared at home which they enjoy [every] eighth day. They live up to the maximum of three *palyas*[4], their bodies marked by two and a half hundred and six ribs. They experience the *suṣama-suṣamā* era, enjoying the fruits of the trees of plenty[5]. Nursing their children during forty-nine days until the end, they die peacefully [and] are born again as gods. To the east and west of the Śītā, eight hundred and thirty-four, and as much as four-sevenths *yojanas* south of the Nīlavat, there are two Yamaka[6] mountains. Both are one thousand *yojanas* high and broad at the base, and half of that broad at the top. On top

---

[1] Viz. five hundred *yojanas* high.

[2] *yugalin* or *yugala*, lit. 'member of a pair'.

[3] Also *yugala-dharman*. See Kirfel, p. 234.

[4] *palya* for *palyopama*. Kirfel, p. 339 explains that one *palyopama* (**paliovama**) is the time that passes when a container of one *yojana* in diameter and height, densely filled with fine hairs that grow within seven days, is completely empty, when every hundred years one hair is removed.

[5] *kalpadru* = *kalpataru*: the wishing tree or the tree of plenty.

[6] Lit. 'twin-mountains', Pkt. Jamaga.

of both there are two palaces made of gold[1] as on Himavat and on so many [others]. In southern direction the lakes Nīla, etc.[2] [are located]. It is said:

> *"The Yamaka [lakes] Nīlavanta, etc. are [located] south of the two Yamaka [mountains]. Every other [Yamaka lake] to the south is of the same size".*

The [lakes] are narrow from north to south, while elongated from east to west.[3] They have the [same] dimensions as Lake Padma and have the same names as the gods residing there. At every side to the east and west of them there are ten Kañcana mountains with the same names as the gods dwelling there.[4] They are one hundred *yojanas* high and one hundred *yojanas* [broad] at the base, while on top they are fifty *yojanas* [broad]. Their peaks lay one hundred *yojanas* from each other, while there is no gap at the base. To the east of the Śītā, five hundred *yojanas* in diameter, in the middle twelve *yojanas* high, gradually becoming smaller, until at the end it is one-half

---

[1] According to Kirfel (p. 235) both Yamaka mountains themselves are made of gold and carry palaces (not necessarily two) on top. Probably the *JDSH* is wrong here. In the rest of the text normally the mountains are made of some kind of precious metal or gem, not the palaces standing on them. So, the alternative reading could be something like '*tayor upari kanaka-mayayoḥ prāsādāḥ*'.

[2] They are called the Yamakahradas (Pkt. Jamagadaha). Five lie in Uttarakuru, five in Devakuru. The lakes of Uttarakuru are: Nīla (Nīlavanta), Uttarakuru, Candra (Canda), Airāvata (Erāvaẏa) and Mālyavat (Mālavanta). See Kirfel, p. 236.

[3] Kirfel (p. 235) explains: "Ihre Längsseiten sind nach Osten und Westen und ihre Breitseiten nach Norden und Süden gerichtet".

[4] Eighty according to Kirfel (p. 236).

yojanas in size, there is a Jambūpīṭha[1] (Jambū pedestal) made of *jambū*-reed[2]. It is surrounded by a lotus terrace, two *gavyūtas* high, and five *dhanus* broad. At all the four cardinal directions the are four gates, two *krośas* high, half of that broad and adorned with banners, festooned decorations and jubilee garlands. Furthermore, in [its] centre there is a Maṇipīṭhikā (pedestal of gems), four *yojanas* high, and eight *yojanas* wide. On that the Jambū tree [stands]. The height and the diameter [of its crest[3]] are eight *yojanas*. Its root is made of diamond. Its root and stem are two *yojanas*.[4] Its branches are six *yojanas* and they are made of gold. The stem and leaves are made of beryl, the sprouts are made of coral and the fruits of gems. On the eastern branch, there is a mansion. Inside there is a *maṇi-pīṭhikā* (pedestal of gems) which is the seat of the god Anādṛta[5]. On the rest [of the branches], there are palaces. In the middle, there is a temple. All have the [same] size as those of Vijayārdha. Around it, there are one hundred and eight [other] Jambū trees. The number of the surrounding Jambū trees is like [it is the case with the lotuses] in Lake Padma.[6] Its overlord is the god Anādṛta. Fifty *yojanas* from there, in the first wood, there are mansions in the four cardinal directions. At the four intermediate directions, in the middle of four lotus

---

[1] Pkt. Jambūpīḍha.

[2] *jambūnada* = *jambūnaḍa*. According to Kirfel (p. 234) it is golden.

[3] The stem is two and the branches are six *yojanas* high (Kirfel, p. 235).

[4] The depth of its root is $^1/_2$ *yojana* (Kirfel, p. 234).

[5] Lit. the 'disrespected'. He is a descendant of Garuḍa .

[6] The Jambū World tree is surrounded by 108 similar but smaller trees, like the central giant lotus in Lake Padma on Himavat is enclosed by the same amount of other lotuses (Kirfel, pp. 219 & 235).

lakes, there are palaces. Between the mansions and palaces there are eight golden[1] peaks having the size of the Ṛṣabha peak[2]. On these, there are temples. In the palaces east, west, etc. from Śāli forest[3] there are *siṃhāsana* (lion) thrones. South of Mandara [mountain] Devakuru [lies]. North of the Niṣadha [the twin mountains] Citra and Vicitra [are located], similar to the Yamakas. The lakes [of Devakuru] are Niṣadha, etc.[4]. In the western half of it, in outlook similar to the Jambū, the Śālmalī tree [stands], abode of Garuḍa[5]. In East and West [Videha], there are thirty-two provinces. For, Prāgvideha (East Videha) is split in two [sectors] by the Śītā, while Aparavideha (West Videha) is divided [in two sectors] by the Śītodā. Again, every part is itself internally split into eight by four Vakṣaskāra [mountain ranges] and by three inland rivers flowing down inside [each sector]. So four multiplied by eight produces the number of provinces as given [above]. In like manner the southern and northern [provinces] are divided into three [provinces] by the Gaṅgā and Sindhu, and by the Raktā and

---

[1] *jambū-nada*, gold according to Kirfel, p. 235.

[2] They are eight *yojanas* high, also eight at the base and four at the top. They have a foundation of two *yojanas* and they are made of gold. See Kirfel, ibid.

[3] Śālivana is most probably Bhadraśālavana See Kirfel pp. 229-30.

[4] Niṣadha (Pkt. Nisaha), Devakuru, Sūrya (Pkt. Sūra), Sulasa and Vidyutprabha (Pkt. Vijjuppabha). See Kirfel, p. 236.

[5] According to Kirfel (p. 235) who relies on the *Sthānāṅga*, *Jambūdvīpaprajñapti*, *Lokaprakāśa* and *Trailokyadīpikā*, the Śālmalī tree is inhabited by the god Veṇu, descendant of Garuḍa. So we should read '*gāruḍāvāsā*' and not '*garuḍāvāsā*' as in Ed1.

Raktodā.[1] When the Vaitāḍhya [Mountains] cleave each province again, six regions are produced. It is said:

> *"For every province there is a Vaitāḍhya [range]. In each case there are two rivers equal to the Gaṅgā and Sindhu. They create six regions. There are thirty-two provinces in videha."*.

A province there is sixteen thousand, eight hundred and forty-two plus two-nineteenths *yojanas* [16,842 $^{2}/_{19}$] long and [3,213 $^{1}/_{2}$] *gavyūtas* broad.[2] On the slopes of the Niṣadha and Nīlavat, every province has one Ṛṣabha peak each. Where the Śītā and the Śītodā, and the Gaṅgā and Sindhu in turn meet the two fortresses Māgadha and Prabhāsa [lie]. Varadāma fortress lies right in between them. Here between the two woods of Bhadraśāla and Mukha[3] there are four Vakṣaskāra [mountains]. Between them, there are three rivers. In the spaces in between them, there are eight provinces. When all are multiplied with four, eight woods arise. There are sixteen Vakṣaskāra [mountains], twelve inland rivers [and] thirty-two provinces. Each province has two main rivers. They are named the Gaṅgā and Sindhu [in the southern provinces], both rising from a basin situated close to the Niṣadha [World Mountain

---

[1] Every *vijaya* or province in Videha is, in fact, a copy of either Bharata or Airāvata. This means that in the sixteen northern *vijayas* as many Gaṅgās and Sindhus stream and that in the sixteen southern *vijayas* as many Raktās and Raktodās flow. So also is every province divided by a Vijayārdha or Vaitāḍhya mountain range. See Fig. 8, p. 273.

[2] This is contradicted by the size given for the province of Kaccha by Kirfel (p. 236): 16,592 $^{2}/_{19}$ *yojanas* long and 2,213 *yojanas* and somewhat more broad.

[3] Here the woods at the mouth (*mukha*) of the Śītā and Śītodā are meant, viz. the four Bhūtāraṇyaka forests.

range]. In the sixteen northern provinces, however, the two rivers escaping from a basin located close to Nīlavat, are known by name as the Raktā and Araktā[1]. The names of the Vakṣaskāra mountains over there are [four by four]: 1. Citra, 2. Padma, 3. Nalina and 4. Ekaśaila, 1. Trikūṭa, 2. Vaiśramaṇa, 3. Sudarśana and 4. Añjana, 1. Aṅkavat, 2. Padmavat, 3. Āśīviṣa and 4. Sukhāvaha, 1. Candra, 2. Sūrya, 3. Nāga and 4. Devagiri.[2] Every Vakṣaskāra has four peaks each, 1. [the first always named] Siddhāyatana, 2. [the second] with the same name [as the Vakṣaskāra itself], 3.[the third having the name of] the province to the east [of it] and 4. [the fourth having the name of] the province to the west [of it]. Then there are the intermediate rivers, rising from a basin with an island in the middle where a goddess of the same name resides. They discharge into the Śītā or the Śītodā, each of them hundred and twenty-five *yojanas* broad and ten *gavyūtas* deep [all over][3]. There are twelve of them, viz. the 1. Grāhāvatī, 2. Hradāvatī and 3. Vegavatī, the 1. Taptajalā, 2. Mattajalā and 3.

---

[1] The Raktā and Raktodā are meant here.

[2] Kirfel (pp. 237*ff*) gives the following somewhat differing list, based on the *Sthānāṅga*, *Jambūdvīpaprajñapti*, *Lokaprakāśa* and *Trailokyadīpikā*: from West to East, in the North-East: 1. Citrakūṭa (Pkt. Cittakūḍa), 2. Brahma-k° (Pkt. Vaṃhak°), 3. Nālina and 4. Ekaśaila (Pkt. Egasela); in the South-East: 1. Trikūṭa (Pkt. Tiuḍa), 2. Vaiśramaṇa (Pkt. Vesamana), 3. Añjana and 4. Mātañjana (Pkt. Māyaṃjana) or Ātmañjana; in the South-West: 1. Aṅkavat or Aṅkāvati, Aṅkāpāti, Śabdavat, 2. Pakṣma (Pkt. Pamha) or Pamhāvaī, Pakṣmapāti, Dvijavat, 3. Āśīviṣa (Pkt. Āsīvisa) and 4. Sukhāvaha (Pkt. Suhāvaha) and, in the North-West: 1. Candra (Pkt. Caṇḍa), 2. Sūrya (Pkt. Sūra), 3. Nāga and 4. Devā.

[3] See Kirfel, p. 237.

Unmattajalā, the 1. Kṣīrodā, 2. Siṃhasrotā and 3. Antarvāhinī and, the 1. Ūrmimālinī, Gambhīramālinī and 3. Phenamālinī.[1] The provinces are: 1. Kaccha, 2. Sukaccha, 3. Mahākaccha, 4. Kacchavat, 5. Āvarta, 6. Maṅgalāvarta, 7. Puṣkara, 8. Puṣkaravanta, 1. Vaccha, 2. Suvaccha, 3. Mahāvaccha, 4. Vacchavat, 5. Ramya, 6. Ramyaka, 7. Ramaṇīya, 8. Maṅgalavanta, 1. Padma, 2. Supadma, 3 Mahāpadma, 4. Padmavat, 5. Śaṅkha, 6. Kumuda, 7. Nalini, 8. Salilavanta and, 1. Vapra, 2. Suvapra, 3. Mahāvapra, 4. Vapravat, 5. Valgu, 6. Suvalgu, 7. Gaṇḍila, 8. Gaṇḍilavanta.[2] They are separated by

---

[1] Here also Kirfel (id.) gives a slightly divergent list: from West to East, in the North-East: the 1. Grāhāvatī (Pkt. G(r)āhāvaī), 2. Hradāvatī (Pkt. Dahāvaī) or Hṛdāvatī and 3. Paṅkā(vaī); in the South-East: the 1. Taptajalā (Pkt. Tattajalā) or Taptā, 2. Mattajalā or Mattā and 3. Unmattajalā or Unmattā; in the South-West: the 1. Kṣīrodā (Pkt. Khīroā), 2. Śītaś(s)rotā (Pkt. Sīasoā) or Suvāhinī and 3. Antarvāhinī (Pkt. Antovahiṇī) and, in the North-West: the 1. Ūrmimālinī (Pkt. Ummimāliṇī), 2. Phenamālinī (Pkt. Pheṇamāliṇī) and 3. Gambhīramālinī (Pkt. Gambhīramāliṇī).

[2] Kirfel (id.) gives the following list: from West to East, in the North-East: 1. Kaccha or Kacchā, 2. Sukaccha or Sukacch(ak)ā, 3. Mahākaccha or Mahākacchā, 4. Kacch(ak)āvatī, 5. Āvarta (Pkt. Āvatta) or Āvartā, 6. Maṅgalāvarta (Pkt. Maṃgalāvatta) or Maṅgalāvartā, 7. Puṣkara (Pkt. Pukkhala) or Puṣkala/Puṣkalā, 8. Puṣkaravatī (Pkt. Pukkhalāvaī) or Puṣkalāvatī; in the South-East: 1. Vatsa (Pkt. Vaccha or Vacchā), 2. Suvatsa (Pkt. Suvaccha or Suvacch(ak)ā), 3. Mahāvatsa (Pkt. Mahāvaccha or Mahāvacchā), 4. Vatsakāvatī (Pkt. Vacchagāvaī) or Vatsāvatī, 5. Ramya (Pkt. Ramma) or Ramyā, 6. Ramyaka (Pkt. Rammaga), 7. Ramaṇīya (Pkt. Rammaṇijja), 8. Maṅgālavatī (Pkt. Maṃgalāvaī) or Maṅgulavat; in the South-West: 1. Pakṣma (Pkt. Paṃha) or Padmā, 2. Supakṣma (Pkt. Supaṃha) or Supadm(ak)ā, 3. Mahāpakṣma (Pkt. Mahāpaṃha) or Mahāpadmā, 4. Pakṣmakāvatī (Pkt.

mountains and rivers. The capital cities for every province separately are: 1. Kṣemā, 2. Kṣemapurī, 3. Ariṣṭā, 4. Ariṣṭavatī, 5. Khaḍgī, 6. Mañjūṣā, 7. Auṣadhī, 8. Puṇḍarīkiṇī, 1. Susīmā, 2. Kuṇḍalā, 3. Aparājitā, 4. Prabhākarī, 5. Aṅkavatī, 6. Padmāvatī, 7. Śubhā, 8. Ratnasañcayāḥ, 1.· Aśvapurī, 2. Siṃhapurī, 3. Mahāpurī, 4. Vijayapurī, 5. Rājyā, 6. Virājyā, 7. Aśokā, 8. Vītaśokā and, 1. Vijayā, 2. Vaijayantī, 3. Jayantī, 4. Aparājitā, 5. Cakrapurī, 6. Khaḍgapurī, 7. Avadhyā, 8. Ayodhyā.[1] All these cities form the counterpart of Ayodhyā in

---

Paṃhagāvaī) or Padmakāvatī, 5. Śaṅkha (Pkt. Saṃkha) or Suśaṅkhyā, 6. Kumuda (Pkt. Kumua) or also Nalina(ā), 7. Nalina (Pkt. Naliṇa) or also Kumuda or Kumudā, 8. Nalināvatī (Pkt. Naliṇāvaī) or also Saritā and, in the North-West: 1. Vapra (Pkt. Vappa) or Vaprā, 2. Suvapra (Pkt. Suvappa) or Suvaprakā, 3. Mahāvapra (Pkt. Mahāvappa) or Mahāvaprakā, 4. Vaprakāvatī (Pkt. Vappagāvaī) or Vaprāvatī, 5. Valgu (Pkt. Vaggū) or also Gandhā, 6. Suvalgu (Pkt. Suvaggū) or also Sugandhā, 7. Gaṇḍila or Gandhila or Gandilā, 8. Gaṇḍilavatī (Pkt. Gaṇḍilāvaī) or Gandhilāvatī or Gandhamālinī.

[1] Kirfel (id.) gives the following list corresponding with the one of the provinces: from West to East, in the North-East: 1. Kṣemā (Pkt. Khemā), 2. Kṣemapurī (Pkt. Khemapurī), 3. Riṣṭā (Pkt. Riṭṭhā), 4. Riṣṭapurī (Pkt. Riṭṭhapurī) or Riṣṭāpurī, 5. Khaḍgī (Pkt. Khaggī), 6. Mañjūṣā (Pkt. Maṃjusā), 7. Auṣadhī (Pkt. Osahī), 8. Puṇḍarīkiṇī; in the South-East: 1. Susīmā, 2. Kuṇḍalā, 3. Aparājitā (Pkt. Avarājiā), 4. Prabhaṃkarā (Pkt. Pahaṃkarā), 5. Aṅkāvatī (Pkt. Aṃkāvaī), 6. Pakṣmāvatī (Pkt. Paṃhāvaī), 7. Śubhā (Pkt. Subhā), 8. Ratnasañcaya (Pkt. Rayaṇasamayā); in the South-West: 1. Aśvapurī (Pkt. Āsapurī), 2. Siṃhapuri (Pkt. Sīhapuri), 3. Mahāpurī or Mahā, 4. Vijayapurī or Vijayā, 5. Aparājitā (Pkt. Avarājitā), 6. Arājyā (Pkt. Arājā) or Virājā or Virājyā, 7. Aśokā (Pkt. Asogā) or Śokā, 8. Vītāśokā (Pkt. Vīasogā); in the North-West: 1. Vijayā, 2. Vaijayantī (Pkt. Vejayaṃtī), 3. Jayantī, 4. Aparājitā (Pkt. Aparājiā), 5. Cakrapurī (Pkt. Cakkapurī), 6. Khaḍgapurī

Bharata. The enumeration and counting of all the Vakṣaskāra mountains, intermediate rivers, provinces, and cities has to start from the Mālyavat Vakṣaskāra Mountains onwards.[1] On each side of the Vaitāḍhya mountains of the provinces, there are fifty-five cities since both slopes have the same length. However, since Bharata and Airāvata have the shape of a bow[2] there is a difference in length between the inner and outer side [of their Vaitāḍhya mountains]. Consequently, they possess fifty-five inhabited cities to the one side, while sixty to the other. Above Nīlavat the continent of Ramyaka [lies]. It completely resembles Harivarṣa. The round Vaitāḍhya [mountain] here is named Mālyavat[3]. Beyond that the mountain [range] of Rukmin [lies], counterpart of Mahāhimavat. On its top Lake Mahāpuṇḍarika [lies], counterpart of Mahāpadma [and] home of the goddess Buddhi. There are eight peaks here, named: 1. Siddha[4], 2. Rukma[5], 3. Ramyaka, 4. Narakānta[6], 5. Buddhi, 6. Raupya[7], 7. Hairaṇyavata and 8. Maṇikāñcana[8]. There, south [of Rukmin] the Narakāntā runs to the east like the Harikāntā [in Harivarṣa while] north in western direction the Rūpyakūlā flows like the Rohitā [in Haimavata]. Adjacent to [the Rukmin range] the

(Pkt. Khaggapurī), 7. Avadhyā (Pkt. Avajjhā) or Avandhyā or Ayodhyā, 8. Ayodhyā (Pkt. Aojjhā) or Avadhyā.

[1] Viz. clockwise starting from the North-Eastern part of Mahāvideha.

[2] Lit.: the back of a bow.

[3] Elsewhere this mountain is named the Gandhāpāti (Pkt. Gandhāvaī).

[4] Siddhāyatana; Kirfel, p. 218.

[5] Rukmin; ibid.

[6] Narakāntā: ibid.

[7] Rūpyakūlā: ibid.

[8] Maṇikañcana; ibid.

continent of Hairaṇyavata [lies], completely resembling Haimavata. In its centre there is a round Vaitāḍhya [mountain] namely Vikaṭāpātī[1], residence of the god Prabhāsa. All round Vaitāḍhya [mountains] have the same size and colour. Above that the World Mountain range of Śikharin [lies]. It is made of gold [and] is the abode of Lakṣmī[2]. There Lake Puṇḍarīka is [situated] with the [same] features as Padma. From there, directing herself to the south, the Suvarṇakūlā [flows], looking like the Rohitāṃśā, while the Raktā and Raktavatī, in size like the Gaṅgā and Sindhu, stream northwards. On its top there are eleven peaks similar to the peaks on Himavat [and] known as the Siddhāyatana, Śikharin, Hairaṇyavata, Surādevī, Raktā, Lakṣmī, Suvarṇā, Raktodā, Gandhāpāti, Eravata and Tigiñchi[3]. Airavata, the counterpart of Bharata, is of all continents the most northerly located. However, [its] Vaitāḍhya [mountain range] is characterized by an inverted number of cities. The island named Jambūdvīpa is just one among the innumerable continents and oceans that lie beyond this Jambūdvīpa. All palaces of the gods that rule the gates of victory, World Mountains, peaks, rivers, lakes, trees, provinces, etc. are located there. [As] it is said in the *Jambūdvīpaprajñapti*:

"*[Where, O Lord!] is the palace [named Dakṣiṇārdhabharata of the god of the Dakṣiṇārdhabharata peak*

---

[1] According the *Jambūdvīpaprajñapti*, *Sthānāṅga* and *Lokaprakāśa* this mountain range is called 'Mālyavat'. The *Jambūdvīpasamāsa* and here the *Jambūdvīpasaṃgrahaṇī* call it the Vikaṭāpātī. See Kirfel, p. 228.

[2] Pkt. Lacchī.

[3] Compare with Kirfel, p. 218: Siddhāyatana, Śikharin, Hairaṇyavata, Suvarṇakūlā, Surādevī, Raktā, Lakṣmī, Raktāvatī, Ilādevī, Airāvata and Tigiñccha.

considered to be located? Gautama!] south of mount Mandara, right across the innumerable continents and oceans, on another Jambūdvīpa [continent], going as far as twelve thousand yojanas [south], there the palace [named Dakṣiṇārdhabharata of the god of the Dakṣiṇārdhabharata peak] is said [to be located]"[1].

The detailed description of these [palaces] can be found in the Major commentary on the *Kṣetrasamāsa*[2].

एषां [ते?] क्षेत्राणां द्वात्रिंशतो विजयानां च मध्यवर्त्तिनो वैताढ्याः, ते च क्रमेण चत्वारश्चतुस्त्रिंशच्च वृत्ता वर्त्तुलाकारा इतरे तद्विपरीता दीर्घा इत्यर्थ, इदमुक्तं भवति, चत्वारो वृत्तवैताढ्यास्तेषां स्थानं प्रमाणं च प्रागेवोक्तं क्षेत्रसमासानुसारेण, सिद्धान्तस्त्वनाद्यानां त्रयाणां स्थानकथनेन व्यवस्थितः, तथाहि - शब्दापाती, तद्वत् हरिवर्षे विकटापाती, रम्यके गन्धापाती, हैरण्यवते माल्यवानिति । तथा च तद्ग्रंथः -

---

[1] *JDP*, *sū.* 14.

[2] No doubt the major commentary of Malayagiri is meant here. In the commentary of Śānticandra on the *JDP* edited by Javeri (pp. 83-84) a similar remark is made: अत्र सूत्रे दक्षिणार्धभरतकूटवत् शेषकूटानामतिदेशात् बृहत्क्षेत्रसमासवृत्तौ "एवं शेषकूटान्यपि स्वस्वाधिपतियोगतः प्रवृत्तान्यवसेयानी"ति श्रीमलयगिरिसूरिभिर् उक्तत्वाच् चेति, चेत् उच्यते: ... *atra sūtre dakṣiṇārdhabharata-kūṭa-vat śeṣa-kūṭānām atideśāt bṛhatkṣetra-samāsa-vṛttau "evaṃ śeṣa-kūṭāny api sva-svādhipati-yogataḥ pravṛttāny avaseyāni" iti śrī-malayagiri-sūribhir uktatvāc ceti cet, ucyate:* ... "If one argues [that the other peaks need not to be described] because the other peaks are analogous to the Dakṣiṇārdhabharata peak [described] here in the *sūtra* and because in the commentary on the *Bṛhatkṣetrasamāsa* the Venerable Malayagiri Sūri says that also the other peaks have to be understood to occur in union with their own tutelary deities, we supply the following information ...".

"कहि णं भंते, हरिवासे वियढावई नामं वट्टवेयड्ढे पन्नते? गोयमा, हरिसलिलाए महानईए पच्चत्थिमेणं हरिकंताए महानईए पूरित्थीमेणं[1], हरिवासस्स बहुमज्झदेसभागे, इत्थ णं वियडाव[ा]ईणामं वट्टवेयड्ढे पण्णत्ते, [...]"[2]

तथा,

"कहि णं भंते, रमए वासे गंधावई नामं वट्टवेयड्ढे पन्नत्ते? गो., नरकंताए पच्चत्थिमेणं, नारीकंताए पुरित्थीमेणं, रम्मयवासस्स बहुमज्झदेसभागे गंधावईनामं वट्टवेयड्ढे पन्नत्ते, [...]"[3]

तथा,

"कहि णं भंते, ए[हे]रण्णवए वासे मालवंतपरियाए नामं वट्टवेयड्ढे पन्नत्ते, [...]"[4]

इति, तत्त्वं पुनः केवलिनो विदन्ति। दीर्घवैताढ्यास्तु द्वात्रिंशत् विदेहेषु प्रतिविजयमेकैकस्य भावात्, द्वौ च भरतैरावतयोः, सर्वमीलने चतुस्त्रिंशत्,

---

[1] For पुरत्थिमेणं.

[2] *JDP*, 4th Vakṣaskāra, *sū.* 82, ed. Javeri, p. 304 (This one and the two quotations below are also found in the commentary on the *BKSJ*, verse 175, p. 179.): कहि णं भन्ते! हरिवासे वासे विअडावई णामं वेट्टवेअद्धपव्वए पण्णत्ते? गो०! हरिए महाणईए पच्चत्थिमेणं हरिकंताए महाणईए पुरत्थिमेणं हरिवासस्स २ बहुमज्झदेसभाए एत्थ णं विअडावई णामं वेट्टवेअद्धपव्वए पण्णत्ते, ... [छाया: कुत्र ननु भदन्त! हरिवर्षे विकटापाती नाम वृत्तवैताढ्यः प्रज्ञप्तः? गौतम, हरिसलिलायाः महानद्यः पश्चिमेन हरिकान्तायाः महानद्यः पूर्वेण, हरिवर्षस्य बहुमध्यदेशभाग, अत्र ननु विकटापाती नाम वृत्तवैताढ्यः प्रज्ञप्तः, ...].

[3] *JDP*, 4th Vakṣaskāra, *sū.* 111, ed. Javeri, p. 377: कहि णं भन्ते! रम्मए वासे गन्धावईणामं वट्टवेअद्धपव्वए पण्णत्ते गोअमा! णरकन्ताए पच्चत्थिमेणं णारीकन्ताए रम्मगवासस्स बहुमज्झदेसभाए एत्थ णं गन्धावईणामं वेट्टवेअद्धे पव्वए पण्णत्ते, ... [छाया: कुत्र ननु भदन्त, रम्यकवर्षे गन्धापाती नाम वृत्तवैताढ्यः प्रज्ञप्तः गौतम, नरकान्तायाः पश्चिमेन, नारीकान्तायाः पूर्वेन रम्यकवर्षस्य बहुमध्यदेशभागे गन्धापाति नाम वृत्तवैताढ्यः प्रज्ञप्तः, ...].

[4] *JDP*, 4th Vakṣaskāra, *sū.* 111, ed. Javeri, p. 378: कहि णं भन्ते! हेरण्णवए वासे मालवन्तपरिआए णामं वट्टवेअद्धपव्व पं०? ... [छाया: कुत्र ननु भदन्त, हैरण्यके वर्षे माल्यवत्पर्यायः नाम वृत्तवैताढ्यः प्रज्ञप्तः?, ...].

वक्षस्कारगिरयः षोडश चित्रादयो ये विजयच्छेदिनः, तथा द्वाविति द्विसंख्यौ, काविस्याह - '**चित्तविचित्त**'-इति प्राकृतशैल्या विभक्तिलोपः। ततः चित्रश्च विचित्रश्च चित्रविचित्रौ, एतयोर्हि निषधमुत्तरेण शीतादाया अपरस्यां चित्रगिरिः प्राच्यां तु विचित्रः, तथान्यौ द्वौ यमकौ नीलवतो दक्षिणतः शीतायाः प्रागपरस्थितौ, एतेषां चतुर्णां समुदितानामपि 'यमका'-इति क्वचित्संज्ञा दृश्यते। कनकगिरयः काञ्चनगिरयस्तेषां द्वे शते शतद्वयं, तद्यथा - कुरुषु समुदिता नीलवदादयो दश ह्रदा, एकैकस्य ह्रदस्य वामतो दक्षिणतश्च प्रत्येकं दश कनकनगास्ततः पार्श्वद्वये ऽपि विंशतिः विंशतिः सर्वमीलने जातं शतद्वयं, तथा गजदन्ताकारत्वाद् गजदन्ता विद्युत्प्रभादयश्चत्वारस्ते हि मेरोर्विदिक्षु स्थिताः, तथेति सादृश्योपन्यासार्थः। चः समुच्चये, सुष्ठु मनोहरः सुवर्णरत्नमयत्वात्, मेरुर्मंदरो, वर्षधरा हिमवदादयः षट्। सर्वसंख्यामाह - 'पिंडे'-इत्यादि पिण्डे सर्वसमूहे एकोनसप्तत्यधिके द्वे शते भवत इति शेषः॥ १२॥

eṣāṃ kṣetrāṇāṃ dvā-triṃśato vijayānāṃ ca madhya-vartino vaitāḍhyāḥ, te ca krameṇa catvāraś catus-triṃśac ca vṛttā vartulākārā itare tad-viparītā dīrghā ity artha, idam uktaṃ bhavati, catvāro vṛtta-vaitāḍhyās teṣāṃ sthānaṃ pramāṇaṃ ca prāg evoktaṃ kṣetrasamāsa^anusāreṇa, siddhāntas tv anādyānāṃ trayāṇāṃ sthāna-kathanena vyavasthitaḥ, tathā hi - śabdāpātī, tad-vat harivarṣe vikaṭāpātī, ramyake gandhāpātī, hairaṇyavate mālyavān iti. tathā ca tad-granthaḥ:

"kahi ṇaṃ bhaṃte, harivāse viẏaḍhāvaī nāmaṃ vaṭṭa-veẏaḍḍhe pannate? goẏamā, hari-salilāe mahā-naīe paccatthimeṇaṃ harikantāe mahā-naīe puritthīmeṇaṃ[1], hari-vāsassa bahu-majjha-desa-bhāge, ittha ṇaṃ viẏaḍāvaī ṇāmaṃ vaṭṭa-veẏaḍḍhe paṇṇatte, [...]"[2]

---

[1] For *puratthimeṇaṃ.*

[2] Chāyā: *kutra nanu bhadanta, harivarṣe vikaṭāpātī nāma vṛtta-vaitāḍhyaḥ prajñaptaḥ? gautama, hari-salilāyāḥ mahā-nadyaḥ*

tathā,

"kahi ṇaṃ bhaṃte, ramae vāse gaṃdhāvaī nāmaṃ vaṭṭa-veẏaḍḍhe pannatte? go., narakantāe paccacchimeṇaṃ, nārīkantāe puricchīmeṇaṃ, rammaẏa-vāsassa bahu-majjha-desa-bhāge gandhāvaī nāmaṃ vaṭṭa-veẏaḍḍhe pannatte, [...]"[1]

tathā,

"kahi ṇaṃ bhaṃte, [h]eraṇṇavae vāse mālavanta-pariẏāenāṃ vaṭṭa-veẏaḍḍhe pannatte? [...]"[2]

iti, tattvaṃ punaḥ kevalino vidanti. dīrgha-vaitāḍhyās tu dvātriṃśat videheṣu prati-vijayam ekaikasya bhāvāt, dvau ca bharat-airāvatayoḥ, sarva-mīlane catustriṃśat, vakṣaskāra-girayaḥ ṣoḍaśa citrādayo ye vijaya-cchedinaḥ, tathā 'dvāv' iti dvi-saṃkhyau, kāv ity āha - ***'citta-vicitta'****-iti prākṛta-śailyā vibhakti-lopaḥ. tataḥ citraś ca vicitraś ca citra-vicitrau, etayor hi niṣadham uttareṇa śītādāyā aparasyāṃ citra-giriḥ prācyāṃ tu vicitraḥ, tathānyau dvau Yamakau nīlavato dakṣiṇataḥ śītāyāḥ prāg-apara-sthitau, eteṣāṃ caturṇāṃ samuditānām api 'yamakā' iti kvacit saṃjñā dṛśyate. kanaka-girayaḥ kāñcana-girayas teṣāṃ dve śate śata-dvayaṃ, tad yathā: kuruṣu samuditā nīlavad-ādayo daśa hradā, ekaikasya hradasya*

---

paścimena harikāntāyāḥ mahā-nadyaḥ pūrveṇa, hari-varṣasya bahu-madhya-deśa-bhāge, atra nanu vikaṭāpātī nāma vṛtta-vaitāḍhyaḥ prajñaptaḥ,[...].

[1] Chāyā: *kutra nanu bhadanta, ramyaka-varṣe gandhāpātī nāma vṛtta-vaitāḍhyaḥ prajñaptaḥ? gautama, narakāntāyāḥ paścimena, nārīkāntāyāḥ pūrvena ramyaka-varṣasya bahu-madhya-deśa-bhāge gandhāpāti nāma vṛtta-vaitāḍhyaḥ prajñaptaḥ, [...].*

[2] Chāyā: *kutra nanu bhadanta, hairaṇyake varṣe mālyavat-paryāyaḥ nāma vṛtta-vaitāḍhyaḥ prajñaptaḥ [...]."*

vāmato dakṣiṇataś ca pratyekaṃ daśa kanaka-nagās tataḥ pārśva-dvaye 'pi viṃśatiḥ viṃśatiḥ sarva-mīlane jātaṃ śata-dvayaṃ, tathā gaja-dantākāratvād gaja-dantā vidyutprabhādayaś catvāras te hi meror vidikṣu sthitāḥ, tatheti sādṛśyopanyāsārthaś, caḥ samuccaye, suṣṭu manoharaḥ su-varṇa-ratna-mayatvāt, merur mandaro, varṣadharā himavad-ādayaḥ ṣaṭ. sarva-saṃkhyām āha - 'piṇḍe'-ity ādi piṇḍe sarva-samūhe ekona-saptaty-adhike dve śate bhavata iti śeṣaḥ. 12.

12. The meaning is as follows. These continents and the thirty-two provinces located in the centre (viz. Videha) have Vaitāḍhya mountains. There are four and thirty-four [Vaitāḍhya mountains] respectively, [the first] round or circular in shape, the others, on the contrary, long.[1] It is stated that there are four round Vaitāḍhya [mountains]. Their location and size have been described earlier following the *Kṣetrasamāsa*. The Canon (Siddhānta), however, stops with a description of the location of three without an 'etc.' [added]. They are the Śabdāpātī and, similar to that, the Vikaṭāpātī in Harivarṣa, the Gandhāpāti in Ramyaka and the Mālyavān in Hairaṇyavata.[2] Therefore, the text reads:

---

[1] There are thirty-eight Vaitāḍhya mountain ranges in total: four round ones in central Videha, thirty-two in East and West Videha, and one in Bharata and Airāvata each.

[2] There is, again, some confusion here. The Śabdāpāti (Pkt. Saddāvaī) lies in Haimavata, 1,000 *yojanas* in height and diameter and consisting of gems. The Mālyavat (Pkt. Mālavanta) is located in Harivarṣa. In the *Jambūdvīpasamāsa* this mountain is called the Vikaṭāpāti. In Harivarṣa the Vikaṭāpātī (Pkt. Viaḍāvaī) lies or, the Gandhāpāti according to the *Jambūdvīpasamāsa*. Finally, the Gandhāpāti (Pkt. Gandhāvaī) is found in Ramyaka. For details, see Kirfel, pp. 222 and 228.

"Where, O Lord, in Harivarṣa is the round Vaitāḍhya mountain Vikaṭāpāti considered [to be located]? Gautama, west of the great River Harisalilā, east of the great River Harikāntā and right in the centre of Harivarṣa, there the round Vaitāḍhya mountain Vikaṭāpāti is considered [to be located, ...]"[1].

Similarly:

"Where, O Lord, in Ramyaka continent is the round Vaitāḍhya mountain Gandhāpāti considered [to be located]? Gautama, west of the Narakāntā, east of the Narīkāntā and right in the centre of the Ramyaka continent, there the round Vaitāḍhya mountain Gandhāpāti is considered [to be located, ...]"[2].

Similarly:

"Where, O Lord, in Hairaṇyaka continent is the round Vaitāḍhya mountain [named the] Mālyavat cone considered [to be located]?"[3].

[Regarding this only] the Omniscient know the truth. There are thirty-two long Vaitāḍhya [mountain ranges] in the Videha regions since they occur in every province. There are two in Bharata and Airāvata. [So] there are thirty-four when all are added together. There are sixteen Vakṣaskāra mountains, Citra, etc.[4], separating the provinces. Next, '*dvau*' means the number

---

[1] *JDP*, *vakṣ*. 4, *sū*. 82.

[2] *JDP*, *vakṣ*. 4, *sū*. 111.

[3] Id.

[4] 'Vakṣaskāra', lit. a bag for keeping valuable things, so called because it is borne upon the breast. The word is also applied to sections of Jaina works. The sixteen Vakṣaskāra or Vakṣāra mountains are located in Mahāvideha. The Vakṣaskāra mountains east from Mālyavat are 1.

two. [The author] explains which two: ***'citta-vicitta'***. According to the nature of Prākrit, there is loss of declension [here]. So, [the words] '*citra*' and '*vicitra*' [form the compound] '*citra-vicitra*'. Both [lie] north of Niṣadha. Mount Citra [lays] west of the Śītā while Vicitra east. The other two, the Yamaka [mountains, lie] to the south of Nīlavat, located to the east and west of the Śītā.[1] All the four mentioned above are sometimes acknowledged as the 'Yamakas (the Twins)'. The Kanaka Mountains are [the same as] the Kañcana Mountains. There are two hundred, viz. two centuries of them. In the Kuru regions there are all together ten lakes, Nīlavat, etc. To the left and the right of each of these lakes there are ten Kanakanaga (golden) mountains. Therefore, at the two sides there are twenty, which all-together make up for two hundred. Even so there are four Gajadanta mountains, the Vidyutprabhā, etc., [so called] because they resemble the tusks of an elephant. They are located at the intermediate points of compass of Meru. The word '*tathā* (even so)' [is used in] the sense of a statement of similarity. '*ca* (and)' is used in conjunctive sense. ['*su*' in '*su-*

Citrakūṭa (Pkt. Cittakūḍa), 2. Brahmakūṭa (Pkt. Vaṃha), 3. Nālina (Pkt. Naliṇa) and 4. Ekaśaila (Pkt. Egasela). East of Saumanasa we find the 1. Mātañjana (Pkt. Māyaṃjana), 2. Añjana, 3. Vaiśramaṇa (Pkt. Vesamaṇa) and 4. Trikūṭa (Pkt. Tiuḍa). West of the Vidyutprabha lie 1. Aṅka, 2. Pakṣma (Pkt. Pamha), 3. Āśīviṣa (Pkt. Āsīvisa) and 4. Sukhāvaha (Pkt. Suhāvaha). Finally, West of the Gandhamādana are situated the 1. Devā, 2. Nāga, 3. Sūrya (Pkt. Sūra) and 4. Candra (Pkt. Caṇḍa).

[1] The Yamaka (Pkt. Jamaga) mountains are located in Uttarakuru, to the west and east of the Śītā, each $834^4/_7$ *yojanas* south of Nīla. They are 1,000 *yojanas* high and made of gold. The Citra and Vicitra match the Yamakas and lie in Devakuru. See Kirfel, p. 235.

meru' means] highly praised or beautiful since [Mount Meru] is made of beautiful gems. Meru is Mandara. There are six world-supporting mountain ranges, Himavat, etc. [Now the author] gives the total number: '***piṇḍe***', etc. The expression '***piṇḍe***' means 'in total'. There two hundred and sixty-nine [mountains]. All this was left to be supplied.

SŪTRA 13

उक्तं पर्वतद्वारमधुना कियत्सु पर्वतेषु कियन्ति कूटानि भवन्ति? इति पञ्चमद्वारमाह -

uktaṃ parvata-dvāram adhunā kiyatsu parvateṣu kiyanti kūṭāni bhavanti? iti pañcama-dvāram āha.

Now that the topic of the [world] mountain ranges has been treated, [the author] deals with the fifth topic [answering the questions] how many peaks there are [and] on how many mountains.

सोलस[1]वक्खारेसुं[2], चउ[3] चउ[4] कूडा य[5] हुंति[6] पत्तेयं[7] ।
सोमणस[8]गंधमायण[9], सत्तट्ठ[10] य[11] रुप्पि[12]मह[1]हिमवे[2] ॥ १३ ॥[3]

---

[1] सोलस्स Bhog6 & 7. सोलस १६ Bhog8.

[2] Only Tueb, Bhog7 & 11 have the metrical correct ending -सुं. The other sources have -सु except Brd3 that has -सू.

[3] चउ २ meaning चउ written twice in succession: Brd1, Bhog9 & 14. चओ Bhog13. चओ २ Bhog17.

[4] चओ LD1. चउ ४ Bhog2. चउ २ Brd1.

[5] ई Bhog2. इं Bhog5. इ Bhog12.

[6] होंति Ed1. हुंत्ति LD1, Brd1. हुंती Bhog2.

[7] पत्तेअं LD2. पत्तेय Brd2.

[8] सोमणसं LD1. सोमणस १ Bhog5. सोमणस्स Bhog6 & 17. सोमनस Bhog13. सोमणस is missing in Bhog12 but added as सोमरस १ after गन्धमायण.

[9] गन्धमाणय LD2, Bhog14. गन्धमायणं Bhog6 & 9.

[10] सत्त७ट्ठ Bhog2. सत्त७ ८ and ट्ठ are missing in Bhog5. सत्त७ट्ठ८ Bhog12. सत्तऽट्ठ Bhog13.

[11] य omitted in Bhog5, 6, 8, 12 & 14.

[12] रूप्पि Ed1, 2 & 3, LD2, Bhog13, 15 & 17. रूपि Brd2, Bhog1, 8, 9 & 12. रुपि Brd3, Bhog10 & 14. रूप्पी Bhog6. रूप्पी य Bhog7 & 16.

solasa-vakkhāresuṃ, caü caü kūḍā ẏa huṃti patteẏaṃ; somaṇasa-gaṃdhamāẏaṇa, sattaṭṭha ẏa ruppi-mahahimave. 13.

(षोडशवक्षस्कारेषु चत्वारि चत्वारि कूटानि भवन्ति प्रत्येकतं, सौमनसगन्धमादनयोः सप्ताष्टौ च रुक्मिमहाहिमवतोः ॥ १३ ॥ *ṣoḍaśa-vakṣāreṣu catvāri catvāri kūṭāni bhavanti pratyekam; saumanasa-gandhamādanayoḥ saptāṣṭau ca rukmi-mahāhimavatoḥ. 13.*)

13. On the sixteen Vakṣāra mountains there are four peaks each, on Saumanasa and Gandhamādana seven and on Rukmi and Mahāhimavat eight.

COMMENTARY

'सोलस'-इति - षोडशसु चित्रादिषु वक्षस्कारनगेषु चत्वारि चत्वारि कूटानि पर्वतस्योपरिष्टादुच्चैर्गतानि शृङ्गाणि, 'कूटानि'-इति सामयिकी संज्ञा। तथा सौमनसगन्धमादनयोः सप्त सप्त, इह विभक्तिलोपो वीप्सा तूत्तरत्रापि प्राकृतशैल्या विज्ञेया। चः पुनरर्थे। रुक्मिमहाहिमवतोर्वर्षधरयोरष्टावष्टौ, एकमेकं प्रति प्रत्येकं, ततः प्रत्येकं कूटानि भवन्तीति सर्वत्र योज्यम् ॥ १३ ॥

---

[1] महा Ed2 & 3, Brd2, Bhog4, 5, 6, 7, 10, 13, 14, 15, 16 & 17. माहा Brd3. मइ Bhog9. The other sources have the metrically correct मह.

[2] हिमवे ८ Bhog2. हिमवंते Bhog6. हीमिवे Bhog9. हेमवे Bhog14.

[3] LD1 repeats the first part of verse 12 in verse 13: ***dosaẏa ... dunni***. This passage is erased with yellow pigment. It then continues with what is actually verse 13 but is numbered 14. Also in Bhog5 & 8 this is verse 14. In Bhog1 this is numbered verse 12. Bhog12 introduces this verse with द्वा ४, Bhog15 with द्वार ५.

*'**solasa**'^iti - ṣoḍaśasu citrādiṣu vakṣaskāra-nageṣu catvāri catvāri kūṭāni parvatasyopariṣṭād uccair-gatāni śṛṅgāṇi, 'kūṭāni'-iti sāmayikī saṃjñā. tathā saumanasa-gandhamādanayoḥ sapta sapta, iha vibhakti-lopo vīpsā tūttaratrāpi prākṛta-śailyā vijñeyā. caḥ punar-arthe. rukmi-mahāhimavator varṣadharayor aṣṭāv aṣṭau, ekam ekaṃ prati pratyekaṃ, tataḥ pratyekaṃ kūṭāni bhavantīti sarvatra yojyam. 13.*

13. '***Solasa***' [etc.]. On the sixteen Vakṣaskāra mountains, Citra[kūṭa], etc.[1], there are four peaks each, pinnacles that rise up on top of the mountain ranges. They are commonly known as the 'Kūṭas' (the 'Horns').[2] Likewise on the Saumanasa and Gandhamādana [Vakṣāra Mountains] there are seven [peaks] each[3]. There is loss of declension here [in '*sapta sapta*']. The

---

[1] For the 'etc.', see p. 154.

[2] The name of the first peak on every Vakṣaskāra is Siddhāyatanakūṭa (Pkt. Siddhāyayaṇak°). The second carries the name of its corresponding mountain range. The third and the fourth have the same names as their adjacent provinces. So we have for instance on Citrakūṭa between Kaccha and Sukaccha: 1. Siddhāyatanakūṭa (Pkt. Siddhāyayaṇak°), 2. Citrakūṭa (Pkt. Cittakūḍa), 3. Kacchakūṭa and 4. Sukacchakūṭa. See Kirfel, pp. 238*ff.*

[3] Saumanasa (Pkt. Somaṇasa) lies southeast from Mount Meru and is made of silver (*rūpya*). Its seven peaks are named: 1. Siddha, 2. Saumanasa (Pkt. Somaṇasa), 3. Māṅgalāpāti (Pkt. Maṃgalāvāī), 4. Devakuru, 5. Vimala, 6. Kāñcana (Pkt. Kāṃcaṇa) and 7. Vaśiṣṭa (Pkt. Vasiṭṭha). Gandhamādana (Pkt. Gandhamāyaṇa) is situated to the northwest and is made of gold (*kanaka*). It carries the peaks 1. Siddha, 2. Gandhamādana (Pkt. Gandhamāyaṇa), 3. Gandhelavat (Pkt.

repetition [of the word '*sapta*'] has to be understood here and in what follows as typical for Prākrit. The word '*ca* (and)' is used in the sense of '*punar* (again)'. On the World Mountain ranges Rukmi and Mahāhimavat there are eight [peaks] each. '*Pratyekam* (each one)' means '*ekam ekam* (one by one)'. The same construction applies in all [three] instances: [viz. on mountain range *x*] there are [*n*] peaks each.[1]

Gandhilāvaī), 4. Uttarakuru, 5. Sphaṭika (Pkt. Phaliha), 6. Lohitākṣa (Pkt. Lohiakkha) and 7. Ānanda (Pkt. Āṇanda). See Kirfel, p. 233.

[1] Haribhadra Sūri did not mention ***satta*** (*sapta*) and ***aṭṭha*** (*aṣṭa*) twice in verse 13, nor did he repeat ***patteyaṃ*** (*pratyekam*) in these instances. Prabhānanda points to the necessity to add ***patteyam*** (*pratyekam*) in both cases.

SŪTRA 14

चउतीस[1] वियड्ढेसुं[2], विज्जु[3]प्पह[4]निसढ[5]नीलवंतेसु[6] ।
तह मालवंत[7]सुरगिरि[8], नव नव[9] कूडाइ[10] पत्तेयं[11] ॥ १४ ॥ [12]

---

[1] चउत्तीस LD1, Brd2 & 3, Bhog6. चउतिसं Bhog2. चउतीसं ३४ Bhog5. व(?)त्तीस Bhog12. चउतीसं Bhog13.

[2] वियड्ढेसु Ed1, 2 & 3, Brd1, Bhog1, 4, 8, 9, 13, 14 & 16. विअड्ढेसु LD2. वियढेसु Brd2, Bhog6. वियढेसुं Brd3. वीयटे(?)सु Bhog2. वेयडे(?)सुं Bhog5. वीयड्ढेसू Bhog7. वियड्ढे(?)सूं Bhog10. वेयढे(?)सु Bhog12. वियढे(?)स्सु Bhog15. विढेसु Bhog17. Only LD1, Tueb and Bhog11 have the metrically correct वियड्ढेसुं.

[3] विद्यु Ed1, LD1, Brd1, 2 & 3, Bhog1, 2, 4, 6, 7, 9, 10, 11, 14 & 16. विज्ज Bhog5. विजु Bhog8. विजू Bhog13. चिद्यु Bhog15. विद्य Bhog17. Only Ed2 & 3, LD2 and Tueb have the standard Pkt. form विज्जु < Skt. विद्युत्.

[4] पह LD1 & 2, Brd1, 2 & 3, Tueb, Bhog1, 2 & 8. पहे १ Bhog5. प्पहे १ Bhog12. The other sources have the metrically correct -प्प- for -प्र-.

[5] नीसड्ढ Bhog1 & 16. निसढि २ Bhog5. निसड्ढ Bhog9 & 14. निटड्ढि २ Bhog12.

[6] नीलवंतेसुं LD1, Bhog9(?), 10 & 11. निलवंतेसु Bhog13 & 17. निल(?)वंतेसु Brd2. नीलवंतेय ३ Bhog5 & 12. नीलवंतेसू Bhog7.

[7] मालवत LD1, Bhog15. मालवंते Bhog2. मालवंत ४ Bhog5 & 12. मालंवंतं Bhog10.

[8] सूरगिरि LD1, Bhog9 & 13. सुरगिरी Bhog1, 6, 11, 14 & 16. र is missing in Bhog2. सुरगिरि ५ Bhog5 & 12. सुरगीरी Bhog7. सुरगिर Bhog8. सूरगिरी Bhog15.

[9] नव २ LD1, Brd1, 2 & 3, Bhog7, 9, 13, 14, 15 & 17.

[10] Only LD2 and Bhog9 & 10 have the metrically correct ending -आइ. कूडाइं Ed1, 2 & 3, LD1, Brd1, 2 & 3, Tueb, Bhog2, 4, 6, 11(?), 14 & 15. Bhog15 adds कुंति. कूडाय Bhog1, 5, 7, 8, 12, 13, 16 & 17.

[11] पत्तेय LD1. पत्तेअ LD2. य(प?)त्तेयं Bhog2.

[12] This is numbered verse 15 in LD2, Bhog5 and Bhog8, verse 13 in Bhog1.

caütīsa viẏaḍḍhesuṃ, vijjuppaha-nisaḍha-nīlavaṃtesu;
taha mālavaṃta-suragiri, nava nava kūḍāi patteẏaṃ. 14.

(चतुस्त्रिंशद्वैताढ्येषु विद्युत्प्रभनिषधनीलवन्तेषु। तथा माल्यवत्सुरगिरयोर्नव नव कूटानि प्रत्येकम्॥ १४॥ *catus-triṃśad vaitāḍhyeṣu vidyutprabha-niṣadha-nīlavanteṣu; tathā mālyavat-suragirayor nava nava kūṭāni pratyekam. 14.*)

14. On the thirty-four Vaitāḍhya mountains, on the Vidyutprabha, Niṣadha and Nīlavanta, and likewise on both the Mālyavat and Suragiri there are over and over again nine peaks each.

COMMENTARY

'चउतिस'-इति - चतुस्त्रिंशति वैताढ्येषु विजयभरतैरवतविच्छेदकेषु दीर्घवैताढ्येषु, तथा विद्युत्प्रभश्च निषधश्च नीलवांश्च ते तथोक्तास्तेषु, तथेति सादृश्ये, माल्यवांश्च सुरगिरिश्च माल्यवत्सुरगिरी, तयोस्तथोक्तयोः प्राकृतशैल्या विभक्तिलोप, एतेषु प्रत्येकमेकोनचत्वारिंशति पर्वतेषु नव नव कूटानि भवन्ति॥ १४॥

*'**caütīsa**'-iti - catus-triṃśati vaitāḍhyeṣu vijaya-bharata-airavata-vicchedakeṣu dīrgha-vaitāḍhyeṣu, tathā vidyut-prabhaś ca niṣadhaś ca nīlavāṃś ca te tathoktās teṣu, tatheti sādṛśye, mālyavāṃś ca suragiriś ca mālyavat-suragirī, tayos tathoktayoḥ prākṛta-śailyā vibhakti-lopa, eteṣu pratyekam ekona-catvāriṃśati parvateṣu nava nava kūṭāni bhavanti. 14.*

14. '***caütīsa***' [etc.]. On the thirty-four Vaitāḍhya mountains [in Videha], the long Vaitāḍhya mountains dividing Bharata and Airavata in provinces, and likewise on the Vidyutprabha, the

Niṣadha and the Nīlavant, on these as they are named - '*tathā*' means 'similarly' - and on both the Mālyavat and the Suragiri - [in compound this is:] on the '*mālyavat-suragiri*' - on those two as they are named - there is loss of declension [here] since this is typical for Prākrit - on [all] these thirty-nine [mountains] separately there are nine peaks each.

SŪTRA 15

तथा -
tathā -
Even so,

हिम[1]सिहरिसु[2] इक्कारस[3], इय[4] इगसट्ठी[5] गिरिसु[6] कूडाणं[7] ।
एगत्ते[8] सव्वधणं[9], सय[10] चउरो[11] सत्त[12]सट्ठी[13]य[14] ॥ १५ ॥[15]
hima-siharisu ikkārasa, iẏa iga-saṭṭhī girīsu kūḍāṇaṃ,
egatte savva-dhaṇaṃ, saẏa caüro satta-saṭṭhī ẏa. 15.

---

[1] हेमगिरि Bhog6. हिम ११ Bhog12.
[2] सिहरीसु Ed3, Bhog1, 5 & 13. सिहरिसि Bhog6. सिंहरिसु Bhog17.
[3] ईक्कारस LD1, Brd3, Bhog7, 16 & 17. स is missing in LD2. इकारस Bhog2. इगारस ११ Bhog5. गारस with इ missing in Bhog6. ईगारस Bhog12.
[4] इयं Brd2, Bhog10. इअ Bhog8.
[5] इगसट्ठि Ed3, Bhog1, 2, 9, 10 & 14. ईगसट्ठी LD1, Brd3. इगसठि Bhog7. इगसवि Bhog15.
[6] गिरिसु Ed2, Bhog4, 6, 8, 10 & 13. गिरिसुं Bhog15 & 17. गिरीसू LD1. गिरीसुं Brd3. सु is missing in Bhog2. गीरीसू Bhog16.
[7] कूडाण Bhog9 & 10. कुण्डाणं Bhog15.
[8] एगेत्ते LD1. एगंते Brd2. एकत्तेBhog2. एवंत्ते Bhog6. एगते Bhog7 & 8.
[9] सव्वधणू LD2, Bhog8. सव्वधणुं Tueb. सव्वधनं Bhog2. सव्वं(?)धणं Bhog6. सव्वधण Bhog15. सव्वधणु Bhog17.
[10] सयं LD1, Bhog6. सेय LD2.
[11] चओरो LD1. चउरो followed by य Tueb.
[12] सत Brd2. सट्ठ(?) Bhog9. सड Bhog13.
[13] सट्ठा LD2, Brd1, Bhog6, 9, 10 & 13. सट्ठि Bhog2, 12 & 14.
[14] अ LD1, Brd3, Bhog11 & 15. य ४६७ Tueb, Bhog8. यं Bhog17.
[15] In LD2 and Bhog1 this verse is numbered 14. In Bhog5 & 8 it is numbered verse 16.

(हिमवच्छिखरिणोरेकादशेत्येकषष्टिगिरिषु कूटानातं, एकत्वे सर्वधनं शतानि चत्वारि सप्तषष्टिश्च ॥ १५ ॥ *himavac-chikhariṇor ekādaśety eka-ṣaṣṭi giriṣu kūṭānām; ekatve sarva-dhanaṃ śatāni catvāri sapta-ṣaṣṭiś ca. 15.*)

15. [There are] eleven [peaks] on Himavat and Śikharin. Therefore, there are sixty-one peaks on the mountains. All in all there are four hundred and sixty-seven [peaks].

COMMENTARY

'**हिम**'-इति - हिमेति पदैकदेशो ऽपि पदसमुदायोपचारात् हिमवान् , यथा भीमो भीमसेनः दृष्टश्च, हिमवांश्च शिखरी च हिमवच्छिखरिणौ तयोस्तथोक्तयोर्, इह प्राकृतत्वात्सूत्रे बहुवचनतं, यत उक्तं - "**दुव्वयणे बहुवयणम्**"-इति। प्रत्येकमेकादश[शै?]कादश कूटानि भवन्ति। समस्तकूटगिरीणां कूटानां च सर्वाग्रमाह - '**इय इगसट्ठी**'-इत्यादि। इति वक्ष्यमाणप्रकारेण एकेनार्गला षाष्टिरेकषष्टिस्तस्यामेकषष्टौ गिरिषु आधारभूतेषु पर्वतेषु एकत्वे सर्वांके सर्वधनं निखिलसमुदायः सप्तषष्ट्यर्गलानि चत्वारि शतानि ४६७ कूटानां भवन्तीति शेषः॥ १५॥

'***hima***'*-iti - himeti padaika-deśo 'pi pada-samudāyopacārāt himavān, yathā bhīmo bhīmasenaḥ dṛṣṭaś ca, himavāṃś ca śikharī ca himavac-chikhariṇau tayos tathoktayor, iha prākṛtatvāt sūtre bahu-vacanam. yata uktaṃ -* "***duvvayaṇe bahu-vayaṇam***" *iti. pratyekam ekādaśa[ai?]kādaśa kūṭāni bhavanti. samasta-kūṭa-girīṇāṃ kūṭānāṃ ca sarvāgram āha -* '***iya iga-saṭṭhī***'*-ity ādi. iti vakṣyamāṇa-prakāreṇa ekenārgalā ṣāṣṭir eka-ṣaṣṭis tasyām eka-ṣaṣṭau giriṣu ādhāra-bhūteṣu parvateṣu ekatve sarvāṅke sarva-dhanaṃ nikhila-samudāyaḥ sapta-ṣaṣṭy-argalāni catvāri śatāni 467 kūṭānāṃ bhavantīti śeṣaḥ. 15.*

15. '***Hima***' [etc.]. '*hima*' is only part of the [whole] word. [It stands for] '*hima-vat*' because it is used for a combination of words, as for instance '*bhīma*' is used for '*bhīma-sena*'.[1] '*himavat*' and '*śikharin*' - [in compound they form the dual] '*himavac-chikhariṇau*' - of these two named as such [the number of peaks will be given]. Here in the manual the plural [is used] since it is Prākrit[2], because it is said that "the plural [stands] for the dual"[3]. [Himavat and Śikharin] have eleven peaks each. [The author] gives the total number of all mountains [supporting] the peaks and the peaks [themselves]: '***iẏa iga-saṭṭhī*** (sixty-one)', etc. In this manner [the author] says that there are sixty plus one or sixty-one. When these sixty-one mountains or mounts carrying [peaks] are added to the total number, then - overall or in total - there are four hundred and sixty-seven, 467 peaks. This is what is supplied.

---

[1] Bhīma is the second son of Pāṇḍu. He is also called 'Bhīmasena' meaning 'having a formidable army'.

[2] In Prākrit the dual number is lost and replaced by the plural.

[3] *dvi-vacane bahu-vacanam*. **duvvaẏana** = *dvivacana*.

SŪTRA 16

अथ सर्वकूटसंख्यानयनाय करणमाह -

atha sarva-kūṭa-saṃkhyānayanāya karaṇam āha -

Next [the author] explains the method to calculate the total number of peaks.

चउ[1]सत्त[2] अट्ठ[3] नवगे,गारस[4]कूडेहि[5] गुणह[6] जहसंखं[7] ।
सोलस[8] दु दु[9] गुणयालं[10], दुवे[11] य[12] सग[13]सट्ठि[14] सय चउरो[15] ॥ १६ ॥[16]

---

[1] चओ LD1. चउ ४ Bhog5. चव(?) Bhog6. हिमसिह written before चउ in Bhog12. चऊ Bhog16.

[2] सत Brd2. सत्त ७ Bhog5 & 12.

[3] अड Bhog1. अट्ठ ८ Bhog5 & 12. गट्ठ Bhog6.

[4] णवगे ९ गारस Bhog5. नवगेगारस्स Bhog6. नवगेइगारस Bhog10. नवमेगारस Bhog14.

[5] Bhog2, 5, 10, 13 & 17 have the metrically correct कूडेहि. The other sources have the ending -एहिं. डे is missing in Bhog10. कुण्डेहि Bhog17.

[6] गुण in stead of गुणह in LD1, Bhog5, 8, 12 & 13. गुणेहें Bhog15. गुंणह Bhog16.

[7] संखे Bhog1. सखं Bhog6.

[8] सोलस १६ Bhog5. सोलस्स Bhog6. सोलस्स १६ Bhog12.

[9] Second दु is missing in Bhog2. दुग २ दुग २ Bhog12.

[10] गुणयाल LD2, Brd2 & 3, Tueb, Bhog1, 2, 7, 9, 10, 11, 13, 15 & 17. गूंणयाल LD1. गणयाल ३९ Bhog5. गुणयाल ३९ Bhog12. गुंणयाल Bhog16.

[11] दुवे २ Bhog5 & 12.

[12] अ LD2 & 15. ग Bhog4. इ Bhog16.

[13] सट्ट(?) Bhog6. इग Bhog7. स omitted in Bhog16.

[14] सट्ठी Ed3. LD1, Brd2, Bhog7 & 16. सट्ठ Tueb, Bhog4 & 6.

[15] चउरो LD1, Bhog10 & 13. चउरो ४६७ Tueb, Bhog5.

[16] In LD2, Bhog5 & 8 this is numbered verse 17, in Bhog1 verse 15.

caüsatta aṭṭha navage, gārasa-kūḍehi guṇaha jaha-saṃkhaṃ;
solasa du du guṇay̆ālaṃ, duve y̆a sagasaṭṭhi say̆a caüro. 16.

(चतुःसप्ताष्टनवकैकादशकूटैर्गुणयत यथासंख्यतं, षोडश द्वे द्वे एकोनचत्वारिंशतं द्वे च सप्तषष्ट्यिधकानि शतानि चत्वारि ॥ १६ ॥ *catuḥ-saptāṣṭa-navakaikādaśa-kūṭair guṇayata yathā-saṃkhyam; ṣodaśa dve dve ekona-catvāriṃśataṃ dve ca sapta-ṣaṣṭy-adhikāni śatāni catvāri. 16.*)

16. Multiply in the relative order [of the two series][1] eleven, two, two, fifty-eight and two, with four, seven, eight, nine and eleven peaks. [The result is] four hundred sixty-seven.

COMMENTARY

'चउसत्त'-इति - चतुःसप्ताष्टनवकैकादशभिः कूटैर्यथासंख्यं यथाक्रमं यथोपन्यासमिति यावद् गुणयत, गुणकारप्रवृत्तान् कुरुत, हे गणितज्ञा इति गम्यते। कानित्याह - **'सोलस'**-इत्यादि - षोडश द्वौ द्वौ एकोनचत्वारिंशतं द्वौ चेति, तद्यथा षोडशानां चतुर्भिर्गुणने चतुःषष्टिर्, द्वयोस्तु सप्तभिर्गुणने चतुर्दश, तथा द्वयोरेवाष्टभिर्हनने षोडश, एकोनचत्वारिंशतो नवभिरभ्यासे सैकपञ्चाशानि त्रीणि शतानि, द्वयोः पुनरेकादशानां गुणकारे जाता द्वाविंशतिरिति। एतावता सर्वांकेन का संख्या भवतीत्याह - **'सगससट्ठि'**-इत्यादि, सप्तषष्ट्यधिकानि चत्वारि शतानि कूटानां भवन्तीति गथार्थः ॥ १६ ॥

'caüsatta'-*iti - catuḥ-saptāṣṭa-navakaikādaśabhiḥ kūṭair yathā-saṃkhyaṃ yathā-kramaṃ yathopanyāsam iti yāvad*

---

[1] *yathā-saṃkhyam*: ind., number for number, so that in two series of an equal amount of numbers, the first number of the first series corresponds to the first of the second, etc.

guṇayata, guṇa-kāra-pravṛttān kuruta, he gaṇita-jñā iti gamyate. kān ity āha - ***'solasa'****-ity ādi - ṣoḍaśa dvau dvau ekona-catvāriṃśataṃ dvau ceti, tad yathā ṣoḍaśānāṃ caturbhir guṇane catuḥ-ṣaṣṭir, dvayos tu saptabhir guṇane catur-daśa, tathā dvayor evāṣṭabhir hanane ṣoḍaśa, ekona-catvāriṃśato navabhir abhyāse saika-pañcāśāni trīṇi śatāni, dvayoḥ punar ekādaśānāṃ guṇa-kāre jātā dvāviṃśatir iti. etāvatā sarvāṅkena kā saṃkhyā bhavatīty āha -* ***'sagasaṭṭhi'****-ity ādi, sapta-ṣaṣṭy-adhikāni catvāri śatāni kūṭānāṃ bhavantīti gathārthaḥ. 16.*

16. ***'caüsatta'*** [etc.]. This has to be understood in the following manner: "Ho, [you] knowing the science of computation, multiply in the relative order, number by number, in the order as they are put down, with four, seven, eight, nine and eleven peaks. Use the numbers of the first series[1] as multipliers. [The author] explains which original numbers: ***'solasa'***, etc.: sixteen, two, two, fifty-eight, and two. For, when [we] multiply sixteen with four [we have] sixty-four. When [we] multiply two with seven [we have] fourteen. Similarly, when [we] multiply two with eight [we have] sixteen. When [we] multiply thirty-nine with nine [we have] three hundred and fifty-one. When [we] again multiply two with eleven [we] obtain twenty-two. [The author] explains which sum [we obtain] with all these coefficients: ***'sagasaṭṭhi'***,

[1] *pravṛtta*: what has been set out [first]. Compare with *pravṛtti*: the original (first) quantity, T. Hayashi (1995), Glossary-Index p. 511.

etc. Therefore, the meaning of the verse is that there are four hundred and sixty-seven peaks.[1]

---

[1] Or:

mountains (*parvatas* and *giris*)			**peaks** (*kūṭas*)	
Vakṣāra	16	X	4	64
Saumanasa and Gandhamādana	2	X	7	14
Rukmin and Mahāhimavat	2	X	8	16
Vaitāḍhya (34) and Vidyutprabha Niṣadha Nīlavat Mālyavat Suragiri	39	X	9	351
Himavat & ũikharin	2	X	11	22
			total	467

SŪTRA 17

इदानीं गिरिशिरःस्थितानि कूटान्यभिधाय भूमिस्थकूटसंख्यानमाह –
idānīṃ giri-śiraḥ-sthitāni kūṭāny abhidhāya bhūmi-stha-kūṭa-saṃkhyānam āha -
Now, having explained the peaks located on top of the mountains, [the author] treats the number of peaks situated on ground level.

चउतीसं[1] विजएसुं[2], उसु[3]कूडा अट्ठ[4] मेरु[5]-जंबुंमि[6] ।
अट्ठ य देवकुराए[7], हरिकूड[8]हरिस्सहे[9] सट्ठी[10] ॥ १७ ॥[11]

---

[1] चउतीसुं Ed1 & 2, Tueb, Bhog8. चउतिसं Brd2 & 3, Bhog2. चउत्तिसं Bhog14.
चउतीस LD2, Bhog4, 10 & 17.
[2] विजयेसुं Ed1. विजयेसु Ed3, LD1, Bhog9, 14 & 17. विजयसु LD2, Bhog8(?) & 16. विजएसु Brd1, Bhog4, 7, 10, 13 & 15. विजएसूं Brd3. विजणसु Bhog2.
[3] उसह Ed2, Bhog14 & 15. उससह Ed3. ओसुलभ(?) LD1. उसुभ Brd2 & 3. उसू Bhog7 & 10. उस Bhog8.
[4] यट्ठ Bhog7. यअट्ठ Bhog15.
[5] मेरू Ed1, Brd1 & 2, Bhog1, 4, 7, 15, 16 & 17. डे(?)रू Bhog2.
[6] Ed2 & 3 have the variant जम्बुम्मि. जम्बूमि LD1, Brd1 & 3, Bhog4, 8, 9, 10, 15, 16 & 17. जम्बुमि Brd2, Bhog7, 13 & 14. जम्बूमि ८ LD2. जम्बूमी Bhog2. जम्बूंमि Bhog11.
[7] देवकुराण LD1, Bhog2. देवकुराणं Brd3. देवकुरुणं Brd3. कूराए Bhog1 & 13. कुराइं Bhog4. कूराइं Bhog14 & 15. कुराय Bhog10.
[8] हरिकूम Bhog2. हरीकूड Bhog4. हरिकूडा Bhog9, 10 & 13. हरिकुण्ड Bhog15. हरिकूण्ड Bhog17.
[9] हरीस्सए LD1, Brd2 & 3. हरिसहे Bhog1, Bhog4. हरिस्सह Bhog7. हरिस्सए Bhog9, 11 & 15. हरिसए Bhog10, 13 & 17.
[10] सट्ठी ६० Tueb. सट्ठि Bhog1, 2, 9, 10, 13 & 14.
[11] This verse is numbered 18 in LD2 & Bhog8, 16 in Bhog1 while it is missing in Bhog5, 6 & 12.

caütīsaṃ vijaesuṃ, usukūḍā aṭṭha meru-jaṃbuṃmi;
aṭṭha ẏa devakurāe*[1]*, harikūḍa-harissahe saṭṭhī. 17.

(चतुस्त्रिंशद् विजयेषु ऋषभकूटान्यष्टौ मेरौ जम्ब्वातं, अष्टौ च देवकुरुषु हरिकूटहरित्सहयोः षष्टिः ॥ १७ ॥ *catus-triṃśad vijayeṣu ṛṣabha-kūṭāny aṣṭau merau jambvāṃ; aṣṭau ca deva-kuruṣu harikūṭa-haritsahayoḥ ṣaṣṭiḥ. 17.*)

17. There are sixty [peaks situated on ground level]: thirty-four Ṛṣabha peaks in the provinces, eight near [Mount] Meru as well as near to the Jambū [tree], eight in Devakuru and [one] on both the Harikūṭa and Haritsaha [each].

COMMENTARY

'**चउतीसं**'-इति - ऋषभकुटानि प्रागुक्तस्थानानि विजयेषु जिनाद्युत्तम-पुरुषोत्पत्तिक्षेत्रेषु चतुस्त्रिंशद् भवन्ति। तथा मेरौ मन्दरगिरौ जम्ब्वामनाद्दृतदेवनिवासवृक्षे प्रत्येकमष्टावष्टौ, चः समुच्चये, देवकुराविति, तदाधेये शाल्मलिवृक्षे ऽष्टावष्टसंख्यानि तथाहि - मेरुकूटानि शीताशीतोदोभयकूलवर्त्तीनि दिग्गजनामानि, उत्तरकुरौ जम्बूवृक्ष-सत्क[सक्त?[2]]वनमध्ये प्राक् प्रपंचितान्यष्टौ कूटानि, एवमेव देवकुरौ शाल्मलिवनमध्ये ऽष्टावेव, हरिकूटहरिस्सहकूटे विद्युत्प्रभ-माल्यवतोर्वक्षस्कारयोरुपरिस्थिते, सामस्त्येन किं जातमित्याह - '**सट्ठी**'-इति षष्टिस्तिस्रो विंशतय इति गाथार्थः। इह यत् हरिकूटहरिस्सहौ भूमिस्थकूटानां मध्ये निबद्धौ तन्न घटते, तयोर्वक्षस्कारयोरुपरिभावात्, तदुक्तं -

---

[1] Devakurā f. = Devakuru m.

[2] Also LD2 has the enigmatic स्त्क. Maybe it is a wrong reading for सक्त: mfn. clinging or adhering to, sticking in (loc. or comp.), belonging to (gen.).

"**विज्जुप्पहेहरिकूडो हरिस्सहो मालवंतवक्खारे**"[1]
इति। तथैताद्दशाधिानं भूमिकूटमपरं जम्बूद्वीपमध्ये न दृश्यते, बृहत्क्षेत्रसमासाद्यनुसारतो, ये तु वक्षष्कारशिरःस्थे हरिकूटहरिस्सहकूटे, ते गिरिकूटप्रस्तावे सप्तषष्ट्यधिकचतुःशतकूटमध्ये पठिते, तत '**इय अडवन्नं धरणिकूटा**'-इति पाठो युक्तः। एतदर्थमाह, इत्युक्तप्रकारेण धरणिस्थानि कूटानि धरणिकूटान्यष्टापञ्चाशद् भवन्ति। तथा च यद्यपि भूमिस्थिताः शिलोच्चयः सर्वे ऽपि पर्वता भण्यन्ते, तथाप्येषां क्षेत्रसमासादिषु कूटानीति संज्ञा। इयं गाथा पुराणपुस्तकेषु न दृश्यते परमुपयोगिनीति कृत्वा व्याकृतेति। गतं पञ्चमं पर्वतद्वारं॥ १७॥

'***caütīsaṃ***'*-iti - ṛṣabha-kuṭāni prāg-ukta-sthānāni vijayeṣu jinādy-uttama-puruṣotpatti-kṣetreṣu catus-triṃśad bhavanti. tathā merau mandara-girau jambvām anādṛta-deva-nivāsa-vṛkṣe pratyekam aṣṭāv aṣṭau, caḥ samuccaye, deva-kurāv iti tad-ādheye śālmali-vṛkṣe 'ṣṭāv aṣṭa-saṃkhyāni, tathā hi - meru-kūṭāni śītā-śītodobhaya-kūla-vartīni diggaja-nāmāni, uttara-kurau jambū-vṛkṣa-satka[sakta?]-vana-madhye prāk prapañcitāny aṣṭau kūṭāni, evam eva deva-kurau śālmali-vana-madhye 'ṣṭāv eva, harikūṭa-harissahakūṭe vidyutprabha-mālyavator vakṣaskārayor uparisthite, sāmastyena kiṃ jātam ity āha - '**saṭṭhī**'-iti ṣaṣṭis tisro viṃśataya iti gāthārthaḥ. iha yat hari-kūṭa-harissahau bhūmi-stha-kūṭānāṃ madhye nibaddhau tan na ghaṭate, tayor vakṣaskārayor upari-bhāvāt, tad uktaṃ:*

"***vijjuppahe harikūḍo harissaho mālavanta-vakkhāre***"[1]

---

[1] बृहत्क्षेत्रसमास, verse 157 (*BKSJ*, p. 166), in full:
विज्झुप्पभि हरिकूडो, हरिस्सहो मालवंतवक्खरो।
नंदणवणबलकूडो, उव्विद्धो जोयणसहस्सं॥ १५६॥
(विद्युत्प्रभे हरिकूटं हरिस्सहं माल्यवंतवक्षस्कारे। नंदनवने बलकूटं उद्विद्धानि योजनसहस्रम्॥ १५६॥).

*iti. tathaitādṛśābhidhānaṃ bhūmi-kūṭam aparaṃ jambūdvīpa-madhye na dṛśyate, bṛhatkṣetrasamāsa-ādy-anusārataḥ, ye tu vakṣaskāra-śiraḥ-sthe hari-kūṭa-harissaha-kūṭe, te giri-kūṭa-prastāve sapta-ṣaṣṭy-adhika-catuḥ-śata-kūṭa-madhye paṭhite, tata "**iya aḍavannaṃ dharaṇi-kūṭā**[2]"-iti pāṭho yukta, etad artham āha, ity ukta-prakāreṇa dharaṇi-sthāni kūṭāni dharaṇi-kūṭāny aṣṭāpañcāśad bhavanti. tathā ca yady api bhūmi-sthitāḥ śiloccayaḥ sarve 'pi parvatā bhaṇyante, tathāpy eṣāṃ kṣetrasamāsādiṣu kūṭānīti saṃjñā. iyaṃ gāthā purāṇa-pustakeṣu na dṛśyate param upayoginīti kṛtvā vyākṛteti. gataṃ pañcamaṃ parvata-dvāraṃ. 17.*

17. '**caütīsaṃ**' [etc.]. In the provinces, the lands where eminent men like the Jina, etc. are born, there are thirty-four Ṛṣabha peaks, their condition described earlier[3]. Even so near Meru or Mount Mandara and near to the Jambū, the tree in which the god Anādṛta[4] dwells, there are eight [peaks] each. [The word] '*ca*'[is used] in conjunctive sense. In Devakuru, near the Śālmali tree[5] situated there, there are eight - the

---

[1] *BKSJ*, verse 156, p. 166, fully:
vijjhuppabhi harikūḍo, harissaho mālavanta-vakkharo;
nandaṇavaṇa-balakūḍo, uvviddho joyaṇa-sahassaṃ .156.
(vidyut-prabhe harikūṭaṃ harissahaṃ mālyavanta-vakṣaskāre; nandana-vane balakūṭam udviddhāni yojana-sahasram.156.).

[2] *ity aṣṭāpañcāśad dharaṇi-kūṭāni.*

[3] See p. 131.

[4] Anādṛta or Anādia in Pkt., lit. the 'disrespected', is a descendant of Garuḍa. See Kirfel, p. 235.

[5] Or Śālmalī, the Seemul or silk-cotton tree, Bombax Heptaphyllum or Salmalia Malabarica, a lofty and thorny tree with red flowers. This

number eight - [peaks]. More specific, the Meru peaks situated on both banks of the Śītā and the Śītodā are called the Diggajas[1]. In Uttarakuru, in the forest belonging to the Jambū tree there are eight peaks treated earlier[2]. In the same manner there are eight [peaks] in the forest of the Śālmali [tree] in Devakuru. The Hari peak and Harissaha[3] peak are located on the Vidyutprabha and Mālyavat Vakṣaskāra Mountains [respectively]. [Answering the question] how many there are in total, [the author answers]: '***saṭṭhī***', sixty or three times twenty. This is the meaning of the verse. As regards [the opinion] here that the Hari and the Harissaha peaks are located amid the peaks standing on ground level, this is not possible since both these Vakṣaskāra mountains are located higher. It is said:

> "*The Harikūṭa is [situated] on the Vidyutprabha, the Harissaha on the Mālavanta Vakṣaskāra mountains.*"[4]

Indeed, no other peak on ground level is found with such a name inside Jambūdvīpa. On the contrary, according to the *Bṛhatkṣetrasamāsa*, etc., the Hari and Harissaha peaks located

---

Śālmalī tree grows in the western half of Devakuru. Its surroundings are similar to those of the Jambū tree. It is the abode of the god Veṇu, like Anādṛta a descendant of Garuḍa. See Kirfel, ibid.

[1] Or the Dighastikūṭas (Pkt. Disāhatthikūḍas). They are named, turning from East to South: 1. Padmottara (Pkt. Paümuttara), 2. Nīla(vat) (Pkt. Nīlavanta), 3. Suhasti (Pkt. Suhatthi), 4. Añjana(giri), 5. Kumuda, 6. Palāśa (Pkt. Palāsa), 7. Vaḍaṃśa (Pkt. Vaḍi(ṃ)sa) and Rocana (Roaṇa). See Kirfel, p. 230.

[2] See p. 145.

[3] Skt. Harit.

[4] The second half verse of *BKSJ*, verse 156 completes with: "Balakūṭa is in Nandana forest. They are thousand *yojanas* high".

on top of the Vakṣaskāra Mountains are referred to as mountain peaks[1] [and] mentioned as [occurring] amid [a list] four hundred and sixty-seven peaks. So the reading: "Hence there are fifty-eight peaks on ground level", is correct. [Now the author] explains the meaning. In the manner explained there are fifty-eight ground-peaks, viz. peaks situated on ground level. Therefore,, even if all rock-accumulations situated on ground level are called mountains, even then these are considered to be 'peaks' in the *Kṣetrasamāsa*, etc. This verse is not found in the ancient books. Knowing that it is useful later, it is explained. The fifth topic of the mountains is finished [now].

---

[1] And not as Bhūmikūṭas or Dharaṇikūṭas, peaks on ground level.

SŪTRA 18

अधुना षष्ठं तीर्थसंख्याद्वारमाह -

adhunā ṣaṣṭhaṃ tīrtha-saṃkhyā-dvāram āha -

Now [the author] treats the sixth topic of the number of fortresses.

मागह[1]वरदाम[2]पभा,स[3]तित्थ[4] विजएसु[5] एरवय[6]भरहे ।
चउतीसा[7] तिहि[8] गुणिया[9], दुरुत्तर[10]सयं[11] तु[12] तित्थाणं[13] ॥ १८ ॥[14]

māgaha-varadāma-pabhā,sa-tittha vijaesu eravaẏa-bharahe;
caütīsā tihi guṇiẏā, du-r[1]-uttara-saẏaṃ tu titthāṇaṃ. 18.

---

[1] मागह १ Tueb, Bhog2, 5 & 12. मागेह Bhog17.

[2] वरदाम २ Tueb, Bhog2, 5 & 12. वरदांम Brd3, Bhog1, 7, 13, 16 & 17.

[3] पभास ३ Tueb, Bhog2 & 5. पभासं Brd1. पभासे Bhog13. य(?)भास Bhog15.

[4] तिथ Brd3. तीत्थ Bhog8.

[5] विजयेसु Ed2, Bhog6, 8, 9, 13, 14 & 16. विजएसू LD1, Bhog15. विजएसुं Brd2, Tueb. विजएसूं Brd3. विजयेसू Bhog7. विजयसू Bhog10. विजयएसु Bhog17.

[6] ऐरवय LD2, Bhog9. एसवय Bhog2. इरवय Bhog6. एरवए Bhog12.

[7] चउतिसा Brd2, Bhog2. चउत्तीसा Brd3. चउतीस Bhog7. चउतीस ३४ Bhog5. चोतीसा Bhog12.

[8] तीहिं Ed1 & 2, Tueb. तिहिं LD1, Brd1 & 2, Bhog1, 5, 6, 7, 12, 13, 14 & 16. तिहां Brd3. तिगुहि Bhog8. तिं(?)हिं(?) Bhog9.

[9] गुणीया Bhog1, 7, 9, 10, 13, 14, 15 & 16. गूंणिया LD1. गुणिआ LD2. गूणिया Bhog12.

[10] दुरूतर Brd2. दुरुतर Bhog2, 15 & 17. गुरुतरू Bhog6.

[11] सय LD1, Brd2 & 3, Bhog2 & 15. स omitted in Bhog8.

[12] तु १०२ Bhog5. तु omitted in Bhog6.

[13] तित्थाणं १०२ Tueb, Bhog8. तीत्थणं Bhog2. तीत्थाणं Bhog12.

[14] This verse is numbered 19 in LD2, Bhog6 & 8, 18 in Bhog1 and 17 in Bhog12. It is introduced with दार ५ in Bhog2, with दारं ५ in Bhog5, with द्वा ५ in Bhog12 and with द्वार ६ in Bhog15.

(मागधवरदामप्रभासतीर्थानि विजयेषु ऐरावतभरतयोः। चतुस्त्रिंशत् त्रिभिर्गुणिता द्युत्तरशतं तु तीर्थानाम्॥ १८॥ *māgadha-varadāma-prabhāsa-tīrthāni vijayeṣu airāvata-bharatayoḥ; catus-triṃśat tribhir guṇitā dvy-uttara-śataṃ tu tīrthānām. 18,*)

18. The fortresses Māgadha, Varadāma, and Prabhāsa [lie] in the provinces and in Airāvata and Bharata. This means that multiplied by three there are one hundred and two fortresses [in total].

COMMENTARY

मागह^इत्ति - मागधश्च वरदाम[-श्च]च प्रभासश्च मागधवरदामप्रभासास्त एव तीर्थानि मागधवरदामप्रभासतीर्थानि, प्राकृतशैल्या सूत्रे विभक्तिलोपः, तथा तीर्थशब्दः प्रत्येकं सम्बन्धनीयः, तेन - मागधतीर्थं १ वरदामतीर्थं २ प्रभासतीर्थं ३ चेति, क्व चैतानि सन्ति? इत्याह - विजया महाविदेहमध्यवर्त्तिनः खण्डविशेषाः, ते च सर्वसंख्यया द्वात्रिंशत् तेषु, तथा ऐरवतं च भरतं चेति समाहारद्वन्द्वः, तस्मिन्नैरवतभरते, श्रोतारमनुलक्ष्य चरमे प्रथमे च क्षेत्रे सन्तीति शेषः। उत्तरार्द्धेन सर्वसंख्यानयनाय करणमाह - चउतीसा^इत्यादि, तीर्थानां सर्वाग्रे द्वाभ्यामुत्तरमधिकं शतं दश दशकलक्षणं द्युत्तरशतं, तुः पादपूरणे भवतीत्यध्याह्रियते। कथमित्याह - चतुर्भिरधिका त्रिंशत् त्रिभिर्गुणिता गुणकारविषयीकृता स[न्]तीति गाथार्थः॥ १८॥

'Māgaha'*^iti - māgadhaś ca varadāma[ś] ca prabhāsaś ca māgadha-varadāma-prabhāsās ta eva tīrthāni māgadha-varadāma-prabhāsa-tīrthāni, prākṛta-śailyā sūtre vibhakti-*

---

[1] *du-* appears frequently for *do-* in compounds (See Pischel, 1900, §436); *-r-* is a sandhi consonant here.

lopaḥ, tathā 'tīrtha'-śabdaḥ pratyekaṃ sambandhanīyaḥ, tena: māgadha-tīrthaṃ 1 varadāma-tīrthaṃ 2 prabhāsa-tīrthaṃ 3 ceti, kva caitāni santi? ity āha - vijayā mahāvideha-madhya-vartinaḥ khaṇḍa-viśeṣāḥ, te ca sarva-saṃkhyayā dvātriṃśat teṣu, tathā 'airavataṃ' ca 'bharataṃ' ceti samāhāra-dvandvaḥ, tasminn airavata-bharate, śrotāram anulakṣya carame prathame ca kṣetre santīti śeṣaḥ. uttarārdhena sarva-saṃkhyānayanāya karaṇam āha - ***caütīsā^*** *ity ādi, tīrthānāṃ sarvāgre dvābhyām uttaram adhikaṃ śataṃ daśa-daśaka-lakṣaṇaṃ dvy-uttara-śataṃ, tuḥ pāda-pūraṇe bhavatīty adhyāhriyate. katham ity āha - caturbhir adhikā triṃśat, tribhir guṇitā guṇa-kāra-viṣayī-kṛtā sa[n]tīti gāthārthaḥ. 18.*

18. '**Māgaha**' [etc.]. [The proper names] 'Māgadha', 'Vara-dāma', and 'Prabhāsa' [together constitute the compound] 'Māgadha-Varadāma-Prabhāsa'. These are the fortresses, [or in compound] the 'Māgadha-Varadāma-Prabhāsa-fortresses'. As is typical for Prākrit there is loss of declension in the aphorism for the word 'fortress' applies to [to all three particular cases] separately, viz. 1. Māgadha fort, 2. Varadāma fort, and 3. Prabhāsa fort. [The author] explains where they are [located]. The provinces are the distinct districts lying in Mahāvideha and they number thirty-two in total. In these [provinces these fortresses lie]. 'Airavata' and 'Bharata' [both together constitute] a Dvandva compound: in this, viz. in Airavata and Bharata. On behalf of the audience we add this: there are [fortresses] in the last as well as in the first area.[1] In

---

[1] Bharata has three fortresses at the coast: Māgadhatīrtha (Pkt. Magahatittha) in the east at the mouth of the Gaṅgā, Prabhāsatīrtha (Pkt. Pabhāsatittha) in the west at the mouth of the Sindhu and

the later half [of the verse the author] explains the way to calculate the total number: ‘***caütīsa***’, etc. Overall there are one hundred, viz. ten times ten and two or, one hundred plus two fortresses. [The word] ‘*tu* (however)’ is an expletive[1]. This is what is supplied. [The author] explains how: thirty plus four, multiplied with three, being turned into the multiplier. This is the meaning [of verse eighteen].

Varadāmatīrtha (Pkt. Varadāmatittha) in between. See Kirfel, p. 227. The position and the names of these three fortresses are identical in Airāvata and in the thirty-two Vijayas, which are, in fact, copies of Bharata and Airāvata.

[1] In this case used to the fill out the line or the measure of the verse and translated here as "This means that ...".

SŪTRA 19

अथ सप्तमं श्रेणिद्वारमाचिख्यासुराह -
atha saptamaṃ śreṇi-dvāram ācikhyāsur āha -
Next, wishing to inform [the audience] on the seventh topic of the rows [of palaces, the author] says:

विज्जाहर[1]अभिओगिय[2], सेढीओ[3] दुन्नि[4] दुन्नि[5] वेयड्ढे[6] ।
इय[7] चउगुण[8] चउ[9]तीसा[10], छत्तीस[11]सयं[12] तु[13] सेढीणं[14] ॥ १९ ॥[1]

---

[1] विद्याहर LD1, Brd1, Bhog2, 6, 7, 9, 10, 14, 15, 16 & 17. विजाहर Brd2, Bhog12. विज्जाहर १ Bhog5. र omitted in Bhog11.

[2] अभियोगिय Ed3. अभिओगिअ LD2, Brd1. अभिउगीयं Brd2. अभिउगीय Brd3 & 15. अभिउगिअ Tueb, Bhog10 & Bhog14. अभिउगिय Bhog6 & 17. अभिओगीय Bhog1 & 4. अभिओगिय २ Bhog5 & 12. Bhog8 has अगी१य omitting भिओ. अभिओगिओअ Bhog9.

[3] सेढीउ Brd2 & 3, Bhog17. सेढिओ Bhog2, 7 & 10. सेड्ढीओ Bhog9 & 14. से(?)ढे २ Bhog12. सेंढीउ Bhog15.

[4] दुनि LD1, Bhog10 & 17. दुण्णि Bhog5. दुणि Bhog12. दुन्नि २ meaning दुन्नि written twice. The same for दुन्नी २ in Bhog14.

[5] दुनि Bhog2. दुनि or दुति in Bhog9. दुणि Bhog12.

[6] वेअड्ढे LD2, Bhog15. वयड्ढे Brd2. वियड्ढे Bhog1, 9, 10 & 13. वयढे Brd3. यवेढे Bhog6.

[7] ईय Brd3, Bhog11. इइ Tueb, Bhog2 & 4. इअ Bhog7.

[8] गूंण LD1.

[9] चऊ LD1. ची and उ are missing in Bhog17.

[10] साती LD1. गुणसा in Tueb and गुण without सा In Bhog2. तिसा Bhog10. त्तीसा Bhog12 & 15. तीसा is missing in Bhog17.

[11] छतीस Brd2 & 3, Bhog6. छत्तिस Bhog2, Bhog10.

[12] मयं Bhog12. सय Bhog15.

[13] तुं Brd1, 2 & 3. च Bhog6.

[14] सेढीणं १३६ Tueb. सेढिणं १३७(?) Bhog2. सेढीओ Bhog5. सेढीणं १३९(?) Bhog8. सढिणं Bhog10. सेड्ढीणं Bhog14.

vijjāhara-abhiogiẏa, seḍhīo dunni dunni veẏaḍḍhe;
iẏa caü-guṇa caütīsā, chattīsa-saẏaṃ tu seḍhīṇaṃ. 19.

(विद्याधराभियोग्यश्रेण्यौ द्वे द्वे वैताढ्ये। इति चतुर्गुणचतुस्त्रिंशत् षट्त्रिंशदुत्तरशतं तु श्रेणीनाम्॥ १९॥ *vidyādharābhiyogya-śreṇyau dve dve vaitāḍhye; iti catur-guṇa-catustriṃśat ṣaṭtriṃśad(-uttara)-śataṃ tu śreṇīnām. 19.*)

19. On every Vaitāḍhya [mountain range], there are two rows [of palaces] of the Vidyādhara and Ābhiyogya [deities], viz. four times thirty-four [make up] one hundred and thirty-six rows.

COMMENTARY

विज्जहार^इत्ति - विद्याधराः खेचरा, अभियोगः पारवश्यं, तत्र नियुक्ता आभियौगिकास्ते चेह संप्रदायात् सौधर्मेशानयोर्देवलोकयोः प्रेष्यप्रायाः सुरा ज्ञेयास्तेषां श्रेणयः प्रागुक्तस्वरूपाः वैताढ्ये विजयाढ्यपर्वते एकैकस्मिन्निति गम्यते, द्वे द्वे प्रत्येकं ज्ञातव्य इति शेषः, तथाहि - एकैकस्मिन् वैताढ्य एकस्यामेकस्यां दिशि एकैका विद्याधरश्रेणिः, एकैका चाभियौगिकदेवनिवासश्रेणिः समुदिता, पार्श्वद्वये ऽपि चतस्रश्चतस्रो भवन्ति। अपरार्द्धेन संख्यानयनाय करणमाह - 'इत्येत्यादि' इत्यनेन प्रकारेण चतुस्त्रिंशत् चतुर्गुणा चतुर्भिर्गुणिता किं भवति? इत्याह - श्रेणीनां षट्त्रिंशदधिकं शतं भवति। गतं श्रेणिद्वारं॥ १९॥

vijjahāra^iti - vidyādharāḥ khecarāḥ, abhiyogaḥ pāravaśyaṃ, tatra niyuktā Ābhiyaugikās te ceha sampradāyāt saudharma-

[1] In LD2 and Bhog8 this verse is numbered 20, 17 in Bhog6 and 18 in Bhog12. Bhog2 introduces this verse with दार ६, Bhog5 with दारं ६, Bhog12 with द्वा ६ and Bhog15 with द्वार ७.

Īśānayor deva-lokayoḥ preṣya-prāyāḥ surā jñeyāḥ teṣāṃ śreṇayaḥ prāg-ukta-svarūpāḥ vaitāḍhye vijayāḍhya-parvate ekaikasminn iti gamyate, dve dve pratyekaṃ jñātavya iti śeṣaḥ. tathā hi: ekaikasmin vaitāḍhya ekasyām ekasyāṃ diśi ekaikā vidyādhara-śreṇiḥ, ekaikā cābhiyaugika-deva-nivāsa-śreṇiḥ samuditā, pārśva-dvaye 'pi catasraś catasro bhavanti. aparārdhena saṃkhyānayanāya karaṇam āha - **iya**^*ity ādi ity anena prakāreṇa catus-triṃśat catur-guṇā caturbhir guṇitā kiṃ bhavati? ity āha - śreṇīnāṃ ṣaṭ-triṃśad-adhikaṃ śataṃ bhavati. gataṃ śreṇi-dvāraṃ. 19.*

19. '**Vijjahāra**' [etc.]. The Vidyādharas[1] are aerial beings. '*Abhiyoga* (charge)[2]' means '*pāravaśya* (service)[3]'. Those employed in that are retainers. According to traditional belief they are known as deities destined to serve the Saudharma and Īśāna gods in their heavenly abodes. The rows of these [are meant]. Their nature has been described earlier.[4] [They dwell] on every Vaitāḍhya or Vijayāḍhya mountain range. This is what is meant [in the first half of the verse]. To this [we] add that this has to be conceived as two [rows] for each [category of gods] separately. For, on every Vaitāḍhya mountain range on every side[5] there is declared to exist one single Vidyādhara row and one single row where the Ābhiyaugika gods live. [So]

---

[1] *vidyādhara*, lit. 'possessed of science or spells'. See Deleu, 1976, p. 279.

[2] Derived from the root *abhi-yuj.*, 'to order, to charge'.

[3] *pāravaśya*, lit. 'the being in the power of others, dependence'.

[4] See p. 145.

[5] '*diś*' must be interpreted as '*pārśva*' here.

on the two sides there are assembled four [rows] in each case.[1] In the second half [verse the author] explains how to make the calculation: '*iẏa*' [viz.] *iti*, etc.: thirty-four, four times or multiplied with four. What [do we get] in this manner? [The author] answers: there are one hundred and thirty-six rows [of palaces]. [Now] the topic of the rows is dealt with.

---

[1] There are thirty-four Vaitāḍhya mountain ranges: one in Bharata, one in Airāvata and thirty-two in Videha. On the first platform on the two sides the Vidyādharas live. On the second platform also on both sides the Ābhiyogya gods dwell.

SŪTRA 20

अधुना गाथार्द्धेनाष्टं विजयद्वारमाह -
adhunā gāthārdhenāṣṭaṃ vijaya-dvāram āha -
Now, in the [first] half of the [next] verse [the author] treats the eighth topic of the provinces.

चक्की[1]जेयव्वाइं[2], विजयाइं[3] इत्थ[4] हुंति[5] चउतीसं[6] ।[7]
cakkī-jeẏavvāiṃ, vijaẏāiṃ ittha huṃti caütīsaṃ;

(चक्रिजेतव्या विजया अत्र भवन्ति चतुस्त्रिंशत्। *cakri-jetavyā vijayā atra bhavanti catustriṃśat;*)

20a. Here there are thirty-four provinces, [lit.] 'to be conquered by a world ruler[8]'.

---

[1] चकी Bhog2.
[2] जेअव्वाइं Ed2, LD2, Tueb, Bhog1, 9, 10, 13, 14 & 15. जयव्वइं LD1. जेयाव्वा(?)इं Brd2. जेयव्वा(?)इं Brd3. जेयवाइ Bhog2. जेयव्वायं Bhog4. जोय and व्वाइं are missing in Bhog6. जेयवाइ Bhog12. जियव्वाइं Bhog17.
[3] विजयाइ Brd2, Brd3, Bhog10 & 12. विजया Bhog1. विज्जया Bhog6.
[4] LD1 omits इ. ईत्थ Brd3. इय Bhog13.
[5] हुति Brd2. हुति इत्थ Bhog2. होइ Bhog5. होतिति Bhog6. हूंति Bhog7. होई Bhog12. हुंत्ति Bhog17.
[6] चउतीसा Ed1 & 3, Bhog14 & 15. चओतीसं LD1. चउतिसं Brd2, Bhog7. चउतीसं ३४ Tueb, Bhog5. चउतिसं ३४ Bhog2. चओत्तीसं ३४ Bhog4. चउत्तिसा Bhog6. चउतीसुं ३४ Bhog8. चउतीस Bhog10.
[7] Bhog5 opens this verse with दारं ७, Bhog12 with द्वा ७, Bhog15 simply with द्वार.
[8] Or, in a more restricted sense 'to be conquered by a governor of a province'.

COMMENTARY

चक्की^इत्ति - इत्थ^इत्यत्र जम्बूद्वीपे ऽस्मिन् प्रकरेण वा विजयाश्चतुस्त्रिंशद् भवन्ति। किंविशिष्टाः? इत्याह - चक्की^इत्यादि, चक्रं सहस्रयक्षाधिष्ठितः प्रहरणविशेषः, तदस्त्यस्येति चक्री सार्वभौमो, यः षट्खण्डां भुवं भुनक्तीत्यर्थः, तेन जेतव्या वशमानेतव्या इति। तथा चतुस्त्रिंशदिति वदता सूत्रकारेण भरतैरवते क्षेत्रे ऽपि विजयत्वेनारोपित, उत्तमपुरुषनिषेवितत्वात्, न चैतदनागमिकं[1], यदुक्तं समवायाङ्गे -

"जंबूद्दीवे णं दीवे चउतीसं चक्कवट्टिविजया पन्नत्ता, तं जहा बत्तीसं महाविदेहे भरहेरवई"[2]

इति। इह सूत्रे सविशेषणस्य विजयशब्दस्य नपुंसकत्वं प्राकृतत्वान्न दोषायेति ॥ २० ॥

cakkī^*iti* - ***ittha^****ity atra jambūdvīpe 'smin prakareṇa vā vijayāś catustriṃśad bhavanti. kiṃ viśiṣṭāḥ? ity āha -* ***cakkī'^****ity ādi, cakraṃ sahasra-yakṣādhiṣṭhitaḥ praharaṇa-viśeṣaḥ, tad asty asyeti cakrī sārva-bhaumo, yaḥ ṣaṭ-khaṇḍāṃ bhuvaṃ bhunaktīty arthaḥ, tena jetavyā vaśamānetavyā iti. tathā catustriṃśad iti vadatā sūtra-kāreṇa bharata^airavate kṣetre 'pi vijayatvenāropita, uttama-puruṣa-niṣevitatvāt, na caitad anāgamikaṃ, yad uktaṃ samavāyāṅge -*

---

[1] Ed1 reads: न चैतदागमिकं. This would change the meaning fundamentally.

[2] This the first sentence of *sū.* 73 of the *Samavāyāṅgasūtra*, Jaina-Śāstroddhāra-Samiti ed. (with Skt. commentary by Pūjyaśrī Ghāsīlālјī and with Hindī and Gujaratī translation), Rajkot, 1973, p. 698. The ed. reads "**... *mahāvidehe, do bharahe Eravae***". Chāyā: जम्बूद्वीप ननु द्वीपे चतुस्त्रिंशत् चक्रवर्तिविजयाः प्रज्ञप्ताः, तद्यथा - द्वात्रिंशद् महाविदेहे भरत एरवते च.

***"jaṃbūddīve ṇaṃ dīve caüttīsaṃ cakka-vaṭṭi-vijayā pannattā, taṃ jahā - battīsaṃ mahāvidehe bharah'-eravaī"*[1].

iti. iha sūtre sa-viśeṣaṇasya vijaya-śabdasya na-puṃsakatvaṃ prākṛtatvān na doṣāyeti.

20a.'***cakkī***' [etc.]. '***ittha***' means 'here', viz. [here] in Jambūdvīpa or [here] in this case, there are thirty-four provinces. As to the question, how they are characterised [the author] says: '***cakkī***', etc. A '*cakra* (discus)' is a particular kind of weapon having the force of a thousand Yakṣas[2]. Who possesses this, is a sovereign ruling over the whole earth[3]. He governs the world with its six parts[4]. So far the meaning. [So the literal meaning of '*vijaya*' is as follows:] be conquered or to be overpowered by him. The author or the writer of the manual says [that there are] thirty-four [in number] because also Bharata and Airāvata are regions considered as provinces since they are ruled by excellent men. Moreover, this is not contrary to [what] the Canon [says]. In the *Samavāyāṅga,* it is stated:

---

[1] *Samavāyāṅga*, 73: *jambūdvīpa khalu dvīpe caturtriṃśat cakra-varti-vijayāḥ prajñaptāḥ, tad yathā - dvātriṃśad mahāvidehe bharata Eravate ca.*

[2] With the Jainas, a subdivision of the Vyantara gods.

[3] A *cakrin*, lit. a 'discus bearer', is a sovereign of the world, a king and the governor of a province. It is clear that *bhūmi* and *bhū* are used here in the sense of *vijaya*, viz. Bharata, Airāvata and the thirty-two provinces of Mahāvideha.

[4] Viz. the six Khaṇḍas or districts of every Vijaya or province.

"*On the isle of Jambūdvīpa thirty-four sovereign domains*[1] *are recognized, viz. thirty-two in Mahāvideha and [in addition two] in Bharata and Airāvata*".

The neuter gender of the particular word '*vijaya* (dominium)' in the manual here is not faulty since this is Prākrit.

अथ नवमं ह्रदद्वारं गाथापाश्चात्यार्द्धेनाह -
atha navamaṃ hrada-dvāraṃ gāthā-pāścātyārdhenāha -
Next, in the last half of the verse [the author] treats the ninth topic of the lakes.

महद्दह[2] छप्पउमाई[3], कुरूसु[4] दसगं[5] ति सोलसगं[6] ॥ २० ॥[7]
mahadaha chap paümāī, kurusu dasagaṃ ti solasagaṃ. 20.

---

[1] Lit. 'dominions of world sovereigns'.

[2] ह is missing in Brd1. मंहद्दह Bhog5, Bhog12. महाह(?)ह Bhog6.

[3] छ for छप- in LD1, Brd2 & 3, Bhog5 & 7. छप- is missing in Bhog6. च्छप- Bhog12. पओमाइं LD1. पउमाइ Ed3, LD2, Brd2 & 3, Bhog7 & 15. पओमाइ Bhog1. पउमाई ३ Bhog2. पउमाइं Bhog4, 5, 8, 13, 16 & 17. उ is missing in Bhog9. पउंमाइं Bhog10.

[4] LD2, Brd2, Bhog5, 11 & 17 have कुरूसु that, contrary to कुरुसु, would be metrically correct. कुरुसुं of Bhog12 is metrically possible. The other sources have कुरुसु.

[5] दसग LD1, Bhog12. दसगं १० Bhog2. दशगं Bhog4, 6, 9 & 14. दसंगं Bhog13.

[6] सालसगं Ed3. सोलसगं १६ Tueb, Bhog5 & 8. सोलसग १६ Bhog2. शोलसगं Bhog11. सोल्लसगं Bhog12.

[7] In LD2 this verse is numbered 21, 18 in Bhog6 and 19 in Bhog12. Bhog2 introduces the second half of the verse with दारं ८, Bhog5 with दारं ८, Bhog7 & 16 with द्वार ८, Bhog12 with द्वा ८.

(महाद्रहाः षड् पद्मादयः कुरुषु दशकमिति षोडशकम् ॥ *mahā-drahāḥ*[1] *ṣaḍ padmādayaḥ kuruṣu daśakam iti ṣoḍaśakam. 20.*)

20b. There are six great lakes, Padma, etc. There are ten [lakes] in the Kuru regions. Therefore, there are sixteen [all together].

COMMENTARY

महद्दह^इति - पद्मो हिमवद्गिरिशिरःस्थ आदिर्येषां ते पद्मादयश्, **छेति** षट्संख्याका, आदिग्रहणान्महापद्मतिगिंछिकेसरिमहापुण्डरीकपुण्डरीकाणां ग्रहः। क एते? इत्याह - **महद्दह^इति** महान्त इतरह्रदापेक्षया गुरुका ह्रदा नदा महाह्रदाः, तथा कुरवो देवकुरव उत्तरकुरवश्च तेषु दशसंख्यामानमेषां दशकं ह्रदानामिति गम्यते, पञ्च ह्रद देवकुरुषु, पञ्चोत्तरकुरुषु चेत्यर्थः। अथ सर्वाग्रमाह, मासः प्राग्वत्, षोडशकमिति मिलिताः सर्वे ऽपि षोडश इह भवन्तीति ॥ २० ॥

maha-daha^*iti - padmo himavad-giri-śiraḥ-stha*[2] *ādir yeṣāṃ te padmādayaś,* ***cha***^*iti ṣaṭ-saṃkhyākā, ādi-grahaṇān mahāpadma-tigiñchi-kesari-mahāpuṇḍarīka-puṇḍarīkāṇāṃ grahaḥ. ka ete? ity āha -* ***maha-daha***^*iti mahānta itara-hradāpekṣayā gurukā hradā nadā mahā-hradāḥ, tathā kuravo deva-kurava uttara-kuravaś ca teṣu daśa-saṃkhyā-mānaṃ, eṣāṃ daśakaṃ hradānām iti gamyate, pañca hrada deva-kuruṣu, pañcottara-kuruṣu cety arthaḥ. atha sarvāgram āha, samāsaḥ prāg-vat, ṣoḍaśakam iti militāḥ sarve 'pi ṣoḍaśa iha bhavantīti. 20.*

---

[1] *draha = hrada.*

[2] Ed1: -स्तं.

20. ***'maha-daha'*** [etc.]. 'Padma, etc.' means: those [lakes] of which Padma, located on top of the Himavat Mountains, is the first [in the series]. The word ***'cha'*** means six in number. [The word] '*ādi* (etc.)' comprises Mahāpadma, Tigiñchi, Kesari, Mahāpuṇḍarīka and Puṇḍarīka.[1] As to the question what they are [the author] answers: [they are] ***'maha-daha'***. This means the following. The great lakes are mighty bodies of water, much larger than other lakes. Moreover, the Kuru regions, viz. Devakuru and Uttarakuru, the [great lakes] of these [regions] are ten in number. That is to say, they have a decade of lakes: five lakes in Devakuru and five in Uttarakuru. So far the meaning. Now [the author] expresses the conclusion with one pithy word [viz. ***'solasagaṃ'***]. The composition [of this word] is as [explained] before.[2] There are, overall, sixteen [great lakes] here or, expressed in one word: one sixteen-in-number.

---

[1] In Kirfel, p. 220: Padma, Mahāpadma, Ti(ṅ)giccha, Keśarin, Mahāpuṇḍarīka and Puṇḍarīka.

[2] Viz. as it was the case with *daśakaṃ*, '*daśa*' means ten or, in other words, a *daśaka* is a decade. So, if '*ṣoḍaśa*' means sixteen, a *ṣoḍaśaka* means something like a 'sixteen-in-number'.

SŪTRA 21

इदानीं दशमं नदीद्वारमाह -
idānīṃ daśamaṃ nadī-dvāram āha -
Now [the author] treats the tenth topic of the rivers.

गङ्गा[1] सिंधू[2] रत्ता[3], रत्त[4] वई[5] चउ[6] नईउ[7] पत्तेयं[8] ।[9]
चउदसहि[10] सहस्सेहिं[11], समगं[12] वच्चंति[13] जलहिंमि[1] ॥ २१ ॥[2]

---

[1] गंगां Brd2. गंगा १ Bhog2 & 5.
[2] सिन्धु Ed3. सिन्धु Brd3, Bhog1, 7, 9, 10, 12, 16 & 17. सिन्धू २ Bhog2 & 5. सिधु Bhog14.
[3] रता ,Brd2 & 3. रता ३ Bhog2. रत्ता ३ Bhog5.
[4] रत Brd2 & 3, Bhog17. रक्त Bhog2. स(?)त्त Bhog7. रत्ता Bhog13.
[5] वइ LD2, Brd2 & 3, Bhog1, 7, 8, 10, 15 & 16. वई ४ Bhog2, 5 & 12.
[6] चओ LD1, Bhog4(?). चऊ Bhog10.
[7] नइओ Ed1, Bhog1, 7, 10, 13 & 16. नईओ of Ed2 & 3, LD1 & 2, Brd1, Bhog2, 6, 9, 11 & 14 is metrically possible if ओ is pronounced short. नइउ Brd2 & 3, Bhog15 & 17. नद्दी Bhog4. नईय Bhog5. नउ Bhog8. नइय Bhog12.
[8] पतेयं Brd3.
[9] Bhog2 & 5 introduce this verse with दारं ९, Bhog7 & 16 with द्वार ९, Bhog12 with द्वा ९, Bhog15 simply with द्वार.
[10] चउदसहिं Ed1, 2 & 3, LD1 & 2, Brd1 & 2, Tueb, Bhog5, 7, 8, 11 & 16. चओदशहिं Bhog4. चउदशहिं Bhog6. चउदसेहिं Bhog9. चउदसई Bhog10. च उदहन(?)इ Bhog14. However, the ending -ईं is metrically impossible.
[11] सहस्सेहिं १४००० Tueb. संहस्सेहि १४००० Bhog2. सहसिहे Bhog10. सहस्सेहि Bhog14 & 17.
[12] समग्गं Bhog1 & 12. समगां Bhog5. समगा Bhog6 & 17. समग Bhog9 & 10.
[13] वचंति Bhog2 & 5.

gaṃgā-siṃdhū-rattā,-rattavaī caü naīu patteẏaṃ;
caüdasahi sahassehiṃ, samagaṃ vaccaṃti jalahiṃmi. 21.

(गङ्गासिन्धुरक्तारक्तवती चतस्रो नद्यः प्रत्येकतं, चतुर्दशभिः सहस्रैः समकं व्रजन्ति जलधौ ॥ २१ ॥ *gaṅgā-sindhu-raktā-raktavatī catasro nadyaḥ pratyekam; catur-daśabhiḥ sahasraiḥ samakaṃ vrajanti jaladhau. 21.*)

21. The four rivers, the Gaṅgā, the Sindhu, the Raktā and the Raktavatī flow into the ocean each joined by fourteen thousand tributaries.

COMMENTARY

गङ्गा^इति - गङ्गासिन्धुरक्तारक्तवत्यः प्रागुक्तस्वरूपाश्चतुःसंख्याका नद्यः सरितः प्रत्येकं पृथक् पृथक् चतुर्दशभिश्चतुर्दशभिर्नदीसहस्रैः सममेव समकं सार्द्धं जलधिं व्रजन्ति गच्छन्ति प्रविशन्तीति यावत् ॥ २१ ॥

gaṃgā^itti - *gaṅgā-sindhu-raktā-raktavatyaḥ prāg-ukta-svarūpā[ś] catuḥ-saṃkhyākā nadyaḥ saritaḥ pratyekaṃ pṛthak pṛthak catur-daśabhiś catur-daśabhir nadī-sahasraiḥ samam eva samakaṃ sārdhaṃ jaladhiṃ vrajanti gacchanti praviśantīti yāvat. 21.*

---

[1] जलहिम्मि Ed3. जलहिंसिं LD1. जलहिमं Brd2 & 3. जलहिमि Bhog2, Bhog10, 13 & 14. जलहंमी Bhog4. जलहिंमी Bhog7 & 16. जलहिंमि १४००० Bhog8. जलहिमिं Bhog9. जलहिमे Bhog14. जलहमि Bhog17.

[2] In LD2 and Bhog8 this verse is numbered 22, 20 in Bhog6 & 12.

21. '***gaṃgā***' [etc.]. The rivers or streams, whose nature has been described earlier[1], are four in number: the Gaṅgā, the Sindhu, the Raktā, and the Raktavatī[2]. Each of them, one by one, goes to or proceeds towards or enters into the ocean along with or together with or joined by fourteen thousand tributaries. This is the explanation.

---

[1] See the commentary on *sū.* 11 & 12.

[2] There seems to be some confusion here. The river Raktā (Pkt. Rattā) flows eastwards through Airāvata. 'Raktavatī', however, is the name of a mountain peak (*kūṭa*) on the Śikharin mountain range. The other river crossing Airāvata in western direction is the Raktodā (Pkt. Rattoā). Significant for the confusion here is that the *Jambūdvīpasamāsa* calls the peak elsewhere referred to as the Raktavatī, the 'Raktodā'. See Kirfel, p. 218.

SŪTRA 22

एवं[1] अब्भिंतरिया[2], चउरो[3] पुण[4] अट्ठ[5]वीस[6]सहसेहिं[7],
पुणरवि[8] छप्पन्नेहिं[9], सहसेहिं[10] जंति[11] चउ[12] सलिला[13] ॥ २२ ॥[14]
evaṃ abbhiṃtariyā, caüro puṇa aṭṭhavīsa-sahasehiṃ;

---

[1] ए omitted in Bhog2. एव Bhog10 & 15.

[2] अब्भंतरगा Ed1. अब्भिंतरय LD1. अब्भिंतरिआ LD2, Bhog15. अब्भीतरिया Brd2. अब्भितरिया Brd3, Bhog10. अब्भिंतरया Tueb. अभितंरिया Bhog2. अब्भं(?)तरिया Bhog4. अब्भिंतरीया Bhog11, 17. अभिंत्तरिया Bhog12. The form अब्भंतरिया is not impossible, but while अब्भंतर and अब्भिंतरिय are both attested Pkt. forms, अब्भंतरिय is not.

[3] चओरो Bhog4.

[4] पुण ४ Bhog2. पण Bhog4. पुण omitted in Bhog5 & 12. ग is missing in Bhog8. पूण Bhog15.

[5] अठ Bhog5. अड Bhog12.

[6] विस Brd2, Bhog2 & 4. वीसई Bhog5. वीसइ Bhog12.

[7] सहस्सेहिं Ed2 & 3, LD2, Brd3, Bhog1, 4, 5, 7, 11, 13, 14, 15 & 16. सहेसेहिं Brd2. सहसेहिं २८००० Tueb. सहस्सेहि २८००० Bhog2. स(?)हस्सेहिं Bhog6. सहस्सेहिं २८००० Bhog8. सहस्सेंहिं LD1, Bhog9. सहसेहि Bhog10. सहस्सेहि Bhog12 & 17.

[8] पूणरवि LD1. पुणरवी Bhog2 & 7.

[9] छपनेहिं Brd2. छपन्नेहिं Brd3. छप्पण्णेहिं ५६००० Tueb. छप्पन्नेहि Bhog2, 11, 16 & 17. छप्पण्णेहिं Bhog12.

[10] सहस्सेहिं Ed1, 2 & 3, LD2, Brd3, Bhog1, 5, 6, 7, 12, 13, 15, 16 & 17. सहस्सेंहिं LD1, Bhog9. सहसेंहि Brd2. सहस्सेहि Bhog2 & 11. सहस्सेहे Bhog10. सहसेहि Bhog14. Only Brd1, Tueb, Bhog4 & 8 have the metrically correct सहसेहिं.

[11] जति LD1. जंति ५६००० Bhog2. जंती Bhog14.

[12] चओ LD1.

[13] सलिला ४ Bhog2. सलीला Bhog6. सलिला ५६००० Bhog8. सलिलां Bhog13. सलिलाउ Bhog15.

[14] In LD2 and Bhog8 this verse is numbered 23, 21 in Bhog6 & 12.

puṇar avi chappannehiṃ, sahasehiṃ jaṃti caü salilā. 22.

(एवमाभ्यन्तरिकाश्चतस्रः पुनरष्टाविंशतिसहस्रैः। पुनरपि षट्पञ्चाशता सहस्रैर्यान्ति चतस्रः सलिलाः॥ २२॥ *evam ābhyantarikāś catasraḥ punar aṣṭā-viṃśati-sahasraiḥ; punar api ṣaṭ-pañcā-śatā-sahasrair yānti catasraḥ salilāḥ. 22.*)

22. So also the four intermediate [rivers] flow, again together with twenty-eight thousand [tributaries]. In addition, the four rivers run [towards the ocean] together with fifty-six thousand tributaries.

COMMENTARY

एवं अब्भिंतरया^इति[1] - एवमिति एवमित्यनेन प्रकारेण यथा एता गङ्गाद्या एकप्रमाणाश्चतस्रो जलधिं प्रविशन्ति, तथा अभ्यन्तरं गच्छन्तीत्यभ्यन्तरगा, मध्यवर्त्तिन्यश्चतस्रो नद्यो रोहितांशारोहितारूप्यकूलासुवर्णकूलालक्षणाः, पुनर्विशेषणे, किं विशिनष्टि? तदाह - प्रत्येकमष्टाविंशत्या नदीसहस्रैः समन्विता जलधिं प्रविशन्तीति प्राच्यगाथासम्बन्धो ऽध्याहार्यः। तत्र रोहितांशारोहिते हैमवतक्षेत्रं रूप्यकूलासुवर्णकूले हैरण्यवतं च मध्येकृत्य प्रवहन्ति। तन्मध्यवर्त्तीनां पुनराधिक्यं दर्शयति - **पुणरवि**^इत्यादि पुनरपि प्रागुक्तनदीभ्यो मध्यगामिन्यश्चतस्रो हरिकान्ताहरित्सलिलानारीकान्तानरकान्ताभिधानाः सरितः पृथक् पृथक् षट्पञ्चाशता नदीसहस्रैः सह यन्ति जलनिधिमिति शेषः। तथा हरिकान्ताहरित्सलिले हरिवर्षं, नारीकान्तानरकान्ते पुना रम्यकं द्विधा विदधते। एवं महाविदेहव्यतिरिक्तेषु षट्सु क्षेत्रेषु त्रीणि लक्षाणि द्विनवतिसहस्राणि ३९२००० नद्यो भवन्ति॥ २२॥

[1] '**एवं अब्भिंतरयेति**' does not occur not in Ed1.

***evaṃ abbhiṃtarayā*^*iti* - *evam iti - evam ity anena prakāreṇa yathā etā gaṅgādyā eka-pramāṇāś catasro jaladhiṃ praviśanti, tathā abhyantaraṃ gacchantīty abhyantara-gā, madhya-vartinyaś catasro nadyo rohitāṃśā-rohitā-rūpyakūlā-suvarṇakūlā-lakṣaṇāḥ, punar viśeṣaṇe, kiṃ viśinaṣṭi? tad āha - pratyekam aṣṭāviṃśatyā nadī-sahasraiḥ samanvitā jaladhiṃ praviśantīti prācya-gāthā-sambandho 'dhyāhāryaḥ. tatra rohitāṃśā-rohite haimavata-kṣetraṃ rūpyakūlā-suvarṇakūle hairaṇyavataṃ ca madhye-kṛtya pravahanti. tan-madhya-vartīnāṃ punar ādhikyaṃ darśayati -* ***puṇar avi*^*ity ādi punar api prāg-ukta-nadībhyo madhya-gāminyaś catasro harikāntā-haritsalilā-nārīkāntā-narakāntābhidhānāḥ saritaḥ pṛthak pṛthak ṣaṭ-pañcāśatā nadī-sahasraiḥ saha yanti jala-nidhim iti śeṣaḥ. tathā harikāntā-haritsalile harivarṣaṃ, nārīkāntā-narakānte punā ramyakaṃ dvidhā vidadhate. evaṃ mahāvideha-vyatirikteṣu ṣaṭsu kṣetreṣu trīṇi lakṣāṇi dvi-navati-sahasrāṇi 392000 nadyo bhavanti. 22.*

22. '***evaṃ abbhiṃtarayā***' [etc.]. [The word] '*evam* (so also)' means 'in this [same] manner', viz. as these four, the Gaṅgā, etc., [all four] having the same size and entering into the ocean. So also, [the rivers] that run in between [them] or 'those flowing intermediate'. Four rivers are situated in the middle, namely the Rohitāṃśā, the Rohitā[1], the Rūpyakūlā, and the Suvarṇakūlā[2]. [The word] '*punar* (again)' [is used] in specifying sense. What does it specify? [The author] explains: they flow towards the ocean each together with twenty-eight

[1] Also Rohit.

[2] Also Svarṇakūlā.

thousand tributaries [each]. In this manner, the connection with the preceding verse has to be understood. Here, running in the middle [of them], the Rohitāṃśā, and the Rohitā, and the Rūpyakūlā and Suvarṇakūlā flow through the continent of Haimavata and through Hairaṇyavata [respectively]. However, [the author] indicates the importance of [the rivers] located in between them [saying] '***puṇar avi*** (in addition)', etc. In addition, the four rivers running in the middle with regard to the rivers already mentioned, named the Harikāntā, Haritsalilā[1], Nārīkāntā[2] and Narakāntā, flow into the ocean each together with fifty-six thousand tributaries [each]. Similarly, the Harikāntā and the Haritsalilā divide Harivarṣa, and the Nārīkāntā and the Narakāntā [divide] Ramyaka again in two. Therefore, excluding Mahāvideha, there are three lakhs and ninety-two thousand - 392,000 - rivers in the six continents.

---

[1] Or simply Harit.

[2] Or simply Nārī.

SŪTRA 23

इदानीं महाविदेहनदीनां संख्यामाह -

idānīṃ mahāvideha-nadīnāṃ saṃkhyām āha -

Now [the author] discusses the number of rivers in Mahāvideha.

कुरु[1]मज्झे चउरासी[2], सहसाइं[3] तह[4] य[5] विजय[6]सोलससु[7] ।
बत्तीसाण[8] नईणं[9] चउदस[10], सहसाइ(?)[11] पत्तेयं[12] ॥ २३ ॥[13]

---

[1] कुरूं Brd2. गुरु Bhog10.

[2] चउरासि Ed3, Bhog2, 7 & 10. चउरासी ८४००० Bhog8. चउराशी Bhog17.

[3] सहस्साइं Ed1, 2 & 3, Bhog1, 5, 7, 9, 11, 13, 14, 15, 16 & 17. सहस्सइं LD1. सहस्साइ LD2, Brd1. सहस्सांइ Brd2. सहस्संइ Brd3. सहस्साई ८४००० Bhog2. सहसा Bhog4. Only Tueb, Bhog8 & 10 have the metrically correct सहसाइं.

[4] दाह Bhog2.

[5] य is missing in LD2, Bhog2, 8, 11, 14 & 17.

[6] वीजय LD1, Bhog2. विजय ८४००० Tueb.

[7] सोलससुं Brd2. सोलसस Brd3. सोलसेसु Bhog2. सोलससू Bhog10 & 13.

[8] बतिसाण Brd2 & 3, Bhog15. बतीसाण Bhog2 & 14. बत्तीसांण Bhog16.

[9] नइणं LD1, Brd2 & 3, Bhog1, 9 & 10. नदीणं Bhog11. नइंणं Bhog15.

[10] चउदश Bhog4. चउद्द Bhog5.

[11] सहस्साइं Ed1, 2 & 3, LD1, Bhog1, 7, 11, 13, 15 & 16. सहिस्साइं Bhog17. सहस्साइ LD2, Brd1, 2 & 3, Bhog5. सहस्साइं Tueb. सहासाइं Bhog10. सहस्साई १४००० Bhog2. सहसाण Bhog4. सहसे(?)हि Bhog8. सहस्साई(?) Bhog9. सहस्सेहिं Bhog14. None of the sixteen sources has the metrically correct and possible form सहसाइ.

[12] पत्तेअं Ed1, LD2. Ed2 gives both पत्तेयं and पत्तेअं. पत्तेंय Ed3. पत्तेय Brd2. पत्तेयं १४००० Tueb.

[13] In LD2 and Bhog8 this verse is numbered 24. It is missing in Bhog6 & 12.

kuru-majjhe caüräsī, sahasāiṃ taha ẏa vijaẏa-solasasu;
battīsāṇa naīṇaṃ, caüdasa-sahasāi(?) patteẏaṃ. 23.

(कुरुमध्ये चतुरशीतिसहस्राणि तथा च विजयषोडशेसु। द्वात्रिंशतो नदीनां चतुर्दशसहस्राणि प्रत्येकं ॥ २३ ॥ *kuru-madhye catur-aśīti-sahasrāṇi tathā ca vijaya-ṣoḍaśasu; dvātriṃśato nadīnāṃ catur-daśa-sahaṣrāṇi pratyekaṃ. 23.*)

23. In Kuru there are eighty-four thousand [rivers] and in each of the sixteen provinces in particular out of the thirty-two there are fourteen thousand rivers.

COMMENTARY

कुरु^इति - कुरव इत्युत्तरकुरवः, पदैकदेशे ऽपि पदसमुदायोपचाराद्यथा भामा सत्यभामेति। तेषां मध्ये विचाले चतुरशीतिसहस्राणि नद्यः। तथेतिशब्दो विशेषद्योतकः। चः पादपूरणे। विजयेषु प्राग्विदेहमध्यवर्त्तिषु षोडशेसु, द्विरष्टसंख्यावच्छिन्नेषु द्वात्रिंशतो गङ्गासिन्धुप्रायाणां प्रत्येकं चतुर्दशसहस्राणि भवन्ति, तथाहि - एकस्मात् कच्छदेशविजयात् प्रत्येकं चतुर्दशभिश्चतुर्दशभिः सहस्रैः सह द्वे नद्यौ रक्तारक्तवतीनाम्न्यौ शीतायां प्रविशतः। प्राक् सामस्त्येन तत्राष्टाविंशतिसहस्राणि नद्यो भवन्ति। एष एव क्रमः सर्वेषु विजयेषु। यथा पूर्वविदेहेषु विजयाः षोडश (१६), प्रतिविजयं चाष्टाविंशतिसहस्राणि नद्यो, ऽपरविदेहमाश्रित्योक्तं च -

"विजयाविययइक्केका, अट्ठावीसइ नइसहस्सेहिं,
आउरमाणसलिला, अवरेणुदहिं समणुपत्ता ॥ १ ॥"[1]

---

[1] बृहत्क्षेत्रसमास, verse 250 (*BKSJ*, p. 240):
विजया वि य एक्केका, अट्ठावीसाइनइसहस्सेहिं।
आऊरमाणसलिला, अवरेणुदहिं अणुप्पत्ता ॥ २५० ॥
(विजयादपि च एकैकस्मात् अष्टाविंशतिनदीसहस्रैः। आपूर्यमाणसलिला अपरेणोदधिमनुप्राप्ता ॥ २५० ॥).

इति। ततो ऽष्टाविंशतेः सहस्राणां षोडशभिर्गुणकारे जाताश्चतस्रो लक्षा अष्टाचत्वारिंशत्सहस्राधिकाः ४४८००० नद्यः। पूर्वोक्ताश्चतुरशीतिसहस्रा उत्तरकुरुमध्यगा नद्य एतासां मध्ये प्रक्षिप्यन्ते, जातानि द्वात्रिंशत्सहस्राधिकानि पञ्चलक्षाणि ५३२००० नदीनातं, तथाऽनेनैव पर्यायेण देवकुरुष्वपरमहाविदेहानां सम्बंधिषु विजयेष्वपि एतावत्य एव ५३२००० सरितः। ततो ऽस्याङ्कराशिद्वयस्य मीलने जातानि दशलक्षाणि चतुःषष्टिसहस्राधिकानि १०६४०००। तस्यैतदङ्कराशिमध्ये पूर्वोक्तानि त्रीणि लक्षाणि द्विनवतिसहस्राधिकानि क्षिप्यन्ते, ततो भवन्ति समस्तजम्बूद्वीपे षट्पञ्चाशत्सहस्राधिकानि चतुर्दशलक्षाणि १४५६००० सर्वाग्रेण नद्य इति॥ २३॥

kuru^*iti - kurava ity uttara-kuravaḥ, padaika-deśe 'pi pada-samudāyopacārād yathā bhāmā satya-bhāmeti. teṣāṃ madhye vicāle catur-aśīti-sahasrāṇi nadyaḥ. tatheti-śabdo viśeṣa-dyotakaḥ. caḥ pāda-pūraṇe. vijayeṣu prāgvideha-madhya-vartiṣu ṣoḍaśasu, dvir-aṣṭa-saṃkhyāvacchinneṣu dvātriṃśato gaṅgā-sindhu-prāyāṇāṃ pratyekaṃ catur-daśa-sahasrāṇi bhavanti. tathā hy: ekasmāt kaccha-deśa-vijayāt pratyekaṃ catur-daśabhiś catur-daśabhiḥ sahasraiḥ saha dve nadyau raktā-raktavatī-nāmnyau śītāyāṃ praviśataḥ. prāk sāmastyena tatrāṣṭāviṃśati-sahasrāṇi nadyo bhavanti. eṣa eva kramaḥ sarveṣu vijayeṣu. yathā pūrvavideheṣu vijayāḥ ṣoḍaśa (16), prativijayaṃ cāṣṭāviṃśati-sahasrāṇi nadyaḥ. aparavideham āśrityoktaṃ ca -*

"***vijayȧ vi ẏaïkkekā, aṭṭhāvīsaï naïsahassehiṃ;***
āuramāṇa-salilā, avareṇudahiṃ samaṇupattā. 1."[1]

---

[1] *BKSJ*, verse 250, p. 240:
vijayā vi ẏa ekkekkā aṭṭhāvīsāi-nai-sahassehiṃ;
āūramāṇa-salilā avareṇ'udahim aṇuppattā. 250.

iti. tato 'ṣṭāviṃśateḥ sahasrāṇāṃ ṣoḍaśabhir guṇa-kāre jātāś catasro lakṣā aṣṭācatvāriṃśat-sahasrādhikāḥ 448000 nadyaḥ. pūrvoktāś catur-aśīti-sahasrā uttarakuru-madhya-gā nadya etāsāṃ madhye prakṣipyante, jātāni dvātriṃśat-sahasrādhikāni pañca-lakṣāṇi 532000 nadīnām. tathānenaiva paryāyeṇa devakuruṣv apara-mahāvidehānāṃ sambandhiṣu vijayeṣv api etāvatya eva 532000 saritaḥ. tato 'syāṅkarāśi-dvayasya mīlane jātāni daśa-lakṣāṇi catuḥ-ṣaṣṭi-sahasrādhikāni 1064000. tasyaitad-aṅkarāśi-madhye pūrvoktāni trīṇi lakṣāṇi dvi-navati-sahasrādhikāni kṣipyante, tato bhavanti samasta-jambūdvīpe ṣaṭ-pañcāśat-sahasrādhikāni catur-daśa-lakṣāṇi 1456000 sarvāgreṇa nadya iti. 23.

23. '***kuru***' [etc.]. The word '*kuru*' refers to the region of Uttarakuru[1] because it is used as an abbreviation, like Bhāmā for Satyabhāmā[2]. Inside them or in the interior of them there are eighty-four thousand rivers. The word '*tathā*' expresses a specification. The word '*ca* (and)' serves to fill out the metre of the verse. In the sixteen provinces situated in East Videha[3] out of the thirty-two, [that is] taken separately as the sum of

---

(*vijayād api ca ekaikasmāt aṣṭāviṃśati-nadī-sahasraiḥ; āpūryamāṇa-salilā apareṇodadhim anuprāptā. 2500.*).

[1] Lit. 'the northern Kurus'. In fact, the word 'Uttarakuru' applies to the inhabitants of that region. The name of a people used in the plural usually refers to the land itself.

[2] Lit. 'having true lustre'. Satyabhāmā is the name of a daughter of Satrājit and one of the eight wives of Kṛṣṇa.

[3] Prāgvideha = Pūrvavideha. See Kirfel, p. 218.

twice eight [provinces][1], there are fourteen thousand [tributaries] for each [river] corresponding to the Gaṅgā and Sindhu.[2] For, from one province, [for instance] the land of Kaccha, two rivers called the Raktā and the Raktavatī stream into the Śītā, each of them together with fourteen thousand [tributaries]. Therefore, there are twenty-eight thousand [tributaries] in all [per province] in the east. The same arrangement applies for all provinces, viz. sixteen provinces in East Videha and twenty-eight thousand rivers for each province. Regarding West Videha, it is said:

"*The stream [viz. the śītodā] reaches the ocean in the west filled by twenty-eight thousand rivers from each province.*"

So, when twenty-eight thousand is multiplied with sixteen, four lakhs and forty-eight thousand - 448,000 - rivers are obtained. The eighty-four thousand rivers already mentioned flowing in Uttarakuru are excluded from these. [If these are included] five lakhs and thirty-two thousand - 532,000 - rivers are obtained. Moreover, in turn, in Devakuru [and] in the provinces connected with West Mahāvideha there are as many as 532,000 rivers. So, when the same number is added, ten lakhs and sixty-four thousand - 1,064,000 - [rivers] are obtained. If the three lakhs and ninety-two thousand [rivers]

---

[1] Apart from Devakuru and Uttarakuru, Mahāvideha consists of a Western and an Eastern part, each containing sixteen provinces. West and East Videha are again divided in a northern and a southern sector, each containing eight provinces.

[2] The full construction would be '... *gaṅgā-sindhu-prāyāṇāṃ pratyekaṃ nadīnāṃ catur-daśa-sahasrāṇi bhavanti*'. In fact the author should add: or the Raktā and Raktavatī since he mentions them in the next clause.

mentioned earlier[1] are added to the total number of this, then in the whole of Jambūdvīpa there are fourteen lakhs and fifty-six thousand - 1,456,000 - rivers in all.

---

[1] See the commentary on *sū.* 22.

SŪTRA 24

एवं व्याख्याने कृते विजयच्छेदिनीनां ग्राह[ा]वत्यादिनां षण्णां नदीनां प्ररुपणा उपेक्षिता भवत्यतस्तद्वर्णनाय वाचनान्तरेण[1] द्वितीयं प्रकारमाह -

evaṃ vyākhyāne kṛte vijaya-cchedinīnāṃ grāha[ā]vaty-ādināṃ ṣaṇṇāṃ nadīnāṃ prarupaṇā upekṣitā bhavaty atas tad-varṇanāya vācanāntareṇa dvitīyaṃ prakāram āha -

Explained in this manner the exposition of the six rivers, the Grāhāvatī etc. separating the provinces, is disregarded. Therefore, in order to describe them [the author] puts it in a second manner, in another wording.

चउदस[2]सहस्स[3]गुणिया[4], अडतीस[5] नईउ[6] विजय[7]मज्झिल्ला[8] ।
सीओयाए निवडंति[9], तह य सीयाइ[10] एमेव ॥ २४ ॥[11]

caüdasa sahassa-guṇiyā, aḍatīsa naīo vijaya-majjhillā;

---

[1] For बाचनान्तरेण in Ed1.

[2] चऊदस LD1. चउद्दस Bhog5. चउदसह Bhog11. दसचउद Bhog12.

[3] सहस Brd2 & 3, Bhog4 & 13. सहिसा Bhog17.

[4] गूंणिया LD1. गुणिआ LD2, Bhog11. गुणीया Brd2, Bhog1, 4, 7, 13 & 17. गुणीआ Bhog8. गुंणिया Bhog16.

[5] अड्ढतीस Bhog15.

[6] नइओ Ed2 & 3, Brd1, Bhog1 & 13. नइंओ LD1. नइउ Brd2 & 3, Bhog8 & 15. नईओ Bhog2, 5, 9, 11, 12, 14 & 16.

[7] विजया Brd2. वीजय Bhog7.

[8] मज्झील्ला Brd2, Bhog12. मज्झिला Brd3. मज्झि(?)ल्ला Bhog13 & 14. मझिला Bhog14.

[9] In Brd1 the phrase 'सीओयाए निवडंति' is omitted, but is added as a correction in the margin.

[10] LD2: सीआइ.

[11] This verse is numbered 25 in LD2, Bhog7 & 8, and 22 in Bhog12. It is missing in Bhog6.

sīoẏāe nivaḍaṃti, taha ẏa sīẏāi emeva. 24.

(चतुर्दशसहस्त्रगुणिता अष्टात्रिंशन्नद्यो विजयमध्यकाः। शीतोदायां निपतन्ति तथा च सीतायामेचमेव॥ २४॥ *catur-daśa-sahasra-guṇitā aṣṭātriṃśan nadyo vijaya-madhyakāḥ; śītodāyāṃ nipatanti tathā ca śītāyām evam eva. 24.)*

24. Thirty-eight multiplied with fourteen thousand rivers intersecting the provinces discharge into the Śītodā and in the same manner in the Śītā.

COMMENTARY

चउदस^इति - अन्य आचार्या एवमाचक्षते - अष्टात्रिंशद्विजयमध्यवर्त्तिन्यः शीतोदायां निपतन्ति प्रविशन्ति, किंविशिष्टास्ताः? इत्याह - चतुर्दशभिर्नदीसहस्त्रैर्गुणिता अभ्यस्ताः। पुनः कीदृश्यस्ताः? तद्यथा - द्वात्रिंशद्गृक्ताद्या नद्यः, तथा षट् ग्राह[ा]वत्याद्याः। एवं सामस्त्येन अष्टात्रिंशत् षोडशविजयेषु सन्ति। ततश्चतुर्दशसहस्त्रैर्गुणिता अष्टात्रिंशत् जातानि पञ्चलक्षाणि द्वात्रिंसत्सहस्त्राधिकानि ५३२०००, तथेति सादृश्ये, यथा शीतोदायामेवमेवेति, अनेनैव प्रकारेण पञ्चलक्षाणि द्वात्रिंशत्सहस्त्राधिकानि ५३२००० शीतायामपि भवन्तीति, ततो राशिद्वयस्याप्येकीकरणे चतुःषष्टिसहस्त्राधिकानि दशलक्षाणि १०६४००० सरितो भवन्ति। इत्थं च व्याख्यायमाने कुरुमध्यगाश्चतुरशीतिसहस्त्राणि सरितो न गृहीताः, तासां स्थाने ग्राह[ा]वत्यादयः षडन्तर्नद्यः प्रत्येकं चतुर्दशनदीसहस्त्रसमन्विताश्चतुर्दशषट्कानि चतुरशीतिरिति गणनाक्रमेण चतुरशीतिनदीसहस्त्रसंख्यां पूरयित्वा यथोक्ता संख्या समाहिता। परमयमपि प्रकारो न सम्भवति, यतो ऽन्तर्नद्यो गङ्गादिभ्यो सकाशाद् द्विगुणविस्ताराः प्रतीयन्त, "**पणवीससयं च सलिलाओ**"[1] इति वचनात्, ततो द्विगुणो

---

[1] पञ्चविंशतिशतं च सलिलानि। Origin of this *vacana* untraced.

ऽष्टाविंशतिनदीसहस्रलक्षणः प्रत्येकतं, आसां परिवारो न्याय्यः। आह चोमास्वातिवाचकः -

"नद्यो विजयच्छेदिन्यो रोहितावत्कुण्डद्वीपा स्वनामदेवीवासा अष्टाविंशतिनदीसहस्रानुगाः प्रत्येकं सर्वत्रसमाः पञ्चविंशत्यधिकं योजनशतं विस्तृता अर्द्धतृतीययोजनावगाहाः ग्राहह्रदपङ्कवत्यः"[1]

इत्यादि। अतः षण्णामप्येतासामष्टषष्टिसहस्रादिकं लक्षम् एकं सरितः परिवारः, तथा पञ्चलक्षानि सद्वात्रिंशत्सहस्राणि पुनः सकुरूणां विजयानामन्तर्नदीरहितानां भवन्ति। एवं राशिद्वयस्य मीलने पूर्णानि सप्तलक्षाणि सरित एतावत्य एवापरविदेहे देवकुरुसमन्विते, ततः समस्तमहाविदेहे चतुर्दशलक्षाणि १४०००००सलिलाः। पुनस्त्रीणि लक्षाणि द्विनवतिसहस्राधिकानि भरतादीनां शेषाणातं, एवं सर्वाङ्के सप्तदशलक्षाणि द्विनवतिसहस्राधिकानि १७९२००० नद्यो भवन्तीति। उक्तं च सूत्रे -

"चउदसलक्खा छपन्नसहसजंबुदीवंमि।
हुंति उ सत्तरसलक्खा बाणवइसहस्स सलिलाओ॥ १॥"[2]

इति। तथा सिद्धान्तानुसारेण पुनरेवं ज्ञायते, यद्ग्राहवत्यादीनां द्वादशनदीनां परिवारो न सम्भवति। यत एतद्व्यतिरिक्ता जम्बूद्वीपे या अन्याः सरितः सन्ति, तासां प्रवाहान्मुखे सर्वासां दशगुणो विस्तारः सुप्रतीत एव। उक्तं च वाचकमुख्येन -

"सर्वा नद्यः प्रवाहदशगुणा मुखे विस्तारपञ्चाशाड्भागावगाहा"[3]

इति। एतासां तु तथा न, किन्तु प्रवाहमध्ये मुखे चैकरूपः पञ्चविंशत्यधिकयोजनशतलक्षणः प्रत्येकं विस्तारो नान्यः कश्चिद्विशेषो, न च परिवारो ऽप्यासां दृश्यते क्षेत्रसमासबृहद्वृत्त्यनुसारेण, अतः प्रतीयते,

---

[1] जम्बूद्वीप्समास (*JDSU*, p. 17, line 13) with a slightly different reading and with the full sentence: नद्यो विजयच्छेदिन्यो रोहितावत्कुण्डद्वीपाः स्वनामदेवीवासाष्टाविंशतिनदीसहस्रानुगाः प्रत्येकं सर्वसमाः पञ्चविंशशतविस्तृताः अर्द्धतृतीययोजनावगाहा ग्राहह्रदपङ्कवत्यस्तप्तमत्तोन्मत्तजलाः क्षीरोदासिंहश्रोतान्तर्वाहिण्य ऊर्मिफेनगभीरमालिन्यः।

[2] Origin of quotation untraced. छाया: चतुर्दशलक्षाः षट्पञ्चासत्सहस्रा जम्बूद्वीपे। भवन्ति तु सप्तदशलक्षा द्विनवतिसहस्राः सलिलाः॥ १॥

[3] Source untraced.

यद्येतास्वन्या अनेकानि सहस्राणि नद्यः प्रविशेयुस्तदा कथं क्रमेण परतस् परतो गच्छन्तीनां विस्तारविशेषो गङ्गादीनामिव न सम्पद्यतेति? अन्यच्च पूर्वविदेहे भद्रशालवनसमीपवर्तिनोः कच्छमङ्गलावतीविजययोस्तथा मुखवनोपकण्ठस्थयोः पुष्कलावतीवच्छनाम्नोश्च विजययोरन्तर्नदीनामभाव एवास्त्य, अत एतेषु चतुर्ष्वपि प्रत्येकं सामस्थ्येन[अष्टाविंशतिर्][1] अष्टाविंशतिसहस्राणि नद्यः सन्ति। गङ्गासिन्धुसम्बन्धिन्यो नापरा यावती च कच्छविजये भूमिरन्तर्नदीमतां सुकच्छादीनां द्वादशानामप्यन्येषां च तावत्येव नाधिका, अतः कथं तेषु बहुतरा नद्यो ग्राह[ा]वत्याद्यन्तर्नदीसंयोगे ऽपि विशेषभूमेरभावात्सम्भवन्ति? अत्राह - नैतत्संवादकोटीमाटीकते, यतो जम्बूद्वीपप्रज्ञप्तावप्यन्तर्नदीनां प्रत्येकमष्टाविंशतिनदीसहस्रलक्षणः परिवारो भणितस्तथा च तद्वाक्यम् -

"गाहावई महानई पवूढासमाणी सुकच्छमहाकच्छविजये दुहा विभयमाणी (२) अट्ठावीसाए सलिला सहस्सेहिं समग्गा दाहिणेणं सीयमहानई समुप्पेई।".[2]

अपरे अनूचानाः पुनरित्थं प्रवदन्ति - यथा अष्टाशीतिग्रहाश्चन्द्रस्यैव परिवारतया प्रसिद्धा अपि सूर्यस्य एत एव परिवारः न पुनरन्यः पृथग् प्रतीयते। उक्तं च समवायाङ्गवृत्तौ - "अष्टाशीतिमहाग्रहा एते यद्यपि चन्द्रस्यैव परिवारो ऽन्यत्र श्रूयते तथापि सूर्यस्यापीन्द्रत्वादेत एव परिवारतयाऽवसेया"[3]

---

[1] The word अष्टाविंशतिर् is superfluous here. This is probably a case of dittography.

[2] जामबूद्वीपप्रज्ञप्ति, सू. ९५, ed. Javeri, p. 345: **... गाहावई महाणई पवूढा समाणी सुकच्छमहाकच्छविजए दुहा विभयमाणी २ अट्ठावीसाए सलिलासहस्सेहिं समग्गा दाहिणेणं सीअं महाणइं समप्पेइ, ...** छाया: ... ग्राहावती महानदी प्रव्यूढा समी सुकच्छमहाकच्छौ विजयौ द्विधा विभजन्ती २ अष्टाविंशत्या सलिलासहस्रैः समग्रा [सहिता दक्षिणेन भागेन - मेरोर्दक्षिणदिशि] दक्षिणेन शीतां महानदीं संप्राप्नोति, ...

[3] This is found in the टीका of Abhayadeva Sūri on the समवायाङ्गसूत्र, सू. ८८, ed. Āgamodaya Samiti Series, Mehesana, 1918, p. 93: ..., अष्टाशीतिर्महाग्रहाः, एते च यद्यपि चन्द्रस्यैव परिवारो ऽन्यत्र श्रूयते तथापि सूर्यस्यापीन्द्रत्वादेत एव परिवारतयाऽवसेया इति।

इति। तथा गङ्गासिन्धुसम्बन्धिन्य एवाष्टाविंशतिरष्टाविंशतिर्नदीसहस्राणि अन्तर्नदीनामपि परिवार इति। एवमपरविदेहे ऽपि ज्ञातव्यमिति ॥ २४ ॥

'caüdasa' *[etc.] - anya ācāryā evam ācakṣate - aṣṭātriṃśad vijaya-madhya-vartinyaḥ śītodāyāṃ nipatanti praviśanti, kiṃ viśiṣṭās tāḥ? ity āha - catur-daśabhir nadī-sahasrair guṇitā abhyastāḥ, punaḥ kīdṛśyas tāḥ? tad yathā: dvātriṃśad raktādyā nadyaḥ, tathā ṣaṭ grāha[ā]vaty-ādyāḥ, evaṃ sāmastyena aṣṭātriṃśat ṣoḍaśa-vijayeṣu santi. tataś catur-daśa-sahasrair guṇitāḥ aṣṭātriṃśat jātāni pañca-lakṣāṇi dvātriṃsat-sahasrādhikāni 532000. tatheti sādṛśye, yathā śītodāyām evam eveti. anenaiva prakāreṇa pañca-lakṣāṇi dvātriṃśat-sahasrādhikāni 532000 śītāyām api bhavantīti. tato rāśi-dvayasyāpy ekī-karaṇe catuḥṣaṣṭi-sahasrādhikāni daśa-lakṣāṇi 1064000 sarito bhavanti. itthaṃ ca vyākhyāyamāne kuru-madhya-gāś catur-aśīti-sahasrāṇi sarito na gṛhītāḥ, tāsāṃ sthāne grāha[ā]vaty-ādayaḥ ṣaḍ-antar-nadyaḥ pratyekaṃ caturdaśa-nadī-sahasra-samanvitāś caturdaśa-ṣaṭkāni catur-aśītir iti gaṇanā-krameṇa catur-aśīti-nadī-sahasra-saṃkhyāṃ pūrayitvā yathoktā saṃkhyā samāhitā. param ayam api prakāro na sambhavati, yato 'ntar-nadyo gaṅgādibhyo sakāśād dvi-guṇa-vistārāḥ pratīyante,* **"paṇa-vīsa-sayaṃ ca salilāo"**[1] *iti vacanāt, tato dvi-guṇo 'ṣṭāviṃśati-nadī-sahasra-lakṣaṇaḥ pratyekaṃ, āsāṃ parivāro nyāyyaḥ. āha ca^umāsvāti-vācakaḥ:*

> *"nadyo vijaya-cchedinyo rohitā-vat-kuṇḍa-dvīpā sva-nāma-devī-vāsāḥ aṣṭāviṃśati-nadī-sahasrānugāḥ pratyekaṃ sarvatra-samāḥ pañca-viṃśaty-adhikaṃ yojana-śataṃ*

[1] *pañca-viṃśati-śataṃ ca salilāni.*

vistṛtāḥ ardha-tṛtīya-yojanāvagāhāḥ. grāha-hrada-paṅkavatyaḥ [...]."[1]

ity ādi. ataḥ ṣaṇṇām apy etāsām aṣṭa-ṣaṣṭi-sahasrādikaṃ lakṣam ekaṃ saritaḥ parivāraḥ, tathā pañca-lakṣāni sa-dvātriṃśat-sahasrāṇi punaḥ sa-kurūṇāṃ vijayānām antar-nadī-rahitānāṃ bhavanti. evaṃ rāśi-dvayasya mīlane pūrṇāni sapta-lakṣāṇi sarita etāvatya eva^aparavidehe devakuru-samanvite, tataḥ samasta-mahāvidehe caturdaśa-lakṣāṇi 1400000 salilāḥ. punas trīṇi lakṣāṇi dvi-navati-sahasrādhikāni bharatādīnāṃ śeṣāṇāṃ, evaṃ sarvāṅke sapta-daśa-lakṣāṇi dvi-navati-sahasrādhikāni 1792000 nadyo bhavantīti. uktaṃ ca sūtre -

"***caü-dasa-lakkhā cha-panna-sahasa-jaṃbudīvaṃmi;***
huṃti u sattarasa-lakkhā bāṇavaï-sahassa salilāo.1."[2]

iti. tathā siddhāntānusāreṇa punar evaṃ jñāyate, yad grāha[ā]vatyādīnāṃ dvādaśa-nadīnāṃ parivāro na sambhavati. yata etad-vyatiriktā jambūdvīpe yā anyāḥ saritaḥ santi, tāsāṃ pravāhān mukhe sarvāsāṃ daśa-guṇo vistāraḥ supratīta eva. uktaṃ ca vācaka-mukhyena-

"*sarvā nadyaḥ pravāha-daśa-guṇā mukhe vistāra-pañcāśad-bhāgāvagāhā*"

iti. etāsāṃ tu tathā na, kintu pravāha-madhye mukhe caika-rūpaḥ pañca-viṃśaty-adhika-yojana-śata-lakṣaṇaḥ pratyekaṃ

---

[1] *JDSU*, p. 17, line 13: *nadyo vijaya-cchedinyo rohitāvat-kuṇḍa-dvīpāḥ sva-nāma-devī-vāsāṣṭāviṃśati-nadī-sahasrānugāḥ pratyekaṃ sarva-samāḥ pañca-viṃśa-śata-vistṛtāḥ ardha-tṛtīya-yojanāvagāhā grāha-hrada-paṅkavatyas tapta-mattonmatta-jalaḥ kṣīrodā-siṃha-śrotāntar-vāhiṇya ūrmi-phena-gabhīra-mālinyaḥ.*

[2] Chāyā: *catu-daśa-lakṣāḥ ṣaṭ-pañcāsat-sahasrā jambūdvīpe; bhavanti tu sapta-daśa-lakṣā dvi-navati-sahasrāḥ salilāḥ. 1.*

vistāro nānyaḥ kaścid viśeṣo, na ca parivāro 'py āsāṃ dṛśyate kṣetra-samāsa-bṛhad-vṛtty-anusāreṇa, ataḥ pratīyate, yady etāsv anyā anekāni sahasrāṇi nadyaḥ praviśeyus tadā kathaṃ krameṇa paratas parato gacchantīnāṃ vistāra-viśeṣo gaṅgādīnām iva na sampadyateti? anyac ca pūrvavidehe bhadraśāla-vana-samīpa-vartinoḥ kaccha-maṅgalāvatī-vijayayos tathā mukha-vanopakaṇṭha-sthayoḥ puṣkalāvatī-vaccha-nāmnoś ca vijayayor antar-nadīnām abhāva evāsty, ata eteṣu caturṣv api pratyekaṃ sāmasthyena[aṣṭāviṃśatir] aṣṭāviṃśati-sahasrāṇi nadyaḥ santi. gaṅgā-sindhu-sambandhinyo nāparā yāvatī ca kaccha-vijaye bhūmir antar-nadī-matāṃ sukacchādīnāṃ dvādaśānām apy anyeṣāṃ ca tāvaty eva nādhikā, ataḥ kathaṃ teṣu bahutarā nadyo grāha[ā]vaty-ādy-antar-nadī-saṃyoge 'pi viśeṣa-bhūmer abhāvāt sambhavanti? atrāha - naitat saṃvāda-koṭīm āṭīkate, yato jambūdvīpaprajñaptāv apy antar-nadīnāṃ pratyekam aṣṭāviṃśati-nadī-sahasra-lakṣaṇaḥ parivāro bhaṇitaḥ, tathā ca tad vākyam -

> "***gāhāvaī mahā-naī pavūḍhā samāṇī sukaccha-mahākaccha-vijaye duhā vibhaẏamāṇī (2) aṭṭhāvīsāe salilā-sahassehiṃ samaggā dāhiṇeṇaṃ sīya-mahā-naī samuppeī.***"[1]

---

[1] *JDP*, *sū.* 95, ed. Javeri, p. 345: ... ***gāhāvaī mahā-ṇaī pavūḍhā samāṇī sukaccha-mahākaccha-vijae duhā vibhaẏamāṇī 2 aṭṭhāvīsāe salilā-sahassehiṃ samaggā dāhiṇeṇaṃ sīaṃ mahā-ṇaiṃ samappei, ...*** Chāyā: ...*grāhāvatī mahā-nadī pravyūḍhā samī sukaccha-mahākacchau vijayau dvidhā vibhajantī 2 aṣṭāviṃśatyā salilā-sahasraiḥ samagrā [sahitā dakṣiṇena bhāgena - meror dakṣiṇa-diśi] dakṣiṇena śītāṃ mahā-nadīṃ samprāpnoti...*

apare anūcānāḥ punar itthaṃ pravadanti - yathā aṣṭāśīti-grahāś candrasyaiva parivāratayā prasiddhā api sūryasya eta eva parivāraḥ na punar anyaḥ pṛthag pratīyate. uktaṃ ca samavāyāṅga-vṛttau -

> *"aṣṭāśīti-mahāgrahā ete yady api candrasyaiva parivāro 'nyatra śrūyate tathāpi sūryasyāpīndratvād eta eva parivāratayā 'vaseyā"*[1]

iti. tathā gaṅgā-sindhu-sambandhinya evāṣṭāviṃśatir aṣṭāviṃśatir nadī-sahasrāṇi antar-nadīnām api parivāra iti. evam aparavidehe 'pi jñātavyam iti. 24.

'***caüdasa***' [etc.]. Other masters have put it this way: there are thirty-eight [main rivers] located inside the [sixteen eastern] provinces that discharge or flow into the Śītodā (Śītā?).[2] Answering the question how they are qualified [the author] states: multiplied or manyfolded with fourteen thousand [tributary] rivers. Which are these? Thirty-two rivers, the Raktā, etc.[3], and the six [intermediate rivers], the Grāhāvatī,

---

[1] *Ṭīkā* of Abhayadeva Sūri on the *Samavāyāṅgasūtra, sū.* 88, ed. Āgamodaya Samiti Series, Mehesana, 1918, p. 93: ..., *aṣṭāśītir mahāgrahāḥ, ete ca yady api candrasyaiva parivāro 'nyatra śrūyate tathāpi sūryasyāpīndratvād eta eva parivāratayā 'vaseyā iti.*

[2] It seems that these other masters locate the Śītodā in Pūrva- or East Videha and the Śītā in Apara- or West Videha. Firstly, the standard description of Videha always starts in the northeast and evolves clockwise. Secondly, the Grāhāvatī, etc., belong to northeast Videha. Otherwise, the possibility that the Śītā and Śītodā are simply interchanged is conceivable too.

[3] Viz. the Raktā and Raktāvatī, corresponding to the two rivers of the same name flowing in Airāvata in North Videha and, likewise, the Gaṅgā and Sindhu in South Videha.

etc.[1] So in all there are thirty-eight [rivers] in the sixteen [eastern (?)] provinces. So, thirty-eight multiplied by fourteen thousand yields five lakhs and thirty-two thousand - 532,000. The word '*tathā* (likewise)' is used to express similarity: as in case of the Śītodā. In the same way there are five lakhs and thirty-two thousand [rivers] - 532,000 - in case of the Śītā also. Therefore, when the two numbers are added up, there are ten thousand and sixty-four lakhs of rivers - 1,064,000. When treated in this manner the eighty-four thousand rivers flowing in the Kurus are not included. In stead of these, when we take the six intermediate rivers, viz. the Grāhāvatī etc., in account, each possessing fourteen thousand tributaries, then six times fourteen [yields] eighty-four. When counted in this order the number of eighty-four thousand rivers is completed and the number as it was given before is reached. Also this alternative way [of reckoning] is not possible, because the intermediate rivers are deemed to be twice as long as compared to the Gaṅgā etc., since it is said that "the [intermediate] rivers are hundred and twenty-five [*yojanas*]".[2] So, twice the amount of twenty-eight thousand of rivers each. The [double length of the river] course of these [intermediate rivers] is correct, since Master Umāsvāti says:

> "*The rivers Grāha[ā]-, Hrada[ā]- and Paṅkavatī*[3] *are separating the provinces [in northeast Videha].*[1] *They have*

---

[1] Viz. the Grāhāvatī, Hradāvatī, Vegavatī, Taptajalā, Mattajalā and Unmattajalā mentioned in the commentary on the *sū.* 11 & 12.

[2] This means that the intermediate rivers have twice the amount of tributaries as the Gaṅgā and Sindhu or Raktā and Raktodā rivers of Mahāvideha, viz. 28,000 each.

[3] Or, Grāhāvatī, Hradāvatī and Paṅkāvatī. See Kirfel, pp. 237-238.

an island in a basin like the Rohitā[2] *where a goddess with the same name dwells. Each of them is accompanied by twenty-eight thousand tributaries. They are equally one hundred and twenty-five yojanas broad all over, while they are two and a half yojanas deep* ",

etc. So, the tributaries of these six [intermediate rivers] number one lakh and sixty-eight thousand [*yojanas*]. There are again five lakhs and thirty-two thousand [of inland rivers] excluding the intermediate rivers of the provinces belonging to the Kuru regions.[3] Therefore, when these are multiplied with the number two there are in total as much as seven lakhs of rivers in West Videha, Devakuru included. Consequently, there are fourteen lakhs - 1,400,000 - of rivers in the whole of Mahāvideha. The other [regions], viz. Bharata, etc., however, have three lakhs and ninety-two thousand [rivers in total]. So, in all there are seventeen lakhs and ninety-two thousand [rivers]. In a manual, it is stated that:

"*In Jambūdvīpa there are fourteen lakhs and fifty-six thousand [rivers, so it is said]. however, [in fact] there are seventeen lakhs and ninety-two thousand.*"

---

[1] Viz. Sukaccha and Mahākaccha, Kacch(ak)āvatī and, Āvarta and Maṅgalāvarta. See Kirfel, p. 238.

[2] See supra p. 139.

[3] This cannot be correct. The new reckoning starts with the six intermediate rivers Grāhāvatī etc., multiplied with 28,000 tributaries, since they are twice as long as the Gaṅgā. The result is 168,000. Then the other thirty-two rivers inside the provinces have to be multiplied with 14,000. This makes 448,000, not 532,000. So, the total number of 616,000 rivers plus the 84,000 of the Kuru regions makes 700,000 in West and in East Videha each. So, in total there are 1,400,000 rivers in Mahāvideha.

However, the Canon learns that the course of the twelve [intermediate] rivers, viz. the Grāhāvatī, etc. is not according to the regular pattern[1] since it is well known indeed that the size of all the other rivers in Jambūdvīpa at the mouth is ten times their size at the source. A prominent Master has said that:

> "*The width of all rivers at the mouth is [the width at] the source multiplied by ten, [while their] depth is one fiftieth of the breath.*"

These [intermediate rivers in Mahāvideha], however, are not like that. On the contrary, they are all uniform [in size] in the middle of their course as well as at their mouth. Their width is fixed at one hundred and twenty-five *yojanas*[2] without any further distinction. Moreover, their course [with the number of tributaries] is not described in accordance with the *Bṛhadvṛtti* (Major Commentary) on the *Kṣetrasamāsa*.[3] So [the question] arises that if several thousands of other [tributary] rivers would discharge in them, why then a difference in the width [of those rivers] while they are gradually progressing [towards their

---

[1] *na sambhavati*.

[2] The intermediate rivers of Mahāvideha, viz. the Grāhāvatī, Hradāvatī, Paṅkavatī, Unmattajalā, Mattajalā and Taptajalā in East Videha and, the Antarvāhinī, Śītāsrotā, Kṣīrodā, Ūrmimālinī, Phenamālinī and Gambhīramālinī in West Videha have an equal width of 125 *yojanas* all over, from source to mouth, and they are 2 $^1/_2$ *yojanas* deep. See Kirfel, p. 237*ff*.

[3] Probably the *Kṣetrasamāsa* (also *Bṛhatkṣetrasamāsa*) by Jinabhadra is meant, but it is not clear which *Bṛhadvṛtti* is referred to: the *vṛtti* of Haribhadra Sūri (comp. Saṃ. 1185), of Siddha Sūri, of Malayagiri, of Vijayasiṃha, of Devānanda, of Devabhadra or of Ānanda Sūri.

mouths] would not be possible as [in case] of the Gaṅgā, etc. On the other hand the two provinces Kaccha and Maṅgalāvatī situated close to the Bhadraśāla forest as well as the provinces named Puṣkalāvatī[1] and Vaccha[2] located near the forest of the mouth [of the Śītā][3], [all] in Pūrvavideha, have no intermediate rivers.[4] Hence, these four [provinces] have each twenty-eight thousand tributaries in all.[5] And if the land in the province of Kaccha, which is considered to be an inter-river [territory and] not different [from lands] related to the Gaṅgā and the Sindhu [on the one hand, and [the land] of the other twelve [provinces] of Sukaccha, etc. [on the other hand] are not much different, why then is it possible that they contain many more [tributary] rivers [as] connected with the intermediate rivers of the Grāhāvatī, etc. For, their lands are not different. Regarding this I [the author must] admit that this does not solve the problem[6], because also in the *Jambūdvīpaprajñapti* it is stated that the course the intermediate rivers is characterised by twenty-eight thousand [tributary] rivers. This is the quotation concerned:

> "*The main river Grāhāvatī, equal in width all over, dividing the provinces of Sukaccha and Mahākaccha in two, reaches the main river Śītā in the south fully provided with twenty-eight thousand tributaries.*"[7]

---

[1] = Puṣkaravatī.

[2] = Vatsa.

[3] Mukhavana.

[4] = Puṣkaravatī.

[5] Viz. twice the number of 14,000 tributaries of the equivalent rivers of the Gaṅgā and Sindhu inside these four provinces.

[6] Lit. 'that this does not make clear the point in question'.

[7] *JDP*, *sū*. 95.

Other scholars teach the following, viz. that as concerns [its] surroundings the moon is known to posses eighty-eight planets [and that] in the same way the course of the sun is considered not to be different, viz. not to be unlike. In the commentary on the *Samavāyāṅga* it is stated:

> "*The great planets are eighty-eight. This is said to be the surroundings of the moon elsewhere. Likewise these [eighty-eight planets] are to be reckoned in case of the surroundings of the sun because of its mighty character.*"

In the same manner, the surrounding [tributaries] of the intermediate rivers as compared to the Gaṅgā and Sindhu are also twenty-eight and again twenty-eight [in number]. One has to consider the same for West Videha.

SŪTRA 25

अत्र सूत्रकारो ऽमुमेवार्थं स्पष्टयन् सकलजम्बूद्वीपनदीनां संख्यामाह -
atra sūtra-kāro 'mum evārtham spaṣṭayan sakala-jambūdvīpa-nadīnāṃ saṃkhyām āha -
Now the author of the manual, settling the matter, sums up all the rivers of Jambūdvīpa.

सीया[1] सीओया[2] वि[3] य[4], बत्तीस[5]सहस्स[6]पंच[7]लक्खेहिं[8] ।
सव्वे[9] चउदस[10]लक्खा[11], छप्पन्न[12]सहस्स[13] मेलविया[14] ॥ २५ ॥[15]
sīyā sīoyā vi ya, battīsa-sahassa-paṃca-lakkhehiṃ;
savve caüdasa-lakkhā, chappanna-sahassa melaviyā. 25.

---

[1] सीआ LD2. सिया Brd2, Bhog2. सीयो Bhog8.
[2] सीयोया Ed3. सीओआ LD2, Bhog13. सीउया Brd1, 2 & 3, Bhog6, 10, 12, 15 & 17. सीयोआ Bhog8.
[3] वी LD2, Brd2 & 3, Bhog2 & 8.
[4] अ LD2, Bhog8. या Bhog13.
[5] बतिस Brd2. बत्ती(?)सस Bhog2. स omitted in Bhog9. बतीस Bhog10.
[6] सहस Tueb, Bhog4. स is missing in Bhog12 & 15.
[7] पच Bhog14 & 15.
[8] लखेहिं Brd2 & 3, Bhog4 & 6. लक्खेहिं ५३२००० Tueb, Bhog8(?). लक्खेहि Bhog2, 7 & 17. लखेहि Bhog10.
[9] सचे Bhog2. सव्व Bhog10.
[10] चओदस LD1. चउदश Bhog4. चउद्दस Bhog10.
[11] लखा Brd3, Bhog2. लक्खा १४५६००० Bhog8.
[12] छप्पन Ed3. छपन्न Brd2 & 3, Bhog2 & 15. छप्पण्ण Bhog5. च्छप्पन्न Bhog6. छपण Bhog12.
[13] सहस Bhog4 & 13. सहसा Bhog10.
[14] मेलविआ LD2, Bhog11 & 13. मलविया १४५६००० Tueb. मेलवीया Bhog8. मेलविय Bhog15.
[15] This verse is numbered 26 in LD2, Bhog7 & 8, 22 in Bhog6 and 23 in Bhog12.

(शीता शीतोदापि च द्वात्रिंशत्सहस्राधिकपञ्चलक्षैः। सर्वाश्चतुर्दशलक्षाणि षट्पञ्चाशत्सहस्राणि मेलिताः॥ २५॥ *śītā śītodāpi ca dvātriṃśat-sahasrādhika-pañca-lakṣaiḥ; sarvāś caturdaśa-lakṣāṇi ṣaṭ-pañcāśat-sahasrāṇi melitāḥ. 25.*)

25. The Śītā as well as the Śītodā [flow to the ocean] together with five hundred thirty and two thousand [tributaries]. All together, there are fourteen lakhs [and] fifty-six thousand [tributaries].

COMMENTARY

सीया^इति - शीता नदी पञ्चभिर्लक्षैर्द्वात्रिंशता सहस्रैर्नदीभिः समं जलधिं व्रजतीति[1] पूर्वतरगाथायाः सम्बन्धो गृह्यते। तथा शीतोदापि पृथगेतावतैव परिवारेणावगन्तव्या, ततः सर्वसंख्यया किं जातमित्याह - **सव्वे**^इत्यादि सर्वे नदीवाचिनो ऽङ्का इति गम्यते, यदि वा प्राकृतत्त्वाल्लिङ्गव्यत्यये सर्वा नद्यः। **मेलविया**^इति मेलिता इति णिगन्तोऽपि मूलार्थद्योतकः। यथा रामो राज्यमकारयदकरोदित्यर्थः, ततो मिलिताः समुदिताश्चतुर्दशलक्षानि षट्पञ्चाशत् सहस्राण्यष्टसप्ततेर्नदीनां परिवारः, ताश्चेमाः गङ्गाद्या ह्रदसम्भवास्तथा कुण्डप्रभवा गङ्गासिन्धुप्रमाणाः प्रतिविजयं द्वे द्वे इति कृत्वा द्वात्रिंशति विजयेषु चतुःषष्टिः। ग्राह[ा]वत्याद्या द्वादश तु परिवारहीना अन्तर्नद्य एवमेता नवतिर्महानद्यो भवन्ति जम्बूद्वीपे। परं पूर्वोक्तात् षट्पञ्चाशत्सहस्राधिकचतुर्दशलक्षलक्षणात् परिवारादेताः समधिका विज्ञेया न पुनस्तन्मध्ये गणनीयाः। **"यतो गङ्गासिन्धुरत्ता रत्तवई"**[2] इति गाथया चतुर्दशसहस्रसंख्यः परिवारो मूलनदीव्यतिरिक्त उक्त इत्यादि। आशाम्बरमतानुसारिणो ऽप्येवमेवाहुः, तथा च तद्ग्रंथः -

---

[1] In stead of व्रजन्तीति.

[2] Origin of quotation untraced.

"जम्बूद्दीवनराहिव, सम्खा सव्वनइ चउदह य लखा ।
छपन्नं च सहस्सा, नवइ नईओ कहंति जिणा ॥ १ ॥"[1]
२५ ॥

sīyā^*iti - śītā-nadī pañcabhir lakṣair dvātriṃśatā sahasrair nadībhiḥ samaṃ jaladhiṃ vrajatīti pūrvatara-gāthāyāḥ sambandho gṛhyate. tathā śītodāpi pṛthag etāvataiva parivāreṇāvagantavyā, tataḥ sarva-saṃkhyayā kiṃ jātam ity āha -* ***savve***^*ity ādi sarve nadī vācino 'ṅkā iti gamyate, yadi vā prākṛtattvāl liṅga-vyatyaye sarvā nadyaḥ,* **melaviyā**^*iti melitā iti ṇig-anto 'pi mūlārtha-dyotakaḥ, yathā rāmo rājyam akārayad akarod ity arthaḥ, tato militāḥ samuditāś catur-daśa-lakṣāni ṣaṭ-pañcāśat sahasrāṇy aṣṭa-saptater nadīnāṃ parivāraḥ, tāś cemāḥ gaṅgādyā hrada-sambhavās tathā kuṇḍa-prabhavā gaṅgā-sindhu-pramāṇāḥ prativijayaṃ dve dva iti kṛtvā dvātriṃśati vijayeṣu catuḥ-ṣaṣṭiḥ, grāha[ā]vaty-ādyā dvādaśa tu parivāra-hīnā antar-nadya evam etā navatir mahā-nadyo bhavanti jambūdvīpe. paraṃ pūrvoktāt ṣaṭ-pañcāśat-sahasrādhika-catur-daśa-lakṣa-lakṣaṇāt parivārād etāḥ samadhikā vijñeyā na punas tan-madhye gaṇanīyāḥ, yato "****gaṃgā-siṃdhu-rattā-rattavaī****"[2] iti gāthayā catur-daśa-sahasra-saṃkhyaḥ parivāro mūla-nadī-vyatirikta ukta ity ādi. āśāmbara-matānusāriṇo 'py evam evāhuḥ, tathā ca tad-granthaḥ -*

---

[1] Origin of quotation untraced. Chāyā: जम्बूद्वीपनराधिप संख्या सर्वनदी चतुर्दश च लक्षा षट्पचाशत् च सहस्राणि नवतिः नद्यः कथयन्ति जिनाः ।

[2] Origin of quotation untraced.

"jaṃbūddīva-narāhiva, saṃkhā savva-naï caü-daha ẏa lakhā; chapannaṃ ca sahassā, navaï naīo kahaṃti jiṇā. 1."[1]

25.

'**Siẏā**' [etc.]. The river Śītā flows to the ocean together with five lakhs and thirty-two thousand tributaries. In this manner, the link with the previous verse is made. So also, the Śītodā on her part must be considered to have the same amount of tributaries.[2] Next [the author] explains what follows from the number 'all': '**savve**', etc. We surmise that '*sarve nadī*' is a mistake[3] of expression. Or else, in case there is a change of gender as it happens in Prākrit, [it stands for] '*sarvā nadyaḥ*'.[4] The ***-i-*** affix in '***melaviẏā***' overall has the same meaning as in '*melitā* (assembled)', as [for instance] the meaning of [the alternative expression that] Rāma exercised or carried out government.[5] Hence [when] assembled, viz. all together, there

---

[1] Origin of quotation untraced. Chāyā: *jambūdvīpa-narādhipa saṃkhyā sarva-nadī catur-daśa ca lakṣā ṣaṭ-pañcāśat ca sahasrāṇi navatiḥ nadyaḥ kathayanti jināḥ.*

[2] This is the number of direct tributaries, viz. 84,000, increased with the number of indirect tributaries, viz. 448,000 that reach the Śītā vs. Śītodā via the 64 Gaṅgās, Sindhus, Raktās and Raktodās in the 32 Vijayas of Mahāvideha.

[3] Lit. a hook or curve.

[4] Normally in Sanskrit as well as in Prākrit '*nadī* (**ṇaī**)' is a female word. So we should read '*sarvā nadyaḥ* (***savvāo ṇaīo***)' in the plural. However, in Prākrit change of gender often occurs.

[5] Reference is made to the *ṇi(ṅ)*affix (*anta*) in the Sanskrit grammatical terminology. This affix forms verbal adjectives of causatives or denominatives on *-(p)ayati*. The Pkt. ***melaviẏa*** formally derives from

are fourteen lakhs and fifty-six thousand. [Now] the tributaries of the seventy-eight rivers[1]. Moreover, they, these, [viz.] the Gaṅgā, etc. have their source in a lake. For every other province there are two of the size of the Gaṅgā and Sindhu, etc. arising from a basin. Knowing this, there are sixty-four in the twelve provinces. On the other hand, there are twelve inland rivers like the Grāhāvatī, etc., which have no tributaries. Thus, there are ninety main rivers in Jambūdvīpa.[2] On the other hand, these [main rivers] should not be added to the fourteen lakhs and fifty-six thousand tributaries mentioned before since they cannot be not be counted among them, because in the verse "*The Gaṅgā, Sindhu, Raktā and Raktāvatī*[3] *[...]*" the number of the fourteen thousand tributaries is reckoned separately from the main rivers. The followers of the Digambara[4] sect agree with this. Accordingly, their manual learns:

**melāpita* which is a causative verbal adjective of the root *mel.* of the 10th verbal class: *melāpayati*. The same root also forms the causative form *melayati* with as verbal adjective **melita-*. So, both forms **melāpita* and **melita* basically have the same meaning. See Turner (1966), vol. I, entry 10332 and Renou, L. (1942), p. 152.

[1] These are the 64 Gaṅgās, Sindhus, Raktās and Raktodās in the 32 Vijayas in Mahāvideha and the 14 main rivers of Jambūdvīpa including the main Gaṅgā and Sindhu in Bharata, and the main Raktā and Raktodā in Airāvata.

[2] Viz., these *mūla-nadīs* are the above mentioned 78 rivers increased with the 12 inland rivers of Mahāvideha.

[3] = Raktodā.

[4] Āśāmbara = Digambara.

"O, Lord of Jambūdvīpa, the Liberated declare that the number of all rivers is fourteen lakhs and fifty-six thousand rivers and that there are ninety [main] rivers [extra]."

SŪTRA 26

सम्प्रति महानदीनां प्रवहमुखयोर्विस्तारमाह -
samprati mahā-nadīnām pravaha-mukhayor vistāram āha -
Now [the author] describes the width of the source and the mouth of the main rivers.

छज्जोयणे[1] सकोसे[2], गङ्गासिंधूण[3] वित्थरो[4] मूले[5] ।
दस[6]गुणिओ[7] पज्जंते[8], इय[9] दुदु[10]गुणणेण[11] सेसाणं[12] ॥ २६ ॥[13]
chaj-joyaṇe sa-kose, gaṃgā-siṃdhūṇa vittharo mūle;
dasa-guṇio pajjaṃte, iẏa du-du-guṇaṇeṇa sesāṇaṃ. 26.

---

[1] छजोयणे LD1, Bhog7, 11, 12, 15 & 16. छज्जोअण LD2. छद्योयणे Brd1, Bhog10. छजोयण Brd3, Bhog5. छज्जोअणे Tueb, Bhog1. छयोयणे Bhog2. छज्जोयणे Bhog4. च्छयोयण Bhog6.
[2] सक्कोसे LD1 & 2. सकोशे १ Tueb. सकोसं Bhog6, 11 & 17. छकोसे Bhog10. सकोस Bhog15. सङ्कोसे Bhog12.
[3] सिन्धु LD1, Bhog1, 8, 10, 14 & 17. सिधु Brd3. सिधू Bhog4.
[4] वीत्थरो Bhog2. वित्थडो(?) Bhog5. वित्य(?)डो(?) Bhog12.
[5] मुले Brd2 & 3, Bhog2, 4, 12 & 14. मूल Bhog15 & 17.
[6] दश Bhog12 & 13.
[7] गूणीऊ LD1. ओ is missing in LD2. गुणिउ Brd2 & 3, Bhog5, 10. गुणीओ Bhog1, 8, 12 & 16. गुणिय Bhog6. गुंणीओ Bhog7. गुणीउ Bhog15 & 17.
[8] पद्यं Bhog2, 4 & 7. पद्यत्ते Bhog6. पज्जे(?)ते Bhog9. पजंति Bhog10 & 13.
[9] इइ Tueb. इय is missing in Bhog5 & 12. इयं Bhog6. ईय Bhog7.
[10] दुदू LD1. दुगुणादुगुणेहिं Bhog5. दुगणादुगहिं Bhog12. Second दु omitted in Bhog6.
[11] गूणेंण LD1. गुणेण Brd2, Bhog15. गुणेणण Brd3. गुणे Bhog2. गुंणणेण Bhog4 & 16. गुणणेणं Bhog6. गुंणेण Bhog7. गुणणण Bhog8. गुणेणेण Bhog10.
[12] सेसेहिं Bhog5. सहस्सेहिं Bhog12.
[13] This verse is numbered 27 in LD2, 23 in Bhog6 and 24 in Bhog12.

(षड्योजनानि सक्रोशानि गङ्गासिन्ध्वोर्विस्तरो मूले। दशगुणितः पर्यन्त इति द्विद्विगुणनेन शेषाणाम्॥ २६॥ *ṣaḍ-yojanāni sa-krośāni gaṅgā-sindhvor vistaro mūle; daśa-guṇitaḥ paryanta iti dvi-dvi-guṇanena śeṣāṇām. 26.*)

26. The width of the Gaṅgā and the Sindhu at their source is six *yojanas* and one *krośa*.[1] At the end [their width] is multiplied by ten. In the same way [the width] of the other [main] rivers at their source and mouth is obtained] by multiplying repeatedly by two.[2]

COMMENTARY

छज्जोयणे^इति - गंगासिन्ध्वोः सादृश्याद्रक्तारक्तावत्योरपि मूले प्रवहे ह्रदान्निःसार इति यावत्, सक्रोशानि सगव्यूतानि षड्योजनानि विस्तरः प्रपञ्चः, पर्यंते समुद्रादिप्रवेशे दशगुणितो दशगुणः सार्द्धद्वाषष्टियोजनरूपो विस्तारो भवति। तथाभ्यन्तराणां रोहितांशादीनां स्वरूपमाह - इय^इत्यादि। इत्यनया दिशा शेषाणां द्वाभ्यां द्वाभ्यां गुणनं तेन[3] द्वि द्वि गुणनेन विस्तारः शेषाणामवशिष्टानामनुक्तानामिति यावत् लभ्यत इति शेषः। तद्यथा

[1] Or as Kirfel (p. 222) has it: $^{25}/_{4}$ *yojanas*. One *yojana* equals four *krośas* or four *gavyūtas*. See also Kirfel, p. 337.

[2] The Gaṅgā and Sindhu are $^{25}/_{4}$ *yojanas* wide at the source. The Raktā and Raktodā, being the identical counterparts of both the main rivers of Bharata, have the same width at their source: $^{25}/_{4}$ *yojanas*. The width at the source of the other main rivers doubles repeatedly towards the centre starting from Bharata and Airāvata. The Rohitāṃśā, Rohit, Rūpyakūlā and Suvarṇakūlā have $^{25}/_{2}$ *yojanas*, the Harikāntā, Harit, Nārī and Narakāntā 25 *yojanas* and, the Śītodā and Śītā: 50 *yojanas*. The same procedure holds for the mouths.

[3] LD2 adds द्वि द्वि गुणनं between गुणनं and तेन.

रोहितांशारोहितारूप्यकूलासुवर्णकूलानां प्रवहे सार्द्धद्वादशा, पर्यंतेपञ्चविंशं शतं योजनानि विस्तारः। तथा तन्मध्यानां हरिकान्ताहरित्सलिलानारीकान्तानरकान्तानां ह्रदतोरणान्निर्गमे पञ्चविंशतिर्, जलधिप्रवेशे तु सार्द्धशतद्वयं योजनानि। पुनः शीताशीतोदयोस्तोरणान्निःसारे पञ्चाशत्पर्यंते पञ्चशतानि योजनानां प्रपञ्च इति गाथार्थः ॥ २६ ॥

chaj-joẏaṇe^*iti - gaṅgā-sindhvoḥ sādṛśyād raktā-raktāvatyor api mūle pravahe hradān niḥsāra iti yāvat, sa-krośāni sa-gavyūtāni ṣaḍ-yojanāni vistaraḥ prapañcaḥ, paryante samudrādi-praveśe daśa-guṇito daśa-guṇaḥ sārdha-dvā-ṣaṣṭi-yojana-rūpo vistāro bhavati. tathābhyantarāṇāṃ rohitāṃśādīnāṃ svarūpam āha -* ***iẏa^****ity ādi. ity anayā diśā śeṣāṇāṃ dvābhyāṃ dvābhyāṃ guṇanaṃ tena dvi dvi guṇanena vistāraḥ śeṣāṇām avaśiṣṭānām anuktānām iti yāvat labhyata iti śeṣaḥ. tad yathā rohitāṃśā-rohitā-rūpyakūlā-suvarṇakūlānāṃ pravahe sārdha-dvādaśa, paryante pañca-viṃśaṃ śataṃ yojanāni vistāraḥ. tathā tan-madhyānāṃ harikāntā-haritsalilā-nārīkāntā-narakāntānāṃ hrada-toraṇān nirgame pañca-viṃśatir, jaladhi-praveśe tu sārdha-śata-dvayaṃ yojanāni. punaḥ śītā-śītodayos toraṇān niḥsāre pañcāśat paryante pañca-śatāni yojanānāṃ prapañca iti gāthārthaḥ. 26.*

26. '***Chaj-joẏaṇe***' [etc.]. At the source of the Gaṅgā and the Sindhu, where [their waters] stream out of their [corresponding] lakes, [and] to be precise - since they are similar - of the Raktā and Raktāvatī too, their width [or] breadth is six *yojanas* and one *krośa* [or] one *gavyūta.* At the end, when they enter into the ocean, etc.[1] their width is

[1] It is not clear what this 'etc.' implies since all main rivers of Jambūdvīpa flow into the same Lavaṇoda ocean.

multiplied by ten, [or] is ten times lager, consisting of sixty-two and one half [*yojanas*].[1] Even so [the author] explains the nature of the [rivers] lying in between, the Rohitāṃśā, etc.: '*iỳa*' (thus), etc. With this reference [introduced with the word] 'thus' one learns just so much that the width of the remaining [rivers], those left out [or] not yet mentioned [is obtained] by over and over again multiplying by two, by the multiplication with two and once more with two for the remaining. This is the full meaning. To wit, the breadth of the Rohitāṃśā, Rohitā, Rūpyakūlā and Suvarṇakūlā is twelve and a half [*yojanas*], at the end one hundred and twenty-five [*yojanas*] at the source. So also is [the width] of the Harikāntā, Haritsalilā, Nārīkāntā and Narakāntā lying in between them twenty-five [*yojanas*] where they come out of the gates of the mountain lakes. When they reach the ocean, however, they are two hundred and fifty *yojanas* [wide]. Moreover, when they flow out of the gates of the mountain lakes, the width of the Śītā and the Śītodā is fifty [and] at the end five hundred *yojanas*. This is the meaning of the verse.

---

[1] See Kirfel, p. 222: $^{125}/_{2}$ or 62 ½ *yojanas*.

SŪTRA 27

इदानीं सूत्रकारः स्वयमेव मुग्धावबोधार्थं वर्षधराणामुच्चत्ववर्णावाह -
idānīṃ sūtra-kāraḥ svayam eva mugdhāvabodhārthaṃ varṣa-dharāṇām uccatva-varṇāv āha -
Now, in order to instruct the ignorant, the author of the manual gives of his own accord the height and colour[1] of the World Mountains.

जोयण[2]सयमुव्विद्धा/उच्चिट्ठा[3], कणय[4]मया[5] सिहरि[6]चुल्लहिमवंता[7] ।
रुप्पि[1]महाहिमवंता[2], दुसउच्चा[3] रुप्प[4]कणय[5]मया ॥ २७ ॥[6]

---

[1] So all descriptions of the different mountains as 'golden', 'made of beryl', etc. do not necessarily have to be taken literally, but can be interpreted as a descriptions of their outward appearance, viz. their colour.

[2] जोअण LD2.

[3] उव्विद्धा Ed1, LD2, Bhog4 & 12. उविद्धा LD1, Brd2, Tueb, Bhog2. उच्चिट्ठा Ed2 & 3, Brd1, Bhog1. उच्चिद्धा Brd3, Bhog13, 14, 16 & 17. उचिद्धा Bhog5 & 15. उच्चि(?)ट्ठा(?) Bhog6, 7, 8, 10 & 11. उव्विद्धा and उच्चिट्ठा are both possible. उव्विद्ध < उद्विद्ध (tossed upwards, high, elevated) is attested in Skt. There is no problem regarding derivation: -द्व- > -व्व-, and no problem regarding meaning. Indeed, उच्चिट्ठ < उद् + स्था, *उद् + तिष्ठ > *उद् + चिट्ठ is attested in Pkt. as from उत् + स्था (in the sense of Hd. खड़ा होना) but is not attested as an adjective in Skt. However, चिट्ठ (= अत्यन्त, 'very great') is attested in Pkt.

[4] य omitted in Bhog6. कणग Bhog7, 10, 13 & 16.

[5] ममया LD1.

[6] सिहिरि. LD1, Brd1, Bhog10. सिहरी Bhog6. सिहर Bhog8. सीहरि Bhog13 & 14. सिंहरी Bhog17.

[7] चुल्लसिहरीहिमवंता Bhog4. चूल्ल LD1, Bhog10 & 15. चुल Bhog2. चुत्त Bhog6. चुल्ल Bhog13. हेमवंतेय Bhog6. हिंमवंता Bhog7, 10 & 16.

joẏaṇa-saẏam uvviddhā/uccitthā, kaṇaẏa-maẏā sihari-cullahimavaṃtā;
ruppi-mahāhimavaṃtā, du-saüccā ruppa-kaṇaẏa-maẏā. 27.

(योजनशतमुच्छ्रितौ कनकमयौ शिखरिक्षुल्लहिमवन्तौ। रुक्मिमहाहिमवन्तौ द्विशतोच्चौ रूप्यकनकमयौ ॥ २७ ॥ *yojana-śatam udviddhau/ucchritau kanaka-mayau śikhari-kṣullahimavantau; rukmi-mahāhimavantau dvi-śatoccau rūpya-kanaka-mayau. 27.*)

27. Śikharin and Kṣullahimavanta are one hundred *yojanas* high and are made of gold. Rukmin and Mahāhimavanta are two hundred [*yojanas*] high and are made of silver[7] and gold.

---

[1] रूप्पि Ed1 & 3, Bhog16, 13 & 17. रूप्पी LD2, Bhog8. रूपि Brd2, Bhog12. रुपि Brd3, Bhog2 & 5. रुप्पी Bhog4 & 6. रूपी Bhog7. रुपी Bhog10.

[2] महहिमवंते Bhog8. महाहिमवंते LD2, Brd1, 2 & 3, Bhog7, 16 & 17. महाहिमवंत Tueb. महाहिवंतां Bhog2. महाहेमवंते Bhog6. महाहिंमवंता Bhog10. महाहिमवंतो Bhog11.

[3] सओच्चा LD1, Bhog4 & 13. सुच्चा(?) LD2. सयउच्चा Bhog1 & 14. सउच्चा Bhog2, 10 & 15(?). सुउच्चा(?) Bhog8. स्सउच्चा Bhog12.

[4] रूप्प Ed3, LD2, Brd2, Bhog6 & 8. रुप Bhog2 & 17. प omitted in Bhog7 & 16.

[5] कणयं Brd2. कणग Bhog6, 7, 16 & 17.

[6] This verse is numbered 28 in LD2, Bhog7, 8 & 16, 24 in Bhog6 and 25 in Bhog12. Bhog2 introduces the verse with दारं १०, Bhog5 with डारं १०, Bhog12 with द्दा १०.

[7] *rūpya* = *raupya*. The *Trailokyadīpikā* describes Rukmin and Mahāhimavat as consisting of *arjuna* and *rajata* respectively, both meaning silver. See Kirfel, p. 215.

COMMENTARY

जोयण^इति - शिखरी पर्यंतवर्त्ती वर्षधरः । **चुल्ल^**इति क्षुल्लो महाहैमवतापेक्षया लघुः हिमवान् क्षुल्लहिमवान् एतौ योजनशतमुद्विद्धावुच्छ्रितौ, कीदृशावित्याह - कनकं स्वर्णं तन्मयौ तद्वर्णावित्यर्थः, तथा **रुप्पि^**इत्यादि, रुक्मिमहाहैमवन्तौ द्वे शते योजनानामिति गम्यते । उच्चावुच्छ्रितौ द्विशतोच्चौ तथा रूप्पकनकमयौ क्रमेण, तथाहि - रुक्मी रूप्यमयः । महाहिमवांस्तु हिरण्यमय इति ॥ २७ ॥

joẏaṇe^iti - śikharī paryanta-vartī varṣa-dharaś, ***culla^****iti kṣullo mahāhaimavatāpekṣayā laghuḥ himavān kṣullahimavān, etau yojana-śatam udviddhāv ucchritau, kīdṛśāv ity āha - kanakaṃ svarṇaṃ tan-mayau tad-varṇāv ity arthaḥ. tathā* ***ruppi^****ity ādi, rukmi-mahāhaimavantau dve śate yojanānām iti gamyate, uccāv ucchritau dvi-śatoccau tathā rūpya-kanaka-mayau krameṇa. tathā hi: rukmī rūpya-mayaḥ, mahāhimavāṃs tu hiraṇya-maya iti. 27.*

27. '***joẏaṇa***' [etc.]. The meaning is as follcws. Śikharin is a World Mountain range situated at the [northern] end. [The word] '***culla***' means small. The [Small or] Kṣullahimavat is a Himavat that is 'small' with regard to the [Great or] Mahāhaimavata. Both are one hundred *yojanas* high [or] elevated. [The author] explains how they are [characterized]: golden, made thereof, viz. having the colour of that. Even so '***ruppi***', etc. Now it is stated that Rukmin and Mahāhaimavanta [measure] two hundred *yojanas*. They are two hundred [*yojanas*] high or elevated and both are made of silver and gold successively. For, Rukmin is made of silver, while Mahāhimavat is made of gold.

SŪTRA 28[1]

सव्वे[2] वि पव्वय[3]वरा[4], समय[5]खित्तंमि[6] मंदर[7]विहूणा[8] ।
धरणि[9]तले[10] अवगाढा[11], उस्सेह[1]चउत्थ[2]भायमिति[3] ॥[4]

---

[1] Prabhānanda Sūri gives the verse that actually represents *sū*. 28 at the end of his comment on *sū*. 27: इह यद्यप्यवगाहो नोक्तः सूत्रकारेण, तथाप्युच्छ्रयस्य चतुर्थांशमानो ऽवगम्यः । उक्तं च -
"सव्वेवि पव्वयवरा, समयखित्तंमि मंदरविहूणा ।
धरणितले अवगाढा,उस्सेह चउत्थयं भायं ॥ १ ॥".
iha yady apy avagāho noktaḥ sūtra-kāreṇa, tathāpy ucchrayasya caturthāṃśa-māno 'vagamyaḥ. uktaṃ ca -
"savvevi pavvaẏa-varā, samaẏa-khittaṃmi maṃdara-vihūṇā;
dhara-ṇitale avagāḍhā, usseha-caütthaẏaṃ bhāẏaṃ.1."
iti: "Here, although the author does not mention the depth [of the World Mountains], it must be considered to be one fourth of the size of their height. It is said: ...".

[2] सवे Bhog2 & 10.

[3] वियपव्वय LD2. पवय Bhog2. पव(?)य Bhog1 & 8. पवण Bhog5. प्पव्वय Bhog17.

[4] व is missing in Ed3, Brd1, Bhog4, 11, 12 & 17. भरा Bhog7 & 16.

[5] य omitted in Bhog9.

[6] खित्तम्मि Ed2. खितंमि Brd2 & 3. खित्तंमी Bhog1, 4 & 13. क्खित्तंमि Bhog7 & 17. खित्तमि Bhog15.

[7] मणिदरं Bhog4. मदइ Bhog12. हिर(?) Bhog14.

[8] There seems to be some confusion between हू and दू. वीहूणा Ed2 & 3, LD1. विदू(?)णा Bhog1, 8, 9, 11, 12, 13, 14 & 15. वीदू(?)णं Bhog2. विदुणा Bhog4. विदूणी Bhog5. विदुंणा Bhog10. विदूंणा Bhog7.

[9] धरणी Ed3, LD1 & 2, Bhog1, 4, 7, 12, 16 & 17. धरणा Brd2 & 3.

[10] तलम् Ed3. यले LD1, Brd1, 2 & 3, Bhog2, 9, 11, 15 & 17. ताले Tueb. त omitted in Bhog8.

[11] उवगाढा Ed2 & 3. Initial अ omitted or elided in LD1, Brd2 & 3, Tueb, Bhog7, 14, 15 & 16. यवगाढा Brd1, Bhog9, 11 & 17. सुवगाढा Bhog4.

savve vi pavvaẏa-varā, samaẏa-khittaṃmi maṃdara-vihūṇā[5]***;***
dharaṇi-tale avagāḍhā, usseha-caüttha-bhāẏam iti. 28.

(सर्वे ऽपि पर्वतवराः समयक्षेत्रे मन्दरविहीनाः। धरणीतले ऽवगाढा उत्सेधचतुर्थभागे॥ *sarve 'pi parvata-varāḥ samaya-kṣetre mandara-vihīnāḥ; dharaṇī-tale 'vagāḍhā utsedha-caturtha-bhāgam iti. 28.*)

28. All main mountains in the temporal world[6] except Mandara are immersed under the surface of the earth one-fourth part of their height.

---

[1] उसेह Brd2 & 3, Bhog2 & 10. ओच्चशेय(?) Bhog4.

[2] There seems to be confusion here between त्थ and च्छ. चओच्छ(?) LD1. चउत्थयं LD2. चउच्छ(?) Brd1, Bhog1, 2, 7, 9, 10, 11, 16 & 17. चउत्थयं Tueb. चओथो(?) Bhog4. वउत्थयं Bhog5. चउच्छय Bhog8. त्थ(?)यल(?) Bhog12.

[3] There are two possibilities here, both of them metrically correct: 1) -भायमिति (Chāya -भागमिति) in LD1 & 2, Brd1, 2 & 3, Tueb, Bhog1, 8 & 9, and 2) -भायंमि (Chāya -भागे) in Ed2 & 3, Bhog13 & 14. Other forms: भायंमी Bhog7 & 16, भायमि Bhog10, भायंमिति Bhog11, भायं Bhog12, भागमिति Bhog15, भायमित्ति Bhog17.

[4] This verse is numbered 29 in Ed2 & 3, LD2, Bhog2, 7, 8 & 16. It is numbered 27 in Bhog12. It is missing in Ed1 and Bhog6. It is introduced with उत्तर(?) in LD1, with उत्तं च in LD2, Brd1, 2 & 3, Tueb, Bhog9, 10, 11, 15 & 17, with वत्तं च Bhog8, with उत्तं in Bhog13 and with उत्तं चः in Bhog14. The Āryā metre is defective in the fourth *gaṇa*. This defect can be remedied by the reading -क्खित्तंमि in stead of -खित्तंमि but only Bhog7 and 17 adopt this version.

[5] For ***vihūṇa*** = *vihīna*. See Pischel §120.

[6] Viz. the human world: समयक्षेत्र = कालोपलक्षित भूमि = मनुष्यलोक or मनुष्यक्षेत्र.

SŪTRA 29

चत्तारि[1] जोयण[2]सए[3], उव्विद्धो/उच्चिट्ठो[4] निसढ[5] नीलवंतो[6] य[7]।
निसढो[8] तवणिज्ज[9]मओ[10], वेरुलिओ[11] नीलवंत[12]गिरी[13] ॥ २८ ॥

cattāri joẏaṇa-sae, uvviddho/uccitṭtho nisaḍha nīlavaṃto ẏa;
nisaḍho tavaṇijjamao, verulio nīlavaṃta-girī. 29.

(चत्वारि योजनशतान्युच्छितो निषधो नीलवांश्च। निषधस्तपनीयमयो वैडूर्यको नीलवान् गिरिः॥ २८॥ *catvāri yojana-śatāny*

---

[1] चतारि Brd2. चत्तारी Bhog1 & 12. चातारि Bhog2. चत्तारिय Bhog14.

[2] जोअण LD2, Tueb, Bhog4 & 8.

[3] सये Bhog6 & 13. सया Bhog12. सय Bhog14.

[4] Ṭhere is again confusioṇ here, cf. verse 27. उव्विद्धो Ed1, LD2, Tueb, Bhog2, 4 & 17. उव्विद्धा Bhog12. ओंविद्धो LD1. उंविद्धा Brd2. उविद्धो(?) Bhog8 & 10. उच्चिट्ठो Ed2 & 3, Brd1, Bhog1, Bhog7(?), 9(?) & 11(?). उच्चि(?)द्धो Bhog6, 13, 14, 15 & 16. उंच्चिद्धा Brd3. उच्चिद्धा Bhog5.

[5] नीसढ Bhog2. निसह Bhog5.

[6] निलवंतो Brd2, Bhog10 & 12. नीलवंता Bhog5. निलवंतेसु Bhog7. नीलवंतेसु Bhog16.

[7] अ Ed2, LD1. य or अ omitted in Bhog7, 12 & 16.

[8] नीसढो Bhog2. निसड्डो(?) Bhog12. निसड्ढो Bhog16.

[9] तवणिद्य LD1 & 2, Brd1, 2 & 3, Bhog4, 6, 10, 14 & 15. तवणीद्य Bhog1. तवणिज Bhog2, 12 & 16. तवणिय Bhog8. तवणीज्ज Bhog17.

[10] मउ Brd2 & 3, Bhog6, 8, 15 & 17.

[11] वेरूलिओ Brd2. वेरुलिउ Brd3, Bhog17. वेरुलीओ Bhog1, 4, 7 & 11. वेरूलिउ Bhog6. विरुलीओ Bhog8. विरुलिउ Bhog15.

[12] नीलवंतो Ed3, Bhog10. नी omitted in LD1. नीलवत LD2. नीलवंत्त(?) Bhog6. निलवंत Bhog15. नीलवंतो य of the first half of the verse repeated and गिरी omitted.

[13] गिरि Ed2, LD2, Bhog2, 8, 9, 12, 13 & 17. गीरि Bhog4 & 15. गीरी Bhog7. गिर Bhog14.

udviddho/ucchito niṣadho nīlavāṃś ca; niṣadhas tapanīya-mayo vaiḍūry(ak)o nīlavān giriḥ. 29.)

29. Niṣadha and Nīlavat are four hundred *yojanas* high. Niṣadha is made of purified gold, Mount Nīlavat is made of beryl.

COMMENTARY

चत्तारि^इति - निषधश्चत्वारि योजनशतानि उद्विद्ध उच्चो, न केवलमयं, नीलवांश्च तावदेवोच्चः। चः समुच्चये। तथा निषधस्तपनीयमयो जात्यस्वर्णनिर्माणो रक्तवर्ण इत्यर्थः। माल्य(नील)वान् गिरिस्तु वैडूर्यमयो नीलवर्ण इति॥ २९॥

cattāri^*iti - niṣadhaś catvāri yojana-śatāni udviddha ucco, na kevalam ayaṃ, nīlavāṃś ca tāvad evoccaḥ. caḥ samuccaye. tathā niṣadhas tapanīya-mayo jātya-svarṇa-nirmāṇo rakta-varṇa ity arthaḥ. mālya(nīla)vān giris tu vaiḍūrya-mayo nīla-varṇa iti. 29.*

29. '***cattāri***' [etc.]. The meaning is as follows. Niṣadha is four hundred *yojanas* high [or] elevated. Moreover, not alone this [one since also] Nīlavat is of the same height. [The particle] '*ca* (and)' [is used] in conjunctive [sense]. Niṣadha is made of purified gold[1], [viz.] made of the finest gold, [and] has a red

[1] Viz., gold purified with fire.

colour. Mount Mālyavat (Nīlavat ?)[1] however, is made of beryl [and] has a blue colour.

---

[1] The confusion of the mountain range of Nīlavat with Mount Mālyavat is inexplicable here. For Niṣadha and Nīlavat, see Kirfel, pp. 215 & 217.

SŪTRA 30[1]

संप्रति स्वाभिधानप्रकाशनपुरःसरं सूत्रकारो ऽर्थकरणोपसंहारमाह -
saṃprati svābhidhāna-prakāśana-puraḥsaraṃ sūtra-kāro 'rtha-karaṇopasaṃhāram āha -
Now the author of the manual states the epilogue, [again] referring to the contents [and] at the same time revealing his name:

खंडाई[2]गाहाहिं[3], दसहिं[4] दारेहि[5] जंबुदीवस्स[6] ।
संघयणी[7] सम्मत्ता[8], रइया[1] हरिभद्द[2]सूरीहिं[3] ॥ ३० ॥[4]

---

[1] This is verse 29 in Ed1 and verse 31 in LD2.

[2] खण्डाइं Ed3, Bhog1, 8, 16 & 17. खण्डाइ LD2, Brd2 & 3, Tueb, Bhog7, 10, 14 & 15.

[3] गाहाए Ed1, LD2, Bhog2, 5, 10, 12, 13 & 14. गाहाइं LD1, Brd3, Bhog7, 15, 16 & 17. गाहाई Brd1. गाहाइ Brd2, Bhog9 & 11. गाहाप(?) Tueb. गाहाहे Bhog1. गाहा Bhog6.

[4] दसहि LD1, Brd2 & 3, Bhog2 & 17. दसेहिं Bhog7 & 15. दशहिं Bhog13. दसए Bhog14.

[5] All sources except Bhog2, 4, 11 & 17 have the ending -हिं here (See next note). दारिहिं Brd2. द्वारेहिं Tueb. दोरेहिं Bhog14.

[6] जम्बूदीवस्स Ed1 & 2, LD1 & 2, Brd1, Bhog1, 6, 8, 13 & 17. जम्बुद्दीवस्स Ed3, Bhog7 & 16. जम्बुदीवस Brd2 & 3. जम्बुदिवस Bhog2. जम्बूद्दीवस्स Bhog4, 9, 12 & 15. जम्बूंदीवस्स Bhog10. Only Tueb, Bhog5, 11 & 14 read जम्बुदीवस्स. The first half of the verse can only be metrically correct if we read ...-हि जम्बु-... in which case we have the regular metrical sequence ˘ – ˘ in the sixth *gaṇa*.

[7] संगहणी Tueb, Bhog5, 6 & 12. य omitted in Bhog2. संघयणि Bhog15.

[8] The regular form समत्ता is found in LD1, Brd3, Bhog2, 4, 5, 7, 8, 9, 12, 13, 14, 15, 16 & 17. समता Brd2, Bhog10. ...त्ता, रइया हरि... omitted in Bhog6. Brd2 & 3: समता.

khaṃḍāī-gāhāhiṃ, dasahiṃ dārehi jaṃbudīvassa;
saṃghayaṇī sammattā, raïyā haribhadda-sūrīhiṃ. 30.

(खण्डादिगाथाभिर्दशभिद्वारैर्जम्बूद्वीपस्य। संग्रहणी समाप्ता रचिता हरिभद्रसूरिभिः ॥ ३० ॥ *khaṇḍādi-gāthābhir daśabhir dvārair jambūdvīpasya; saṃgrahaṇī samāptā racitā haribhadra-sūribhiḥ. 30.*)

30. The *Saṃgrahaṇī* (Summary) of Jambūdvīpa composed by Haribhadra Sūri on the ten topics by means of the verses on the continents, etc. is [now] completed.

COMMENTARY

खंडाई^इति[5] - जम्बूद्वीपस्याद्यद्वीपक्षेत्ररूपस्य[6] संग्रहणिः समाप्ता, इष्टार्थकथनेन पूर्णा, कैः? इत्याह - दशभिर् दशसंख्यावच्छिन्नैर् द्वारैरुक्तस्वरूपैः। किंविशिष्टैः? खंडाई^इति[7] खण्डादीनामुद्देशका गाथा खण्डा[8]दिगाथा, तया तथोक्तया, "दीर्घह्रस्वौ मिथो वृत्तौ" इति दीर्गत्वं 'ई',

---

[1] रईया LD1, Bhog12, 13, 14 & 17. रईआ LD2. रइआ Bhog8 & 10.

[2] हरीभद्द LD1. हरिभद Bhog2 & 6. हरिभद्र Bhog13.

[3] सूरिहिं Ed1, Brd3, Bhog7, 10, 13, 16 & 17. सुरिहिं Brd2. सुरिहि Bhog2. सूरेहिं Bhog12. सूरीहिं is the only metrically correct form with lengthening metri causa of इ in the ending -ईहिं.

[4] This verse is numbered 29 in Ed1, 31 in LD2, Bhog7, 8 & 16, 26 in Bhog6 and 28 in Bhog12. The final clause रइया हरिभद्दसूरीहिं ॥ ३० ॥ is missing in Bhog15.

[5] Ed1: खण्डाइत्ति.

[6] LD2: जम्बूद्वीपक्षेत्ररूपस्य.

[7] LD2: खण्डाइत्ति.

[8] In stead of खंदा...

खंडा जोयणवासा^इत्यनया सूत्रादिकथितया गाथया उपलिखितैरिति, कैः? कृतेयं? इत्याह - श्री हरिभद्रसूरिभिः रचिता सूत्रतया निबद्धेति भद्रम्॥ ३०॥

khaṇḍāī*^*iti *jambūdvīpasyādya-dvīpa-kṣetra-rūpasya saṃgrahaṇiḥ samāptā, iṣṭārtha-kathanena pūrṇā. kaiḥ? ity āha - daśabhir daśa-saṃkhyāvacchinnair dvārair ukta-svarūpaiḥ, kiṃ viśiṣṭaiḥ?* ***khaṇḍāī*^*iti*** *khaṇḍādīnām uddeśakā gāthā khandādi-gāthā, tayā tathoktayā, "dīrgha-hrasvau mitho vṛttau" iti dīrgatvaṃ 'ī',* ***khaṇḍā joẏaṇa-vāsā*^*ity*** *anayā sūtrādi-kathitayā gāthayā upalikhitair iti. kaiḥ? kṛteyam? ity āha - śrī haribhadra-sūribhiḥ racitā sūtratayā nibaddheti bhadram. 30.*

30. '***khaṇḍāī***' [etc.]. The 'Summary of Jambūdvīpa', the region of the first world island[1], is finished, viz. is completed with the exposition intended. With what? [The author] explains: with the ten - viz. restricted to the number of ten - topics, their nature described. [These ten topics are described] by what specifically? '***khaṇḍāī***' [etc.]. A verse explaining the continents, etc. is a verse *on* the continents etc. [So, these ten topics] are explained by this [verse] as such. [Note that] the '*ī*' is long according to the rule that [in Prākrit] long and short [vowels] can be interchanged.[2] [These ten topics] are described in verse [2, viz.] "The sectors, the *yojanas* and the continents

---

[1] Viz. the most central world island of the other countless concentrically expanding world islands of Jambūdvīpa.

[2] In Prākrit vowels are lengthened or shortened mostly for metrical reasons, as is the case here with the '*ī*' in ***khaṃḍāī***. The regular neuter plural ending is ***-āi(ṃ)***.

[etc.]", expressed as an aphorism, etc. As to the question who has written this ['Summary', the author] answers: it is composed or written by the venerable Haribhadra Sūri in the *sūtra* style, and happily so[1].

---

[1] The use of the expression '*iti bhadram*', 'blessed, auspicious' etc., refers to author, Haribhadra Sūri himself.

Appendices

APPENDIX

Appendix 1: The circumference of Jambūdvīpa, with root extraction drawn from of 10^{10}:

Table 1

				3		1		6		2		2		7		
			s	*v*	*s*	*v*	*s*	*v*	*s*	*v*	*s*	*v*	*s*	*v*		
			1	0	0	0	0	0	0	0	0	0	0	0		
A	3^2=		-	9	(	-										
	3x2=	6)		1	0	(	1	=10/6								
	6x1=			-	6											
					4	0										
B	1^2=				-	1										
	31x2=	6 2)			3	9	0	(	6	=390/62						
					3	7	2									
						1	8	0								
C	6^2=						3	6	(	-						
	316x2=	6 3 2				1	4	4	0	(	2	=1440/632				
						1	2	6	4							
							1	7	6	0						
D	2^2=									4	(	-				
	3162x2=	6 3 2 4)					1	7	5	6	0	(	2	=17560/6324		
							1	2	6	4	8					
								4	9	1	2	0				
E	2^2=											4	(	-		
	31622x2=	6 3 2 4 4)						4	9	1	9	6	0	(	7	*
								4	4	2	7	0	8			
									4	8	4	5	2	0		
F	7^2=												4	9	(	-
	316227x2=	6 3 2 4 5 4)							4	8	4	4	7	1		

s = *sama*, even

v = *viṣama*, oneven

* = 491960/63244

Table 2

			4 8 4 4 7 1	*yoj.*	
G	316227x2=	6 3 2 4 5 4) =	1 9 3 7 8 8 4	***gav.***	(3
	632454x3		1 8 9 7 3 6 2	*gav.*	
			4 0 5 2 2	*gav.*	
H	316227x2=	6 3 2 4 5 4) =	8 1 0 4 4 0 0 0	***dhan.***	(128
	632454x128		8 0 9 5 4 1 1 2	*dhan.*	
			8 9 8 8 8	*dhan.*	
I	316227x2=	6 3 2 4 5 4) =	8 6 2 9 2 4 8	***aṅg.***	(13
	632454x13		8 2 2 1 9 0 2	*aṅg.*	
			4 0 7 3 4 6	*aṅg.*	
	316227x2=	6 3 2 4 5 4) =	8 1 4 6 9 2	**½ *aṅg***	(1
	632454x1		6 3 2 4 5 4		
	remainder =		1 8 2 2 3 8		

yoj. = yojana
gav. = gavyūta
dhan. = dhanus
aṅg. = aṅula

Appendix 2: Materials for the study of the Jaina Haribhadras

Below the relevant information on the Jaina Haribhadras (Sūris) as found in the *JRK* is listed. The list refers to the pages in the *JRK*. It also gives the main name (Haribhadra or Haribhadra Sūri), eventually his epithet, his place in the succession of predecessors and successors, and of teachers and pupils, works and commentaries. Finally, yet importantly, it furnishes dates and places if found. Undated and anonymous commentaries are not mentioned.

JRK p.	*author*	*epithet*	*relationships*	*works*	*dates & places*
2	Haribhadrasūri			*Ṭīkā* on the *Aṅgavidyā* of Śāntisūri (astrology)	
9	Haribhadrasūri	Bhavaviraha	pupil of Jinabhaṭa	*Ṭīkā* on the *Anuyogadvārasūtra*	
9	Haribhadra	Śvetabhikṣu		*Anekāntajayapatākā* + *Svopajña* (Skt.) with *Vṛtti* - *Tippaṇa* of Municandra, pupil of Devasūri with a *Ṭīkā* of Yajñadevamuni	
9	Haribhadra		pupil of Jinabhadra	*Anekāntajayapatākāpraveśa* (Skt.)	
14	Haribhadra	Mahattarā-[yākinī]putra	mentioned in the *Amamasvāmicaritra* of Muniratnasūri		comp. Saṃ. 1252

18	Haribhadra			*Aṣṭakaprakaraṇa* with *Ṭīkā* of Jineśvarasūri	 comp. Saṃ. 1080
20	Haribhadrasūri			*Ahiṃsāṣṭaka* (= part of the *Aṣṭakaprakaraṇa*)	
21	Haribhadra		pupil of Jinadeva of the Bṛhad Gaccha	*Vṛtti* on the *Āgamanikavastuvicārasāraprakaraṇa* (= *Ṣaḍaśīti*) of Jinavallabhagaṇi of the Kharatara Gaccha	comp. Saṃ. 1172 at Ahnilvad
35-37	Haribhadra	Mahattarā-yākinīputra	pupil of Jinadatta, pupil of Jinabhaṭa	*Niryukti Ṭīkā* (= *Śiṣyahitā* = *Bṛhadvṛtti*) on the *Avaśyakasūtra* (= *Ṣaḍāvasyakasūtra*) with a *Avacūrṇi* of Jñānasāgara with a *Avacūrṇi* of Dhīrasundara	 comp. Saṃ. 1440 comp. Saṃ. 1500
47	Haribhadrasūri		successor of Abhayadevasūri		
48, 159	Haribhadra	Mahattarā-yākinīputra		*Upadeśapada* (Pkt., = *Haribhadrasūrikathā*) with a *Ṭīkā* of Vardhamānasūri with a *Vyākhyā* of Municandra and Rāmacandragaṇi	 comp. Saṃ. 1055 comp. Saṃ. 1174
53	Haribhadrasūri			Upadnānapañcāśaka (= part of the	

				Pañcāśakasūtra)	
72-73	Haribhadra		pupil of Jinadeva	*Ṭīkā* on the (*Bṛhat* or *Prācīna-*)*Karmavipāka* of Gargarṣi *Ṭīkā* on the (*Bṛhat* or *Prācīna-*)*Karmastava* of Jinavallabha	before Saṃ. 1288
94	Haribhadra	Bhavaviraha	alluded to in the *Kuvalayamālākathā* of Dākṣiṇyacinharūri		comp. Saṃ. 835
98	Haribhadra			*Vṛtti* on the *BKSJ*	comp. Saṃ. 1185
119	Haribhadrasūri		pupil of Candrasūri of the Bṛhad Gaccha	*Candraprabhacaritra* (Pkt.)	comp. during the reign of King Kumārapāla of Gujarat
124	Haribhadra			*Caityaprabhṛtistotra* (Pkt.)	
125, 337	Haribhadra			*Lalitavistarā (Vṛtti)*[1] on the *Caityavandanāsūtra* with *Pañjikā* of Municandra	
127	Haribhadra			*Caityavandanāvidhipañcāśaka* (= part of the *Pañcāśakasūtra*)	

[1] Composed for Siddharṣi.

130	Haribhadra			*Ṭīkā* (Pkt.) on the *Jambūdvīpaprajñapti*	
131, 336	Haribhadrasūri			*Jambūdvīpasaṃgrahaṇī* (Pkt., 30 gāthās, = *Laghusaṃgrahaṇī*) with *Vṛtti* of Prabhānanda	comp. Saṃ. 1390
144	Haribhadra	Mahattarā-yākinīputra		*Laghu-* or *Pradeśa-Vṛtti* on the *Jīvābhigamasūtra*	
147	Haribhadra			*Jñānadarśanacāritrasaṃvāda* (Skt.)	
148	Haribhadra			*Jñānapañcakavivaraṇa*[1]	
149	Haribhadrasūri			*Jñānādityaprakaraṇa* (Pkt.)	
152	Haribhadra			*Tattvaprakāśaka* = *Saṃbodhatattva*	
153	Haribhadra			*Tattvabodha* (= *Nijatīrthikakalpitakumatinirāsa*)	
159	Haribhadra			*Ṣaddarśanasamuccaya* with the com. *Tarkarahasyadīpikā* of Guṇaratna	
159	Haribhadra or Haribhaṭṭa (?)			*Tajikasāra* (astrology)	lived Śaka 1445[1]

[1] Quoted in the *Gāthāsarasrī* of Samayasundara.

166	Haribhadra			*Darśanaśuddhi*	
167	Haribhadra			*Darśanasaptatīkā* (= *Samyaktatvasaptati*) with *Ṭīkā* of Śivamaṇḍanagaṇi	
169-170	Haribhadra	Yākinīputra		*Ṭīkā* on the *Daśavaikālikasūtra* ascribed to Sayyaṃbhavasvāmin	
175	Haribhadrasūri			*Dīkṣāvidhānapañcāśaka* (= part of the *Pañcāśakasūtra*)	
185	Haribhadra			*Dvijavadanacapaṭikā* (= *Vedāṅkuśa*)	
191	Haribhadrasūri			*Dharmabindu* with a *Ṭīkā* of Municandrasūri	
194	Haribhadrasūri			*Dharmasaṃgrahaṇī* with a *Ṭīkā* of Malayagiri	
198	Haribhadra			*Dhūrtākhyāna* (Pkt.)	comp. during the reign of King Sammattarāya of Citoḍa

[1] According to Dikshit in his Marathi '*History of Ancient Astronomy*', p. 490.

200	Haribhadra		pupil of Jinabhadra	*Vivaraṇa*[1] or Laghuvṛtti on the Nandīsūtra with *Vṛtti - Ṭippaṇa* (= *Durgapadavyākhyā*) of Śrī Candrasūri	
217	Haribhadra		pupil of Candrasūri of the Vaṭa Gaccha	*Nemināthacaritra* (Pkt. & Ap.)	comp. Saṃ. 1216 at Ahnilvad[2]
220	Haribhadrasūri			*Ṭīkā* on the *Nyāyapraveśasūtra* of Śaṅkarasvāmin[3] with *Pañjikā* of (Pārśvadevagaṇi) Candrasūri	comp. Saṃ. 1169
222	Haribhadra			*Vṛtti* on the *Nyāyavatārasūtra* of Siddhasena Divākara	
227	Haribhadra	Mahattarā-yākinīputra		*Pañcaliṅgī*	
228	Haribhadra	Yākinīputra		*Pañcavastuka* with own *Vṛtti - Śiṣyahitā*	

[1] Mentioned by Malayagiri in his *Ṭīkā* on the same.
[2] At the request of minister Pṛthvīpāla during the reign of King Kumārapāla of Gujarat.
[3] Wrongly attributed to Diṅnāga.

228	Haribhadra		pupil of Mānadeva	*Pañcaśataprakaraṇa*	
229	Haribhadrasūri			*Pañcasaṃgraha*	
230	Haribhadrasūri	Yākinīputra		*Ṭīkā* on the *Pañcasūtra*	
230	Haribhadrasūri			*Pañcasthānaka*	
230-231	Haribhadra			*Pañcāśakasūtra* (19 Pañcāśakas) with *Vṛtti* of Abhayadevasūri with *Cūrṇi* (Pkt.) of Yaśodeva with own (?) *Ṭīkā*	 comp. Saṃ. 1124 comp. Saṃ. 1172
232	Haribhadrasūri			*Paṭṭāvalī*	
238	Haribhadrasūri	Mahattarā-yākinīputra		*Paralokasiddhi*	
249	Haribhadra			*Vṛtti* - *Śiṣyahitā* (partly of Vīragaṇı) on the *Piṇḍaniryukti* ascribed to Badrabāhu	comp. Saṃ. 1160 (?)[1]
255	Haribhadrasūri			*Pūjāpañcāśikā*[2] (= part of the *Pañcāśakasūtra* ?) with *Vṛtti* of Abhayadevasūri	

[1] Corrected by Nemicandrasūri and Jinadattasūri at Ahnilvad.
[2] Quoted by Dharmakīrti in his *Saṃghācāravidhi*.

258	Haribhadra		pupil of Jinabhaṭa	*Pradeśavyākhyā*[1] on the *Prajñāpanāsūtra*	
259	Haribhadrasūri			*Vṛtti* on the *Pratikramaṇasūtra*	
261	Haribhadrasūri			*Pratiṣṭhākalpa*	
262	Haribhadrasūri			*Pratyākhyāna*	
273	Haribhadra		pupil of Mānadeva of the Bṛhad Gaccha	*Ṭīkā* on the *Praśamarati*	comp. Saṃ. 1185
281	Haribhadra		pupil of Jinadeva Upādhyāya of the Bṛhad Gaccha	*Ṭīkā* on the *Bandhasvāmitva*	
286	Haribhadra		author of the *Munipaticaritra*	*Vṛtti* on the *Bṛhatsaṃgrahaṇī* of Jinabhadragaṇi	
286	Haribhadra	Yākinīputra		*Boṭikanirākaraṇa* = *Boṭipratiṣedha*	
287	Haribhadra			*Brāhmaṇyajātinirākaraṇa*	
298	Haribhadrasūri			*Bhuvanabhānucaritra*	
300,	Haribhadra(sūri)		pupil of Jinadeva,	*Maṇipaticaritra* (Pkt., = *Munipaticaritra*)	comp. Saṃ. 1172

[1] Mentioned by Malayagiri who also composed a *Vṛtti* on the same..

311			pupil of Mānadeva of the Bṛhad Gaccha		
302	Haribhadra		pupil of Candrasūri	*Mallināthacaritra* (Pkt.)	comp. during the reign of King Kumārapāla
317	Haribhadrasūri			*Yatidinakṛtya* (= *Yatidinacaryā* ?)	
321	Haribhadrasūri			*Yogadṛṣṭisamauccaya* with *Svopajña Ṭīkā* with *Ṭīkā* of Sādhurājagaṇi	
322	Haribhadrasūri			*Yogabindhu* with *Svopajña Vṛtti*	
322	Haribhadrasūri			*Yogaviṃśikā* (= part of his *Viṃśativiṃśikā*)	
323	Haribhadra			*Yogaśataka* (Pkt.)	
334	Haribhadrasūri			*Lagnaśuddhi* (= *Lagnakuṇḍali*)	
338	Haribhadra			*Lokatattvanirṇaya* (Skt.)	
349	Haribhadrasūri	Yākinīputra		*Viṃśativiṃśikā* with *Vyākhyā* of Yaśovijaya	

363	Haribhadra			*Vīrāṅgadakathā*	
365	Haribhadra			*Vedabāhyatānirākaraṇa*	
369	Haribhadra	Mahattarā-yākinīputra		*Śataka*[1]	
377	Haribhadra			*Prākṛtavṛttidīpikā* on the *Śabdānuśāsana* of Hemacandrasūri	
383	Haribhadrasūri			*Śāstravārtāsamuccaya* with a *Ṭīkā Svopajña* with a *Vṛtti* (= *Syādvādakalpalatā*) of Yaśovijaya	
392	Haribhadrasūri			*Śrāvakadharma* (Pkt. = *Śrāvakadharmavidhi* = part of the *Pañcāśakasūtra*) with *Ṭīkā* of Yaśodevasūri (Pkt.)	comp. Saṃ. 1172
392	Haribhadrasūri			*Śrāvakadharmatantra* with *Ṭīkā* of Mānadevasūri	
393	Haribhadra		pupil of	*Ṭīkā* on the *Śrāvakaprajñapti* of Ūmāsvāti	

[1] Mentioned in the Prabandhakośa.

			Jinabhadrasūri	Vācaka[1]	
394	Haribhadra			*Śrāvakasāmācārī*	
399	Haribhadra		pupil of Jinaḍeva of the Bṛhad Gaccha	*Śreyāṃsacarita*	comp. Saṃ. 1172
402	Haribhadrasūri			*Ṣaḍdarśanasamuccaya* with com. *Tarkarahasyadīpikā* of Guṇaratnasūri with *Ṭīkā* of Somatilaka (Vidyātilaka) with *Ṭīkā* of Maṇibhadra with *Ṭīkā* of Rājahaṃsa with *Avacūri* (Anon.) with *Avacūrṇi* of Brahma Śāntidāsa	 comp. Saṃ. 1392 comp. Saṃ. 1295
405	Haribhadrasūri			*Ṣoḍaśakaprakaraṇa* with *Vivaraṇa* of Yaśobhadrasūri with *Vṛtti* of Abhayadevasūri (?) with com. *Yogadīpikā* of Yaśovijaya	

[1] Also ascribed to Haribhadra.

407	Haribhadrasūri			*Saṃsāradāvānalastuti* (?) with com. of Jñānavimalasūri with *Ṭīkā* of Pārśvacandra	
412	Haribhadrasūri			*Sanatkumāracaritra* (= part of the *Nemināthacaritra*)	
419	Haribhadrasūri		pupil of Jinadattasūri	*Samarādityacaritra* (Pkt.) with *Ṭippaṇī* (Skt.) of Kṣamākalyāṇa & Sumativardhana	comp. Saṃ. 1874
427	Haribhadrasūri			*Sambodhatattva* (= *Saṃbodhaprakaraṇa* = *Tattvaprakāśa*)	
425	Haribhadra (or Devendra ?)			*Samyaktvapañcaviṃśatikā*	
426	Haribhadrasūri			*Samyaktvasaptatikā* (= *Darśanasaptatikā*) with *Vivaraṇa* of Saṅghatilakasūri with *Avacūri* of Guṇanidhānasūri-śiṣya (= *Vivaraṇa* above ?) with *Vṛtti* of Devendra (?) with *Ṭīkā* of Śivamaṇḍanagaṇi	comp. Saṃ. 1422

				with *Bālavabodha* of Ratnacandragaṇi	comp. Saṃ. 1676
428	Haribhadra			*Sarvajñasiddhi*	
429	Haribhadrasūri			*Sādhutattva* = *Darśanaśuddhi* ?	
429	Haribhadra			*Sādhunikṛtya*	
430	Haribhadra			*Sādhupravacanasāra*	
430, 432	Haribhadra			*(Sādhu)Sāmācārī*	
435	Haribhadra			*Vṛtti* on the *Sārdhaśatakaprakaraṇa* of Jinavallabhasūri	comp. Saṃ. 1172
437	Haribhadra (?)			*Ṭīkā* on the *Siddhaprābhṛti*	
438	Haribhadra	Mahattarā-yākinīputra		*Siddhasukhaviṃśikā* (= part of the *Viṃśativiṃśikā*)	

Data indirectly related to Haribhadra (Sūri)

46-47, 68, 344,359	Bālacandra(sūri)	pupil and successor of Haribhadrasūri of the Candra Gaccha	*Ṭīkā* on the *Upadeśakandalī* of Āsaḍa[1] *Karuṇavajrāyudhanāṭaka* *Vasantavilāsakāvya* *Ṭīkā* on the *Vivekamañjarī* of Āsaḍa[2]	 comp. Saṃ. 1296
98, 131	Vijayasiṃha(sūri)	pupil of Haribhadrasūri of the Candra Gaccha	*Vṛtti* on the BKSJ *Ṭīkā* on the JDSU	comp. Saṃ. 1215 comp. Sam. 1215
47, 53	Abhayadevasūri	teacher of Āsaḍa	*Upadhānapañcāśaka* = com. (?) on the *Upadhānapañcāśaka* of Haribhadra	
44	Devabhadra	pupil of Abhayadeva		
44	Śrīcandra	pupil of Prabhānanda		
110	Nemicandra	pupil of Prabhānanda	*Jīvatattvapradīpikā* (= *Ṭīkā* on the *Gommaṭasāra* of Saiddhāntika Nemicandra) based on the Kanarese *Jīvatattvapradīpikā* of Keśava Varṇin	comp. Śaka 1281
234	Devasūri	mentions Haribhadrasūri as his teacher in Āgama in his *Padmaprabhacaritra*		

[1] Composed at the advice of Abhayadevasūri. Āsaḍa is the son of Kaṭikarāja of the Bhillamāla family.

[2] Composed at the request of Jaitrasiṃha, son of Āsaḍa. The Vivekamañjarī was composed in Saṃ. 1248.

			comp. Saṃ. 1254
236	Dharmacandra	pupil of Haribhadrasūri; requested Ratnadevagaṇi to compose a *Ṭīkā* on the *Padyālaya* (= *Vajjālagga*) compiled by Jayavallabha	comp. Saṃ. 1393
335	Śāntisūri	pupil of Haribhadra, pupil of Bhadreśvara of the Candra Gaccha	
376	Mānabhadra	pupil of Haribhadrasūri	
379	Devacandra	teacher of the famous Hemacandra mentions Haribhadra author of the *Samarādityakathā* in his *Śāntināthacarita* (Pkt.)	in Saṃ. 1160
380	Māṇikyacandra	mentions Haribhadra in his *Śāntināthacarita* (Skt.); author of the *Pārśvanāthacaritra*	comp. Saṃ. 1276
419	Pradyumnasūri	*Samarādityacaritra* = abridgment in Skt. of the *Samarādityacaritra* (Pkt.) of Haribhadrasūri	comp. Saṃ. 1324
423	Mallavādin	Haribhadra in his *Anekāntajayapatākā* quotes the *Vṛtti* of Mallavādin on the *Saṃmatimahātarka* of Siddhasena Divākara	

434	Kṣemendra	pupil of Haribhadra; author of a *Ṭippaṇaka* on the *Sārasvatavyākaraṇa*	comp. Saṃ. 1692

Figures

For the figures I am for a great deal indebted to the loka section of the *Jainendra Siddhānta Kośa* of Jinendra Varṇī, 1955, Dillī, Bharatīya Jñānapīṭha Prakāśana.

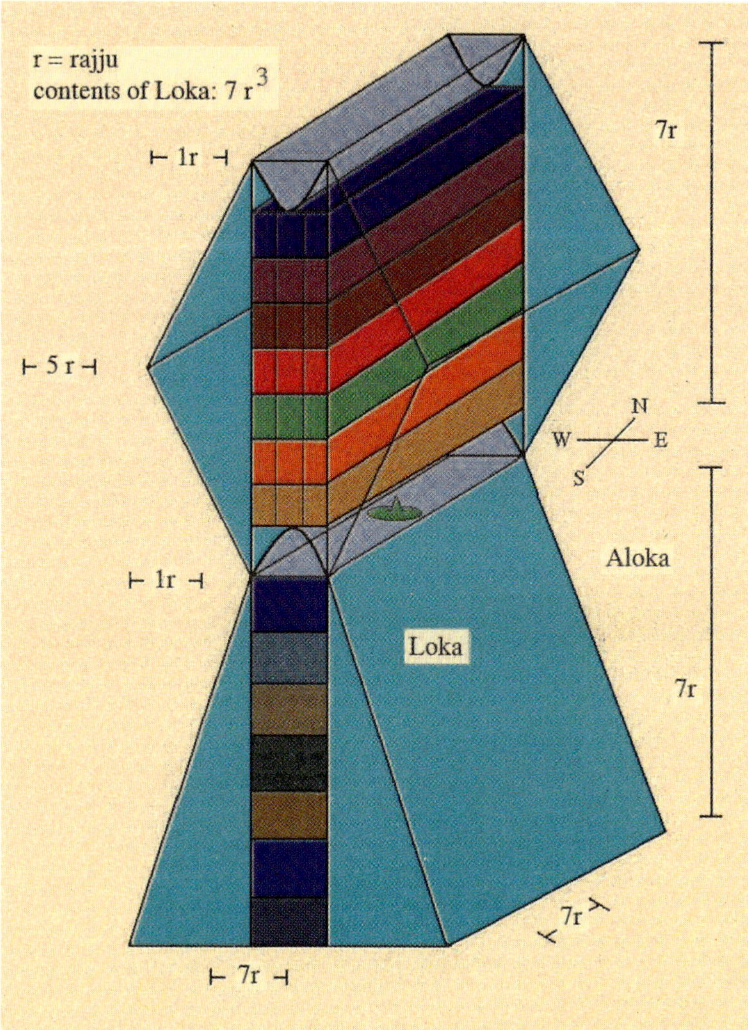

Fig. 1 The Jaina Universe

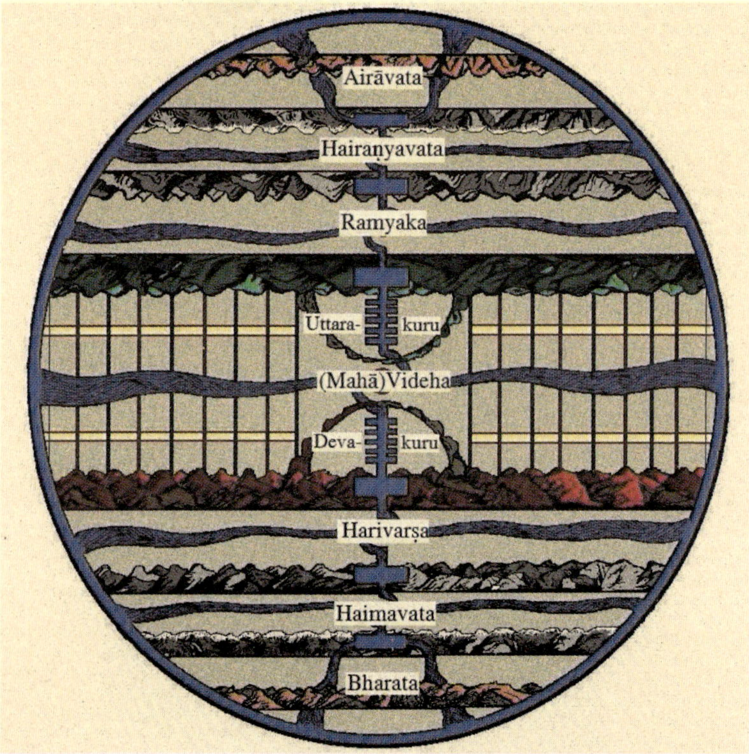

Fig. 2 Jambūdvīpa - The Continents

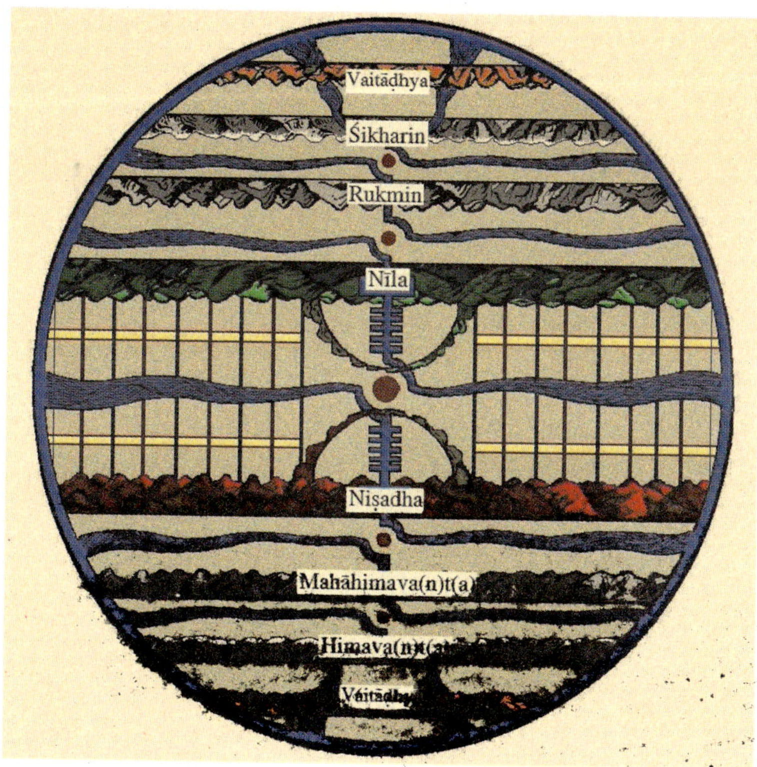

Fig. 3 Jambūdvīpa - The Main Mountain Ranges

Fig. 4 Jambūdvīpa - The Main Rivers

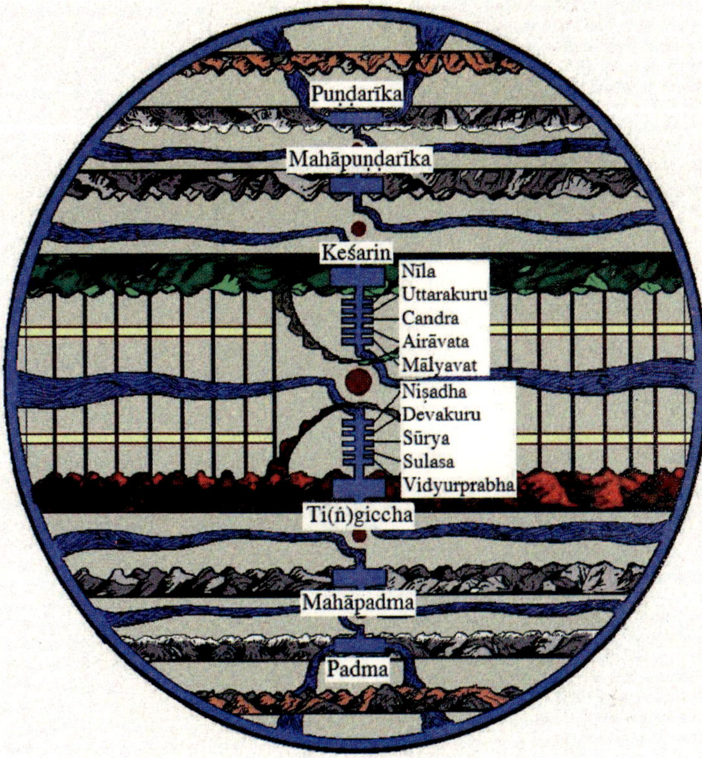

Fig. 5 Jambūdvīpa - The Lakes

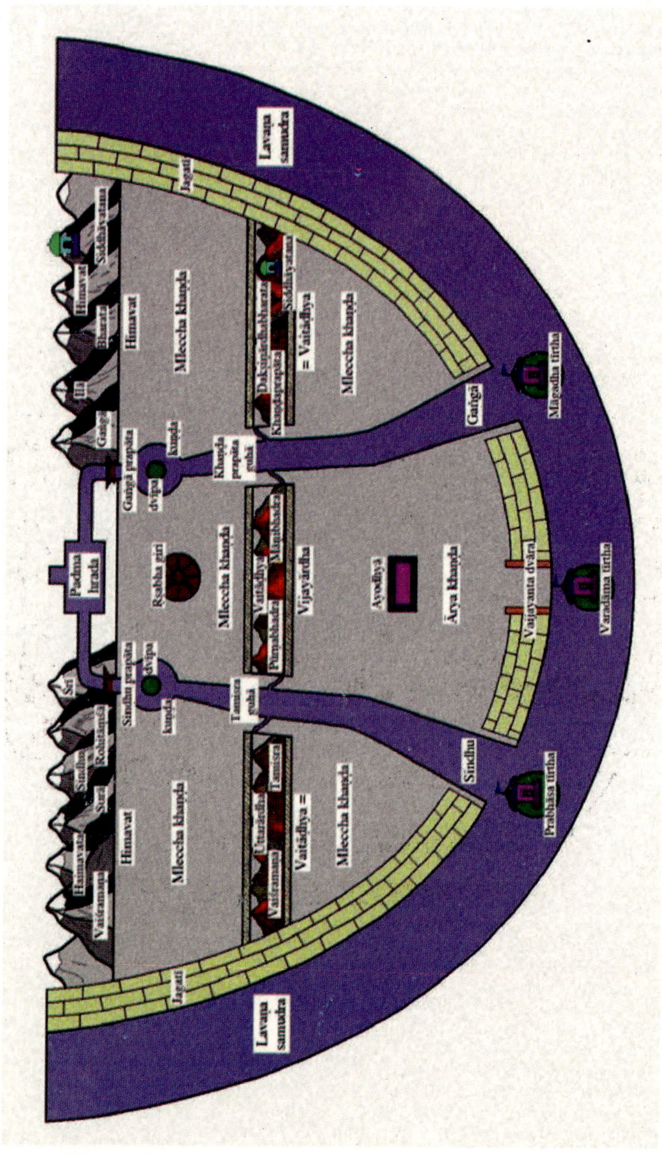

Fig. 6 Bharata

Fig. 7 Mahāvideha - The Provinces

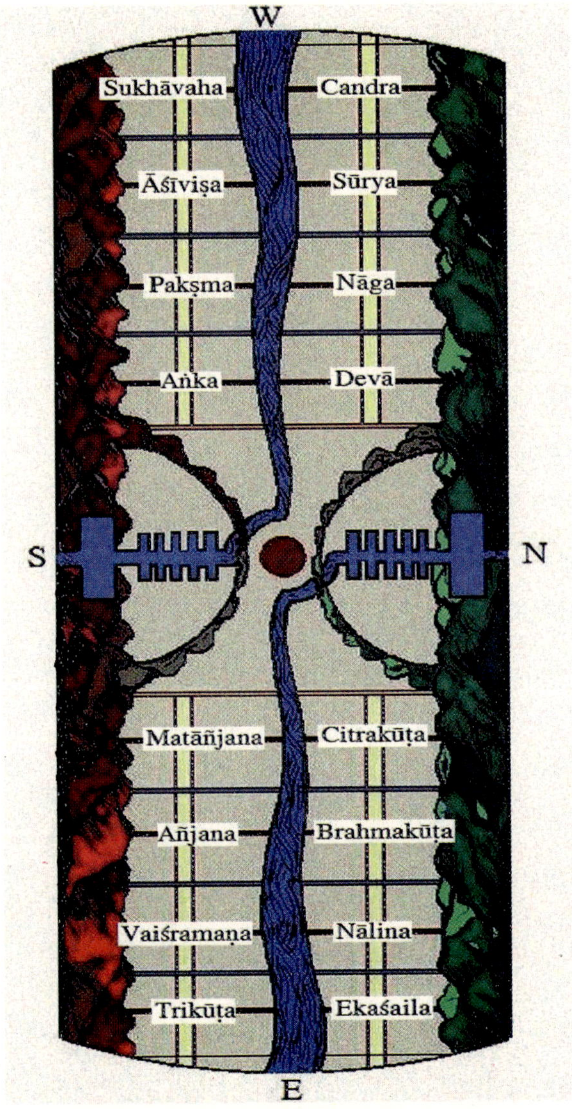

Fig. 8 Māhavideha - The Mountain Ranges

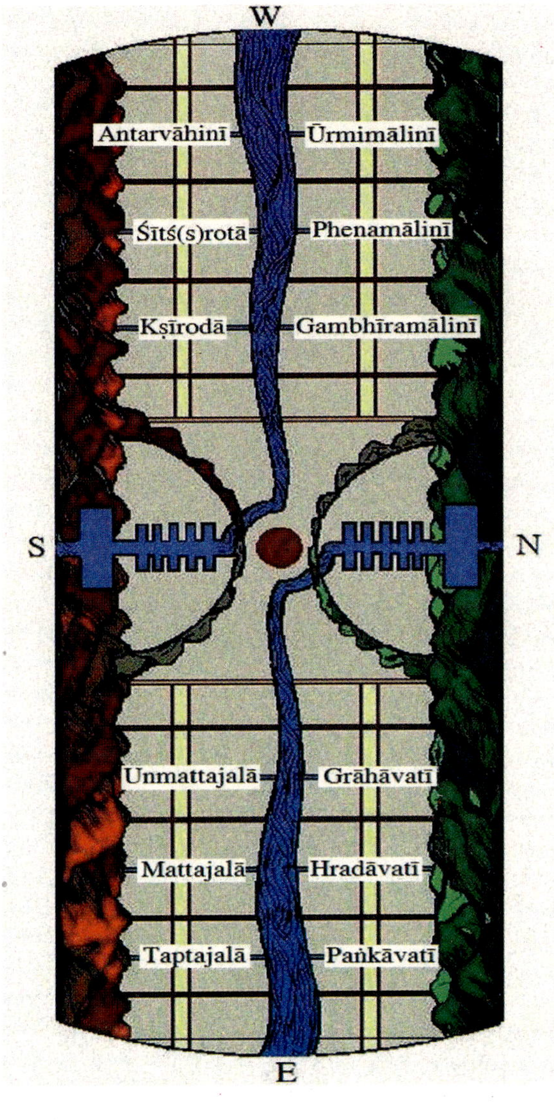

Fig. 9 Mahāvideha - The Inland Rivers

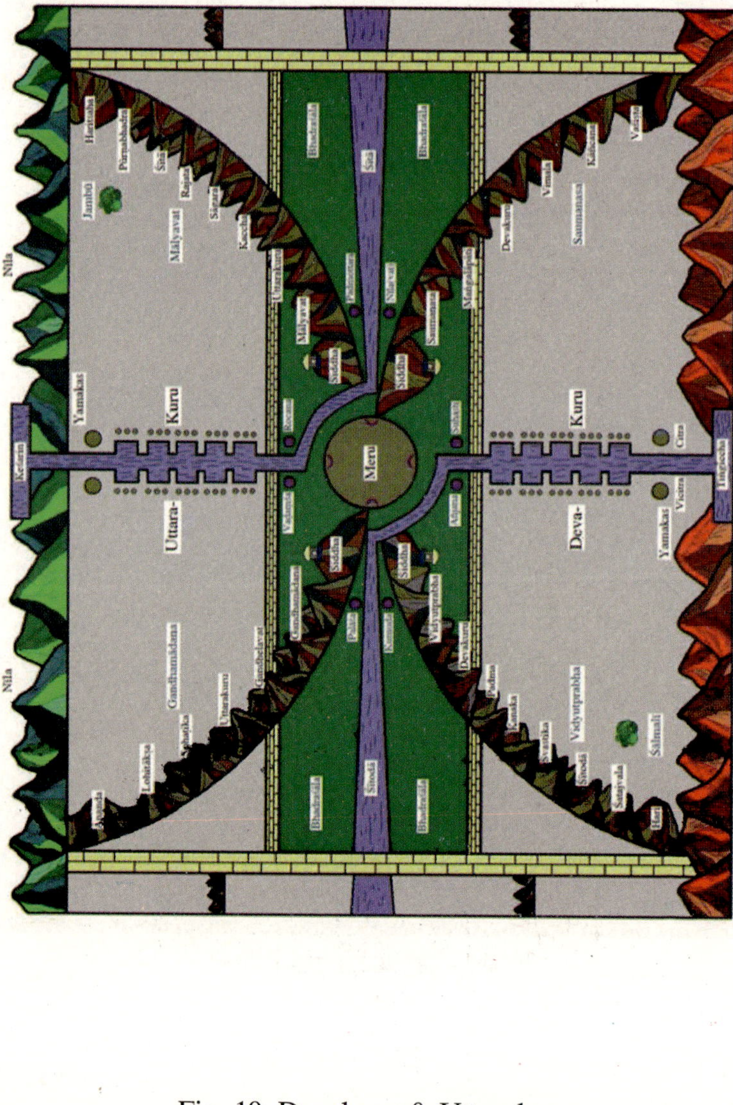

Fig. 10 Devakuru & Uttarakuru

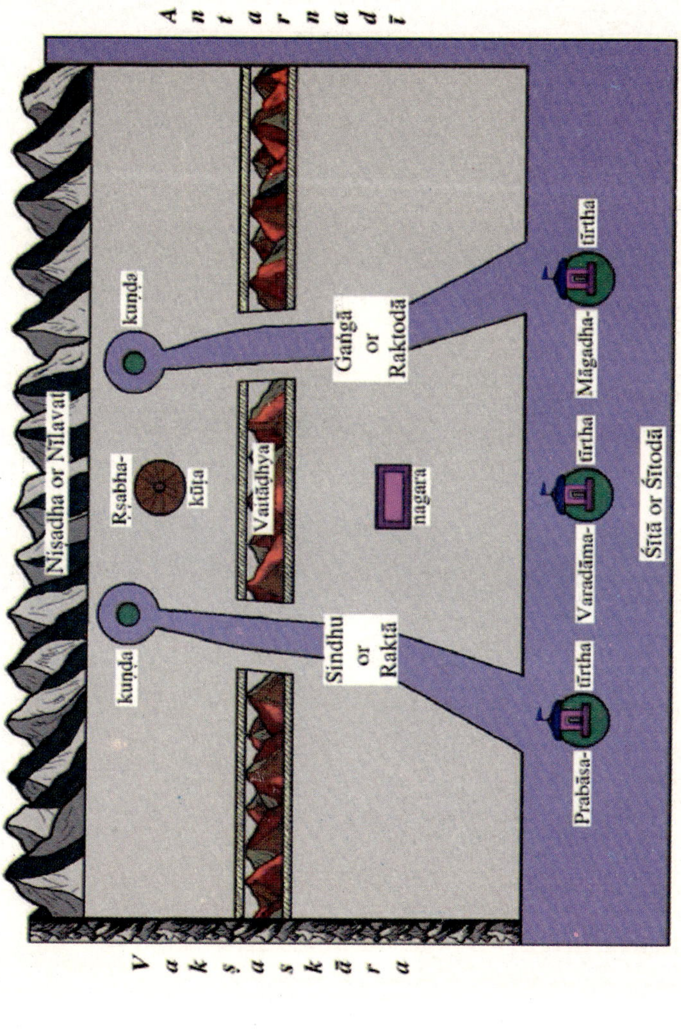

Fig. 11 A Province in Mahāvideha

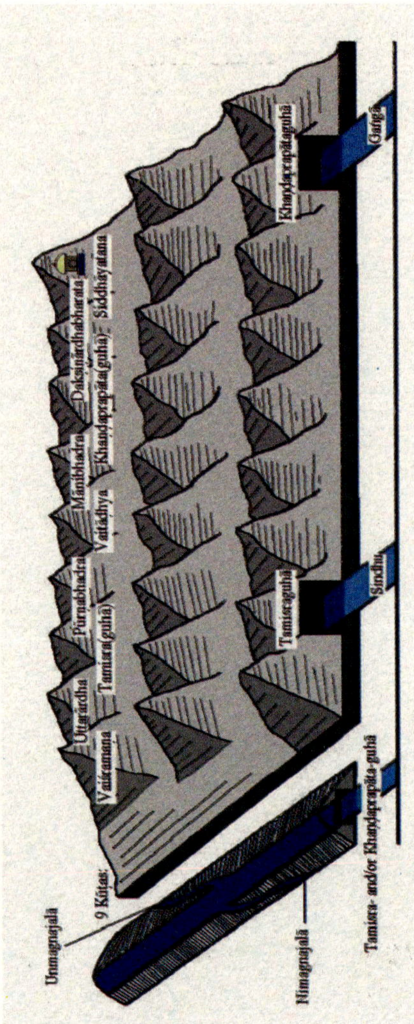

Fig. 12 The Vaitāḍhya or Vijayārdha Mountains

Bibliography

Primary sources

The list of primary sources for the study of Jaina cosmology, cosmography and geography is tentative and incomplete. It is based on primarily on the materials provided by the *JRK*. Wherever possible I have completed the information.

Abbreviations and meanings

chs.: chapters; *com.*: commentary; *comp.*: composed; Pkt.: Prākrit; Skt.: Sanskrit; *vs.*: verses. *avacūri*: gloss or short commentary; *bālāvabodha*: instruction of the young; *cūrṇi*: commentary on the old Prākrit commentaries on Jain texts; *ṭippaṇa*: gloss, comment; *ṭīkā*: commentary; *vṛtti*: commentary, comment, gloss, explanation (esp. on a Sūtra); *vṛtti* or *vivṛti*: commentary (*svopajña vṛtti*: own commentary); *vyākhyā*: explanation, exposition, gloss, comment, paraphrase. A question mark indicates uncertain data. The '+' indicates that there is a *com.* of a certain type on the basic text.

Bṛhatsaṃgrahaṇī, see *Saṃgrahaṇī* by Jinabhadragaṇi.

Candraprajñapti (Pkt. *Caṃdapaṇṇaṭṭī*): ed. in Ahmedabad, 1883 (with Skt. *com.* of Malayagiri and with *Bālāvabodha* in Gujarati).

Gaṇitānuyoga - Selection and classification of Geographical and Astronomical data from Jaina Sutras. Edited by Muni Kanhailal 'Kamala'. Tr. in Hindi by Dr. Mohanlal Mehta.

Ed. Pt. Shobhacandra Bharilla, Sanderao (Rajasthan), 1968.

Jambūdvīpajīvāgaṇitapada (?).

Jambūdvīpaparidhi (?).

Jambūdvīpaprajñapti (being the 6th Upāṅga of the Śvetāmbara canon): ed. in the DLP[1] Series 52 & 54, Bombay, 1920 (with *com.* of Śānticandra); ed. by R.B. Dhanpatisinha, Calcutta (with *com.* of Malayagiri); + *cūrṇi*; + *ṭīkā* of Malayagiri; + *ṭīkā* of Haribhadra (Pkt.); + *vṛtti* of Hīravijaya Sūri, Saṃ. 1639; + *vṛtti* of Puṇyasāgara, Saṃ. 1645; + *ṭīkā* (= *Prameyaratnamañjūṣā*) of Śānticandra, Saṃ. 1660; + *ṭīkā* of Brahmamuni; + *vṛtti* of Dharmasāgara (= *com.* of Hīravijaya ?), Saṃ. 1639; + *vṛtti* (Anon.).

Jambūdvīpaprajñaptisaṃgraha (13 *chs.*, ca. 2426 *vs.*) by Padmanandin (Pkt. Paümaṇaṃdi, ca. 1000 AD[2]); ed. with Hindi paraphrase by Upadhye, A.N. & Jain, Hiralal: *Paümaṇaṃdi's Jaṃbūdīva-Paṇṇatti-Saṃgaho (An Important Prākrit Text dealing with Jaina Cosmography etc.), Authentically Edited for the first time with Various Readings, Appendices etc.* (Jīvarāja Jaina Granthamālā, 7) Sholapur: Jaina Saṃskṛti Saṃrakṣaka Saṃgha, 1958.

Jambūdvīpasamāsa (88 *vs.*, Pkt.) of Umāsvāti Vācaka (= *Kṣetrasamāsa*, = *bhāṣya* on the *Tattvārthādhigama-sūtra*): ed. Pub. by Satyavijaya Granthamālā, Ahmedabad, 1922 (with *com.* of Vijayasiṃha Sūri); + *ṭīkā* of Śrīvijaya = Vijayasiṃha, Saṃ. 1215.

[1] Devachanda Lālabhāi Jaina Pustakoddhāra.

[2] See Upadhye, A.N. & Jain, Hiralal, 1958, p. 14.

Jambūdvīpasaṃgrahaṇī (30 *vs.*) of Haribhadra Sūri (= *Kṣetrasaṃgrahaṇī* or *Kṣetrasamāsa* ?): ed. by Bhimsi Manek, Bombay (with the *com.* of Prabhānanda), 1908 (?); ed. in the JDPS Series (with the *com.* of Prabhānanda, Bhavnagar, 1915; ed. Śrī Jaina-grantha-prakāśana-samitiḥ, 1988; ed. Shah, M.J, Mahesāṇā, Śrī Bābūlāl Jeśiṃgalāl Mehetā, 1997; + *vṛtti* by Prabhānanda Sūri; + *vṛṭṭi* (Anon.).

Jambūdvīpavicāraprakaraṇa.

Jīvābhigamasūtra (3th Upāṅga, a piecemeal exposition of Jaina geography).

Karmagrantha of Devendra Sūri: ed. Bhāvnagar, Saṃ. 1966.

Kṣetrasamāsa (264 *vs.*, also *Kṣetrasamāsavivaraṇa*) by Ratnaśekhara Sūri: ed. by Bhimsi Manek in '*Laghuprakaraṇasaṃgraha*', Bombay 1903; ed. in the JAS Series, no. 46; + *vṛtti svopajña*; + *bālāvabodha* by Pārśvacandra; + *bālāvabodha* by Udayasāgara; + *ṭippaṇa* or *avacūri* (Anon.); see also *Shri Laghu Xetrasamas or Jain Geography.*

Kṣetrasamāsa (341 *vs.*) by Śrīcandra Sūri.

Kṣetrasamāsa (also *Bṛhatkṣetrasamāsa*) by Jinabhadra(-gaṇi): ed. JDPS, Bhavnagar (with the *com.* of Malayagiri), Saṃ. 1977; + *vṛtti* of Haribhadra Sūri (*comp.* Saṃ. 1185); + *vṛtti* of Siddha Sūri (fl. A.D. 1136); + *vṛtti* or *ṭīkā* of Malayagiri; + *vṛtti* of Vijayasiṃha; + *vṛtti* of Devānanda; + *vṛtti* of Devabhadra; + *vṛtti* of Ānanda Sūri (fl. A.D. 1070).

Kṣetrasamāsa (Anon.): + *vṛtti* (Anon.).

Kṣetrasamāsa (Anon., by Jinadāsa ?): + *ṭīkā* by Jinadāsa.

Kṣetrasamāsa (Pkt., 387 *vs.*) by Somatilaka Sūri (= *Navyakṣetrasamāsa* or *Bṛhatkṣetrasamāsa*): + *avacūri* by

Guṇaratna Sūri; + *avacūri* by Jñānasāgara, Saṃ. 1465; + *vṛtti* (= *avacūri* by Guṇaratna ?).

Kṣetrasamāsa (Pkt., 656 *vs.*) by Padmadeva Sūri.

Kṣetrasamāsa (Skt., 7 *chs.*) by Devānanda, Śaka 1320: + *svopajña vṛtti*.

Kṣetrasamāsa by Candraprabhā (= *Kṣetrasamāsa* by Devānanda ?).

Kṣetrasamāsa by Hemācārya (?).

Kṣetrasamāsa by Jayaśekhara (= *Kṣetrasamāsa* by Ratnaśekhara Sūri).

Kṣetrasamāsa by Umāsvāti (Skt.), see *Jambūdvīpasamāsa*.

Kṣetrasamāsasaṃgrahaṇī, see *Jambūdvīpasaṃgrahaṇī*.

Laghukṣetrasamāsa by Ratnaśekhara, ed. in the collection '*Laghuprakaraṇasaṃgraha*', Bombay, Saṃ. 1959.

Laghusaṃgrahaṇī by Haribhradra Sūri (= *Jaṃbūdvīpasaṃgrahaṇī* ?): + *bālāvabodha*.

Laghusaṃgrahaṇaratna = *Saṃghayaṇarayaṇa* = *Saṃgrahaṇī* or *Saṃghayaṇī* by Candra Sūri (pupil of Hemācārya); + *avacūri* (Anon.).

Lokaprakāśa of Vinayavijaya: ed. by Hīrālāla Haṃsarāja, Jāmnagar, Saṃ. 1967.

Pravacanasāroddhāra by Nemicandra Sūri: ed. with *com.* of Siddhasena Sūri, 1922 (?).

Sūryaprajñapti (Pkt. *Sūrapaṇṇatti*): + *ṭīkā* of Malayagiri, ed. Surat: Āgamodaya Samiti, 1919.

Samavāyāṅgasūtra: ed. Kanhaiyā Lāla (1973): Jainācārya-jainadharma-divākara-pūjyaśrī-Ghāsīlālajī-mahārāja-viracitayā munikumuda-candrikākhyayā vyākhyayā samalaṃkṛtaṃ hindīgurjarabhāṣānuvāda-sahitam; Śrī-Samavāyāṅgasūtram; niyojakaḥ ... Śrīkanhaiyālālajī-mahārājaḥ. Rājakoṭ.

Saṃgrahaṇ(i)īratna by Candra Sūri (274 *vs.*, 7 chps.): ed. in the DLP[3] Series, 27, Bombay, 1915; ed. in the JDPS Series, 42, Bhavnagar; ed. by Bhimsi Manek, Bombay, 1903 (349 gs.); + *vṛtti* by Devabhadra (pupil of Candra Sūri); + *vyākhyā* by Śivanidhānagaṇi; + *avacūri* by Dharmānandagaṇi; + *bālāvabodha* (= *Saṃgrahaṇī-sūtravivaraṇa* ?) by Dayāsiṃhagaṇi, Saṃ. 1497; + *bālāvabodha* by Śivanidhānagaṇi, Saṃ. 1680; + *avacūri* by Cāritramuni; + *vṛtti* (?).

Saṃgrahaṇī (also *Bṛhatsaṃgrahaṇī*) by Jinabhadragaṇi: ed. in Bhavnagar (?), Saṃ. 1973; ed. by Manacand Velchand, Gopipura (with the *com.* of Malayagiri), Surat, Saṃ. 1972; ed. in the JAS Series [4], 47 (with the *com.* of Malayagiri), Bhadraṃkara Prakāśana, 1978-79; + *ṭīkā* by Malayagiri; + *vivṛti* by Śālibhadra, Saṃ. 1139; + *vṛtti* by Haribhadra; + *vṛtti* by Jinavallabha (?); + *ṭīkā* (Anon.).

Saṃgrahaṇī by Abhayadeva Sūri (= *Prajñāpanātṛtīya-padasaṃgrahaṇī* ?).

Saṃgrahaṇī by Rāmacandra (Skt. verse).

Saṃgrahaṇīpadavicāra by Devakuśala; + *vṛtti* of Devabhadra.

Shri Brihatsangrahani Sutram or Jain Astronomy (*Trailokya-dīpikā*), by His Holiness Jainacharya Shrimad Chandrasuri. With Gujarati tr. and 70 coloured plates. Tr. Muni Shri Yashovijayji. Baroda, 1939.

Shri Laghu Xetrasamas or Jain Geography by His Holiness Jainacharya Shrimad Ratnashekher-Surishvaraji. With Gujarati tr. and 50 coloured plates. Baroda, 1934 (Shriman Muktikamal Jain Mohanmala, 31).

---

[3] Devachanda Lālabhāi Jaina Pustakoddhāra Fund Series.

[4] Jaina-Dharma-prasāraka Sabhā Series.

Stānāṅga (3th Aṅga: no systematic exposition but main Jaina work for names and concepts, base of all other non-canonical works on Jaina cosmography and geography[5]).

Tattvārthādhigamasūtra of Umāsvāti (Adhy. 3 and 4); ed. by Keshavlal Premchand Mody in Calcutta 1903 (Bib. Ind.); tr. by Jacobi in Z.D.M.G., 60, 1906 (based on the ed. of Keshavlal Premchand Mody); ed. with tr. by Jaini, J.L.: *Tattvarthadhigama Sutra; A Treatise on the Essential Principles of Jainism, by Sri Umasvami Acharya.* The Sacred Books of the Jainas, Vol. II, Arrah, 1920. Reprint in the Bibliotheca Jainica, New York: AMS Press, 1974; tr. by Nathmal Tatia, San Francisco: Harper Collins Publishers, 1994.

Tattvarthavritti of Shri Shrutasagar Suri. The Commentary on the Tattvarthasutra of Shri Umasvami with translation in Hindi. Edited, with introduction by Mahendra Kumar Jain with the help of Udayachandra Jain. Benares, 1949 (Jnana-Pitha-Moorti Devi Jain Granthamala Sanskrit Grantha 4).

Tiloyapaṇṇatti (Skt. *Trilokaprajñapti*): *Jadivasaha's Tiloya-paṇṇatti (An Ancient Prakrit Text Dealing with Jaina Cosmography, Dogmatics, etc.).*[6] Ed. by Prof. A.N. Upadhye & Prof. Hiralal Jain with paraphrase in Hindi by Pt. Balchandra. 2 vol. I, Sholapur, 1956; II 1951 (Jīvaraja Jain Granthamala 1).

Trailokyadīpikā by Candra Sūri, see *Shri Brihatsangrahani Sutram.*

[5] Kirfel, p. 208.

[6] In a ms. listed by S.R. Banerjee, 1987, no. 360, p. 501 ascribed to Kundakunda.

Trailokyadīpikā of Indravāmadeva (Digambara).
Trailokyadīpikānāmasaṃgrahaṇī.
Trailokyasāra of Nemicandra (Digambara, Pkt.): + *com.* of Sāgarasena.
Uttarajjhāyā: *The Uttarādhyayanasūtra*. Ed. Jarl Charpentier. Uppsala, 1922, 2 vol. (Archives d'études orientales 18:1, 18:2). English tr. in Jaina Sūtras II. Tr. from the Prākrit by Hermann Jacobi. London, 1895 (reprint, Delhi, 1964; Sacred Books of the East, 45).

Secondary sources

Alsdorf, L. (1974): *Kleine Schriften*. Ed. by Albrecht Wezler. Wiesbaden, (Glasenapp-Stiftung, 10), pp. 71-100 ('Zur Geschichte der Jaina-Kosmographie und -Mythologie'), and pp. 136-159 ('Further Contributions to the History of Jain Cosmography and Mythology').
Art Tantrique - Le Point Cardinal. Paris, 17 february - end march 1970. Texts by Henri Michaux, Octavio Paz, Souren Melikian.
Bajpai, K. D. et al. (eds., 1967) : *The Geographical Encyclopaedia of Ancient and Medieval India. Based on Vedic, Puranic, Tantric, Jain, Buddhistic Literature and Historical Records*. Part I: A-D. Varanasi: Indic Academy.
Banerjee, S.R. (1987): *A Descriptive Catalogue of Sanskrit Manuscripts in the Collections of the Asiatic Society, Vol. XIII: Jaina manuscripts (Sanskrit and Prakrit)*. Calcutta: The Asiatic Society.
Barnett (1907): 'Note on the Jain Cosmography'. In his tr. of the Antagaḍaadsao and Anuttarovavāiyadasāo, Oriental Translation Fund N.S. 17.

Barooah, A. (1971 [1877]): *Ancient Geography of India.* Gauhati: Publication Board, Assam.

Basham, A.L. (1978): *La Civilisation de l'Inde ancienne.* (collection "Les grandes civilisations") Paris: Editions Arthaud.

Basham, A.L. (1969 [1954]): *The Wonder that was India. A Survey of the Indian Sub-continent before the Coming of the Muslims.* London: Sidgwick & Jackson.

Bhattacharyya, N.N. (1991): *The Geographical Dictionary, Ancient and Early Medieval India.* New Delhi : Munshiram Manoharlal.

Bhayani, H.C. & Modi, M.C. (1970 & 1971): *Haribhadra's Nemināhacariya.* (2 vols., Lalbhai Dalpatbhai Series 25 & 23) Ahmedabad: Lalbhai Dalpatbhai Bharatiya Samskriti Vidyamandir.

Burnett, Ch. et al, eds. (2004): *Studies in the History of the Exact Sciences in Honour of David Pingree.* Leiden: Brill.

Caillat, C., Upadhye, A.N. & Bal Patil (1974): *Jainism.* Delhi & Bombay (Bhagwan Mahavira 2500th Nirvana Mahotsava Samiti, Bombay, 1974).

Caillat, C. (1970): 'Le jinisme', in the Encyclopédie de la Pléiade, Histoire des Religions, I, Volume publié sous la direction de Henri-Charles Puech, Paris.

Caillat, Colette & Kumar, Ravi (1981): *The Jain Cosmology* (English rendering by R. Norman). New York: Harmony Books.

Chakledar, H.C. (1963): *The geography of Kalidasa.* Calcutta: Indian Studies Past & Present.

Chanchreek, K.L. & Jain, M.K. (2004): *Jain Agamas; An Introduction to Canonical Literature.* New Delhi: Shree Publishers.

Charpentier, Jarl: *Uttarajjhāyā: The Uttarādhyayanasūtra.* Uppsala, 1922, 2 vol. (Archives d'études orientales 18:1, 18:2). English tr. in Jaina Sūtras II. Tr. from Prākrit by Hermann Jacobi. London, 1895 (reprint, Delhi, 1964, Sacred Books of the East, 45).

Chatterjee, Asim Kumar (1978): *A comprehensive history of Jainism, up to 1000 A.D.* Calcutta: Firma KLM.

Cosmologie jaina, XVe-XIXe siècle. Art moderne, Jaubert, 1977. 13 may-12 july. Texts by Armand Neven & Nik Douglas.

Deleu, Jozef (1976): 'Die Mythologie des Jinismus', in *Wörterbuch der Mythologie.* Under the direction of H.W. Haussig. Stuttgart: Ernst Klett Verlag, pp. 207-284. Also pub. separately as 'Sonderdruck aus Wörterbuch der Mythologie'.

Deleu, Jozef (1970): *Viyāhapannatti (Bhagavaī). The fifth Anga of the Jaina Canon. Introduction, Critical Analysis, Commentary & Indexes.* Bruges, (Rijksuniversiteit te Gent. Werken Uitgegeven door de Faculteit van de Letteren in Wijsbegeerte, No. 151).

Dey, Nundo Lal (1899): *The geographical dictionary of ancient and mediaeval India, with an appendix on modern names of ancient Indian geography.* Calcutta: W. Newman & co.

Dixix, K.K. (1974): tr. of Pt. Suklalji's Commentary on Tattvārtha Sūtra of Vācaka Umāsvāti. Ahmedabad (L.D. Series 44).

Dundas, Paul (1992): *The Jains.* London & New York: Routledge.

Emeneau, M.B. (1935): *A Union List of Printed Indic Texts and Translations in American Libraries.* American

Oriental Series Vol. 7, New Haven: American Oriental Society.

Glasenapp, H. von (1964 [1925]): *Der Jainismus. Eine indische Erlösungsreligion.* Hildesheim: Georg Olms Verlagsbuchhandlung, 1964).

Gode, P.K. (1953-54): Studies in Indian Literary History (2 vols., SJS 38). Bombay: Bharatiya Vidya Bhavan.

Grafenhorst, Rainer (1996): *Das kosmographische System der Puranas: zur Funktion und Struktur indischer Kosmographie.* Hamburg: Zeitgemaber Druck (Studien zur Indologie und Iranistik, 4).

Guérinot, A. (1926): *La Religion djaina. Histoire. Doctrine; Culte, Coutumes, Institutions.* (Avec 25 planches hors-texte). Paris: Paul Geuthner.

Jain, Chandra Jagdish (1947): *Life in ancient india as depicted in the Jain canons, with commentaries; an administrative, economic, social and geographical survey of ancient India based on the Jain canons.* Bombay: New Book Company.

Jain, Chandra Jagdish (1981): *Prakrit Narrative Literature; Origin and Growth.* New Delhi: Munshiram Manoharlal Pub.

Jain, G. R. (1991^2): *Cosmology, Old and New; A modern commentary on the fifth chapter of Tattvarthadhigama-Sutra of Acarya Umasvati.* New Delhi: Bharatiya Jnanpith.

Jain, Jyotindra & Fischer, Eberhard (1978): *Jaina Iconography.* (Iconography of Religions XIII, fasc. 12, 13) Leyde: Institute of Religious Iconography, State University of Groningen.

Jain, Mahendra Kumar & Jain, Udayachandra (1949): *Tattvarthavritti of Shri Shrutasagar Suri; The*

Commentary on the Tattvarthasutra of Shri Umasvami, with tr. in Hindi. Edited, with introduction. Benares, (Jnana-Pitha-Moorti Devi Jain Granthamala Sanskrit Grantha 4).

Jaina, Jyotiprasada (1975): *Religion and culture of the Jains.* New Delhi: Bharatiya Jnanpith Publication.

Jaini J.L., ed. (1974 [1920]): Umāsvāmin (Umāsvāti): *Tattvārthādhigama-sūtram,: A Treatise on the Essential Principles of Jainism.* Sacred Books of the Jainas, Vol. 2, AMS edition, New York.

Jaini, L.C. (1983): *Astronomy and Cosmology.* Jaipur: Rajasthan Prakrit Bharti Sansthan (Exact Sciences from Jaina Sources, Vol. 2, Prakrit Bharti Pushpa, 29).

Jaini, Padmanabh Shrivarma (1979): *The Jaina path of purification.* Berkeley: University of California Press.

Jñānamatī, Āryikā (1985): *Jaina Geography* (tr. into English by S.S. Lishk). Hastinapur (Meerut, U. P.): Digambara Jaina Institute of Cosmographic Research (Vira jnanodaya granthamala, no. 76).

Kapadia, H.R. (2000 [1941]): *A History of the Canonical Literature of the Jainas.* Ahmedabad: Shree Shwetambar Murtipujak Jaina Boarding Series Vol. 17, Sharadaben Chimanbhai Educational Research Centre.

Kapadia, H.R. (1987 [1952]): *Descriptive Catalogue of Manuscripts in the Government Manuscripts Library deposited at the Bhandarkar Oriental Research Institute, 27: Jaina literature and philosophy.* Poona: Bhandarkar Oriental Research Institute.

Kirfel, W. (1920): *Die Kosmographie der Inder; nach den Quellen dargestellt.* Bonn & Leipzig: Kurt Schroeder (reprint, Hildesheim, 1967 & 1990).

Kirfel, W. (1928): 'Die Religion der Jaina's'. In D. Hans Haas: *Bilderatlas zur Religionsgeschichte*, 12. Leipzig.

Law, B.C. (1949): *Some Jaina Canonical Sūtras*. Bombay: The Bombay Branch Royal Asiatic Society (Bombay Branch Royal Asiatic Society Monograph No. 2).

Law, Bimala Churn (1954): *Historical Geography of Ancient India*. Paris: Société Asiatique de Paris.

Muzafer Ali, S. (1966): The Geography of the Puranas. New Delhi: People's Publishing House.

Padmanabh, S. Jaini (1979): *The Jaina Path of Purification*. Berkeley: University of California Press.

Park, Chris C. (1994): *Sacred worlds; an introduction to geography and religion*. London : Routledge.

Pingree, David (1966): 'Sanskrit Geographical Tables'. *Indian Journal of History of Science*, New Delhi 31/2:173-220.

Pischel, Richard (1973 [1900]): Grammatik der Prakrit-Sprachen. Hildesheim: Georg Olms Verlag.

Pollet, G., Eggermont, P. & Van Darnme, G. (1990): *Corpus Topographicum Indiae Antiquae. II: Archeological sites*. Leuven: Departement Oriëntalistiek (OLA 37).

Suklalji, Pt. (1974): *Commentary on Tattvārtha Sūtra of Vācaka Umāsvāti*. (Tr. by K.K. Dixit, L.D. Series 44). Ahmedabad.

Renou, L. (1942): *Terminologie grammaticale du Sanskrit*. Paris: Edouard Champion.

Renou, L. & Filliozat, J. (1953): *L' Inde classique; Manuel des études Indiennes*. - *I*, Paris, 1947; *II*, with le concours d' Olivier Lacombe, Paris-Hanoi (école française d' Extrème-Orient).

Schubring, W. (1935): *Die Lehre der Jainas*. Berlin & Leipzig. (Grundriss der Indo-Arischen Philologie und

Altertumskunde, III 75). Tr. as *The Doctrine of the Jainas* by Wolfgang Beurlen. Delhi, Benares, Patna, 1962. Also tr. as *The Religion of the Jainas* by Amulyachandra Sen and T.C. Burke. Sanskrit College, Calcutta (Calcutta Sanskrit College Research Series 52), 1966.

Schubring, W. (1964): 'Jinismus', in *Die Religionen Indiens. III Buddhismus - Jinismus - Primitivvölker*, by André Bareau, Walther Schubring. Christoph von Fürer-Haimendorf. Stuttgart (Die Religionen der Menschheit, 13, Published under the direction of Christel Matthias Schröder).

Schubring, W. (1977): *Kleine Schriften*. Ed. by Klaus Bruhn. Wiesbaden: Glasenapp-Stiftung, 13, pp. 414-435).

Schwarzberg, Joseph E., ed. (1978): *A Historical Atlas of South Asia*. Chicago/London: University of Chicago Press (The Association for Asian Studies Reference Series, 2).

Seṭh, H.T. (1963): *Pāia-Sadda-Mahaṇṇavo (Prākṛta-Śabda-Mahārṇavaḥ)*. Vārāṇasī: Prākṛta Grantha Pariṣad.

Shah, U.P. (1955): *Studies in Jaina Art*. Benares: Jaina Cultural Research Society.

Sharma, J.P. (1968): *Republics in Ancient India: c. 1500 B.C. - 500 B.C.* Leiden: Brill.

Sircar, D.C. (1967): *Cosmography and Geography in Early Indian Literature*. Calcutta (Indian Studies: Past & Present).

Stevenson, Mrs. Sinclair (1970 [1915]): *The Heart of Jainism*. New Delhi: Munshiram Manoharlal.

Stevenson, J. (1848): 'Some remarks on the relation thats subsists between the Jain and Brahmanical system of Geography'. *Journal of the Bombay Branch of the Royal Asiatic Society*, Vol. 2, pp. 411-15.

Stroobandt, R.: *Corpus Topographicum Indiae Antiquae. Part I: Epigraphical Find-spots.* Gent: A sodalibus Universitatis Gandavensis et Universitatis Lovaniensis. Curantibus A. Scharpé, J. Deleu (Gandav.) et P. Eggermont, G. Pollet (Lovan.), 1974.

Surishvaraji (1934): *Shri Laghu Xetrasamas or Jain Geography by His Holiness Jainacharya Shrimad Ratnashekher.* With Gujarati tr. and 50 coloured plates. Baroda: Shriman Muktikamal Jain Mohanmala, 31.

Tatia, N. (1994): *Tattvārthādhigamasūtra; with the combined commentaries of Umāsvāti/Umāsvāmi, Pūjyapada and Siddhasenagaṇi; translated with an introduction; with a foreword by L.M. Singhvi and an introduction to the Jaina faith.* San Francisco: Harper Collins Publishers.

The Cambridge History of India. Six volumes. Cambridge, 1922-1937.

The History and Culture of the Indian People. Under direction of R.C. Majumdar. Bombay, 1951-1969.

Turner, R.L. (1999, [1966]): *A Comparative Dictionary of the Indo-Aryan Languages; I. Text, II. Indexes, III. Phonetic Analysis, IV. Addenda and Corrigenda.* Delhi: Motilal Banarsidass Publishers.

Pal, Pratapaditya, ed. (1994): *The Peaceful Liberators; Jain Art from India.* Los Angeles County Museum of Art. Nov. 6, 1994 - Jan. 22, 1995.

Tripāṭhī, Chandrabhāl (1975): *Catalogue of the Jaina Manuscripts at Strasbourg.* Leiden: E.J. Brill.

Upadhye, A.N., ed. (195&, 1956): *Jadivasaha's Tiloyapaṇṇatti (An Ancient Prakrit Text Dealing with Jaina Cosmography, Dogmatics, etc.).* Ed. with Hindi paraphrase by Pt. Balchandra. Sholapur: Jīvaraja Jain Granthamala, 1 (2 vols.).

Varṇī, Jinendra (1970): *Jainendra Siddhānta Kośa* (4 vols.). Delhi: Bharatīya Jñānapīṭha Prakāśana.

Velanker, H.D. (1944): *Jinaratnakośa; An Alphabethical Register of Jain Works and Authors, Vol. I. Works*. Poona: Bhandarkar Oriental Research Institute.

Williams, R. (1959): *Two Prakrit Versions of the Maṇipati-carita*. London: Lusac & Company LTD (published for the Royal Asiatic Society).

Williams, R. (1963): *Jaina Yoga; A survey of the mediaeval Śravakācāras*. London & New York: Oxford University Press.

Wilford, F. (1980 [1822]): *On the Ancient Geography of India.* (Asiatic Researches 1822, 14:373-470) New Delhi: Cosmo Publications.

Yashovijayji, Muni Shri, tr. (1939): *Shri Brihatsangrahaṇi Sutram or Jain Astronomy [Trailokya-dīpikā], by His Holiness Jainacharya Shrimad Chandrasuri.* With Gujarati tr. and 70 coloured plates. Baroda, 1939.

Index

The proper names of authors, mountains, rivers, etc., are put in the standard lettertype. Titles of works are put in *italics*. References to Sanskrit and Prākrit words occuring in the translation and the notes are put in *italics* for Skt. and ***bold*** for Pkt. Standard type numbers refer to the pages, while **bold** type numbers refer to the verses.